THE CRIMINAL PROCESS

The Criminal Process
An Evaluative Study

by

Andrew Ashworth

CLARENDON PRESS · OXFORD
1994

Oxford University Press, Walton Street, Oxford OX2 6DP
Oxford New York
Athens Auckland Bangkok Bombay
Calcutta Cape Town Dar es Salaam Delhi
Florence Hong Kong Istanbul Karachi
Kuala Lumpur Madras Madrid Melbourne
Mexico City Nairobi Paris Singapore
Taipei Tokyo Toronto
and associated companies in
Berlin Ibadan

Oxford is a trade mark of Oxford University Press

Published in the United States
by Oxford University Press Inc., New York

British Library Cataloguing in Publication Data
Data available

Library of Congress Cataloging in Publication Data
Ashworth, Andrew
The criminal process; an evaluative study /
by Andrew Ashworth.
Includes index.
1. Criminal justice, Administration of—Great Britain.
2. Criminal investigation—Great Britain.   3. Sentences (Criminal
procedure)—Great Britain.   I. Title.   II. Series.
HV9960.G7A74   1994   364.941—dc20   94–7711
ISBN 0–19–876262–3
ISBN 0–19–876358–1 (pbk.)

Set by Hope Services (Abingdon) Ltd.
Printed in Great Britain
on acid-free paper by
Bookcraft Ltd.,
Midsomer Norton, Avon

Preface

THE pre-trial criminal process has been the subject of considerable empirical research in recent years, although the research has been focused on some issues to the neglect of others. There has, however, been little attempt to provide an integrated treatment of questions of principle and practice. It was in the hope of remedying this deficiency that the plan for this book was conceived. The notorious cases of mis-carriage of justice uncovered in recent years added a distinct human purpose to the endeavour, in so far as they drew attention not only to the defects of the appeals and review procedures but also to the power-ful effects of events and decisions earlier in the process. A short time after the writing began, the Government announced the appointment of the Royal Commission on Criminal Justice and so, by coincidence, the bulk of the writing was carried out in parallel with the work of the Royal Commission. This brought two distinct benefits—a further crop of valuable research into the criminal process, and the opportunity to comment on the recommendations of the Royal Commission—but the original plan for the work was not changed. It is not a textbook, either on criminal procedure or on the pre-trial process. It certainly does not deal with all the topics on which the Royal Commission made recom-mendations. The aim is to discuss six significant and interrelated stages of decision-making in the early part of the criminal process, drawing on empirical research, statute law, case-law, and arguments of principle.

The book concentrates on the law and practice in England and Wales. It does not neglect comparisons with other legal systems, but it is in no sense a comparative work—that would have been a different and much larger enterprise. It does, however, seek to reflect the posi-tion of the United Kingdom as a signatory to the European Convention on Human Rights. In the first three chapters, which constitute the general part of the work, the Convention and the decisions of the European Court of Human Rights form a focal point for the arguments of principle. But the arguments are not restricted by the rights declared in the Convention, and there is wider discussion of ethical issues in the administration of criminal justice.

The second part of the book contains six chapters on particular stages in decision-making. Chapter 4 deals with many of the issues that arise at the investigation stage, with particular emphasis on police questioning and investigation methods. Chapter 5 examines decisions which determine whether a suspect should be prosecuted or dealt with in some other way, and Chapter 6 discusses the prosecutorial review of cases in which a charge has been brought. In Chapter 7 there is an analysis of remand decisions, seeking to scrutinize the justifications for taking away liberty before trial. Chapter 8 turns to the relatively under-discussed question of determining whether a case should be heard in the magistrates' court or in the Crown Court. The sixth decision to be examined is that on plea, in Chapter 9, where the issues raised by 'plea bargaining' are discussed. The book concludes with a final chapter in which the problems of the pre-trial criminal process are re-examined.

I have been fortunate in being able to draw on the experience and support of many colleagues and friends during the writing of the book. Special thanks are due to those who have read and commented on draft chapters—Brian Bix, Penny Darbyshire, Sionaidh Douglas-Scott, Julia Fionda, Nicola Padfield, Elaine Player, Andrew von Hirsch, and Lucia Zedner. I would also like to record my thanks for the efficiency with which the Oxford University Press has handled this project. I ceased to collect new material on 1 October 1993, but a few references to subsequent developments have been inserted where possible.

A.J.A.
January 1994

Contents

PART II. PARTICULAR DECISIONS

PART III. CONCLUSIONS

Abbreviations

ABA	American Bar Association
BJ Crim.	*British Journal of Criminology*
Camb. LJ	*Cambridge Law Journal*
CLP	*Current Legal Problems*
CPS	Crown Prosecution Service
Crim. LR	*Criminal Law Review*
HORS	Home Office Research Study
Howard JCJ	*Howard Journal of Criminal Justice*
ICLQ	*International and Comparative Law Quarterly*
LJ	*Law Journal*
LQR	*Law Quarterly Review*
LR	*Law Review*
MLR	*Modern Law Review*
NILQ	*Northern Ireland Law Quarterly*
NLJ	*New Law Journal*
Oxford JLS	*Oxford Journal of Legal Studies*
PACE	Police and Criminal Evidence Act 1984
PAS Supp.	*Proceedings of the Aristotelian Society Supplement*
PICA	Public Interest Case Assessment
PL	*Public Law*
PSI	Policy Studies Institute
RCCJ	Royal Commission on Criminal Justice
RCCP	Royal Commission on Criminal Procedure
SFO	Serious Fraud Office
U. Chi. LR	*University of Chicago Law Review*
U. Pa. LR	*University of Pennsylvania Law Review*

Table of Cases

Table of Statutes

Table of European Conventions

PART I

General

1

Decisions

THE subject-matter of this book is the criminal process from the first official engagement with a suspected offence or offender through to trial. The treatment is selective rather than comprehensive, focusing on pre-trial procedures and devoting little discussion to trials, sentences, or appeal mechanisms. The selection of issues here is not intended as a comment on their relative importance. The legal and social significance of appeal mechanisms and procedures for correcting miscarriages of justice has been placed beyond doubt by several notorious cases.[1] The principles and practice of sentencing retain a high public profile, and have been examined extensively elsewhere.[2] But it has long been true that the amount of public and academic discussion devoted to criminal trials, particularly trials by jury, far outweighs their numerical significance within the criminal process. The vast majority of defendants are dealt with in magistrates' courts, and the vast majority of defendants in all courts plead guilty. It makes sense, therefore, to examine the processes and procedures that lead to guilty pleas. For most defendants this is the reality of criminal justice. Speaking statistically, a trial of guilt is most unlikely, and a trial by jury in the Crown Court is highly unlikely. The pre-trial stages are far more important than their low visibility would suggest.

This chapter contains a discursive survey of the English criminal process, designed to provide a context in which readers can place the theoretical discussions and the examination of particular stages in the later chapters. It begins with a brief description of the key decisions taken in respect of suspected offences that come to the notice of the authorities. Many of these decisions are discussed in later chapters, and therefore detailed references are not given at this stage, but it is necessary to have an overall view before we go on to explore issues of policy and principle in Chapters 2 and 3. Consideration is then given to the possibility of classifying the different *types* of decision taken at the pre-trial stage, and also to some of the differences in processing crimes of various kinds. There is then some discussion of ways of dealing with

---

[1] P. Thornton, 'Miscarriages of Justice: A Lost Opportunity', [1993] *Crim. LR* 926.

[2] A. Ashworth, *Sentencing and Criminal Justice* (1992).

errors. This is followed by brief outlines of the decision-making personnel and of recent landmarks in English policy in respect of the pre-trial process. The aim is to provide readers with a short overview of procedures and issues.

1. Key Stages in Decision-Making

In most cases the first decision is that of a member of the public—victim, bystander, employer, etc.—to report an offence-like incident to the police or other authorities. In a minority of cases the authorities might learn about a suspected offence through their own activities. The police might be conducting an undercover operation into drug-dealing, for example, or they may be on duty at a public meeting or procession. The Inland Revenue might discover an offence through their checking procedures, or the Pollution Inspectorate may discover an offence through routine inquiries. If the authorities believe that an offence has been committed, they may seek the offender. In some cases the identity of the probable offender is readily apparent: there might be an identification or even a naming by the person who reported the offence, or there may be a high probability that the person to seek is the victim's husband, or the owner of a certain factory, etc.

Once the authorities begin questioning members of the public, issues of rights and procedures are raised.[3] In general a police officer is free to put any questions to any citizen, but no citizen has a duty to answer the questions of the police or to remain where the police wish him or her to remain.[4] Many citizens will answer questions, and this may result in the police officer terminating the inquiry, or informing the suspect that a summons will be issued in respect of the offence, or deciding to arrest the suspect. Whether or not the person answers questions, a police officer is entitled to arrest any person whom he or she has reasonable grounds to suspect of having committed or being about to commit an 'arrestable offence'.[5] When the suspect is brought to the police station, the custody officer has to decide whether the suspect should be released without charge, charged, or (if it is thought necessary to obtain further evidence by questioning) detained for questioning.[6] That detention may be for up to six hours in the first place, and there are procedures for renewal.[7] The custody officer must record these and other decisions on a custody sheet, and the suspect

[3] For an accessible and detailed treatment of the relevant law, see *Emmins on Criminal Procedure* (5th edn. by John Sprack, 1992). For a more critical review of police powers, see K. Ewing and C. Gearty, *Freedom under Thatcher* (1991).
[4] *Rice* v. *Connelly* [1966] 2 QB 414.   [5] PACE, s. 24.   [6] PACE, s. 37.
[7] PACE, ss. 40–4.

must be informed of the right to free and confidential legal advice. The Codes of Practice issued under the Police and Criminal Evidence Act set out standards for the conduct of police investigations. For example, they impose restrictions on the manner in which the police may question a suspect,[8] and on the handling of identification procedures. Many details of these procedures will be examined in Chapter 4, where actual practice as well as the letter of the law will be discussed. The police will question the victim at an early stage, and should inform victims of violent offences of the existence of the Criminal Injuries Compensation Board. The police may also put the victim in touch with Victim Support or other similar agencies. Inquiries in a case may be completed quickly or may spread over a considerable time, in which case the police have a duty to keep the victim informed of the progress of the case.

The outline in the previous paragraph focused on police procedures. Other investigating agencies, such as HM Customs and Excise, are subject to the Codes of Practice, although there is much less legal regulation of inquiries by the many so-called 'regulatory' agencies. The general principle throughout, however, is that a person may only be questioned before charge and not after charge. Once there is sufficient evidence, the suspect should be charged. On the other hand, it must not be thought that charging is the only way of commencing a prosecution. The alternative method is for a police officer to lay an information before a magistrate or justices' clerk, as a result of which a summons will be issued and served on the defendant. The summons procedure is more commonly used for minor offences and arrest for serious offences.

In the early stages before charge there are also various powers of search. The police have been given powers to stop and search persons and vehicles in public places, and PACE Code A sets out guidance on these matters.[9] There are detailed provisions for searches of premises, differentiated according to the seriousness of the alleged offence and excluding certain kinds of material.[10] The 1984 Act also provides for the search of arrested persons, and there are special rules for intimate searches.[11] It should be added that several regulatory agencies have special powers to search premises in connection with inquiries into particular forms of offence. Indeed, the powers of HM Customs and Excise far exceed those of the police.

It has been assumed so far that the progression from sufficient evidence to charge or summons is natural or inevitable, but that is far from being true. An authority with the power to prosecute may decide

---

[8] Taken in conjunction with ss. 76, 78, and 67 (1) of PACE.   [9] PACE, ss. 1–3.
[10] See generally PACE, ss. 8–22.   [11] PACE, s. 55; cf. ss. 54 and 118.

to take no formal action at all, perhaps believing that the experience of detection or an informal warning is sufficient, or it may decide that a formal caution or warning is appropriate. The police have developed the practice of issuing a formal caution to certain offenders, particularly the young, the elderly, and those whose offences are very minor. The police are supposed to consult the victim of the crime before deciding to caution, although the victim's wishes should not be conclusive. Many regulatory agencies have powers to issue formal warnings to employers, companies, farmers, and others in respect of offences, and they may prefer to adopt this approach in the hope of maximizing compliance with the law. Some agencies have powers to exact financial penalties from offenders without bringing a prosecution: the Inland Revenue may offer citizens the opportunity to pay, say, double the amount of tax evaded as a condition of non-prosecution.

If the prosecution proceeds by way of summons, the defendant will be given a date for first appearance in a magistrates' court. If it proceeds by arrest and charge, the custody officer must decide what course to take after the defendant has been charged. There is a duty to ensure that a defendant is brought before a court as soon as practicable, which is often the morning after arrest (or on Monday morning, if the arrest takes place on a Saturday). The defendant may be bailed to appear in court or, if there are reasonable grounds for believing that detention is necessary for certain purposes, the police may keep the defendant in custody until the first court appearance.[12] At first appearance the magistrates' court must either dispose of the case or, if not (and particularly in serious cases which will be committed to the Crown Court for trial), the court must decide whether to release the defendant on bail or to make a custodial remand. The Bail Act 1976 proclaims a presumption in favour of bail, but also sets out various reasons for the refusal of bail.

Legal assistance is available at several stages in the process. Not only is there a right to free legal advice at the police station, but there are duty solicitor schemes to facilitate this and to advise on representation in court. The Legal Aid Act 1988 provides, in effect, that magistrates' courts must grant legal aid to defendants who are going to the Crown Court, and they have a discretion to grant legal aid for summary trials. Defendants with means are expected to make contributions, but a majority of defendants are unemployed or otherwise in receipt of State assistance.

In cases investigated by the police, they take the decision whether or

---

[12] PACE, s. 38.

not to charge the defendant, although they may seek advice from the Crown Prosecution Service before doing so. The papers are then passed to the Crown Prosecution Service. Their function is to review the evidence, to consider the 'public interest', and then to decide how to proceed. They have the power to discontinue prosecutions in magistrates' courts,[13] and may drop a case when it is called on in the Crown Court. They may decide to continue with the prosecution on the charges preferred by the police, or may alter the charges. If it is a Crown Court case it will be necessary to draft the indictment.[14] If the defendant has been remanded in custody, there are now time-limits which apply to the period between first appearance in the magistrates' court and committal (seventy days), and between committal to the Crown Court and trial (112 days).[15] The prosecution may apply for an extension, but if there are insufficient grounds the accused must be released on bail until the trial.

The choice of charge determines the mode of trial. Most minor offences are triable summarily only, in the magistrates' courts. Most serious offences are triable only on indictment, in the Crown Court. The intermediate category of offences triable either way may be tried in a magistrates' court or at the Crown Court: the first decision is that of magistrates, having heard representations, but the defendant has an unfettered right to elect Crown Court trial even if the magistrates regard an 'either-way' case as suitable for summary trial. When a case is committed to the Crown Court for trial, this should not be taken to mean that committal proceedings are held. The vast majority of cases are committed on paper, but both the defendant and the prosecution have the power to insist on full committal proceedings before a magistrates' court to test the strength of the prosecution case.

If a defendant indicates an intention to plead not guilty, there may be various exchanges between prosecution and defence before the date set for trial. In some cases there will be a form of preparatory hearing: in some magistrates' courts there may be a pre-trial review, and in some Crown Court centres a 'Plea and Directions' hearing, intended to define the issues for trial. In many cases there will be discussion between prosecuting counsel and defence counsel on the day before, or the very day of, the Crown Court trial. In some cases there may be a preliminary discussion with the judge. Defence counsel may then discuss the case with the defendant, and a change of plea to guilty may take place. This part of the process, sometimes described as 'plea

[13] Prosecution of Offences Act 1985, s. 23.
[14] For full discussion, see *Emmins on Criminal Procedure*, ch. 6.
[15] Prosecution of Offences Act 1985, s. 22.

bargaining', is unregulated by statute and little regulated by the Court of Appeal.

A defendant who pleads guilty will be sentenced by the magistrates or by the Crown Court judge, after hearing a statement of facts from the prosecution and a plea in mitigation from the defence, and in non-minor cases after receiving a pre-sentence report. A defendant who pleads not guilty will be tried in the appropriate court. Magistrates' courts tend to be less formal, with less strict adherence to the laws of evidence but also with a greater sense of briskness. In the Crown Court the trial will be before judge and jury, and matters are unfolded in greater detail.

A defendant convicted by a magistrates' court may appeal against conviction or sentence to the Crown Court, where the appeal takes the form of a rehearing. If either the defence or the prosecution wish to appeal on a point of law, the magistrates may be asked to state a case to the Divisional Court. A defendant convicted in the Crown Court may appeal against conviction and/or sentence to the Court of Appeal (Criminal Division). After the appeal process has been exhausted there is provision for a case to be referred to the Court of Appeal, for review, by the Home Secretary. It is this procedure that was found wanting in the notorious cases of miscarriage of justice uncovered in the late 1980s and early 1990s.

The various stages in decision-making outlined above apply generally, although reference was made to differences between the powers and practices of the police and of the regulatory agencies. However, there are differences of approach to cases involving certain types of suspect or defendant and certain types of alleged offence. Where the suspect or defendant is a juvenile, aged between 10 and 18, there are special procedures and safeguards. There is also special provision for mentally disordered suspects and defendants. Persons requiring interpreters or suffering from deafness, etc., should also be treated differently. As for types of offence, brief mention may be made of the different legal regimes for motoring offences and for persons suspected of terrorist offence or of serious fraud. Many motoring offences may be dealt with by a fixed penalty without a court appearance, and some of those that have to be brought to court do not require the appearance of the defendant. There are also several other differences of procedure, including particular time-limits for commencing a prosecution. The Prevention of Terrorism Acts give greater powers to the police when questioning persons suspected of involvement in terrorist offences, including the power to detain such persons without charge for up to seven days. The Criminal Justice Act 1987 gives enhanced powers to the

Serious Fraud Office when investigating persons suspected of involvement in frauds involving millions of pounds. The Act authorizes the SFO to require a defendant to furnish documents and to answer questions, and institutes a special procedure for bringing cases of serious fraud to trial.

Before leaving this outline of decisions, their context within a system needs to be emphasized. They are not discrete individual decisions taken in laboratory conditions. Rather, they should be viewed as decisions taken either by individuals or by courts, working within a given professional context. The individual police officer or Crown Prosecutor is likely to be affected, for example, not only by the working practices and expectations of colleagues, but also by decisions taken by others beforehand and decisions likely to be taken at subsequent stages. The factual basis for the decision may well have been constructed by others, in a way that depends partly on selection and interpretation. This point is developed in the last section of the chapter, but it is important to avoid from the outset the dominance of a 'rationalist' notion of decisions taken by individuals independently and based on objective information.[16]

2. Distinguishing Types of Decision

The various legal procedures and practices described in the previous section combine to affect the ways in which particular suspects and defendants are processed by officials. Formal procedures do not determine that treatment, since the working practices of officials are what suspects and defendants actually experience. Those practices may be more or less faithful to the rules, and in some instances the law may leave discretion rather than imposing rules.

It is noticeable, however, that the various decisions outlined above are not all of the same kind. Most of them might be described as 'processual', in that they are decisions about the processing of the case from initial charge through to trial. But there are two or three decisions that may be described more accurately as 'dispositive', in that they are concerned more with the disposal of the case. One strong example of this is the decision either to give a formal caution or warning or to take no formal action, rather than to prosecute. This decision, whether taken by the police or by a regulatory agency, may be regarded as analogous to sentencing. It disposes of the case, which goes no further in the system, with some form of censure. The weakness of the analogy is

---

[16] Cf. R. Baldwin and K. Hawkins, 'Discretionary Justice: Davis Reconsidered', [1984] *PL* 570, at 581.

that no court is involved. Diversion is premised on the belief that the case does not warrant full processing and a court appearance. A second example is the review of a case by the Crown Prosecution Service, followed by a decision to discontinue the prosecution on grounds of insufficient public interest. A third possible example is the prosecutor's decision to accept a bargain which involves the dropping or reduction of one or more charges—a decision which will usually have implications for sentence, and may therefore be described as dispositive to some extent. Decisions on mode of trial may also have this dimension.

The point of making this distinction is that different considerations will apply to processual decisions and to dispositive decisions—as is clear from the analogy between dispositive decisions and sentencing, which has no application to decisions on the processing of cases. None the less, in practice questions of evidential sufficiency and of public interest often intermingle in the minds of decision-makers, and so the distinction may be less sharp in practice than in theory. Moreover, there is at least one type of decision that is neither processual nor dispositive: the remand decision, whether on bail or in custody. This has no direct bearing on whether the prosecution will be continued or discontinued, nor on mode of trial or plea, although in practice it may be affected by these other decisions. Nor is it a means of taking a case out of the system and dealing with it otherwise. It is *sui generis*, and is perhaps best described as a temporal decision, in that it arises solely if and when a case cannot be dealt with at the first court appearance. The adjective temporal refers only to why this decision arises rather than to the nature of the issues involved, but in view of the discussion in Chapter 7 below, this neutrality is probably wise.

3. Miscarriages of Justice

In a number of well-publicized cases, errors have been discovered in the investigations and trials which led to convictions followed by defendants spending long years in prison for serious crimes. It was in the aftermath of these cases that the Government decided in 1991 to appoint a Royal Commission on Criminal Justice, the first Royal Commission for twelve years. Yet in its report the Royal Commission gave neither an analysis nor even a description of these catalytic cases.[17] It seems that the Commission decided that such an exercise ran a considerable risk of provoking 'further unprofitable controversy', which was taken to outweigh any benefits.[18] However, these cases now

[17] Royal Commission on Criminal Justice, *Report*, Cm. 2263 (1993).
[18] Michael Zander, 'Where the Critics got it Wrong', (1993) *NLJ* 1338, at 1339.

form an essential part of the context of criminal justice reform, and it is important to include here a brief survey of the problems they brought to light.[19]

In the case of the 'Guildford Four', the four defendants had been convicted in 1976 of murder by causing an explosion at a public house in Guildford. Their appeal against conviction was turned down. In 1989 their case was referred to the Court of Appeal by the Home Secretary. The Director of Public Prosecutions stated that he no longer sought to support the convictions, and the Court quashed them. The primary ground was that tests on police documents undermined the evidence of police officers that the crucial interviews were recorded contemporaneously, since the handwritten notes had evidently been written after the typed 'records' of the interviews.[20]

In the case of the 'Maguire Seven', the seven defendants, most of whom were members of the Maguire family, had been convicted in 1976 of an offence of possessing explosive substances that was linked by the prosecution to bombings in London and Guildford. Their application for leave to appeal was refused in 1977. After the convictions of the 'Guildford Four' had been quashed, the Home Secretary asked the May Inquiry to consider this case but then referred the case to the Court of Appeal. The Court quashed the convictions in 1992.[21] There were two main grounds. First, the prosecution had failed to disclose to the defence certain scientific evidence, which amounted to a material irregularity. Second, the scientific evidence left open the possibility that the traces of nitro-glycerine found on the defendants and in their house came from an innocent source, which rendered the verdicts unsafe and unsatisfactory. The defendants had spent some thirteen years in prison, and one of them had died there.

In the case of the 'Birmingham Six', the six defendants had been convicted in 1975 of murder by causing an explosion at a public house in the centre of Birmingham. Their appeal against conviction was dismissed. In 1987 the Home Secretary used his power to refer the case back to the Court of Appeal, on the grounds of fresh scientific evidence and fresh evidence that the defendants had been beaten following their arrest. The appeal was dismissed. In 1990 the Home Secretary referred the case to the Court of Appeal again as a result of further fresh

[19] For a more detailed survey, see Joshua Rozenberg, 'Miscarriages of Justice', in E. Stockdale and S. Casale (eds.), *Criminal Justice under Stress* (1993).

[20] *Armstrong, Conlon, Hill and Richardson*, 19 Oct. 1989, discussed ibid. 92–4.

[21] *Maguire et al.* (1992) 94 Cr. App. R. 133. For the May Inquiry, see *Return to an Address of the Honourable House of Commons Dated 12 July 1990 for the Inquiry into the Circumstances Surrounding the Convictions Arising out of the Bomb Attacks in Guildford and Woolwich in 1974*, HC 556 (1990).

evidence. In 1991 the Court of Appeal quashed the convictions.[22] The defendants had maintained from the outset that they were beaten and that the so-called confessions were false. Among the reasons given by the Court of Appeal were the finding that all the notes of an alleged interview could not have been written contemporaneously (this was established by electrostatic analysis, the so-called ESDA test), and the finding that the Forensic Science Service had not disclosed the possibility that alleged traces of explosives could have come from innocent contamination or even from smoking cigarettes. The defendants had served over sixteen years in prison. The Crown Prosecution Service decided that there was sufficient evidence to justify prosecuting three police officers involved in the investigation for perjury and conspiracy to pervert the course of justice, but the judge stayed the prosecution on the ground that the publicity surrounding the Birmingham Six case made it impossible for the three former policemen to receive a fair trial on the specific charges alleged.[23]

In the case of the M62 bombing, Judith Ward had been convicted in 1974 of murder and causing an explosion. She did not appeal. In 1991 the Home Secretary referred her case to the Court of Appeal, and in 1992 her convictions were quashed.[24] The first ground was that the Forensic Science Service had failed to disclose the results of tests that were favourable to the defendant, and there were other failures of disclosure by the police, the Director of Public Prosecutions, and prosecuting counsel. The second ground was that the defendant's mental condition, a form of personality disorder, rendered her alleged confessions unreliable. Medical evidence available at the time of the trial had not been disclosed, and there was fresh medical evidence. Since the prosecution's case rested chiefly on statements by the defendant, the convictions were unsafe and unsatisfactory. Ms Ward had been in prison for eighteen years.

In the case of the 'Tottenham Three' the defendants were convicted in 1986 of the murder of a police officer during disturbances on the Broadwater Farm estate. Their appeals were unsuccessful, but in 1991 the Home Secretary referred their cases back to the Court of Appeal and the convictions were quashed. The principal ground was that ESDA tests on the 'notes of interview' showed that some parts of the alleged records had been written at different times from others. Although much is sometimes made of the fact that the investigation of all the earlier cases took place before the controls introduced by the Police and Criminal Evidence Act, it is noteworthy that the provisions

---

[22] *McIlkenny et al.* (1991) 93 Cr. App. R. 287.   [23] (1992) *The Times* 16 Oct.
[24] *Ward* (1993) 96 Cr. App. R. 1; cf. also *Kiszko* (1992) *The Times* 19 Feb.

of that Act were being tested in late 1985 in the police division where the three defendants were questioned.[25]

In one way the most significant case is that the 'Cardiff Three', convicted in 1990 of the murder of a Cardiff prostitute. Their convictions were quashed by the Court of Appeal on the ground that the tenor and length of the police interviews was such that they should have been excluded from evidence. The Lord Chief Justice held that the techniques of interrogation used by the police amounted to 'oppression' within the meaning of section 76 (2) (a) of the Police and Criminal Evidence Act 1984. On playing one of the tapes recording the interview, the appeal judges were 'horrified'.

Miller was bullied and hectored. The officers, particularly Detective Constable Greenwood, were not questioning him so much as shouting at him . . . Short of physical violence, it is hard to conceive of a more hostile and intimidating approach by officers to a suspect. It is impossible to convey on the printed page the pace, force and menace of the officer's delivery.[26]

The particular significance of this case is that one defensive comment on most of the previous miscarriages of justice was that they occurred before the Police and Criminal Evidence Act and before the tape recording of interviews, with the implication that they could not happen today. Yet the Cardiff Three case not only occurred some years after the implementation of PACE but the interviews, including the manner of the police questioning, were tape recorded—perhaps suggesting that the officers did not think that their approach was anything to be ashamed of.

This simplified sketch of several complex cases suffices to expose some recurrent problems. The most common pre-trial faults lay in the concoction or falsification of evidence by the police officers, in non-disclosure by forensic scientists, and more generally in non-disclosure by the prosecution to the defence. In some cases there was oppressive conduct by the police during questioning, with or without actual violence. These faults have implications for the rules on confessions and the controls on police investigations, and for the ethical orientation of the police, prosecution lawyers, and the Forensic Science Service. The most common post-trial faults lay in the slow and cumbersome procedure for referring cases to the Court of Appeal, and in that Court's reluctance (at least until recently) to overturn jury verdicts, especially if such a decision would imply that the police had not told the truth.

[25] *Silcott, Braithwaite and Raghip* (1991) *The Times* 6 Dec.; in the case of Raghip, the conviction was quashed on the additional ground that psychiatric evidence of his mental condition, not available at the time of the trial, had since come to light.
[26] *Paris, Abdullahi and Miller* (1993) 97 Cr. App. R. 99, at 103.

These faults call into question the existing machinery for dealing with alleged miscarriages of justice. Indeed, the term 'miscarriage of justice' should not be restricted to wrong outcomes, as it commonly is. Wherever there is a departure from proper practice, this should be regarded as a miscarriage of justice irrespective of its effect on the outcome of the case. Thus, speaking generally at this early stage, if a person who is factually guilty is convicted as a result of wrongful police practices, that should count as a miscarriage of justice. On the other hand, the term is also apt to cover cases in which a guilty person is acquitted. Justice can miscarry in either direction.

4. Dealing with Miscarriages of Justice

The problem of errors in the system, whether caused by conscious or by careless departures from the rules, and whether favourable or unfavourable to the defendant, may be dealt with in two ways. Steps should be taken to prevent miscarriages of justice from occurring but, recognizing human fallibility within any system, there ought to be mechanisms for correcting them after they have occurred.

Probably the best-known method of error correction is the appeal against a decision of the trial court: in England there is a strong tradition that appeals against the decisions of magistrates and judges should be open to the defendant and not to the prosecution, because a prosecution appeal is tantamount to placing the defendant in double jeopardy. Other countries are less willing to allow defendants to take advantage of windfalls provided by erroneous rulings or verdicts. For the defendant, however, there is no need to wait for the appeal process in order to challenge the propriety of the treatment received from police, prosecutors, and others at the pre-trial stage. Where the defendant alleges that there have been departures from the rules at the investigation stage—for example, by improper questioning, unlawful search, or failure to allow access to legal advice—this may be raised in court as an objection to the admissibility of the evidence thereby obtained. The court has a duty to exclude a confession obtained by oppression, and has further powers to exclude oral or real evidence where it is likely to be unreliable or might adversely affect the fairness of the trial.[27] There is also the possibility of police disciplinary proceedings in these cases, but from the defendant's point of view any unfair advantage to the prosecution should be removed by excluding the tainted evidence.

[27] PACE, ss. 76, 78, and 82 (3).

Two further means of challenging procedural irregularities are judicial review and inviting the court to stay proceedings. Judicial review is available *inter alia* where a public body exercises its powers unreasonably or by taking account of irrelevant considerations. In recent years the Divisional Court has accepted that decisions to prosecute or not prosecute, by the police, the Crown Prosecution Service, or a regulatory agency, may be susceptible to judicial review on these grounds.[28] A decision by a magistrates' court at committal proceedings, and other decisions of magistrates' courts, may also be challenged by this method. To ask the court to stay proceedings in a case involves invoking the doctrine of abuse of process, and it has been used against the misuse of prosecutorial power (e.g. attempting to circumvent a magistrates' court decision that an either-way case should be tried summarily, by dropping the either-way charge and prosecuting for an indictable-only offence),[29] against unreasonable delay or the unreasonable grant of an extension of custody time-limits,[30] and also in some cases of impropriety at the investigation stage.

The effect of a successful action for judicial review is to nullify the decision taken by the agency or court reviewed. The effect of a stay of proceedings is to terminate the case. The effect of a successful appeal depends on the grounds: where there has been a procedural irregularity the conviction would normally be quashed, but the Court of appeal does have the power (rarely exercised) to order a retrial. The effect of a decision to exclude evidence depends on the centrality of the excluded evidence to the prosecution case: in many instances the prosecution will founder. It should be added that there are other ways in which a court can reflect what it considers to be less fundamental departures from procedure, mitigation of sentence being the most flexible.

This, however, raises questions. For what kinds of departure from procedure should each of the methods of challenge be available? Are there some departures from the PACE Codes of Practice, for example, to which exclusion of evidence would be too severe a response? Are there some forms of unfair or improper conduct in investigation to which mitigation of sentence is an inadequate response? Is the use of the term 'response' sufficiently accurate, or would other terms such as remedy, compensation, or penalty be more appropriate descriptions of

[28] e.g. *R. v. Chief Constable of Kent, ex p. L.* [1993] 1 All ER 756, *R. v. Inland Revenue Commissioners ex p. Mead* [1993] 1 All ER 882, *R. v. Croydon Justices, ex p. Dean* [1993] Crim. LR 759.

[29] e.g. *Brooks* [1985] Crim. LR 385.

[30] *Attorney-General's Reference (No. 1 of 1990)* [1992] 1 QB 630.

the function that the law should perform here? These are among the questions that will be raised periodically throughout the book.

Turning to the preventive approach to errors, brief mention may be made of training, guidelines, and best practice. Legal rules might be regarded as the primary means of preventing errors, but it is because errors (deliberate and accidental) have taken place despite the existence of legal rules and powers that it is necessary to look for wider solutions. Proper training is the basis of prevention. It should help to minimize the number of accidental departures from proper procedure. Training is much sharper if it is possible to rely on fairly detailed guidelines for dealing with cases and taking decisions: the PACE Codes of Practice might be an example of this. In many situations, however, guidelines are laid down by superior authorities as a means of shaping decision-making. They may not cover the ground fully, or may need to be supplemented by 'best practice'—practices developed on the ground by decision-makers that fit most appropriately with the purposes to be achieved. Training in itself is therefore not of great assistance unless there is something definite with which to train the decision-makers. On the other hand, rules, guidelines, and best practices are invariably open to interpretation and manipulation by those who are out of sympathy with the aims they seek to achieve. Most professions have one or more occupational cultures, which may sometimes breed a defensive and sectional approach to tasks. It will therefore be argued below that training must confront these cultures and must seek to inculcate an ethical perspective on decision-making in the criminal process.

5. The Decision-Makers

Victims of crime have a central role as decision-makers, albeit informally. Theirs is usually the initial decision to call the police, and they will often give information to the police that is useful in the investigation. The victim's wishes are stated to be relevant to the decision to caution rather than prosecute, and to the decision to discontinue a prosecution, but those wishes may be overridden by considerations of 'public interest'. The interests of the victim may be taken into account in remand decisions, particularly where there have been threats, but there is no formal procedure for that. It is apparent that victims have no formal role as decision-makers.

The police have considerable power and discretion in relation to suspects and defendants. Decisions about reasonable suspicion, arrest or summons, detention for questioning, and remand in custody before first court appearance are all for the police, although the custody officer is supposed to maintain a certain independence from other officers. The crucial decision whether to prosecute, caution, or take no formal action is also for the police, and this is a decision that can have a profound effect on the course of an individual's life. There are 'national standards' applicable to the cautioning decision, but the working practices of the police may prove to be of greater importance than the letter of the law or the guidelines. The influence of the early decisions taken by the police often endures through later decisions, such as bail, mode of trial, and plea.

Similar power is wielded by the officers of the various regulatory agencies, although they tend to use it for different purposes. Often there are strict liability offences for which they could prosecute, rendering conviction almost certain. But their tendency is to place compliance above punishment, and to use prosecution as a last resort when other methods of bringing about conformity with the legal standards have failed.

The Crown Prosecution Service was created in 1985, and consists of salaried lawyers whose task is to review cases to decide whether the prosecution commenced by the police should be continued, whether the charges should be changed, and to conduct prosecutions in the magistrates' courts. The CPS briefs counsel for prosecutions in the Crown Court and, except for the few cases conducted by Treasury Counsel, barristers acting for the prosecution will be independent counsel who sometimes act for the defence. The CPS makes representations to magistrates' courts at remand hearings and on mode of trial, and will normally be consulted if there is plea negotiation before a Crown Court trial.

Defendants have a number of decisions to make throughout the process. They have to decide whether or not to accept the offer of free legal advice at the police station, and also to decide what (if anything) to say to the police. If a police caution seems to be a possibility, they will be asked whether they admit the offence, and the prospect of a caution may lead them to accept guilt even if they believe they have a possible defence. If they are prosecuted and remanded for trial, they will have the opportunity personally or through their advocate to make representations on bail. If they are charged with an offence triable either way, they will have the absolute right to elect trial by jury in the Crown Court. In the period before trial they will have to decide on their plea, and they may make a decision to change their plea from not guilty to guilty.

Rather less is known about defence lawyers and their methods of operating. They are entitled to accompany a suspect or defendant at the police station during police questioning, and any omission to prevent unfair questioning may be treated as a decision taken by them. More remotely but no less significantly, the organization of a solicitors' practice may determine whether a solicitor or an unadmitted member of staff attends the police station. Since it may be necessary to give advice about, for example, the right of silence, much may turn on the confidence and experience of the legal adviser. The defence lawyer may make representations to the court at remand proceedings and at proceedings to determine mode of trial (if the offence charged is triable either way). The defence lawyer, whether solicitor or retained counsel, will play a role if there is to be any plea negotiation prior to trial in cases where the defendant has entered a plea of not guilty. Indeed, the way in which the defence lawyer puts the alternatives to the defendant may well have a profound effect on the defendant's decision.

Probation officers and social workers have no formal role in decision-making. However, social workers may participate in juvenile bureaux and other multi-agency groups for deciding how to deal with juvenile offenders. Probation officers and social workers may also be involved in supplying information to the Crown Prosecution Service as part of bail information schemes and Public Interest Case Assessment schemes. At the sentencing stage, the pre-sentence report is of increased significance since the Criminal Justice Act 1991.

Magistrates and judges hear the various representations mentioned above and take decisions. Magistrates take decisions on remand (on bail or in custody) and on mode of trial in offences triable either way. In cases tried in magistrates' courts, they decide on the admissibility of evidence and then on guilt or innocence, passing sentence if there is a conviction. Crown Court judges preside over pre-trial reviews or similar hearings in courts where they take place. They may also be approached in chambers by counsel seeking indications of sentence with a view to change of plea. At the trial they decide on the admissibility of evidence and they direct the jury, passing sentence if there is a conviction. Crown Court judges sit on appeals against the decisions of magistrates' courts (usually sitting with two lay magistrates), and in the Court of Appeal judges of the High Court sit with Lords Justices of Appeal to hear appeals from the Crown Court.

6. Changing the System

A further part of the context of the analysis in the chapters to follow is the series of official reports that have had a bearing on reform of the

English criminal process. Some twenty years ago the Criminal Law Revision Committee's report on evidence was published.[31] Its recommendations to remove the 'right of silence' in the police station and to reword the police caution to suspects aroused fierce opposition, and many of the less controversial proposals for reforming the laws of evidence were also lost in the ensuing furore. However, reform of police powers remained a live question in public debate,[32] and in 1977 the Government announced the appointment of a Royal Commission on Criminal Procedure. In its 1981 report, the Commission made proposals for the rationalization of police powers and for the introduction of an independent prosecuting agency.[33] The Police and Criminal Evidence Act 1984 amounts to a statutory code of police powers of arrest, search, and questioning, and it is supported by Codes of Practice issued by the Home Office. Some of the provisions extended police powers whereas others curtailed them. The Prosecution of Offences Act 1985 created the Crown Prosecution Service, and gave it statutory authority for the prosecution of almost all cases commenced by the police. The Royal Commission had argued strongly in favour of an independent prosecution service but, unlike in most other countries, it believed that the police should still retain the initial decision whether to prosecute, caution, or take no formal action.

In April 1990 the disturbances at Strangeways Prison, Manchester, and at other establishments led to an official inquiry by Lord Justice Woolf and Judge Tumin. Among the many points made in their report in 1991,[34] two are particularly relevant in the present context. The first is that the Inquiry was extremely critical of the conditions in which remand prisoners awaiting trial are held. The Government has accepted most of the recommendations on this point, but improvements are slow in coming.[35] The second is that the Inquiry emphasized the need for greater co-operation among agencies dealing with criminal justice. Its main recommendation on this point has been implemented: there is now a national Criminal Justice Consultative Council, supported by a number of area committees at which representatives of various agencies meet and discuss the approach to particular problems. However, the impact of the Council is still not clear, and it seems

[31] Criminal Law Revision Committee, Eleventh Report, *Evidence (General)*, Cmnd. 4991 (1972).

[32] See Michael Zander, 'The Criminal Process: A Subject Ripe for a Major Inquiry', [1977] *Crim. LR* 249.

[33] Royal Commission on Criminal Procedure, *Report*, Cmnd. 8092 (1981).

[34] *Prison Disturbances April 1990: Report of an Inquiry by the Rt. Hon. Lord Justice Woolf (Parts I and II) and His Honour Judge Stephen Tumim (Part II)*, Cm. 1456 (1991).

[35] Home Office, *Custody, Care and Justice*, Cm. 1647 (1991), ch. 7.

not to be consulted on any regular basis before the Government announces changes of policy.

Also in 1990 the Government issued its White Paper on the future of sentencing policy, proposing the adoption of a principal rationale for most sentences (desert or proportionate sentences) and the introduction of clearer structures.[36] The Criminal Justice Act 1991 implemented these proposals, but some changes were made by the Criminal Justice Act 1993 within months of the introduction of the 1991 Act.

The Royal Commission of 1981 had declined to follow the 1972 report in relation to the right of silence, deciding that it would not be wise to abandon this right at the stage of police questioning, before the prosecution case was known to the suspect. However, the Government introduced severe curtailments of the right of silence into Northern Irish law, by an Order in Council made in 1988.[37] In 1989 the report of a Government working group was published, recommending similar curtailment of the right of silence in England and Wales.[38] Before this could be acted upon the succession of cases of miscarriage of justice, summarized in Section 3 above, began to receive wide publicity. Silence became one of the subjects central to the work of the Royal Commission on Criminal Justice, which was appointed in 1991 and reported in 1993.[39] Among over 300 recommendations in its Report may be found some proposals for greater police powers in dealing with suspects, a review of police disciplinary procedures, disclosure by the prosecution and the defence, abolishing the defendant's right to elect Crown Court trial of an 'either-way' offence, and creating a new review body for alleged miscarriages of justice. The Commission did not recommend the abolition of the right of silence, although neither did it recommend the corroboration of all confessions.

The Government has already rejected the Royal Commission's recommendations on the right of silence, and has incorporated in its Criminal Justice and Public Order Bill 1993–94 some clauses which allow courts to draw adverse inferences, based on the 1972 report and on the Northern Ireland changes of 1988. To what extent the other recommendations of the 1993 Royal Commission will be implemented remains unclear.

---

[36] Home Office, *Crime, Justice and Protecting the Public*, Cm. 965 (1990).

[37] A. Ashworth and P. Creighton, 'The Right of Silence in Northern Ireland', in J. Hayes and P. O'Higgins (eds.), *Lessons from Northern Ireland* (1990); J. D. Jackson, 'Curtailing the Right of Silence: Lessons from Northern Ireland', [1991] *Crim. LR* 404.

[38] Home Office Working Group on the Right of Silence, *Report* (1989), reviewed by A. A. S. Zuckerman, 'Trial by Unfair Means', [1989] *Crim. LR* 855.

[39] See above, n. 14.

7. Process and System

Although many who speak and write about criminal justice tend to refer to 'the criminal justice system', it is widely agreed that it is not a 'system' in the sense of a set of co-ordinated decision-makers. Even from the broad survey above it will be apparent that many groups working within criminal justice enjoy considerable discretion, and that they are relatively autonomous. None the less, the inappropriateness of the term 'system' should not be allowed to obscure the practical inter-dependence of the various agencies.[40] Many depend on other agencies for their case-load or for their information, and decisions taken by one agency can impinge on those taken by others. Thus, to take a few examples, the Crown Prosecution Service depends entirely on the police for its case-load, and largely on the police for information, although some information is now being supplied by the Probation Service. Decisions taken by the Crown Prosecution Service affect the case-load of the courts, and may constrain the powers of magistrates' courts and of defendants to determine mode of trial. Many other exam-ples of interdependence and influence will be found throughout the book, and in the first section of the chapter it was emphasized that decisions should be viewed in this context rather than as discrete and objectively based determinations.

References to systems and interdependence are, however, very much in the managerial mode. The criminal process impinges directly on vic-tims, suspects, and defendants. It impinges on them in the form of one or more contacts and decisions. A defendant who has been questioned by the police, charged, kept in police custody, remanded by the court, perhaps offered a plea bargain, and then tried in court is already likely to feel 'punished' irrespective of whether a guilty verdict and sentence follow. A person who is acquitted after such a sequence of events may well feel 'punished' by the process to which he or she has been sub-jected, even if relieved at the outcome. Of course this is a misuse of the term punishment, which is properly confined in the present context to sentences imposed by courts after findings of guilt. But it accords with the results of American research by Malcolm Feeley, encapsulated in the title of his book *The Process is the Punishment*.[41] Suspects and defendants often feel that the way in which they are treated is equiva-lent to punishment, in the sense that it inflicts on them deprivations (of

[40] For further discussion, see H. Pullinger, 'The Criminal Justice System Viewed as a System', and F. Feeney, 'Interdependence as a Working Concept', both in David Moxon (ed.), *Managing Criminal Justice* (1985).

[41] M. Feeley, *The Process is the Punishment* (1979).

liberty, of reputation) similar to those resulting from a sentence. This is particularly true for defendants who have been remanded in custody, and may flow from a single decision such as the decision to prosecute. Alternatively it may be a consequence, not so much of decisions taken in their case, but rather of what they regard as disrespect for their rights by the officials dealing with them. For present purposes, it is sufficient to make the point that the pre-trial process is a *process* to which defendants are *subjected* by officials who have the power of law behind them. It can be viewed as an exercise of State power—necessary, as part of the political system, but no less real for that. It is therefore appropriate to consider standards, accountability, and other issues relevant to dealings between the State and individual citizens.

Victims are also individual citizens whose interests should be protected. There is no shortage of empirical research findings that victims have been and are being treated in the criminal process in ways that can be described as 'punishment'. In the language of victimologists, victims who report crimes are often subjected to 'secondary victimization' at the hands of police, prosecutors, and courts.[42] Whilst some steps have been taken to reduce these effects by improving techniques of police questioning and by granting anonymity to victims of certain offences, there is little doubt that some victims still suffer psychologically and socially from their involvement in the criminal process. In absolute terms this may be unavoidable, even though efforts must be made to minimize it. It is sufficient here to state that the pre-trial process is a *process* to which victims of crime, too, are *subjected* by officials.

If one adds to these processual elements the fact that the one 'temporal' decision—remand before trial—may result in loss of liberty, and the effects that dispositive decisions can have (as a form of sentence without trial), it is evident that there is much at the pre-trial stage that needs to be justified. Chapter 2 on values and Chapter 3 on ethics begin to explore the foundations of possible justifications.

---

[42] See Ch. 2.3 below.

2

Values

WHAT should we expect of a criminal process? What aims should it pursue and what values ought it to respect? In this chapter and the following chapter we consider some of the criteria by which pre-trial criminal justice tends to be judged and ought to be judged. This chapter offers a general outline of the main values, and Chapter 3 examines in greater detail the rights of suspects and defendants. We begin here with an introductory discussion of the criminal law itself.

1. The Purpose and Scope of the Criminal Law

The purpose of the criminal law is to declare those forms of conduct that are thought to require State punishment, setting out the conditions under which people may be punished for comitting the offences. Systems of criminal law are closely allied with sentencing systems and, together, they have the functions of declaring the forms of conduct that attract conviction and punishment and of acting as a general deterrent against those forms of conduct.

How should the boundaries of the criminal law be set? This is not simply an abstract question about the dividing line between law and morality. It has pressing implications for the division of wrongs between the criminal law and tort, contract, and other parts of civil law. There is also the related question of whether there should be an intermediate category of 'civil offences' or 'contraventions', followed by small sanctions but without the full formality and the severity of the criminal law.

This is not an appropriate place to attempt a developed survey of the criteria for criminalization,[1] but an outline is needed. The most obvious criterion is the seriousness of the harm caused, and that clearly depends for its content on a settled concept of seriousness.[2] Many of the harms will be identifiable individual harms, but there is also the need for a conception of public harm to rationalize offences against the

[1] For a recent attempt, see A. von Hirsch and A. Ashworth, 'Criminalizing Remote Harm: The Standard Analysis' (unpublished MS).

[2] See A. von Hirsch and N. Jareborg, 'Gauging Criminal Harm: A Living Standard Analysis', (1991) 11 *Oxford JLS* 1.

administration of justice, against State security, and perhaps against the environment, for example. A second and related criterion is culpability, for (in principle, and subject to the discussion in the next paragraph) it is not the mere causing of harm but its wrongful causing that should be criminal. Exactly what degree or form of culpability ought to be required for criminal liability is a matter for debate. But such is the emphasis on culpability that there may be types of case in which the intention to cause harm is considered sufficient without much overt conduct, as in attempted crimes.

There is room for considerable argument around the margins of these criteria, but their core is sufficiently well established to serve as a basis for the ensuing discussion. One major area of controversy that should be noted is the widespread use of strict liability offences in English law. Probably half of the 7,000 or more offences require no culpability, or at least they allow for nothing more than a defence of due diligence to be proved by the defendant.[3] Most of these offences may be described as 'regulatory', in that they were created in the context of regulating a particular form of industry, trade, or activity. However, some of them are thought serious enough to carry substantial maximum penalties: they ought therefore to have a culpability requirement, and to be treated as proper crimes, because of their implications for defendants' liberty. Other offences that do not now have substantial penalties ought to have, and ought similarly to be upgraded. But some of the offences concern minor transgressions which have come to be dealt with as crimes largely because the criminal courts are there and are able to deal fairly swiftly with minor offences, especially since there is usually a plea of guilty and merely a fine to be imposed. If the focus of criminalization is to be upon conduct that is culpable and causes harm that is not minor, then a lesser form of liability should be found for these types of case—perhaps civil offences, administrative offences, or contraventions, as suggested earlier.[4]

The centrality of culpability to a discussion of the functions of the criminal law is evident in another respect, too. Some of those who argue for less emphasis on defendants' rights in the criminal process point to the incontestability of factual guilt in many cases. A person may have been 'caught in the act', or apprehended in strongly compromising circumstances. Yet these descriptions often apply to the doing

---

[3] See L. H. Leigh, *Strict and Vicarious Liability* (1982); A. Ashworth, *Principles of Criminal Law* (1991), 135–45.

[4] In Germany many 'regulatory' offences are dealt with administratively as *Ordnungswidrigkeiten*: see A. M. von Kalmthout and P. Tak, *Sanctions Systems in the Member States of the Council of Europe* (1992), ii. 441.

of certain acts or the causing of consequences, and they may neglect the culpability element. Thus Herbert Packer has been taken to task for referring to 'factual guilt' in a way that excludes possible defences to criminal liability, such as insanity, mistake, duress, and so on.[5] It is important to bear in mind that the concepts of guilt and innocence ought to include the element of culpability, even if legal systems are often tempted to impose strict liability for certain offences.

Some authors go much further and emphasize that one of the functions of the administration of criminal justice is to ensure that only those deserving of punishment are convicted. What this appears to mean is that juries should bend or misapply the law when the written rules are insufficiently sensitive to cater for the exculpatory facts of the particular case, or (more bluntly and more rarely) where the law is thought to be wrong. Thus Adrian Zuckerman refers to the desirability of being 'judged by reference to the current social standards'[6] as a common argument in favour of jury trial, and this embodies a belief that even the law's provisions on culpability and criminalizing may need to be supplemented. This view is particularly relevant when discussing the rules of criminal procedure and evidence, where the existence of discretion and the consequent need to reach judgments allows non-legal views about the disposal of cases to filter into the system.

The paradigm of criminal law is a set of rules which declares the conduct that is serious enough and culpable enough to be subject to the criminal sanction and provides a general deterrent against it. This framework of rules functions, to a greater or lesser extent (as we shall see), to authorize and to restrict the extent to which State officials may take coercive procedural steps against citizens. Its scope is very wide, even if the so-called strict liability offences are ignored. There are offences against the person, sexual offences, offences against public order, traffic offences, environmental offences, offences against the State, property offences (including fraud), and various offences connected with safety in a modern society. In ideal terms there should be a rational distinction between harms for which only civil liability is provided and those (more serious) harms for which both civil and criminal liability are possible. Procedurally there should be differences because in criminal proceedings the power of the State, which (albeit through the different agencies of the police and the Crown Prosecution Service)

---

[5] P. Arenella, 'Rethinking the Functions of Criminal Procedure: The Warren and Burger Courts' Competing Ideologies', (1983) 72 *Georgeown LJ* 185, at 214; criticizing H. Packer, *The Limits of the Criminal Sanction* (1968), discussed below in s. 2 of this chapter.

[6] A. A. S. Zuckerman, *The Principles of Criminal Evidence* (1989), 43.

is both investigator and prosecutor, is ranged against the individual defendant, usually supported by legal advisers provided at the State's expense. This disparity may be held to justify procedural and evidential rules designed to rectify the imbalance of power. However, different forms of criminal process may be thought appropriate for different kinds of offence—for example, many countries deal separately with certain traffic offences, and separate regimes for fraud offences are becoming common. The justifications for this must be scrutinized with care, since different degrees of protection of rights require justification. As we shall see, one issue frequently raised in this connection is the relevance of different degrees of seriousness of offence.

2. A Theoretical Framework

The previous chapter demonstrated that a large number of decisions have to be taken in the pre-trial process. Many are concerned with the processing function, some with the dispositive function, and then there is the 'temporal' remand decision. The possible consequences of these decisions for the suspect or defendant are considerable—from loss of liberty and loss of job, to family tensions, inability to sleep, and illness—and this is why there must be justifications for particular practices. In principle the State should take no more power over a person at this stage than is absolutely necessary for the carrying out of the proper functions of law enforcement. There has been no finding of guilt yet, and even if there has been an admission of guilt it is for a court to determine whether any measures (and, if so, what) should be taken against the defendant. Nothing done during the pre-trial process should have a punitive element to it, except where a defendant consents to submit to an obligation as a means of diverting the case from the process (the dispositive function). Apart from that, whilst it is acknowledged that many pre-trial processes will inevitably impose restrictions or even deprivations on a suspect or defendant, the proper principle is that any such impositions should be kept to the minimum.

Would it be relevant to argue that such concern for defendants is misplaced, since victims also have to undergo pain and hardship that is not their choice? Surely not. In order to maintain that a person who has been charged with an offence (though not yet convicted) should be treated no better than he or she is alleged to have treated the victim, one would need to argue not only for a form of talionic justice in sentencing but also that this approach to the infliction of punishment should dominate the period before trial. There are formidable difficulties in arguing that people may be punished before they are tried: it is a mark of civilized society that punishment may be inflicted only after a finding of guilt by a court or a satisfactory admission of guilt to an official in cases where some form of fixed penalty is payable.[7]

A less direct argument with a similar tendency is that, given limited resources, we should accord priority to crime prevention and the protection of victims and should not worry over the conditions imposed on suspects and defendants. This is less easy to dispose of, since the obvious answer that the protection of victims and the protection of defendants' rights are both important will often be met by the response that it may be necessary, practically, to make choices.

How ought these choices to be made? What rights and interests should be recognized? Are some rights stronger (or more fundamental) than others? Mere references to balancing, without careful analysis of these issues, are unhelpful.[8] The best-known theoretical framework for evaluating the criminal process is that of Herbert Packer, developed in the 1960s.[9] It has been subjected to considerable criticism and modification in subsequent years, and will not be adopted as a starting-point here, but it remains worthwhile to consider. Packer suggested that tendencies in criminal justice might be evaluated by means of two theoretical models, the Crime Control model and the Due Process model. 'The value system that underlies the Crime Control model is based on the proposition that the repression of criminal conduct is by far the most important function to be performed by the criminal process.'[10] This calls for 'a high rate of apprehension and conviction', placing a 'premium on speed and finality', and therefore preferring informal to formal procedures, with minimal opportunity for challenge. To work efficiently, the Crime Control model should ensure that weak cases are discarded at the earliest opportunity and that strong cases are taken forward to conviction and sentence as expeditiously as possible. The police are in the best position to judge guilt, and, if they form the view after their investigation that a person is guilty, the subsequent stages of the process should be as truncated as possible.

Packer contrasts with this the Due Process model, which takes cognizance of the stigma and loss of liberty that might fall on the

[7] This refers to the widespread use of fixed penalties for road traffic offences and fare evasion on transport systems, and also extends to the practices of the Customs and Excise and Inland Revenue. For the principle that access to a court must be possible if the defendant contests liability, see Ch. 5.2.

[8] This is a major criticism of the Report of the Royal Commission on Criminal Justice, Cm. 2263 (1993). For discussion, see the articles by Reiner, Jackson, Ashworth, and Glynn in [1993] Crim. LR 808–50.

[9] H. Packer, *The Limits of the Criminal Sanction* (1968).   [10] Ibid. 158.

individual defendant as a result of the criminal process, and which insists on fairness criteria and other protections for the suspect or defendant. Thus the emphasis should be on formal and open adjudication of the facts in court, with the possibility of appeal, in order to give maximum protection to the innocent. Some proponents of the Due Process model would claim that it is a more accurate method of discovering the truth than the Crime Control model, but others would emphasize its recognition that errors do occur and its attempt to erect safeguards against mistaken judgments.

A number of objections have been raised against Packer's approach, of which five may be mentioned briefly here. First, Packer failed to give a clear explanation of the relationship between his models. He recognized that 'the polarity of the two models is not absolute',[11] and stated that the ideology of Due Process 'is not the converse of that underlying the Crime Control model', since 'it does not rest on the idea that it is not socially desirable to repress crime'.[12] His model might be reconstructed so as to suggest that Crime Control is the underlying purpose of the system, but that pursuit of this purpose should be qualified out of respect to Due Process. That, too, needs to be evaluated. Second, Packer assumed that the system of pre-trial justice is capable of affecting the crime rate, since he used the term Crime Control. It is true that Packer included powers of arrest and detection rates in his discussion of pre-trial justice, but evidence is needed of a significant relationship between the extent of police powers and the crime rate. Variations in the crime rate may be influenced more greatly by social and economic factors, and it is fairly well established that different styles of policing do not affect crime rates.[13] The notion that different methods of processing defendants before trial might affect crime rates is not only unproven but also question-begging at a more fundamental level: surely Packer's models would be more realistic if he posited, as the primary State interest in pre-trial processes, convicting the guilty rather than controlling crime. Third, and related to this, Packer underestimated the importance of resource management as an element in the criminal process. However, this may have assumed greater significance in the years since Packer wrote, as governments have come under much greater financial pressure.[14] Fourth, Packer's models make no allowance for victim-related matters. Again, this may be because there was far less consciousness of victims' interests and rights in the 1960s,

[11] H. Packer, *The Limits of the Criminal Sanction* (1968) 154.   [12] Ibid. 163.
[13] See e.g. M. Hough, 'Thinking about Effectiveness', (1987) 27 *BJ Crim.* 70.
[14] Cf. however the criticisms of A. E. Bottoms and J. D. McClean, *Defendants in the Criminal Process* (1976), ch. 9, writing only eight years after Packer.

but it is a significant drawback in using Packer's models today. Fifth, it is possible to mount various internal critiques of the two models. One example is the premium on speed, which Packer describes as an element in the Crime Control model. However, delays are also a source of considerable anxiety and inconvenience, and occasionally prolonged loss of liberty, to defendants. A properly developed notion of Due Process would surely insist that there be no unreasonable delay.[15]

Consideration of Packer's models begins to demonstrate the complexity of the criminal process and the problems of devising a satisfactory theoretical framework. The models may help us to identify elements of two important strands, but they neglect other, conflicting tendencies. Rather than pursuing the search for further possible models,[16] however, it is more relevant to introduce certain concepts from the law of criminal evidence. This branch of the law concerns not only the rules and principles according to which evidence may be admitted at a trial but also, directly or by implication, some of the rules and principles according to which investigators may properly gather evidence. It therefore deals with several activities at the pre-trial stage, particularly police investigations. One central principle is what Bentham termed 'rectitude', that is, the need to ensure that evidence is as reliable and as accurate as possible.[17] This involves recognition of the weaknesses of certain types of evidence, and the taking of steps to avoid or minimize them. In the words of Dennis Galligan, 'these are issues *internal* to proof'.[18] Often pulling against rectitude are various other principles and policies, of which some merit discussion at this stage. The first is the principle that the innocent should be protected against wrongful conviction. Ronald Dworkin has argued that the right of an innocent person not to be convicted should be regarded as fundamental.[19] An obvious reason why this is regarded as fundamental— not a mere harm, but a moral harm, as Dworkin expresses it—is that there is a particular injustice in being wrongly convicted and sentenced. For one thing there is a misapplication of blame, which is unjust in its own right. But there are also the consequential wrongs, which may include deprivation of liberty, or at least restrictions on

---

[15] See the discussion of the European Convention on Human Rights, Art. 6 (1), discussed below in Ch. 3.3 (1).

[16] On which see M. King, *The Framework of Criminal Justice* (1981).

[17] For discussion, see W. L. Twining, *Theories of Evidence: Bentham and Wigmore* (1987), and the review article by D. J. Galligan, 'More Scepticism about Scepticism', (1988) 8 *Oxford JLS* 249.

[18] Galligan, 'More Scepticism', at 255.

[19] R. Dworkin, 'Principle, Policy, Procedure', in C. Tapper (ed.), *Crime, Proof and Punishment* (1981).

liberty. Since the presumption in favour of liberty is surely one of the most basic elements in social life, it can be appreciated why wrongful conviction is regarded as such an injustice. The two aspects of deprivation and wrongfulness combine to yield its fundamental significance. It should be noted that this principle does not always pull against rectitude, since its concern is also accuracy of factual determinations. But where total accuracy is known to be unattainable, the principle tells against admitting the evidence.

If it is agreed that this right is fundamental, why should it not be regarded as absolute? Why does no legal system take the right so seriously as to strive to give the maximum procedural protection against such miscarriages of justice? One answer to this is that it would be simply too constricting in other ways if we were unable to devote funds to other social needs until we were completely satisfied that the criminal justice system could not be further improved. Matters such as education, health, social security, transport systems, and even expenditure on other aspects of criminal justice would be curtailed, in order to make way for an elaborate system (or extensive experiments) aimed at eliminating the risk of wrongful conviction. Few societies and few individuals would be content with this order of priority, even if many would like to see far less complacency about the existing criminal process. A second answer is that if the system were always to yield to the risk of wrongful conviction wherever it was found to be present, this would lead to widespread acquittals of the guilty. Avoiding all types of evidence that have been shown to be open to error or manipulation would require no reliance at all on confessions, hearsay evidence, identification evidence, and so on. This would lead to more 'cracked' trials, fewer convictions, and perhaps fewer prosecutions. The likely results would be loss of public confidence, reduced fulfilment of the State's interest in convicting the guilty, and possibly a loss of crime-preventive effects. Maximum protection of the innocent may well have to be compromised, therefore, but this should be confined to the smallest extent. The right of an innocent person not to be convicted is fundamental, but not absolute.

This should not, however, deliver us back to the shadowy world of 'balancing'. Dworkin proposes that, if equal respect and concern is to be shown towards all citizens, at least two rights ought to be recognized. The first is a right to procedures that place a proper valuation on moral harms such as that arising from breach of the right not to be convicted if innocent. This is evidently a formulation that begs questions—which harms are 'moral harms', and what valuation of them is 'proper'? An attempt to answer the former question is made later, through the concept of human rights. As for the valuation of each moral harm, this is plainly a matter for debate. The point, surely, is that discussions about the form of the criminal process and other aspects of policy should not overlook the principled reasons for avoiding the conviction of innocent people—these would be special, moral harms that necessitate special protections. This suggests that, although the avoidance of moral harms cannot realistically be regarded as an absolute goal or priority, it should be regarded as a primary goal from which it is only proper to derogate on the giving of strong justifications.

The second right would be the right to consistent treatment within the declared policies—in effect, a right to the consistent weighting of the importance of moral harm. This enables an individual to call attention to ways in which a certain procedure fails to show the respect for moral harm that is evident in the criminal process generally. As Dworkin accepts,[20] this is a fairly conservative right that provides no benchmark for determining whether twelve or, say, ten or fifteen is the most appropriate number for a jury. However, if it were decided that juries should remain at twelve generally but should be reduced to six in certain types of case, this principle of consistent treatment or non-discrimination would call for strong justifications for the departure. Moreover, wherever the system institutionalizes differences of treatment (e.g. between summary offences and indictable offences), satisfactory justifications should be sought.

A further point, not explicitly to be found in Dworkin but related to the value of liberty, is that the pre-trial system should impose the minimum of burdens on the individuals subject to it. This is relevant to investigation procedures, and also to remand decisions. In principle, no punitive action should be taken until there has been a conviction. The greater the burdens and deprivations imposed at the pre-trial stage, the stronger the justifications needed to uphold them. The most poignant case to consider, examined in Chapter 7, is the remand in custody pending trial. Also connected to the 'minimum burdens' ideal is the principle that individuals should not be placed in double jeopardy by being prosecuted twice for the same crime. Although one reason for this principle is that it may be oppressive for an individual to have to bear the stress of two trials, the reason relevant to the 'minimum burdens' ideal is that it is an abuse of State power to mount two prosecutions in respect of the same offence. The State should take sufficient care in preparing its case the first time, and it is unfair that

---

[20] R. Dworkin, 'Principle, Policy, Procedure', in C. Tapper (ed.), *Crime, Proof and Punishment* (1981) 212.

standing bodies such as the police and prosecution service, with all their resources, should be allowed to harass defendants.[21]

Much discussed in contemporary writings is the principle of integrity. In its simplest form, this states that the agents of law enforcement should not use, and the courts should not condone, methods of investigating crime that involve breaches of the rules. The criminal justice system is a public institution for responding to cases of actual and alleged law-breaking: it would be a deplorable contradiction if the system itself were to take advantage of rule-breaking by its agents. The reasons advanced in support of this principle often appear to be consequentialist. Thus Justices Holmes and Brandeis, in their famous dissenting speech in *Olmstead* v. *United States*, argued thus: 'Our government is the potent, the omnipresent teacher. For good or for ill, it teaches . . . by its example. If the government becomes a law breaker, it breeds contempt for law; it invites every man to become a law unto himself; it invites anarchy.'[22] Adrian Zuckerman takes the argument further, championing the jury as a means of ensuring the moral legitimacy of verdicts and going so far as to state that 'there is no conflict between the need to protect the citizen from crime and the policy of outlawing the fruits of torture and degradation, because convictions based on these fruits would defeat the aims of the administration of justice'.[23] This statement conceals the conflict by dissolving it into the broader notion of the aims of the system. In effect, it asserts that integrity is more important than obtaining convictions (of the guilty) by certain methods. A similar argument has been developed by Ian Dennis,[24] and is advanced by Andrew Choo as one of the bases of his treatise on the doctrine of abuse of process: 'what the public interest demands is that offenders are brought to conviction in a civilized and publicly acceptable manner.'[25] Whilst the theory seems incontrovertible at a certain level—it would be self-contradictory to proclaim the rule of law and yet to condone the use of torture or of burglary in order to obtain evidence—there remain questions as to whether every departure from the rules at the investigative stage can be said to compromise the integrity of the courts.[26]

The reference to methods that are 'publicly acceptable' brings to the

---

[21] Cf. M. L. Friedland, *Double Jeopardy* (1969).

[22] (1928) 277 US, 438, at 484–5.

[23] Zuckerman, *The Principles of Criminal Evidence*, 303; cf. below, ch. 10.4.

[24] I. Dennis, 'A Rationale of the Law of Evidence', [1989] *CLP* 21.

[25] A. Choo, *Abuse of Process and Judicial Stays of Criminal Proceedings* (1993), 13.

[26] Compare, e.g., J. Kaplan, 'The Limits of the Exclusionary Rule', (1974) 26 *Stanford LR* 1026 with Y. Kamisar, 'Comparative Reprehensibility and the Fourth Amendment Exclusionary Rule', (1987) 86 *Michigan LR* 1. For further discussion, see Ch. 4.4.

surface an abiding difficulty with the principle of integrity. In so far as it is claimed to have an empirical foundation in the views of the public, the case in its favour has not been made out. In order to test the proposition, one would have to question either people in general, or perhaps persons who have been involved in criminal justice as jurors, to find out whether and in what circumstances they are concerned about the methods used by the police and others involved in law enforcement. It seems perfectly possible that the results would be coloured by well-publicized cases of the time, or by particular cases in which the respondents had been involved, although both these possibilities could be minimized by the use of case-studies. It also seems possible that the results would show a lack of concern for methods, except the most flagrantly invasive or brutal, and greater concern for convicting the guilty. Thus the assertion of Justices Holmes and Brandeis that anarchy might result if the use of unfair or unlawful methods by law enforcement agents were condoned could be well wide of the mark. If the principle of integrity is to be regarded as important, it must be supported on the ground that it is right rather than because the consequences of following or not following it are thought to be beneficial.

The principle of integrity is right for a number of reasons. It can be discerned beneath several of the provisions in the European Convention on Human Rights, to be discussed in Chapter 3. Those provisions insist that the system should be fair, and they do so partly because of the consequences of conviction (especially of wrongful conviction) for the individual, and partly because of the unequal strength of the State, as investigator and prosecutor, and the defendant. It can also be argued that such a central institution as the criminal justice system ought to be beyond reproach, not merely because of its own concern with law-breaking but also because it is a central political institution of a State that is a member of the European and international communities. The lawmakers should ensure that the legal rules conform to standards such as those set by the European Convention on Human Rights. Law enforcers, investigators, and other officials should ensure that their conduct conforms with the rules and guidelines laid down. The courts and other bodies should uphold the integrity of the system by declining to allow advantage to be taken of breaches of the rules by officials. There is therefore a political value in the principle of integrity, in so far as it serves to prevent officials within the criminal justice system from undermining the compromises embodied in the duly created rules.

The argument above, then, is that it is better not to rely on Packer's two models but instead to develop an approach that reflects the range of factors that may legitimately impinge on decision-making in criminal justice. The temptation to reach for the concept of 'balancing' must be resisted: the first task is to explore the claims of various factors to influence the shape of rules and principles for the criminal process. In this section we have considered the principle of rectitude, the principle of avoiding the conviction of the innocent (manifesting itself in the principle of proper weighting and the principle of consistent treatment), and the integrity principle. These will be developed in greater detail, and by reference to the European Convention on Human Rights, in Chapter 3.

The task remaining for the present chapter is to examine some of the other principles and policies relevant to the criminal process. In doing so, it should be borne in mind that the pre-trial processes discussed here mostly involve decisions with either of two purposes—the processing of cases through the system, and the diversion of cases from the system. First we turn to the right of victims, and then to the protection of the vulnerable. After that we discuss some values connected with diversion, and the relevance of systems of accountability and information.

3. The Rights of Victims

What should be the rights of victims in the criminal justice system and, more particularly, in pre-trial processes? This depends on a proper appreciation of the respective rights of the State, offenders, and victims.

Until recent years there had been a relative neglect of victims' needs for support, respect, and compensation. Now, urged on by the United Nations,[27] by the Council of Europe,[28] and by the US President's Task Force on Victims of Crime,[29] there is increasing recognition that the victims of crime have rights to respectful and sympathetic treatment from law enforcement agents; to support and help in the aftermath of the offence; to proper information about the progress of their case; to facilities at courtrooms that separate them from other members of the public; and to compensation for the crime, either from the offender or (if that is not possible) from the State, at least for crimes of violence.[30]

[27] United Nations, *Basic Principles of Justice for Victims of Crime and Abuse of Power* (1985).
[28] Council of Europe, *The Position of the Victim in the Framework of Criminal Law and Procedure* (1985).
[29] Which gave rise, e.g., to the federal Victim and Witness Protection Act of 1982.
[30] See generally D. Miers, 'The Responsibilities and the Rights of Victims of Crime', (1992) 55 *MLR* 482.

These rights to services should be regarded as an important element in social provision for the disadvantaged, and it should be the concern of people working in the criminal justice system to ensure that they are recognized and fulfilled. But completely different justifications are needed if it is claimed that victims have procedural rights in the criminal process. Should the victim have the right to be consulted on the decision whether or not to prosecute, on the bail/custody decision, on the acceptance of a plea to a lesser offence or to fewer offences, or on sentence? The answer to these questions depends on the proper purposes of the criminal process. On one version of the restorative paradigm, the overall purpose might be described as 'the restoration into safe communities of victims and offenders who have resolved their conflicts'.[31] This places a form of mediation between victim and offender at the centre of criminal procedure, with compensation from offender to victim as a significant element. Clearly victims' procedural rights would be extensive in such a system, although many versions of restorative justice also recognize the importance of restoring the damage to the community, and decisions on this must surely be the function of a court.[32] However, this is not the only possible restorative model of criminal justice: an alternative approach would be to maintain that the prosecution should be charged with representing the interests of victims in a fairly conventional system, arguing for compensation and for protection where appropriate.

On a punishment paradigm, in contrast, the emphasis is on the crime as an offence which the State, through the courts, should visit with censure if appropriate. This is not to dispute or to overlook the victim's right to receive compensation from the offender, which is primarily a civil law matter but which may properly be incorporated into the criminal process for pragmatic reasons of speed and efficiency. However, the State has the primary interest in prosecution and sentence. This is because those who commit offences may be said to deserve punishment, and for reasons of general prevention and deterrence. Those arguments will not be pursued further here:[33] the key point is that punishment is a transaction between the State and the offender, on which the victim's personal view should be no more significant than the judge's personal view or those of any other

[31] The words of Daniel van Ness, 'New Wine and Old Wineskins: Four Challenges of Restorative Justice', (1993) 4 *Criminal Law Forum* 251.

[32] See van Ness, 'New Wine' who recognizes this as a matter for the court; cf. the critical observations of A. Ashworth, 'Some Doubts about Restorative Justice', (1993) 4 *Criminal Law Forum* 277.

[33] For elaboration, see A. von Hirsch, *Censure and Sanctions* (1993); for brief discussion, see A. Ashworth, *Sentencing and Criminal Justice* (1992), ch. 3.

individual. The court, not any individual, has the right to order punishment. The form and intensity of the sentence should embody a judgement, according to the law, of the relative heinousness of the offence, and should comport fairly with the sentences imposed on others who have committed similar crimes. Admittedly all the key concepts here (e.g. seriousness of offence, severity of sentence, proportionality) are essentially contestable, but it is possible to develop criteria that can be debated in their social context.[34] What a particular victim would like to see as the punishment is not a relevant consideration: the victim might be vindictive or forgiving, demanding or afraid of the offender, well informed or unable to grasp the differences between types of sentence, and it would be unfair and wrong that punishments should vary according to these factors.

A similar analysis can be applied to decisions taken at earlier stages, since the pre-trial process should also be a matter chiefly between the State and the offender. The decision to prosecute should be taken in the public interest, not according to the desires of the victim. However, most systems have one or more 'complainant offences', typically assault, for which no prosecution will be brought unless there is an official complaint from the aggrieved party.[35] The justifications for regarding these offences differently seem unconvincing: they are personal offences, and in practice a prosecution cannot succeed unless the victim is willing to testify, but those considerations apply to many crimes. As we shall see, there is a further complication in England because an enforceable order for the offender to pay compensation to the victim can only be made if a prosecution is brought. But the general principle is unaffected by these two points. Similarly, the decision between bail or custody should be taken in the public interest, but that decision should be informed by any fears the victim may have about harassment or retaliation if the alleged offender is granted bail. As for decisions on acceptance of plea, these are entirely parallel to sentencing decisions. If consultation with the victim on any of these issues suggests that the victim should be able to influence the outcome, it should be resisted. However, there may be good arguments for allowing victims to have an input into proceedings on questions of fact—for example, to submit a victim impact statement that details the precise harm resulting, for purposes of compensation—but even then it should be ensured that the contents of such statements are subjected to proper evidential requirements. Just as a defendant should not be allowed to

---

[34] See e.g. von Hirsch and Jareborg, 'Gauging Criminal Harm', 1; Ashworth, *Sentencing and Criminal Justice*, ch. 4.

[35] See P. J. P. Tak, *The Legal Scope of Non-prosecution in Europe* (1986), 53.

make unsupported allegations about the victim's role in an offence, so equally the victim should not be permitted to make unsubstantiated claims about things done or harm or loss inflicted by the defendant.[36]

In several jurisdictions the role of the victim is greater than has been proposed here. Victim impact statements are permitted in New Zealand and in some Australian states, as well as many states of the USA, and they may contain information relevant not merely to compensation but also to sentence (e.g. detailing the after-effects of the crime). Some jurisdictions also provide for consultation with victims before such decisions as prosecuting or not and accepting a 'plea bargain' or not. Some American states go further and allow the victim impact statement to include a recommendation on sentence, or indeed grant to victims a right of allocution that allows the victim to address the court before sentence.[37] On the view taken here, such a development should be opposed on the ground that either it infiltrates irrelevant considerations (personal views) into the sentencing process, or it raises victims' expectations unfairly, or both. However, there are versions of 'restorative theory' that do not depend on the greater involvement of victims in decision-making, and such approaches lie much closer to the view taken above.[38] The interests of the victim ought to be recognized as forming part of the public interest, so that prosecutors should take account of victim-oriented matters in their judgements at various stages of the criminal process. This is why threats against the victim constitute a strong reason for opposing bail, for example.

4. Fairness and the Protection of the Vulnerable

The implications of the principle of legality and the principle of equality before the law will be explored in Chapter 3, especially in relation to the avoidance of discriminatory practices in the criminal process.[39] However, there are certain classes of person who are specially vulnerable and in whose cases there should be favourable discrimination—as by the provision of extra advice, support, or protection. Two such classes are juveniles and the mentally disordered.

Young victims of crime have received little attention, as a group, until the last five or ten years. There is now increasing awareness that child abuse within families in a social problem of significant dimensions, and that young people also suffer as the victims of a wide range

---

[36] For further discussion and references, see A. Ashworth, 'Victim Impact Statements and Sentencing', [1993] *Crim. LR* 498.

[37] See further ibid.   [38] L. Zedner, 'Restoration and Retribution' (1994) *MLR*.

[39] See Ch. 3.3.4.

of crimes (such as burglary of their and their parents' homes).[40] Changes such as the pre-recording of child witness statements and live video links in courts form part of the response to this.[41] Increasing awareness of the problems encountered by children as complainants and as witnesses has led to improved police practices and to procedural changes in relation to the reception of children's evidence in court.[42] It is because of their tender age and dependency that young victims ought to receive special support in the investigative parts of the process and procedural concessions at the trial.

Suspects and defendants under a certain age (18 in England and Wales) also require special protection during the criminal process for the same general reason. They need support when being questioned by the police, and the presence of an adult is desirable to ensure that they have some measure of protection and advice. Code of Practice C under the Police and Criminal Evidence Act 1984 provides for the presence of an 'appropriate adult' whenever a juvenile is interviewed by the police, and introduces several other special requirements. As with all legal provisions and guidelines, it is essential to determine whether they operate as intended, and there is some evidence that certain police divisions try to discourage juveniles from summoning legal advice themselves and from having both an appropriate adult and a legal adviser present.[43] There is at present no provision for advice before deciding whether or not to accept a caution or other form of diversion. It is important that young suspects be properly advised at all the significant stages, whether dispositive or processual, in the criminal process.

The case for support and advice for the mentally disordered is no less compelling. These are people who may be at an intellectual or other disadvantage in their dealings with agents of law enforcement. It is quite unfair that they should suffer as a result of such a disadvantage, particularly in the light of the strong policy in favour of the diversion of the mentally disordered.[44] Code of Practice C under the Police and Criminal Evidence Act 1984 introduces special protections for mentally disordered or mentally handicapped persons who are interviewed by the police. Once again it is important to be satisfied that these protections

[40] J. Morgan and L. Zedner, *Child Victims* (1992).

[41] See J. R. Spencer, *Children's Evidence in Legal Proceedings* (1989).

[42] Home Office, *Report of the Advisory Group on Video Evidence* (the Pigot Report) (1989); J. Spencer and R. Flin, *The Evidence of Children* (1990); D. J. Birch, 'The Criminal Justice Act 1991: Children's Evidence', [1992] *Crim. LR* 262.

[43] D. Brown, T. Ellis, and K. Larcombe, *Changing the Code: Police Detention under the Revised PACE Codes of Practice*, HORS 129 (1993).

[44] Home Office Circular 66/1990, *Provision for Mentally Disordered Offenders*.

are being granted to those who need them: one survey found that around 15 to 20 per cent of suspects were 'mentally incapable of understanding the significance of questions put to him or his replies', the words of Code C, compared with a mere 4 per cent whom the police identified as such.[45] Thus it is not merely special legal protection but also practical awareness training that is needed to secure these rights.

5. Dispositive Values

We now turn away from the framework within which process values operate, and consider some values relevant to the 'dispositive' aspects of pre-trial decisions.[46] The focus here is on police cautioning, discontinuance of cases, and other forms of diversion from the formal process. To a large extent the values relevant here reflect the purposes at the stage of sentencing, which is the best-known and most widely publicized dispositive decision, but there should also be a philosophical connection with the principles discussed above in relation to process values. In particular, the right of an innocent person not to be punished is relevant to both types of decision.

1. *Prevention of crime*: the prevention of crime is among the reasons for having a criminal justice system, with police, courts, and sentences. It is also an underlying reason for diversion, but this is not to say that it should be determinative in individual cases. These two points should be kept separate. It is one thing to argue that the system of diversion should operate in such a way that it contributes to the overall prevention of crime, at least by dealing with offenders in ways that do not increase the chances of further law-breaking by them or by others. It is another thing to maintain that the prospect of a particular person not reoffending should be a necessary or sufficient reason for diverting that offender from the formal criminal process. The latter point comes into direct conflict with the principle of proportionality in (4) below. The point here is that, since dispositive decisions without trial may be regarded as part of or analogous to the sentencing system, they should not increase the probability of people committing offences. This may have implications for the nature and overall severity level of methods of diversion.

2. *Freedom and fairness*: this principle has a direct connection with process values. The system should ensure that, as far as possible, a person's decision whether or not to accept diversion is a free and

[45] G. Gudjonsson, I. Clare, S. Rutter, and J. Pearse, *Persons at Risk during Interviews in Police Custody: The Identification of Vulnerabilities*, RCCJ Research Study 12 (1993).
[46] See Ch. 1.2 for elaboration.

informed one, and that there is a right of access to a court if guilt is disputed. The idea of a completely free decision may be regarded as unattainable, in the sense that the alternative of going to court will often be
perceived as more stressful, but there are ways of maximizing this freedom. For example, in cases where the prosecutor or police offer diversion and the defendant wishes to contest guilt, there could be a rule
that the court could impose no more severe penalty than was offered
for diversion.[47] The right of access to court has been insisted upon by
the European Court of Human Rights,[48] and is essential so as to ensure
that methods of diversion do not become methods of subversion, as far
as fairness and the protection of the innocent are concerned.

3. *Victim compensation*: any arrangement for diversion should
ensure that the victim does not thereby lose a right to compensation.
The system should remain committed to victims' rights, for the reasons
elaborated in Section 3 above. This does not necessarily mean that
offenders should be required to pay full compensation to their victims
as an element in diversion: as will be argued, the victim's right to compensation is a fundamental right but not an absolute one.[49] But it does
mean that arrangements for diversion should not be made in a way
that precludes an enforceable agreement for compensation, unless
there is a strong argument for overriding the right in this situation.

4. *Proportionality of imposition*: there should be a sense of proportion between the seriousness of the offence and that which the
offender is asked to agree to as the condition of diversion. This is not
merely a means of ensuring that consent is as voluntary as can be. It is
also a basic element of desert: a person who has committed an offence
deserves to be punished, but only to an extent that may be described as
appropriate to the seriousness of the offence committed (seriousness
being composed of harm and culpability). The idea of deserved punishment is grounded in the belief that those who commit crimes are
rightly liable to punishment in the same way that those who commit
civil wrongs are rightly liable to be made to pay damages. These are elementary propositions of corrective justice.[50]

The impositions on those who are 'diverted' must be proportionate
to one another, in the sense that more serious cases should involve
more onerous sanctions and less serious cases should involve less
onerous sanctions. This is known as 'ordinal proportionality',[51]

---

[47] Unless considerations of public expenditure are deemed relevant to such decisions:
see the discussion of plea bargaining in Ch. 9.

[48] See the decisions cited in Ch. 5 n. 24.   [49] See below, Ch. 3.3.2.

[50] For discussion, see von Hirsch, *Censure and Sanctions*.

[51] For discussion, see A. von Hirsch and A. Ashworth, *Principled Sentencing* (1992), ch.
4, esp. 207–19.

although its application to diversion is likely to be somewhat muted since most of the offences and the sanctions are relatively minor. Combined with this is the requirement of 'cardinal proportionality', that the absolute level of severity of sanctions should not be disproportionate to the crimes involved.[52] Since those who commit serious offences should not be diverted from the criminal process, it follows that the penalties on diversion should be of modest severity only.

It will be evident that, although the parameters of desert are fairly clear at a conceptual level, their application in practice leaves room for variations according to the cultural and political context. What is regarded as a sufficiently minor offence for diversion or too severe a sanction for diversion may to a large extent be culturally determined, the latter being related to the function of crime prevention discussed in (1) above. The principle of proportionality should, however, be regarded as a fundamental one—not absolute, since questions of priority will necessarily arise, but fundamental. If 'legality' values are to be respected, the questions of priority should be decided on principle and not *ad hoc*. A great deal has been written about these issues in the context of sentencing,[53] but a few general points should suffice here. Public protection from 'dangerous' offenders is often regarded as a justification for departing from proportionality,[54] but that is unlikely to be a significant factor in decisions at this level. Reparation has already been discussed, in the context of victim compensation, and so that leaves deterrence and rehabilitation to be considered.

The deterrent rationale for punishment conflicts with desert in several ways. Individual deterrence argues that the punishment on the individual should be such as to deter him or her from further offences. This conflicts with desert in cases where the offender seems unlikely to reoffend and therefore needs no deterrence (desert might require a more severe response), and in cases where the offender seems likely to reoffend and therefore requires a substantial sentence (desert might require a less severe response, commensurate with the seriousness of the offence). Desert theorists would argue against individual deterrent sentencing on the ground that it places hopes of crime prevention above the general right of the offender not to be sentenced disproportionately to

---

[52] See ibid. and von Hirsch, *Censure and Sanctions*, chs. 3 and 4.

[53] e.g. Ashworth, *Sentencing and Criminal Justice*, ch. 3; Ashworth and von Hirsch, *Principled Sentencing, passim*; M. Cavadino and J. Dignan, *The Penal System: An Introduction* (1992), ch. 2.

[54] See ss. 1 (2) (*b*) and 2 (2) (*b*) of the Criminal Justice Act 1991; for criticisms, see Ashworth, *Sentencing and Criminal Justice*, 159–67.

the crime committed.[55] The awkward area is, however, the approach to offenders with a previous record: individual deterrent theory has a widespread attraction here, escalating the response to successive offences, whereas desert theory argues that after a few offences the offender has forfeited all claims to indulgence but should not be sentenced more severely than is proportionate to the latest offence.[56] On desert theory, the first or second offender should have mitigation, but the repeated offender should not suffer aggravation of sentence beyond what is proportionate. In practice, this is less of a problem in the sphere of diversion because the penalties overall should remain low. But there is a serious question whether (young) repeat offenders ought to receive multiple cautions or other forms of diversion from prosecution, and whether previous criminal record should affect other dispositive decisions such as plea bargaining. Desert theorists would minimize the effect, save for allowing mitigation for first and second offenders.

General deterrence is more commonly regarded as a rationale for the overall level of punishments, but occasionally it is cited as a reason for a specially severe sentence in a particular case—an exemplary sentence, aimed at deterring others from this type of offence. Such sentences are now widely criticized, and the problem is unlikely to present itself in the context of diversion. More relevant is the argument that diversion and its sanctions are so undemanding that this may undermine the general deterrent effect of the law, leading offenders to believe that they have a licence to commit certain types of offence. This is the point of (1) above, and some desert theorists would adapt the notion of cardinal proportionality so as to ensure a minimum level of sanctions that makes the system credible. However, this is an argument that is often advanced and rarely substantiated by evidence: before accepting that sanction levels are too low and are leading to more law-breaking than would otherwise take place, there must be a careful review of the evidence on the patterns of thought and behaviour of offenders and potential offenders.

The rehabilitative rationale justifies intervention in the lives of offenders so as to alter their attitudes or behaviour in a way that ensures future law-abidance. Having reached its ascendancy in the 1960s, this rationale then lost support because of the sparsity of evidence that rehabilitative programmes worked and because of the variable and sometimes excessive periods for which offenders were

[55] For extensive discussion and readings, see Ashworth and von Hirsch, *Principled Sentencing*, ch. 2.

[56] For discussion, see M. Wasik, 'Guidance, Guidelines and Criminal Record', in K. Pease and M. Wasik (eds.), *Sentencing Reform: Guidance or Guidelines?* (1987).

subjected to control. The rehabilitation of offenders remains a declared aim of many of those working in the criminal justice system, but it is better seen as an aim to be achieved within the framework of a sanction that is fairly proportioned to the offence. It should therefore be a collateral rather than a determining aim. Some forms of diversion are rehabilitative in aim, and for similar reasons it should be ensured that rehabilitative programmes do not make greater demands on diverted offenders than other forms of diversion for comparable offences.

6. Accountability

It will be evident in the course of the book that many stages of the criminal process are characterized by discretion. This is often justified by reference to the multifactorial nature of many decisions in the criminal process. However, this does not mean that values such as predictability, certainty, and principled decision-making have to be jettisoned: to a large extent they may be secured through systems of accountability.[57] Such values as the protection of declared rights (of victims and suspects or offenders) and the prevention of abuse of power by officials might be threatened if the policies or the practices of a law enforcement agency diverge from the purposes of the system. Methods of accountability include proper scrutiny of general policies, rules and/or guidelines for decision-making, active supervision of practice, avenues for challenging decisions, and openness rather than secrecy at key stages.

In a democratic form of society, issues of public policy should be decided by the legislature. However, in matters of law enforcement the tendency has been for Parliament to avoid such issues and to leave them to each agency itself, usually without any check other than the formal requirement to submit annual reports to the House of Commons. Thus agencies such as the Inland Revenue, Customs and Excise, and the Health and Safety Executive are relatively free to determine their own policies—'semi-autonomous', as Dennis Galligan puts it[58]—although some of their procedures will be authorized by statute. The Crown Prosecution Service is similarly regulated: statute requires the Service to formulate a code and to report annually to Parliament, but there is no legislative guidance on substance. The police are also relatively free in this regard, although the Home Office sends guidance by circular to chief constables which is then used as a basis for

[57] D. J. Galligan, 'Regulating Pre-trial Decisions', in I. Dennis (ed.), *Criminal Law and Criminal Justice* (1987).
[58] Ibid.

appraisal by Her Majesty's Chief Inspector of Constabulary. It is, of course, possible for the Government to put pressure on agencies to modify their policies, but that hardly qualifies as a form of accountability. The Crown Prosecution Service has published its general guidelines, in the form of the *Code for Crown Prosecutors*, but this is only a significant step towards accountability if they are worded clearly and if they are followed in practice. The Crown Prosecution Service, in common with other statutory bodies, is also open to scrutiny from various government and parliamentary sources. The Select Committee procedure applies, and thus the Home Affairs Committee has examined the performance of such organizations as the police, the Crown Prosecution Service, the Forensic Science Service, and the Prison Service. Within Government, there is also the role of the Audit Commission in assessing the performance of agencies. The existence of these bodies adds to accountability, even though their direct powers are limited.

Are these agencies accountable to the courts? There is a number of public law doctrines available, but the tendency has been to confine judicial review to the outer limits of unreasonableness (by applying the *Wednesbury* principle).[59] In recent years there have been some moves towards the scrutiny of certain policies for and against prosecution,[60] but the prevailing attitude remains one of reluctance. One could argue that the courts themselves, not being a democratic body, are unsuited to the task of reviewing operational policies. However, in a system with a declared set of rights (such as the US Constitution, or the European Convention on Human Rights if incorporated into English law), the courts could at least function to safeguard those rights against infringement.[61] Thus there is the potential for the courts to scrutinize decisions or policies on such matters as prosecution decisions, mode of trial, plea negotiation, and so forth, ensuring that they do not deprive individuals of procedural or substantive rights.

Claims for greater openness, as a step towards public accountability, are likely to be unwelcome in a sphere that has long known secrecy. Following the Scarman Report,[62] the Metropolitan Police developed local consultative committees, neighbourhood watch schemes, and

---

[59] *Associated Provincial Picture Houses* v. *Wednesbury Corporation* [1948] 1 KB 223.

[60] e.g. *R.* v. *Chief Constable of Kent, ex p. L.* (1991) 93 Cr. App. R. 416, *R.* v. *Inland Revenue Commissioners, ex p. Mead* [1993] 1 All ER 722, and *R.* v. *Croydon Justices, ex p. Dean* [1993] Crim. LR 759, discussed in Ch. 5.

[61] For a recent judicial essay in favour of incorporating the European Convention into English law, see Sir Thomas Bingham, 'The European Convention on Human Rights: Time to Incorporate', (1993) 109 *LQR* 390.

[62] Lord Scarman, *The Brixton Disorders*, Cmnd. 8427 (1981).

other links with the community.[63] There are now schemes for lay visitors in police stations,[64] and 'appropriate adults' must be summoned to interviews of young people and of mentally handicapped people at police stations. Proposals for greater openness in plea bargaining might have similar benefits, in so far as they lead the participants in decision-making to take greater care to follow the rules.

However, it is in the nature of many pre-trial decisions that they involve wide discretion, offer the suspect or defendant a 'take-it-or-leave-it' choice, and may result in the case dropping out of the system altogether. Occasional *post hoc* review may well prove inferior to the articulation of policies, followed by thorough training, by internal supervision arrangements, and by opportunities for challenging decisions. It would certainly not be sufficient to assume that the formulation of guidelines for all the key decisions would ensure accountability and consistency, although that is a necessary step. But even then, there are further questions: who is to formulate the policies? If there is to be accountability at this stage, to whom should it be? There are varied histories of local accountability for the police and the Probation Service, but even a perfect system of local accountability might still lead to variations between one area and another. This suggests that, if the democratic ideal is to be taken seriously, there must be some overall plan or overall body with responsibility for general policies of law enforcement. This theme will be taken up again in the concluding chapter. For the present, it is sufficient to establish the strong arguments in favour of accountability, to point out the need for accountability at the different levels of general policy and individual decision-making,[65] and to advert to its limited and fragmentary nature in the existing system of pre-trial justice.

7. Rights, Decisions, and Information

To propound the principle that information ought to be assured to those who have to take decisions about the exercise of rights or about the progress of cases might seem to be a redundant exercise. Yet research has shown that many of those who have rights do not exercise them because of their ignorance that the right exists, or that its exercise carries no penalty, and so forth; that some defendants do not learn

---

[63] For general discussion, see R. Reiner, *The Politics of the Police* (2nd edn., 1992), 253–61, and L. Lustgarten, *The Governance of the Police* (1986).

[64] R. Morgan, 'Policing by Consent', in R. Morgan and D. Smith (eds.), *Coming to Terms with Policing* (1989).

[65] See G. Richardson, *Law, Process and Custody: Prisoners and Patients* (1993), 43–5.

about information possessed by the police and not used by the prosecution; and that some officials who have to take decisions about cases
receive information predominantly in favour of one party and hardly
ever in favour of the other. Referring to the case of the Maguire Seven,[66]
where non-disclosure by the Forensic Science Service was a reason for
quashing the convictions but one defendant had died in prison, Patrick
O'Connor writes: 'perhaps there is no more moving reminder of the
power that goes with the control of information. It can be a matter of
life and death.'[67]

If it is decided that a suspect, defendant, or victim should have a certain right, one can assume that a significant value is thereby respected.
Yet if there is no machinery for informing the right-holders of their
rights, and if it is shown that many or even some of them are ignorant,
this practical deficiency undermines the very value that the right was
intended to respect. For example, victims of violent crime have access
to the Criminal Injuries Compensation Board for compensation (within
the regulations): an early study showed that only 39 per cent of victims
of violence got to know about the Board's existence,[68] and efforts to
improve information by imposing a duty on the police have not met
with complete success, largely because of incomplete understanding
by police officers of the scheme and its relationship to court compensation.[69] According to the *Victim's Charter* victims have a right to
receive information about the progress of 'their' case, but without adequate mechanisms, especially with regard to liaison between the police
and the Crown Prosecution Service, respect for this right appears
patchy.[70]

Another example is provided by the suspect's right to legal advice in
the police station: attempts were made in the revised Codes of Practice
(under the Police and Criminal Evidence Act 1984) to ensure that suspects are fully informed of the right and its extent. Research since the
introduction of the revised Codes in 1991 shows that some three-quarters of suspects are now informed of the right, and that legal advice is
free; just over a half are told that the legal advice is independent, but
very few are told that the consultation is in private.[71] The position is
therefore improved, but information is still less than complete.

---

[66] See Ch. 1.3.

[67] P. O'Connor, 'Prosecution Disclosure: Principle, Practice and Justice', [1992] *Crim. LR* 464, at 467.

[68] J. Shapland, J. Willmore, and P. Duff, *Victims in the Criminal Justice System* (1985), 124.

[69] T. Newburn and S. Merry, *Keeping in Touch: Police–Victim Communication in Two Area*, HORS 116 (1990), ch. 5.

[70] Ibid. [71] Brown, Ellis, and Larcombe, *Changing the Code.*

Moreover, greater attention should be devoted to techniques of communication: being told is not the same as being caused to understand.[72] Other examples could be given, but the point of principle should now be clear. If it is known that people who should have the opportunity to exercise certain rights fail to realize their existence or to grasp their extent, this undermines the value that the rights are supposed to respect.

Reference has already been made above to the unequal resources of prosecution and defence. When the police do much of the early investigating and questioning, this is hardly surprising. But should the information obtained by the police be treated as belonging to them, or not? In many cases in the 1970s there was no clear obligation on the prosecution to disclose to the defence material they had obtained but did not wish to use in the prosecution. The situation began to improve in 1981 with the publication of Attorney-General's Guidelines on the subject, and the Court of Appeal's decision in the 'miscarriage of justice' case of *Ward* (1993)[73] reasserts the prosecution's duty of disclosure, states that there will be few exceptions to this duty, and suggests that the court should be prepared to make a ruling if the contents of unused material are sensitive. Whilst both the Court of Appeal[74] and the Royal Commission on Criminal Justice[75] have since taken the view that the *Ward* judgment went too far in requiring the prosecution to notify the defence in every case where public interest immunity is claimed, this does not prevent it being said that there is now a general principle that the police and the Crown are merely trustees of the information that comes into their hands.[76] The detailed proposals of the Royal Commission are open to criticism on theoretical and practical grounds,[77] but in the present context it is sufficient to note the recognition of the power of information in the wake of notorious miscarriages of justice that stemmed from non-disclosure to the defence.[78]

A slightly different point about information relates to the input into various decisions. Magistrates' decisions on bail have tended to follow the prosecutor's representations, and one reason for this may be that most of the information comes from the prosecutor. The information

[72] I. Clare and G. Gudjonsson, *Devising and Piloting an Experimental Version of the 'Notice to Detained Persons'*, RCCJ Research Study 7 (1993).

[73] *Ward* (1993) 96 Cr. App. R. 1.

[74] In *Johnson et al.* [1993] Crim. LR 689. [75] RCCJ Report, paras. 6.44 to 6.48.

[76] See the arguments of O'Connor, 'Prosecution Disclosure'.

[77] See J. Glynn, 'The Royal Commission on Criminal Procedure: Disclosure', [1993] *Crim. LR* 841.

[78] e.g. *McIlkenny et al.* (1991) 93 Cr. App. R. 287; *Maguire et al.* (1992) 94 Cr. App. R. 133; *Ward* (1993) 96 Cr. App. R. 1.

necessary to decide in favour of the accused (e.g. information on address, employment, family ties, etc.) is not routinely available to the Crown Prosecution Service or to the courts. Bail information schemes have been developed with a view to filling this gap, particularly in cases where a defendant who is otherwise likely to be remanded in custody might be found a place in a bail hostel.[79] There are now also a few 'Public Information Case Assessment' schemes, designed to provide the Crown Prosecution Service with personal information about a defendant that might lead to discontinuance of the case: without such information, a favourable decision is unlikely. The point of principle is that, where a decision-maker is expected to take account of conflicting considerations, fairness is unlikely to be achieved if the available information relates predominantly to one set of considerations.

8. Conclusions

In this chapter we have considered some elements in a framework of values for the criminal process. The whole point of having the criminal process is to deal with those who commit offences: some are diverted from the process early, either because there is insufficient evidence of guilt or because the case is not serious enough to be brought to court, whereas the cases of others are 'processed' towards trial. In this chapter, apart from discussing certain values relevant to dispositive decisions, the discussion has ranged over the rights of victims, the protection of the vulnerable, the importance of information and the need for accountability. In order to complete this preliminary discussion the rights of suspects and defendants must be discussed, and that is central to Chapter 3.

[79] C. Lloyd, *Bail Information Schemes: Practice and Effect*, Home Office Research and Planning Unit Paper 69 (1992).

3

Ethics

In this chapter there is further exploration of the moral principles that should inform the criminal process. In Chapter 2 some elements of the framework of values were sketched. The emphasis here is on the principles that should govern interactions between individual suspects or defendants and State officials, in the form of police, prosecutors, and others. It is important to begin with the affirmation that committing a crime may itself be regarded as wrongful. This is not a self-evident proposition—much depends on the contents of the criminal law, the political system in which it is situated, and even the method by which it was created[1]—but it will be assumed for the purpose of the discussion that follows. Doubts about the ethical status of strict liability crimes, victimless crimes, and certain other offences were aired in Chapter 2[2] and will be left aside here, in the belief that there is a sufficient core of crimes proscribing behaviour that is morally wrong beyond a peradventure.

Much of the discussion below concerns the ethical principles that ought to shape the way in which officials exercising power within the criminal process should conduct themselves towards citizens. The substance of these principles could be analysed in terms of rights, and the language of rights (used in the European Convention) is adopted from time to time. However, one reason for framing the discussion in terms of ethical principles for State officials is to draw attention to the rival influences on the conduct of State officials: particular interest is taken in the occupational cultures that currently dominate the practices of some officials—the 'Spanish customs', the judgements of moral character,[3] and even the conceptions of 'public interest' and of 'justice'. The chapter opens with a brief inquiry into some philosophical justifications, connecting with Chapter 2. The central section of the chapter examines key provisions of the European Convention on

---

[1] For a developed argument, see Nicola Lacey, *State Punishment* (1988), chs. 4 and 6.
[2] See Ch. 2.1.
[3] On judgements of moral character, see e.g. K. Hawkins, *Environment and Enforcement* (1984), on pollution inspectors and H. Parker, M. Sumner, and G. Jarvis, *Unmasking the Magistrates* (1989), on magistrates. This use of 'moral' is a good reason for adopting the term 'ethical' in this chapter.

Human Rights and kindred conventions. This is followed by inquiries into types of, and reasons for, unethical behaviour. This necessitates careful examination of the practices and statements of practitioners in the criminal justice system. The chapter ends by discussing the role of codes of ethics in bringing about change.

1. Rules and Ethics

Is there any need to discuss ethics or abstract rights when there are so many legal rules, codes, and guidelines impinging on the work of law enforcement agents? Is there really any room for moral disputation when we have such documents as the Police and Criminal Evidence Act 1984 and its Codes of Practice, the *Code for Crown Prosecutors*, the *Victim's Charter*, guideline judgments on sentencing, and the Criminal Justice Acts 1991–3? Three good reasons may be offered for pressing ahead with ethical inquiries.

First, ethical principles should apply to those who make rules and guidelines as well as to those who are subject to them. Thus there should be no suggestion that ethical issues affect only the lower ranks: the decisions of members of the legislature, the Home Secretary, the Director of Public Prosecutions, and the Lord Chief Justice should be equally subject to appraisal on ethical grounds. However, there should be no confusion between legal rules and moral or ethical principles. It is good that legal rules should be based on ethical principles, rather than (say) on short-term pragmatism, but the function of ethical principles is to supply strong reasons for adopting a particular rule. In that sense they are more fundamental, many of them being found in the European Convention of Human Rights and Fundamental Freedoms.

Second, there is no warrant for the view that the criminal justice system is entirely covered by rules and clear-cut guidance. Recent years have seen greater efforts to introduce various forms of guidance and accountability, but there are still vast tracts of discretion, some of it left deliberately so as to enable flexibility, some eked out by practitioners in order to allow them to follow their preferred practices. Wherever there is discretion, there may be choices between following ethical principles and following other policies or preferences.

Third, it is well known that there are strong occupational cultures among the various professional groups in the criminal justice system. The point is clearest in relation to the police. For example, a study of detectives for the Royal Commission on Criminal Justice concluded that a necessary step towards improving the situation would be 'raising CID officers' awareness of the faults in the traditional "detective cul-

ture" ("macho" and "elitist" attitudes, belief that "rules are there to be
bent", excessive secrecy and suspicion of outsiders, and so on) and the
ease with which young officers are sucked into it, almost without realis-
ing it'.[4] In its report, the Royal Commission refers to 'the culture and
approach of the Criminal Bar' as a possible obstacle to the success of
some of its proposals for streamlining pre-trial procedure.[5] In the face
of such well-entrenched cultures, what are the prospects for rules, let
alone guidelines or unfettered discretion? In practical terms these cultures seem to be direct competitors with ethical principles, partly
because they often put sectional interests first, but partly also because
they sometimes challenge the values of those who argue for the recognition of rights. However, as we shall see, professional cultures do have
some ethical content, and often embody a challenge to the more
rights-oriented principles.

2. Developing Ethical Principles for Criminal Justice

What kind of principle may be described as ethical? It should be a principle that is impartial as between persons and for which reasons can be
given. Thus a principle may not properly be described as moral or ethical if it tends to be justified by reference to its benefits for a particular
person or group. Impartiality as between persons may be linked to
respect for the separateness or autonomy of individuals, as we shall
see. But this emphasis on the individual, appropriate as it is in the context of a system in which someone cloaked with State authority and
supported by considerable organizational power may be dealing with a
person who is suspected of a crime, should not lead us to overlook the
justification for having some form of system in the first place. As
argued in Chapter 2, the general public benefit supplies the major reason for having criminal law, police, courts, and other parts of the system. Without such a system, life would be chaotic and insecure, and
the weak would be even more at the mercy of the strong. On the available evidence, it is clearly more beneficial to have a criminal justice
system than to have no criminal law and no official means of law
enforcement.

If the system is justified by reference to its general social
consequences, is there any reason to recognize the rights of individuals, rather than allowing all arrangements to be made purely on the

[4] Mike Maguire and Clive Norris, *The Conduct and Supervision of Criminal
Investigations*, RCCJ Research Study 5 (1992).
[5] Royal Commission on Criminal Justice, *Report*, Cm. 2263 (1993), para. 7.36, on
preparatory hearings.

utilitarian ground of calculating the greatest happiness of the greatest number? One answer to this would be to consider the position of victims of crime. Do they not have a right to be treated fairly and with respect by law enforcement agents, and to receive compensation either from their offender or from the State for the harm done? On a factual level it is well documented that victims have in the past felt that the criminal process operates as a kind of secondary victimization, with all its demands and pressures.[6] It was argued in Chapter 2 that we ought to recognize the right of victims to respect for their dignity: correspondingly it should be a duty upon State officials to avoid or minimize these secondary effects as far as possible. It is wrong to treat victims in a way that leaves them in ignorance about the progress of the case, or forces them to wait in court with supporters of the defendant, or fails to prepare them for the possible strains of giving evidence in court, etc.

Are the arguments different when we come to consider the rights of criminals? If someone is convicted of a serious offence such as rape, child abuse, or grievous bodily harm, why should they be treated with any respect? These questions are hinting at the conclusion that a person who has committed a crime forfeits all rights and can thereafter be subjected by the State to whatever form of punishment or treatment may be ordained. Are there any good reasons for rejecting this conclusion? The strongest argument is that a person who commits a criminal offence should not be laid open to whatever sanction a court chooses to impose, for whatever reason. Surely there should be a right not to be punished more than is proportionate to the seriousness of the offence: in principle, sentences should be related to the comparative seriousness of offences (rather than, say, to their predicted deterrent effects),[7] since this shows respect for the offender as a rational and autonomous being.[8] However, rights such as the right not to be punished disproportionately may be advanced as 'prima facie' rights rather than absolute rights.[9] This reflects the practical point that individual rights may

[6] e.g. J. Shapland, J. Willmore, and P. Duff, *Victims in the Criminal Justice System* (1985), 176–8.

[7] Considerations of space make it difficult to develop these arguments fully here. For a fuller version, with further references, see A. von Hirsch and A. Ashworth (eds.), *Principled Sentencing* (1993), 56–7 and ch. 2 generally.

[8] In the present context, 'autonomy' is being used merely as a restraining idea which can generate various limits on the treatment of individuals, particularly by the State. To argue for the attainment of autonomy as an ideal state would be a separate enterprise: cf. J. Raz, *The Morality of Freedom* (1986), 154–7. Cf. also the counter-argument that the 'respect for autonomy' argument ignores the social and other disadvantages under which many defendants labour: B. Hudson, *Justice through Punishment* (1987).

[9] J. L. Mackie, 'Can there be a Right-Based Moral Theory?', in Jeremy Waldron (ed.), *Theories of Rights* (1984).

conflict and that, in resolving these conflicts, it will sometimes prove necessary to curtail a right or to subordinate it to another. Thus it could be adjudged that a particular offender remains a danger to members of the community in general or to one particular citizen, and might well commit a further serious offence if released after the proportionate sentence. In such a situation of 'vivid danger', the probability of serious harm to other citizens might suffice as a justification for detaining the offender beyond the proportionate sentence, although the fallibility of such predictions is well documented.[10]

Thus, convicted offenders should not forfeit all their rights: their essential humanity ought to be recognized, and they ought not to be treated as mere pawns but should in general be punished no more than is proportionate to the seriousness of their offence. A related issue is how they should be treated, if imprisoned. Do they deserve any minimum standards of facilities, or is it sufficient that they be kept alive as cheaply as possible? This is another awkward question, particularly at a time when so many citizens who have not been convicted of serious offences find themselves living in dreadful conditions, often without sufficient money for decent housing, heat, clothing, and food, and possibly homeless. On an ethical plane it should be affirmed that citizens living in conditions of poverty have no less a claim that the State should treat them with respect and dignity.[11] But that should not alter the rightful claims of imprisoned offenders that the State should treat them with respect in terms of sanitation, food, clothing, and so forth. The increasing disquiet about prisoners 'slopping out' shows how conceptions of decent treatment can alter, and how the notion of a right to certain minimum standards begins to take root.

In describing ethical arguments in favour of proportionate sentences and decent treatment in prison, emphasis has been placed on the morality of the State acting in this way towards people who are rational autonomous beings. In practice, there are also pragmatic arguments running in the same direction that may be no less powerful—the spectre of miscarriages of justice, and the prospect of greater prison stability. The former argument has become more prominent in recent times, as several major miscarriages of justice have been uncovered, with people who have been wrongly convicted spending many years in prison. Few systems can claim to be error-proof, and the possibility of

[10] For this argument, see A. E Bottoms and R. Brownsword, 'Dangerousness and Rights', in J. Hinton (ed.), *Dangerousness: Problems of Assessment and Prediction* (1983), developing remarks by R. Dworkin, *Taking Rights Seriously* (1977), ch. 1.

[11] For the Victorian concept of 'less eligibility'—the argument that conditions in prison should be no better than those for the lowest in society—see L. Radzinowicz and R. Hood, *The Emergence of Penal Policy* (1986), 146–7, 381–2.

convicting and punishing innocent people makes it all the more fitting that the basic rights of convicted persons should be respected. The argument about prison stability received strong endorsement from the Woolf Inquiry into the prison disturbances of 1990. Indeed, it was argued not merely that degrading prison conditions are contributing factors to prison disturbances, but also that they may contribute to further law-breaking on release.[12] The Royal Commission on Criminal Justice similarly argues that 'the fairer the treatment which all the parties receive at the hands of the system, the more likely it is that the jury's verdict . . . will be correct'.[13] These pragmatic considerations may be powerful in practice, and they pull in the same direction as the argument in favour of maintaining the integrity of the criminal justice system, discussed in Chapter 2.

If it is now accepted that behaving ethically requires public officials to observe certain restraints in their dealing with convicted offenders, it would surely apply *a fortiori* that these restraints should operate in the pre-trial stages. Until a person has been convicted by a court, he or she should be treated as if innocent. Now to some people, particular to some practitioners and politicians, this sounds the sirens of pretence and misplaced sympathy. Most of the people who are prosecuted acknowledge their guilt by pleading guilty. Some of them, even, were caught red-handed or readily confessed at the earliest stage. It hardly makes sense to treat them as innocent and to constrain the processes of investigation and arraignment by reference to a presumption that is manifestly inapplicable in their case. This argument, however, should not be accepted. At a factual level it draws attention to the frequency of guilty pleas but ignores the many pleas of not guilty: on its own premiss it could only apply to guilty plea cases. Even at that, it overlooks the possibility of confessions and guilty pleas by the innocent,[14] thus ignoring the case for safeguards. One of the reasons for the criminal trial is to provide a forum for the issue of guilt or innocence to be examined openly. Even if the belief in the suspect's guilt is held strongly by police officers or tax inspectors or prosecutors or others, there are two reasons why this should not alter the presumption of innocence: first, how is the officials' judgement to be tested, or is it to be left merely as a matter of subjective belief? and second, what if it is

[12] 'The conditions which exist at present in our prisons cause a substantial number of prisoners to leave prison more embittered and hostile to society than when they arrived. They leave prison, then, in a state of mind where they are more likely to re-offend.' Home Office, *Prison Disturbances April 1990*, Cm. 1456 (Woolf Report 1991), para. 10.27.

[13] RCCJ Report, para. 1.27.

[14] The former, at least, was recognized by the Royal Commission: ibid., paras. 4.31–4.32.

found that the defendant has based his indication of a guilty plea on a misconception about the law or the evidence? The conclusion must be that there is insufficient reason to abandon the presumption of innocence, even in guilty plea cases, until there has been a determinative court hearing.

One of the principal reasons for having a criminal trial is to require the prosecution to prove its case in open court, if it can, and to allow the defendant the opportunity to contest that case. A system in which decisions on guilt or innocence are taken behind closed doors without a proper opportunity to make a defence fails to achieve this ideal, and one fundamental question raised about the English system is that so many cases are dealt with by cautioning or another form of diversion (see Chapter 5) or by guilty pleas or negotiated pleas of guilty (see Chapter 9). Allied to this, but far more controversial in its ambit, is the presumption of innocence at trial. The Royal Commission on Criminal Justice treated it as axiomatic, without argument, that the prosecution should bear the burden of proof. Beyond that there is even more room for dispute—whether the prosecution should have to prove guilt beyond reasonable doubt, whether the defence (as well as the prosecution) should have a duty to disclose its case, whether the defendant should have the right to remain silent in pre-trial investigations and/or at the trial, without adverse inferences, whether there should be exceptions for particular types of case, and so forth. How can issues of this kind be resolved? Are there any principles that deserve special weight?

Some answers to this have been sketched at a theoretical level both here and in Section 1 of Chapter 2. Some conduct towards suspects and defendants is immoral even in the absence of a criminal justice system: conduct such as torture, random searches, and unjustified detention is morally wrong. Some conduct, on the other hand, is unethical simply because the legitimate political process has decided that certain rights should be respected, and so it is unethical to undermine those rights. The task of establishing and delineating conduct that is immoral in itself is the far more difficult one, but the European Convention on Human Rights, together with the Commission and the Court of Human Rights, establishes a set of principles which have some measure of objective validity, in the sense that the United Kingdom is a signatory to the Convention and has thereby acknowledged its force as a kind of higher law. It may be said to bind the legislature, but not directly the courts, or officials in the system. The case-law of the Court has developed through applications from many different European countries, and this contributes to the idea of Europe-wide minimum standards for the treatment of citizens in the criminal process. For these reasons, the search for ethical principles for the criminal process should focus on the European Convention.

3. Ethical Principles and the European Convention

The European Convention on Human Rights and Fundamental Freedoms was signed in 1950 and came into force in 1953. It was ratified by all member countries of the Council of Europe. In recent years many new countries from the eastern part of the Continent have been granted or have applied for membership of the Council of Europe, and it is anticipated that they will ratify the Convention in due course. The European Commission on Human Rights had received over 57,000 petitions by 1991. Its function is to determine whether or not the application is admissible. Only about 1,000 of the applications have been held admissible, and they are then passed to the European Court of Human Rights for adjudication.[15] The Convention declares a number of rights, covering such matters as freedom of expression, of religion, of peaceful assembly, but our concern here is limited to those relevant to the criminal process. In this connection it is noteworthy that commentators take the view that 'the Convention is at its best when it is operating as a charter for procedural fairness'.[16] The text of the European Convention has been incorporated into the domestic law of some European countries but not into the law of the United Kingdom. This means that defendants or other litigants in this country cannot rely on the Convention in court: all they can do is to petition the European Commission on Human Rights if they allege that an English court or the administrative process has acted in violation of the Convention.

It is not proposed here to go through the European Convention article by article. Instead, an attempt is made to distil general principles from the earlier discussion in Section 1 of Chapter 2 and in Section 2 of this Chapter, together with rights upheld by the European Convention, in order to provide a general framework of ethical principles. Some eleven ethical rights or principles are set out and discussed briefly. Generally speaking, those dealt with first are more fundamental than those discussed later, which tend to be more detailed. We then turn to some possible reasons for derogation from the rights listed. These introduce arguments that will recur at several points during the book.

---

[15] For a general introduction, see Conor Gearty, 'The European Court of Human Rights and the Protection of Civil Liberties: An Overview', (1993) 52 *Camb. LJ* 89.
[16] Ibid., at 98.

1. *Right to be treated with humanity and without degradation*: one of the best-known provisions in the European Convention is Article 3, stating that 'no one shall be subjected to torture or to inhuman or degrading treatment'. There are no exceptions. Torture may be regarded as perhaps the most direct incursion into a person's right to liberty and to security of person (protected by Article 5), since torture involves the deliberate infliction of pain. Does this mean that torture is an absolute moral wrong in all circumstances? It is perhaps not surprising to find Bentham writing that 'torture ought not to be condemned any more than approved in the lump',[17] since utilitarians might be expected to regard torture as justifiable in certain circumstances. Some rights-based moral philosophers, whose primary orientation is away from utility, have argued that there might be circumstances in which torture could be justified.[18] However, the deliberate debasement of individuals that it involves raises formidable problems of justification, and the European Convention is right to condemn torture absolutely. Indeed, if the integrity principle has any cogency, this is the clearest situation in which it should apply so as to prevent a legal system from acting on the results of such inhumane conduct.[19]

Article 3 of the European Convention contains an absolute ban on the three forms of conduct, and the European Court has graded them according to severity, so that not all degrading conduct is inhuman, and not all inhuman conduct amounts to torture. The European Commission, in the *Greek* case, defined inhuman treatment as that which inflicts 'severe suffering, mental or physical', and defined conduct as degrading if 'it grossly humiliates him before others or drives him to act against his will or conscience.'[20] The European Court of Human Rights has held that Article 3 is breached by corporal punishment[21] and by third degree methods of interrogation involving five techniques—being made to stand right up to a wall for hours, being hooded for hours, subjection to persistent noise, deprivation of sleep, and deprivation of food.[22] The 'five techniques' were held, in *Ireland* v. *United Kingdom*, to amount to treatment that was inhuman and degrading but not to torture. Among the dissenting judgments, Judge Zekia held that the five techniques did amount to torture since that concept should not be confined to pain of extreme intensity, whereas

---

[17] Cited from manuscripts by W. L. and P. E. Twining, 'Bentham on Torture', (1973) 24 *NILQ* 305.

[18] Cf. the articles by William Twining and by Barry Paskins, 'Torture and Philosophy', (1978) 52 *PAS Supp.* 143 and 169; and Sanford H. Kadish, 'Torture, the State and the Individual', (1989) 23 *Israel LR* 345.

[19] See Ch. 2.2.

[20] *Greek Case*, Yearbook XII (1969), 196.

[21] *Tyrer* v. *Isle of Man* A.26 (1978).

[22] *Ireland* v. *United Kingdom* A. 25 (1978) 67.

Judge Fitzmaurice doubted whether any or all of the five techniques could properly be termed 'inhuman'. In this case the United Kingdom was also found to have breached Article 5 in several respects, but Article 15 allows a state to derogate from Article 5 where there is a 'public emergency threatening the life of the nation', though only 'to the extent strictly required by the exigencies of the situation'. The derogation was therefore held permissible.[23] This may be thought to underline the wisdom of allowing no exceptions to Article 3, since torture and inhuman treatment are more direct harms to the individual and it is wrong that states should be allowed, in effect, to be judge in their own cause of whether there are circumstances that justify their use.[24]

As far as enforcement is concerned, a step forward was taken in 1989 by the coming into force of the European Convention for the Prevention of Torture and Inhuman or Degrading Treatment or Punishment. This establishes a committee which is allowed to make visits to any member country and to report on conditions which are or may be in breach of the convention: for example, practices in some English prisons were found to contravene Article 3.[25] The committee has recently taken the bold step of making a 'Public Statement on Turkey', calling upon its Government to put a stop to torture and inhuman treatment and to remedy other breaches of the Convention.[26] In view of the difficulty and delay involved in taking a case to the Strasbourg Court, this new proactive approach is to be welcomed.

2. *Right of victims to compensation*: the proper formulation of this right is rather complex. The basic right is that of a victim to be compensated by the offender. This forms part of the general obligation of reparation, the justifying ground of which is described by Neil MacCormick as being 'that individuals have as a matter of principle a right to reasonable security in their persons and possessions and accordingly a right to be compensated when that reasonable security is infringed'.[27] As such, this right is a matter of civil law. However, it is now recognized that criminal justice systems should take steps to ensure that victims receive compensation from those offenders who are convicted, since a criminal court is seized of the matter and it is right that victims should

[23] *Ireland* v. *United Kingdom* A. 25 (1978) 78.

[24] This does not settle the ethical argument of whether the torture of an individual can ever be justified by the consequences, which is much too large an issue to be argued to a conclusion here. See the references in n. 18 above, and the discussion of terrorism in s. 4 below.

[25] See generally Malcolm Evans and Rod Morgan, 'The European Convention for the Prevention of Torture: Operational Practice', (1992) 41 *ICLQ* 590.

[26] Reported in (1993) 15 EHRR 309.

[27] D. N. MacCormick, *Legal Rights and Social Democracy* (1978), 214 and ch. 11 *passim*.

be provided with compensation from this course (where possible) without the trouble of further application. However, some systems (including the English) provide that a court may reduce the amount of a compensation order so as to bring it within the means of the offender. This raises the question whether the victim's right to compensation is absolute or merely fundamental: should a victim's right to full compensation from the offender prevail over all other considerations? The European Convention on Human Rights is silent on the rights of victims, so the question must be approached from other angles. One technical answer is that the right to full compensation exists at civil law and is not exhausted by the grant of partial compensation by a criminal court, which has other interests to respect. For so long as the system is oriented towards the punishment paradigm rather than a restorative paradigm,[28] it is proper that in some respects priority will be given to certain State interests in the form and amount of punishment over the victim's interest in full compensation. In addition to the basic right to receive compensation from the offender, many states have gone on to recognize a limited right to State compensation in cases where the offender is untraceable or unable to pay. The European Convention on the compensation of victims of violent crimes recognizes the State's residual duty to provide compensation for the victims of crimes of violence, but not for other forms of crime (notably, property crimes, against which individuals are presumably expected to insure). However, the primary right is to receive compensation from the offender, which criminal courts are empowered to order. Honouring this primary right may have implications, as we shall see, for some of the dispositive decisions in the pre-trial process.

3. *Right of innocent persons not to be convicted*: this is a restatement of the fundamental right discussed in Chapter 2.[29] It would be a grievous wrong to be found guilty of an offence that one had not committed; and that wrong would be compounded if one suffered deprivation of liberty or restrictions on liberty as a consequence. But whereas the content of the right to be treated with humanity and without degradation is negative in its implications, in the sense that it rules out certain methods of investigating and punishing crime, this right is positive in its implications. It tends to suggest that the State should strive to provide the most error-proof system of trial that is possible, irrespective of the expense. It is one thing to abjure certain types of conduct in investigating crime; it is another thing to require a commitment of huge resources in a social setting in which there are many other strong

---

[28] For discussion and references, see ch. 2 s. 3 above.
[29] See Ch. 2 n. 19, and accompanying text.

claims on public expenditure. Dworkin therefore proposes that the cutting edge of this right should be expressed through two subsidiary principles—the right to procedures which put a proper valuation on the fundamental harm of wrongful conviction, and the right to a consistent application of principles across different types of offence and offender. The second of these rights is discussed further under (4) below. The first proposes a special weighting, when resolving conflicts between rights or interests, of the right not to be wrongly convicted and punished. This right receives some recognition in Article 5 (1) of the European Convention (right to liberty and to security of the person), and, may be seen as the progenitor of others set out below—the right to be presumed innocent, the right not to be arrested or detained unless there are reasonable grounds, the right to a fair trial within a reasonable time, the right to prepare a proper defence, and the principle of equality of arms. Each of these can be explained as a means of ensuring that the criminal process assigns proper importance to avoiding wrongful convictions: they are discussed below, at paragraph (5) and following. Similar considerations argue in favour of the right of an innocent person to have the case dismissed at the earliest possible stage, rather than having to undergo the strain of awaiting and undergoing a trial, and the right of a person whose case falls within the criteria for diversion to have the case diverted from prosecution. These issues will be raised in the appropriate chapters below.

4. *Right to be treated fairly and without discrimination*: the enjoyment of all the rights in the European Convention shall be secured, states Article 14, 'without discrimination on any ground such as sex, race, colour, language, religion, political or other opinion, national or social origin, association with a national minority, property, birth or other status'. One could maintain that this is superfluous, in that proper application of the principle of legality (see (6) below) or of Dworkin's principle of consistent treatment should be sufficient. However, on the one hand there may be matters of 'status' that justify extra safeguards or other preferential treatment for certain groups such as juveniles or mentally disordered people, as we saw in Chapter 2.[30] On the other hand, in increasingly multi-racial societies there are good reasons why a separate fundamental principle should be enunciated. First, the laws of criminal procedure may themselves incorporate rules or exceptions that discriminate against certain groups: for example, rules requiring corroboration in cases of sexual offences, especially against women, and rules on cross-examination of victims in rape tri-

---

[30] Ch. 2.4.

als. Second, in practice the principle of legality is nowhere followed without exception, and discretion plays a large part in the criminal process. This leaves the way open for a welter of proper and improper considerations to influence decisions—as, for example, in the investigation of sexual offences against women in the early 1980s[31]—and a separate declaration of the principle of non-discrimination may therefore be worthwhile.

English law now has a provision that at least recognizes the importance of avoiding discrimination in the criminal process. Section 95 (1) of the Criminal Justice Act 1991 requires the Home Secretary to publish each year such information as he considers expedient 'for the purpose of facilitating the performance by such persons [engaged in the administration of justice] of their duty to avoid discriminating against any persons on the ground of race or sex or any other improper ground'. Statistics and empirical studies should be able to identify discrimination where it occurs.[32] Its prevention requires not only a firm declaration of principle but also training in awareness of discriminatory influences, including such matters as social status and employment status, to which the European Convention extends. Training in racial awareness is a central example of this. The English legislation also refers expressly to sex discrimination, perhaps a more difficult topic in the sense that there appears to be differentiation in favour of females (such as higher rates of cautioning and diversion). Research in analogous fields suggests that the overall figures may be explicable on the ground that females generally commit less serious offences than males, but that there may be subgroups of women who do suffer discrimination because they fail to satisfy the stereotypical role-model of the good woman or good mother.[33]

5. *Right to be presumed innocent*: Article 6 (2) provides that 'everyone charged with a criminal offence shall be presumed innocent until proved guilty according to law'. This right is one way of giving special weight to the fundamental right of innocent persons not to be convicted, a right that can only be honoured by means of adequate protections against mistaken convictions. However, it should be noted that Article 6 (2) of the European Convention does not specify proof beyond reasonable doubt as the appropriate standard. It merely places the burden on the prosecution, and that can be justified by the maxim 'the party that alleges must prove', by the relatively unequal strengths of

---

[31] See Lorna Smith, *Concerns about Rape*, HORS 106 (1989), ch. 1.

[32] See e.g. R. Hood, *Race and Sentencing* (1992).

[33] For a survey in an analogous field, see A. Morris, 'Sex and Sentencing', [1988] *Crim. LR* 163.

prosecution and defence, and by the consequences for the defendant if convicted (e.g. loss of liberty, restrictions on liberty, duty to make payments, stigma). The European Court of Human Rights has gone a little further, however. In *Barbera, Messegue and Jabardo* (1989) it stated that 'the burden of proof is on the prosecution, and any doubt should benefit the accused';[34] and in *Funke, Cremieux and Miailhe* (1993) it went so far as to refer to 'the right of anyone charged with a criminal offence to remain silent and not to incriminate himself',[35] although this reference came in the context of a case on compelling a suspect to yield documents, and it is unclear whether it can be generalized so as to encompass a broad 'right of silence'. If we are to declare unambiguously that guilt must be proved beyond reasonable doubt, there is a need to justify a higher standard of proof in criminal cases than in civil. One reason for this was advanced in the US Supreme Court by Justice Brennan, who described proof beyond reasonable doubt as 'the prime instrument for reducing the risk of convictions resting on factual error'.[36] Whether it is the *prime* instrument is a matter for debate: no less effective might be stringent requirements for the gathering of evidence before trial, or corroboration requirements. However, it undoubtedly has a symbolic significance in drawing attention to the effects of conviction on individuals. As we shall see later, it is also subject to definitional problems. To state that the prosecution shall bear the burden of proof, even beyond reasonable doubt, might constitute a lesser protection if the State is free to define the elements of the crime without constraint—e.g. by creating strict liability offences, or by removing certain elements from the definition of crimes.[37] This, in turn, raises the question whether the right to be presumed innocent is breached by strict liability offences, without any culpability requirement. It can be argued that treating individuals as autonomous human beings requires a measure of respect for their choices, and this is denied by convicting people who have no, or no sufficient, fault.[38]

6. *The principle of legality*: the law should state clearly and in advance the body of rules and exceptions relating to the rights and powers that may be taken over individuals during the criminal process. This principle, sometimes referred to as 'the rule of law', aims to secure the protection of rights and the prevention of abuse of power by

[34] *Barbera, Messegue and Jabardo* A. 146 (1989), p. 33.
[35] *Funke, Cremieux and Miailhe* v. *France* A. 256 (1993).
[36] *In re Winship* (1970) 397 US 358.
[37] See J. Jeffreys and P. Stephan, 'The Burden of Proof in Criminal Cases', (1979) 88 *Yale LJ* 1323, and also A. Ashworth, 'Defining Criminal Offences without Harm', in P. F. Smith (ed.), *Criminal Law: Essays in Honour of J. C. Smith* (1987).
[38] A. Ashworth, *Principles of Criminal Law* (1991), 128–9.

officials. It is one of the core propositions in the rhetoric of criminal justice, aimed at ensuring fairness of treatment, openness in decision-making criteria, and equal treatment of all individuals without discrimination. In its narrow form it is absolute: thus Article 7 of the European Convention provides that 'no one shall be held guilty of any criminal offence on account of any act or omission which did not constitute a criminal offence under national or international law at the time when it was committed', and the terms of Article 15 (2) make it clear that there can be no derogation from Article 7.[39] In the broader form in which the principle is expressed here, exceptions are common. In practice, discretion is a significant part of all pre-trial systems. For example, few countries now maintain a principle of compulsory prosecution as part of the principle of legality, and even then they tend to admit various exceptions to it.[40] Whilst the purposes behind the principle of legality remain as worthwhile ideals, they may sometimes be pursued more appropriately through methods of accountability.[41] The kinds of question that need to be raised are: why is discretion regarded as indispensable? If it is permitted, how should it be regulated? What systems of accountability should be put in place?

7. *Reasonable grounds for arrest and detention*: Article 5 (1) of the European Convention on Human Rights states that 'everyone has the right to liberty and security of the person'. Clearly that cannot apply to some of the persons proceeded against for crimes, and so among the exceptions is Article 5 (1) (c):

the lawful arrest or detention of a person effected for the purpose of bringing him before the competent legal authority on reasonable suspicion of having committed an offence or when it is considered necessary to prevent his committing an offence or fleeing after having done so.

Arrest or detention is therefore not an infringement of an individual's right to liberty, in so far as there is 'reasonable suspicion' that he or she has committed an offence. The term 'reasonable' immediately imports an element of judgement and degree into the protection, but this has not prevented the Court from finding breaches. In *Fox, Campbell and Hartley* v. *United Kingdom* (1990)[42] it was held that detention for up to forty-four hours of 'any persons suspected of being a terrorist' under a

---

[39] Art. 7 also prohibits the imposition of a heavier penalty than was applicable at the time of the offence: see generally P. van Dijk and G. J. H. van Hoof, *Theory and Practice of the European Convention on Human Rights* (2nd edn., 1990), 358–68.

[40] See e.g., L. H. Leigh and L. Zedner, *A Report on the Administration of Criminal Justice in the pre-trial Phase in France and Germany*, RCCJ Research Study 1 (1992), at 41 and 57, discussed further in Ch. 4 below.

[41] See Ch. 2.6.   [42] (1990) 13 EHRR 157.

Northern Ireland law could not be justified unless the arresting authority was willing to disclose the basis for the suspicion. The UK Government maintained that suspicion was based on acutely sensitive material that could not be disclosed, since it would place the lives of others in danger. A majority of the Court decided against the Government since it was not possible to ascertain whether the safeguard in Article 5 (1) (c) had been secured. It may be noted, however, that the European Convention contains no express commitment to the principle of minimum intervention, e.g. by stating that arrest should be reserved for serious offences and not used if some less coercive power (such as the summons) would be sufficient.

8. *Right to be brought before a court*: Article 5 (3) provides that everyone arrested or detained in accordance with Article 5 (1) (c) 'shall be brought promptly' before a court. This applies to persons arrested by the police, who should be brought before a court as soon as practicable. A breach was found in *Brogan* v. *United Kingdom* (1988),[43] where the applicants had been held for four to seven days under the Prevention of Terrorism Act without being brought before a court. This part of Article 5 also applies to those remanded in custody pending trial, although the Article does not specify how frequently such a person should have access to a court and merely states that he or she 'shall be entitled to trial within a reasonable time'. The underlying principle is that of access to a court to determine the lawfulness of detention. However, the force of Article 5 is weakened by the provision in Article 15 allowing states to derogate from it under certain conditions. The United Kingdom's decision to derogate from Article 5 (1) (c) has been challenged in the Court,[44] and is discussed in Section 4(1) below.

9. *Right to prepare a proper defence*: Article 6 (3) lists five rights of every person charged with an offence. These are minimum rights, and the 'fair trial' guarantee in Article 6 (1) has generated further rights, as we shall see below.

   (a) to be informed promptly, in a language which he understands and in detail, of the nature and cause of the accusation against him;
   (b) to have adequate time and facilities for the preparation of his defence;
   (c) to defend himself in person or through legal assistance of his own choosing or, if he has not sufficient means to pay for legal assistance, to be given it free when the interests of justice so require;
   (d) to examine or have examined witnesses against him and to obtain the attendance and examination of witnesses on his behalf under the same conditions as witnesses against him;

---

[43] (1988) 11 EHRR 117.
[44] *Brannigan and McBride* v. *United Kingdom* (1993) The Times 27 May.

(e) to have the free assistance of an interpreter if he cannot understand or speak the language used in court.

Various parts of this article have been subject to interpretation by the European Court of Human Rights, and the relevant decisions will be cited as appropriate in the chapters that follow. The implications of paragraph (d), on the right to have witnesses against him examined, remain a matter for discussion in the context of the hearsay rule and its erosion by the courts and by Parliament.[45] It is also noteworthy that there is a difference between the right to an interpreter, which *is* regarded as an absolute requirement of fairness, and the right to free legal assistance, which must be given only 'when the interests of justice so require'. The European Court has held that the complexity of the case is the principal factor to be taken into account in deciding whether the State should provide legal aid.[46] There were signs that the Court was becoming bolder in its approach under Article 6, particularly when it found that the trial in *Barbera, Messegue and Jabardo* v. *Spain* (1988)[47] was not a 'fair and public hearing' because the trial was too short, the composition of the court changed unexpectedly just before the hearing, and some evidence was heard in the absence of the defendants and the public. However, in the same year it declined to hold that the admission of unlawfully obtained evidence rendered a trial unfair.[48]

10. *Right of the victim to respect in the criminal process*: this right is derived from the Council of Europe's recommendation on the 'Position of the Victim in the Framework of Criminal Law and Procedure'.[49] It should ensure that the victim of a crime is treated with respect by law enforcement agents, prosecutors, and others working in the criminal justice system. It should also ensure that the victim is kept informed of the progress of the case, and is informed of the date and place when the court hearing takes place. If the victim attends court, there should be a waiting area separate from other witnesses and members of the public.[50] If the victim does not attend court, he or she should be notified of the outcome of the case. Some of the details of this right were discussed in Chapter 2, and will not be elaborated further here.[51]

11. *Right to trial within reasonable time*: Article 6 (1) provides that, in

---

[45] See C. Osborne, 'Hearsay and the European Court of Human Rights', [1993] *Crim. LR* 255.

[46] Cf. the Court's decision in *Airey* B. 30 (1982), holding that Art. 6 (1) might be breached in a civil case if the costs of going to court are very high.

[47] (1988) 11 EHRR 360.   [48] *Schenk* v. *Switzerland* (1988) 11 EHRR 242.

[49] Recommendation R (85) 11 of 1985.

[50] This right does not form part of the Council of Europe's recommendations, but may be found in the British Government's *Victim's Charter* (1990).

[51] Ch. 2.3.

determining a criminal charge, 'everyone is entitled to a fair and public hearing within a reasonable time by an independent and impartial tribunal established by law'. What is a 'reasonable time' for the purposes of delay before trial? The European Court of Human Rights has said that reasonableness depends on 'the complexity of the case, the conduct of the applicants and the conduct of the authorities'.[52] In *Tomasi v. France* (1992) the Court held unreasonable a delay of five years and seven months between arrest and verdict, which included two one-year delays at the instance of the public prosecutor.[53] The Court explicitly linked the question of reasonableness to due respect for the presumption of innocence and for individual liberty. In the Convention itself, there is a contrast between the principle that the defendant must have 'adequate time' to prepare a defence (Article 6 (3) (*b*), above) and the principle that a person remanded in custody 'shall be entitled to trial within a reasonable time' (Article 5 (3), above). When we come to discuss issues of pre-trial custody, it will be questioned whether it would be preferable to go further and to recognize a principle of minimum delay. Minimizing delays is not merely a concern for defendants remanded in custody, however. It is a concern for the State, in the sense that the aim of convicting the guilty may be thwarted if trials are so long after the event that witnesses' recollections are fallible (leading to unjustified acquittals) or the sentences imposed have a lower general deterrent effect because of the lapse of time. It is also a concern for victims, who may be left without compensation and with added anxiety (especially if they are to be called to testify) until the trial is completed. It is sometimes said that certain defendants wish to promote delay, either in order to put off their conviction for as long as possible or in the hope that the witnesses will forget what happened: possibilities of this kind underscore the importance of recognizing the interests of the State and of victims in reducing unwarranted delays in the criminal justice system by striving to shorten case-processing times.[54]

12. *The principle of equality of arms*: this is a principle that has emerged from the jurisprudence of the European Court of Human Rights. It is not stated explicitly in the Convention itself, although we have seen that Article 6 (1) requires trials to be 'fair'. The principle is that defendants should have the same access to documents, to records, and to other evidence as the prosecution.[55] It derives strength from the

---

[52] *Eckle Case* A. 51 (1982).   [53] *Tomasi* v. *France* A. 241 (1992).
[54] For discussion, see Council of Europe, *Delays in the Criminal Justice System*, Studies in Criminological Research 28 (1992).
[55] For the relevant decisions of the European Court, see van Dijk and van Hoof, *Theory and Practice of the European Convention on Human Rights* 319–20.

presumption of innocence, and its conception of fairness is that it would be wrong for a system to have one side with either procedural or practical advantages over the other. This would be especially wrong when that party is the State, with its immense power and resources, and the other party is the individual citizen, invariably much the poorer in terms of resources and support. Thus the Court has held that it is a requirement of fairness under Article 6 (1) that 'the prosecution authorities disclose to the defence all material evidence for or against the accused'.[56] Article 6 (3) (*d*), quoted above, comes close to stating the principle when it declares a defendant's right to bring witnesses 'under the same conditions as witnesses against him'. The principle of equality of arms has also been used to declare unfair the proceedings of the Appeal Court in Belgium, where the Advocate-General appears but the appellant has no right to address arguments to the court.[57] The implications of the principle extend much further, however. How is the balance of arms to be measured? If it is thought unequal, should it be rectified by means of legal rules or greater funding for the defence, or by some combination of the two?

4. Derogations and the Sacrifice of Ethics

In what circumstances, if ever, is it justifiable to depart from any of the principles outlined above? The European Convention rightly allows no derogation from Article 3 on torture, inhuman, or degrading treatment, nor from Article 7 on non-retroactivity. However, it does permit limited derogations from other provisions under Article 15, to be discussed in paragraph (1) below. Other possible grounds for derogation have been suggested by the European Court and in general discourse, and they are outlined briefly.

1. *Public emergencies*: the first two paragraphs of Article 15 of the European Convention read as follows:

1. In time of war or other public emergency threatening the life of the nation any High Contracting Party may take measures derogating from its obligations under this Convention to the extent strictly required by the exigencies of the situation, provided that such measures are not inconsistent with its other obligations under international law.

2. No derogation from Article 2, except in respect of deaths resulting from lawful acts of war, or from Articles 3, 4 (paragraph 1) and 7 shall be made under this provision.

---

[56] *Edwards* v. *United Kingdom* A. 247 (1992), 36; see also s. 8 of this chapter, on the right to information.

[57] *Borgers* v. *Belgium* A. 214 (1991).

A few general points may be noticed. It allows derogation from Articles 5 and 6 which, along with Article 3, are those most closely concerned with the criminal process. There are only two types of situation in which derogation is permitted, and it is clearly stated that any derogation should be kept to a minimum. In *Ireland* v. *United Kingdom* (1978)[58] the Court accepted the judgement of the UK Government that the situation in Northern Ireland amounted to a 'public emergency threatening the life of the nation', and held that the conditions for derogation set by Article 15 had not been overstepped in that case. The derogations from Article 5, on detention without being brought before a court and other matters, were therefore held to be permissible. In *Brogan* v. *United Kingdom* (1988)[59] the UK Government was again found to be in breach of Article 5 on the length of detention. The use of Article 15 to derogate was challenged unsuccessfully in separate proceedings, the Court again holding, in *Brannigan and McBride* v. *United Kingdom* (1993),[60] that the extent and impact of terrorist violence in Northern Ireland and elsewhere in the United Kingdom was sufficient to constitute a public emergency requiring exceptional measures such as extended detention under the Prevention of Terrorism Act.

These cases raise the question of how to reconcile the political demand to combat terrorism with commitment to the principle enshrined in the European Convention on Human Rights. Even if the nature of court proceedings is not altered in the case of alleged terrorists, there are various methods of gathering evidence that might fall foul of the Convention, in spirit if not in law.[61]

2. *Seriousness of offence*: an argument sometimes raised is that basic principles should yield in the face of (allegations of) very serious offences. This argument is even raised against the presumption of innocence, particularly in cases involving firearms or drugs, where there is alleged to be great social danger. Those are typically crimes that generate concern in the mass media, but there is also great danger from offences such as murder, rape, and armed robbery. The 'seriousness of offence' argument is a further element in the argument for derogations in terrorist cases. However, it can be contended that, where the consequences of conviction are likely to be severe for the defendant, it is all the more important that rights should be respected. This, then, is a central battlefield between utility and rights, between hopes of increased public protection through more convictions of the guilty and respect for individual rights. The fundamental right of the innocent not to be convicted is important here, because one might

[58] (1978) A. 25, at 78.   [59] (1988) 11 EHRR 117.
[60] (1993) *The Times* 27 May.   [61] A. Vercher, *Terrorism in Europe* (1992), 380.

argue that the right to procedures that put a proper valuation on the moral harm of wrongful conviction should be given weight, as should the right to consistent protection under the law. The risk of convicting the innocent should not be increased because of social concern about a particular type of crime. Some utilitarians and other consequentialists would argue that the conviction and punishment of an innocent person (stated to be guilty) might achieve a salutary general deterrent effect,[62] but this is an objectionable sacrifice of the fundamental rights of an innocent person, as well as perpetrating the futility of allowing the true offenders to go unpunished.

One example of the problems that arise is provided by Article 8 of the European Convention. Whilst Article 8 (1) declares that 'everyone has the right to respect for his private and family life, his home and his correspondence', Article 8 (2) establishes a limited exception, where interference with the right by a public authority 'is in accordance with the law and is necessary in a democratic society . . . for the prevention of disorder or crime'. This exception was considered by the European Court of Human Rights in the context of telephone-tapping in *Malone* v. *United Kingdom*. The Court stated that the inherent secrecy of telephone-tapping leads to a 'danger of abuse that is potentially easy in individual cases and could have harmful consequences for democratic society as a whole'. It therefore emphasized the need for 'adequate guarantees against abuse', and found the United Kingdom in breach for failing to require judicial authority for any tapping.[63] However, on its way to this conclusion the Court accepted the view of the UK Government that 'the increase of crime, and particularly the growth of organised crime, the increasing sophistication of criminals and the ease and speed with which they can move about have made telephone interception an indispensable tool in the investigation and prevention of serious crime'. It is noteworthy that, whereas Article 8 (2) refers simply to the prevention of crime, this statement is confined to 'serious crime'. The line of argument, then, is that telephone-tapping is an invasion of the right to privacy; that the right may be overridden in limited circumstances of necessity; and that the case for an exception is stronger where the crime is serious. However, all the steps in this argument are open to debate, particularly the double-sided significance of the seriousness of the crime. If the crime is serious from society's point of view, the consequences of conviction (and particularly of wrongful conviction) are also likely to be serious for the defendant. The balance of the equation has not altered.

[62] Cf. von Hirsch and Ashworth, *Principled Sentencing*, 55–6 and ch. 2 generally.
[63] Report 82 (1984), para. 81.

None the less, there is an abiding attraction in the argument that serious crimes justify exceptional measures. It has been urged at various times in the United States as a rational way of restricting the operation of the exclusionary rule, the argument being that the principle of judicial integrity should not be applied to exclude unlawfully obtained evidence when the defendant's crime was demonstrably worse than the police officer's wrongdoing.[64] It also appears to be influential in German law, where the 'principle of proportionality' is relevant when the court balances the constitutional interests of the defendant against the seriousness of the offence and the strength of the suspicion.[65] This seems to give little weight to the consequences of conviction for the defendant.

The converse argument can be disposed of quickly: that some offences are so minor that it is unnecessary to grant rights to defendants. It may be socially and economically sound to deal with such infractions swiftly, but this is an argument in favour of removing such offences from the criminal law or, at least, from the criminal courts. The European Court of Human Rights has accepted, as we have seen,[66] that sanctions such as fines can be imposed without a court hearing and without the regular safeguards, so long as there is the possibility of access to a court in the event of a challenge.

3. *Difficulty of proof*: it is sometimes claimed that there should be some derogation from the principles where a type of offence is peculiarly difficult to establish. Offences involving the possession of drugs may be an example: it is easy for the defendant to claim mistake or ignorance about the substance possessed, and there would be few convictions (and massive loss of crime control) if the prosecution had to prove knowledge beyond reasonable doubt in very case. This is open to the same counter-arguments as the previous argument on seriousness of offence, since it takes no account of the consequences for defendants. The 'difficulty of proof' point is also heard in relation to the investigation of serious fraud, and has been used in England to justify special powers for the Serious Fraud Office that can be taken to weaken the presumption of innocence (in so far as they place a suspect/defendant under a duty to speak or suffer adverse inferences).[67] Supporters of these special powers sometimes argue that the kinds of

[64] Y. Kamisar, 'Comparative Reprehensibility and the Fourth Amendment Exclusionary Rule', (1987) 86 *Michigan LR* 1, discussed in Ch. 4.

[65] C. M. Bradley, 'The Emerging International Consensus as to Criminal Procedure Rules', (1993) 14 *Michigan Journal of International Law* 171, at 210–16.

[66] *Le Compte, van Leuven and De Meyere* A. 43 (1981) 23.

[67] Serious Fraud Office, *Annual Report, 1992–93*, ch. 2; *R. v. Serious Fraud Office, ex p. Smith* [1993] AC 1.

people who are likely to have the presumption of innocence thus weakened are those who are unlikely to be at a great disadvantage *vis-à-vis* the investigating agency, since they will be well advised and well funded. Indeed, some of them will avoid prosecution altogether and will be dealt with by administrative or regulatory means—which raises issues of equal treatment and even discrimination under Article 14 of the Convention—whereas others who are prosecuted may find that what the European Court has described as 'the right of anyone charged with a criminal offence to remain silent and not to contribute to incriminating himself' has been taken away.[68]

4. *Speed and economy*: there can be no doubt that one relevant factor, sometimes avowed and sometimes concealed, is the high cost of operating criminal justice systems in times of fiscal stringency. Considerations of cost may lead to the streamlining of procedures—indeed, the Royal Commission on Criminal Justice took the view that this was a powerful factor in favour of diverting more fraud cases away from the criminal process[69]—but this may have the effect of diminishing fairness between those committing offences of similar seriousness, and of reducing the protection of certain rights. On the one hand, one cannot simply dismiss economic factors as being irrelevant. Public expenditure choices have to be made. On the other hand, it would be quite wrong to regard economic considerations, without more, as being sufficient reasons for overriding or curtailing a right. This is because the very concept of a right is an anti-utilitarian claim, an individual's claim against collective or social purposes. Economic considerations may force awkward decisions on priorities, but that does not necessarily lead to sacrifice of rights. Other strategies must be considered, such as decriminalization, fixed penalties, or some other system for dealing with the least serious forms of offending. By that means one can strive to retain proper safeguards for the cases with a certain level of seriousness, with cost considerations determining the dividing line between the two. Once again, the principle should be minimum derogation.

5. Identifying 'Unethical' Practices

The discussion so far has been aimed at establishing some general ethical principles applicable to pre-trial criminal justice, with particular reference to the European Convention on Human Rights. The importance of the subject, however, lies in its practical relevance. Now is the

[68] *Funke, Cremieux and Miailhe* v. *France* A. 256 (1993).
[69] RCCJ Report, para. 7.63.

time to move away from abstract theorizing, and to test some actual practices. What unethical practices in criminal justice can be identified? Exactly why might it be right to describe each one as unethical? What motives typically lie behind unethical practices?

Some nine presumptively unethical practices will be identified very briefly, so as to enable a spectrum of practices to be mentioned. Many of them are discussed in greater detail later in the book, but it is important at this early stage to illustrate the context in which ethical arguments take place. Whether the practices can properly be termed 'unethical' will not be determined until we have discussed the explanations for them, but they are discussed here because they appear unethical. There is no suggestion that all the practices are widespread, but it is believed that they occur on some occasions, and references are given to support this belief.

One of the purposes of introducing new rules on detention in police stations under the Police and Criminal Evidence Act 1984 was to ensure that persons brought to police stations under arrest are only detained if it is necessary to do so, and if there is sufficient evidence for a charge.[70] Research by McKenzie, Morgan, and Reiner shows that custody officers routinely authorize detention without an examination of the sufficiency of evidence, and do so by reference to the need 'to secure or preserve evidence or to obtain evidence by questioning'.[71] This practice is unethical because it deprives suspects of protection against being detained unless that is absolutely necessary, a protection that Parliament intended to give them.[72] The 1984 Act and its Codes of Practice were also designed to lay down standards of fair treatment and to reinforce the courts' discretion to exclude evidence obtained in contravention of the standards.[73] The reason behind these protections is to spare defendants intimidation, not to mention violence, and to enhance the reliability of any evidence that is obtained. Yet the years since 1986 have seen a spate of cases in which police officers have been found to have departed from the Code of Practice on Questioning.[74] Another innovation in the 1984 Act was to require the police to inform

[70] PACE, s. 37.
[71] I. McKenzie, R. Morgan, and R. Reiner, 'Helping the Police with their Inquiries: The Necessity Principle and Voluntary Attendance at the Police Station', [1990] *Crim. LR* 22; see, to the same effect, M. McConville, A. Sanders, and R. Leng, *The Case for the Prosecution* (1991), ch. 3.
[72] The Home Secretary at the time stated the principle that detention must be necessary, 'not desirable, convenient or a good idea but necessary': cited by McKenzie, Morgan, and Reiner, 'Helping the Police', 23.
[73] For discussion, see Peter Mirfield, *Confessions* (1985), and Andrew Sanders, 'Rights, Remedies and the Police and Criminal Evidence Act', [1988] *Crim. LR* 802.
[74] See e.g. Ch. 4, nn. 77, 81, and 83.

each suspect/defendant of certain rights—the right to make a telephone call from the police station, the right to have someone informed of the detention, and the right to have legal advice that is free, independent, and given in a private consultation. After the implementation of the new law in 1986 it was found that not all suspects were being informed of these rights.[75] The relevant Code of Practice was altered in 1991, and Home Office research has shown that the rate of informing suspects has increased but is still less than complete; almost all suspects were told of the right to legal advice, but only 73 per cent were told that it is free, 56 per cent were told that it is independent, and hardly any were told that the consultation would be private.[76] No less significantly, in over a quarter of cases where information was given, it was spoken in an unclear or unduly rapid fashion. There was also evidence that some police officers emphasized the possible problems (such as delay) in summoning legal advice, presumably in order to encourage a suspect to waive the right. All three practices discussed above are probably unethical, and seem to stem from the police's belief that the law inhibits them from adopting the most effective approach to investigation. The law is regarded as an impediment to be circumvented.

Similar motivation may have underlain the failure by the police to disclose to the prosecution or the defence certain evidence in favour of the defence, which was a reason for quashing the convictions in the cases of the Maguire Seven,[77] the Birmingham Six,[78] and Judith Ward.[79] The Attorney-General's Guidelines on disclosure were not in force at the time of the original trials in these cases, but the principle of disclosure did exist. Similarly, in the case of the Maguire Seven the results of certain tests carried out by the Forensic Science Service, with results favourable to the defendants, were not notified to the defence. Nondisclosure of forensic evidence also occurred in the cases of the Birmingham Six and Judith Ward. These omissions can be regarded as unethical.

One of the reasons for allowing suspects the right to consult a lawyer at a police station is to ensure that the conduct of the police towards

[75] See e.g. A. Sanders and L. Bridges, 'Access to Legal Advice and Police Malpractice', [1990] *Crim. LR* 494.

[76] D. Brown, T. Ellis, and K. Larcombe, *Changing the Code: Police Detention under the Revised PACE Codes of Practice*, HORS 129 (1993); to similar effect see M. Zander and P. Henderson, *Crown Court Study*, RCCJ Research Study 19 (1993), 8–10.

[77] *Maguire et al.* (1992) 94 Cr. App. R. 133.

[78] *McIlkenny et al.* (1991) 93 Cr. App. R. 287.

[79] *Ward* (1993) 96 Cr. App. R. 1; cf. the Court of Appeal's change of direction in *Johnson et al.* [1993] Crim. LR 689, and the recommendations in RCCJ Report, paras. 6.50–6.53.

the suspect is scrupulously fair. However, in some cases legal advisers are reluctant to intervene to protect their client, allowing hostile and hectoring modes of questioning to pass without comment.[80] In gross cases this is unethical conduct by the legal adviser. The Royal Commission also chided defence barristers for failing to abide by the regulations for pre-trial hearings introduced at certain Crown Court centres under the authority of a Practice Direction. Even though the Commission made recommendations for improving the situation, it recognized the need to provide sanctions for non-compliance, for otherwise 'the defence lawyers called upon to make it work will in practice ensure that it fails'.[81] Such conduct could be regarded as unethical.

A primary reason for introducing the Crown Prosecution Service was to bring professional prosecutorial review into the system, to prevent weak or inappropriate cases from going to court,[82] and for this they were given a power of discontinuance.[83] However, it is noteworthy that the House of Commons Home Affairs Committee went so far as to recommend that the CPS should 'act co-operatively with the police' in supporting local police initiatives in charging people following incidents of public disorder.[84] If, despite the rising rate of discontinuances, there are still cases in which the CPS fail to discontinue a case where they know that there is insufficient evidence, this may be unethical behaviour.[85] Also, under the existing system for determining mode of trial, various cases have arisen in which the prosecution has preferred an either-way charge, the defendant has elected Crown Court trial, and the prosecution has thereupon dropped the either-way charge and brought a charge that is triable summarily only, in a magistrates' court. Defendants have challenged these tactics by means of judicial review, and the Divisional Court has held that in general the choice of charge lies within the discretion of the prosecutor so long as the substituted charge is not inappropriate and there is no bad faith, oppression, or prejudice.[86] Substituting a lesser charge may therefore be lawful, but it

---

[80] J. Baldwin, *The Role of Legal Representatives at Police Stations*, RCCJ Research Study 3 (1992); M. McConville and J. Hodgson, *Custodial Legal Advice and the Right to Silence*, RCCJ Research Study 16 (1993). Both studies also confirmed that most 'legal advisers' attending to give advice at police stations are not qualified solicitors but clerks, articled clerks, or former police officers on retainers.

[81] RCCJ, para. 7.36.

[82] Royal Commission on Criminal Procedure, *Report*, Cmnd. 8092 (1981), para. 7.6.

[83] Prosecution of Offences Act 1985, s. 23.

[84] House of Commons Home Affairs Committee, Session 1989–90, *The Crown Prosecution Service*, HC Paper 118 (1990), para. 27.

[85] This refers to cases where there is clearly insufficient evidence. Where there is doubt, it may be reasonable to continue with the case.

[86] *R. v. Liverpool Stipendiary Magistrate, ex p. Ellison* [1989] Crim. LR 369; however, where the magistrates have decided that a charge should be tried summarily, it would be

is ethical? Acquittal rates tend to be lower in magistrates' courts,[87] and this may be one reason why the CPS prefer to have many cases heard in those courts. The ethical argument is complex, as we shall see in Chapter 8, but such conduct by the prosecution is presumptively unethical.

6. Understanding 'Unethical' Behaviour

The preceding section has set out some examples of behaviour that might be described as 'unethical', in the sense that it fails to show proper respect for citizens and often removes, circumvents, or weakens certain rights of the suspect or defendant. There may be other practices that lead to miscarriages of justice because of mistakes or casualness within the system, but the focus here is on conduct that may be said to involve some conscious circumvention of the rules. Suspending final judgement on whether these practices are to be termed unethical, we must first inquire into the reasons for them.

Lawyers have tended to regard practices of this kind as the product of individuals, exercising a discretion unconstrained by context or by colleagues, whereas in fact they tend to form part of a process in which several influences such as organizational and occupational rules operate.[88] Thus research into the police has often concluded that much police behaviour is influenced by a 'cop culture' that is spread widely through the organization. There is no need here to enter into an extensive analysis of the elements identified by different researchers. It is sufficient to mention four elements that seem to be at the core of 'cop culture'—(1) support for colleagues and the inappropriateness of close supervision; (2) what is termed 'the macho image', which includes heavy drinking, physical presence, and some attitudes that are sexist and racist; (3) the idea that rules are there to be used and bent; and (4) the sense of mission in police work.[89] The suggestion is that these and similar attitudes are widespread, not that they are universal. There may be differences from division to division, particularly between rural and

an abuse of process for the prosecutor to drop that charge and prefer one that is triable only on indictment: *Brooks* [1985] Crim. LR 385.

[87] J. Vennard, 'The Outcome of Contested Trials', in D. Moxon (ed.), *Managing Criminal Justice* (1985), finding acquittal rates of 57% in the Crown Court and 30% in magistrates' courts.

[88] K. Hawkins, 'The Use of Legal Discretion: Perspectives from Law and Social Science', in K. Hawkins (ed.), *The Uses of Discretion* (1992), at 22.

[89] For detailed discussion, see J. Skolnick, *Justice without Trial* (1966); P. Manning, *Police Work* (1977); S. Holdaway, *Inside the British Police* (1983); D. J. Smith and J. Gray, *Police and People in London: The Police in Action*, PSI study, vol. iv (1983); and R. Reiner, *The Politics of the Police* (2nd edn., 1992), ch. 3.

urban areas. There may be individuals or groups, particularly women and some younger police officers, who accept few or no aspects of the culture. Senior officers may argue that changes are taking place, but the stronghold of the culture has always been in the lower ranks. The phenomenon of police culture has been observed so frequently that its existence as an entity cannot be put in doubt.

In an attempt to unravel the reasons which underlie the culture, we may begin by considering (1), support for colleagues and the inappropriateness of close supervision. In order to set aside the claim that this part of the culture has changed, it is worth recalling that two recent research studies for the Royal Commission on Criminal Justice found that the supervision of junior officers in the conduct of inquiries and in questioning was not the norm and was often regarded as a breach of the trust that should be shown in every officer's skills.[90] This is linked to the idea of police solidarity and the duty to support a fellow officer, although it may have a darker side, as the Royal Commission recognizes in its reference to officers and civilian staff being 'deterred by the prevailing culture from complaining openly about malpractice'.[91] To some extent the isolated position of the police in society may breed a form of solidarity and defensiveness. To some extent the culture may reflect the differing perspectives of police officers 'at the sharp end' and those officers who are managers, with the lower ranks covering for one another and trying to shield from senior officers various deviations from the rules.[92]

Perhaps the strongest evidence for the existence in the British police of (2), what is termed the 'macho image' and includes racist and sexist attitudes, came from the PSI study of policing in London.[93] Other researchers refer to physical dangers of the job, to 'the alcoholic and sexual indulgences' of male police officers, and to the struggle of women police officers to gain acceptance.[94] In respect of racism, however, Robert Reiner suggests that some allegations fail to take proper account of the nature of police work in a society that places ethnic minorities at a disadvantage in many respects.[95]

Central to the cop culture is (3), the idea that rules are there to be used and bent. There are two strands to this. The first emphasizes the use of the criminal law as a resource for legitimating or reinforcing police handling of a situation: the police officer has available a range of

[90] J. Baldwin, *Supervision of Police Investigations in Serious Criminal Cases*, RCCJ Research Study 4 (1992); Maguire and Norris, *Conduct and Supervision*.

[91] RCCJ Report, para. 2.65.

[92] See further Reiner, *Politics of the Police*, 115–17.

[93] Smith and Gray, *Police and People in London*.

[94] Reiner, *Politics of the Police*, 124–5.   [95] Ibid. 156 f.

offences with which to support his or her authority, and may decide
whether or not to invoke one of them as a reason for arrest and
charge.[96] Of course this is hardly applicable to crimes such as murder,
rape, and armed robbery, but it can be applied to the range of public
order offences, obstruction and assault on police officers, and a number of other charges. The primary objective of the police may be to
keep the peace and to manage situations; in this they use and exert
authority; anyone who resists that authority may be charged. The second strand concerns the various procedural rules about questioning,
notably the Codes of Practice under the Police and Criminal Evidence
Act. The reason why these rules are broken from time to time is that
they are seen as unwise impediments to proper police work, standing
in the way of vigorous questioning which will get at the truth, or (sometimes) will produce the results which senior police officers or the media
seem to want. Indeed, it is thought to be a poor reflection on those who
recommend and make the laws that they fail to understand the realities
of police work. This led Smith and Gray to comment that deviations
from proper procedures can be expected to continue 'as long as many
police officers believe that the job cannot be done effectively within the
rules'.[97]

These two strands coalesce to suggest that there is a police motivation that lies beyond and above the formal rules of the criminal justice
system. It flourishes partly because of the discretion actually left to the
police by the system, and partly because of their continued ability to
circumvent what they regard as fetters unjustifiably imposed on them.
This leads us to inquire about (4), the sense of mission in police work. It
is an essentially conservative outlook, in social terms, which celebrates
the position of the police as a 'thin blue line' standing between order
and chaos. The mission is strengthened by seeing the police as being
on the side of the right, serving society and ranged against offenders
and other miscreants who are in the wrong. Reiner describes the subtle
interplay of three themes—'of mission, hedonistic love of action, and
pessimistic cynicism'—that constitute the core of the police outlook.[98]
Many officers join the police with a sense of mission, in terms of
defending the society and its institutions against attack and disorder,
and then develop a kind of cynicism about social trends that seem to

[96] For a classic study that highlights this, see E. Bittner, 'The Police on Skid Row: A
Study in Peacekeeping', (1967) *American Sociological Review* 32.

[97] Smith and Gray, *Police and People in London*, 230; see also Reiner, *Politics of the
Police*, 81–5.

[98] Reiner, *Politics of the Police*, 114.

threaten existing ways of doing things. The Royal Commission appears to accept some such view:

> We recognize that police malpractice, where it occurs, may often be motivated by an over-zealous determination to secure the conviction of suspects believed to be guilty in the face of rules and procedures which seem to those charged with the investigation to be weighted in favour of the defence.[99]

To be sceptical about the moral quality of the police mission would be easy: it certainly contains its contradictions, in that it purports to emphasize established moral values when there is evidence that some officers rejoice in various sexual exploits, and in that it adopts a puritanical attitude towards drug-users when police alcoholism is a long-standing problem.[100] Yet, these contradictions apart, there is a true sense in which the police are performing an essential and central social function. To this extent both the term 'police force' and its modern successor, 'police service', contain elements of realism. There is nothing unhealthy in having a sense of mission about that, any more than it is unhealthy for doctors, nurses, or even lawyers to have a sense of mission. Just as people are right to expect medical care when ill or injured, so citizens are entitled to expect official action when they fall victim to a crime or in the face of threats to good order. Often, this does amount to the protection of the weak against the predatory. But whilst the vital nature of this social function cannot be disputed, its definition can be. The police culture evidently defines it differently from Parliament, for example, since police officers often express contempt for 'legal restrictions'. There is no question that the maintenance of good order counts, but there is room for debate about what counts as the maintenance of good order.

In focusing on the 'cop culture' within the police, the above discussion has said nothing about the cultures among prosecutors, magistrates, judges, forensic scientists, defence lawyers, probation officers, and others working within the system. The fact is that there has been far less empirical research in these other fields. The danger is that this will lead us to overlook the existence and the practical significance of 'defensive' cultures within these other groups. Attention will be called to this danger again, but (for evidential reasons) the bulk of the discussion will continue to focus on the police.

7. Justifying 'Unethical' Behaviour by Challenging the Ethics

We arrive, then, at the point of struggle for the high ground. The police would presumably claim a strong moral element in their mission. Is

---

[99] RCCJ Report, para. 1.24.   [100] Reiner, *Politics of the Police*, 124.

this really open to challenge? What ethics could call into question the vigorous pursuit of this apparently fundamental social function?

Let us begin by constructing a version of the mission. Some of the main elements have been described above, but there is a need for a rounded version that could fit the words and opinions of police officers. The key element is crime control: this is surely the point of the criminal justice system. It means that law observance should be maintained. In this the police are inevitably in the front line, having peace-keeping functions that (in terms of time spent) outstrip the processing of suspected offenders. A second element is that, where the interests of the defendant conflict with those of the victim or society, priority should be given to the latter. A third and connected element, following from the first two, is that the police should pursue this society-centred approach so far as is possible, exploiting any discretion left by the criminal justice system in order to further the conviction of the guilty. Taken together, these elements of crime control and the protection of society may be treated as establishing a powerful case in favour of the police mission. If we are not to descend into anarchy, someone has to do it. Better that it be done in a committed way than without any sense of its social importance.

Assuming that there is some truth in this account, is it defensible? Almost every step suffers from confusion which, when examined, mixes overstatement with understatement and neglects important features of social life. It would be easy to claim that this is because this version of the police mission has been formulated in a way favourable to the thesis being advanced: but the counter-arguments below can be ranged against any other version of the police mission that keeps faith with what considerable numbers of police officers say and do. The counter-arguments are these. The first element refers to crime control as if it were to be pursued without regard to any other values. Is it plausible to advance such an uncomplicated notion? To take an extreme but telling example, does it suggest that the police should be free to use repressive measures wherever they regard them as appropriate, or that torture should be available for use on those suspected of serious crimes? If the answers are negative, then we need to adopt a more sophisticated and sensitive notion than 'crime control'. Many people might accept at first blush that crime control is the ultimate aim of the criminal justice system, but on reflection they would surely recognize that it ought not to be pursued without qualification. That would lead to a police state.

The second element is that priority should be given to the victim or society over the interests of the suspect/defendant. In the vernacular this might be called 'toe-rag theory', since its essence is that the interests of the innocent and good should be preferred over those of the suspect or defendant. As one constable stated some years ago, 'Speaking from a policeman's point of view it doesn't give a damn if we oppress law-breakers, because they're oppressors in their own right.'[101] This seems to suggest that accused persons should have no rights, or few rights, or at least rights that can be overridden when that is necessary in the public interest (as interpreted by the police). This is to turn the idea of rights on its head. The whole idea of rights is that they respect the individual's autonomy and ensure that the individual is protected from certain kinds of inappropriate behaviour and is furnished with certain assistance when he or she is in the hands of public officials. Rights have been termed anti-utilitarian claims, in the sense that they represent claims that the individual be not treated in certain ways even if that might enhance the general good. However, the idea of priority for 'the interests of society' seems to accord the individual suspect or defendant no particular rights, and to deny the whole legitimacy of human rights such as those incorporated in the European Convention and discussed in Section 4 above.[102] Moreover, it does so at a stage before the suspect or defendant has been convicted, thereby affirming a strong presumption of guilt arising from the investigating officer's belief. Is it really acceptable to place so much emphasis on the judgement of one or more police officers, especially when one element in the cop culture is a mutual support and respect for the skills of others which frowns on routine supervision?

These arguments also show the weakness of the third element, always seeking to promote the interests of society against those of the suspect. This is flawed for various reasons. Suspects are members of society. Even members of society who are unlikely to be suspected of crime might accept that those who are suspected should be accorded some rights. Few would agree that it should be for the police to decide which suspects should be accorded rights and which not. The notorious cases of miscarriage of justice leave us well aware that police officers' judgements of someone's guilt or innocence should not be determinative.

The conclusion is therefore irresistible that the 'police mission' described above cannot claim the moral high ground. It overstates the

[101] Reiner, *Politics of the Police*, 111.

[102] This is not to overlook the importance of victims' rights, which may on occasion conflict with those of suspects or defendants. However, this argument should not be taken as far as those who readily convert 'the interests of society' to 'the interests of victims' would wish to take it. One must first decide what the rights of victims should be: see Ch. 2.3.

notion of crime control by assuming that this should be pursued either without qualification or with only such qualifications as the police deem appropriate. It assumes that respect for the rights of suspects is bound to detract from crime control, and does so for insufficient reason. In this it understates the importance of respect for human rights even when accused of a crime. It also calls into question the relative importance of convicting the guilty and of acquitting the innocent. However, some statements of the importance of suspects' rights might equally be said to neglect the social importance of convicting the guilty and dealing with crime. The fundamental reasons for having a criminal justice system are to reduce crime and to deal with offenders. Among the reasons for having a police force are to reduce crime and to apprehend and question suspected offenders. Statements of the rights of suspects and defendants cannot stand on their own, in isolation from the social functions of the system to which they apply.

It is one small step from these ruminations to the conclusion that what is required is a balance between powers of crime control and rights to protect suspects and defendants. But this is a step that should not be taken until there has been full discussion about the nature and significance of the rights. It would be far too casual to assume that, after recognizing the absolute right not to be subjected to torture, all other so-called rights can be traded off as part of some political compromise, wherever gains in crime control seem likely. The investigation of terrorist crimes or mass murders tends to bring these issues sharply into focus: the 'prevention of terrorism' legislation curtails or removes various rights accorded to persons suspected of other crimes, and yet some of the most notorious miscarriages of justice have been perpetrated against people suspected of terrorist crimes. This is a good illustration of the importance of deciding what rights are to be respected, understanding why they should be respected, and only then assessing the weight of arguments for derogation *in extremis*. Whilst it would be wrong to overlook the importance to citizens of peaceful and crime-free living conditions, it is also right that persons suspected of crimes should be granted various facilities, and that the agents of law enforcement should behave towards them in particular ways—both of which the European Convention on Human Rights is designed to secure. The rights of victims, too, are not mere matters to be weighed in the balance, but are important in their own right. The metaphor of balancing can too easily lead policy-makers to overlook the reasons behind the special claims of certain groups.

8. Unethical Standpoints?

We might now consider three standpoints that appear to ooze practicality and good sense, particularly among those who work in particular parts of the criminal justice system. The first, already mentioned in one context, is the argument that certain rules should be circumvented because the rulemakers do not understand the practical problems. The second is that it is wrong to expect police, prosecutors, etc. to operate with 'their hands tied behind their back'. And the third is that, when the Crown Prosecution Service drops a case or when a court gives a lenient sentence, this is bad for morale. All these standpoints are connected, but they deserve brief discussion individually.

Is it right to circumvent rules on the ground that the rulemakers do not understand the day-to-day on-the-ground problems of the criminal process? The claim is heard in various quarters. It is heard among some police officers in relation to the Police and Criminal Evidence Act and its Codes of Practice: these are restrictions imposed by people who expect 'results' and yet do not understand the difficulties the police have to encounter. There are three problems with a claim of this kind. First, there is the constitutional argument: any official or public organization that substitutes its own judgement for one reached through the appropriate democratic channels is behaving unconstitutionally. Second, there is the values argument: that this claim assumes that crime control, in a fairly absolute form, is the only worthwhile value. It gives no weight to the protection of the rights of suspects. And third, there is the evidential argument: is it really true that 'the job' cannot be done if the restrictions are observed? In fact this is less likely to be a matter of evidence than a question of values again, since the claim that the job cannot be done suppresses the unarticulated clause, 'within the prevailing culture'. If a different culture prevailed, perhaps the job could be done. One can only plausibly assert that it cannot be done if one assumes no change in the culture. These three arguments expose the weaknesses of the claim that rules made by out-of-touch rulemakers may be circumvented. They apply no less to the view said to obtain among some magistrates' clerks some years ago, that High Court rulings were there to be circumvented because 'the judges did not understand the practicalities, e.g. of dealing with truculent, often regular, customers, or a busy court schedule'.[103] This, again, seems to have been based on the assumption that the conviction of the guilty is important above all else.

---

[103] The words of a magistrates' clerk, quoted by A. Rutherford, *Criminal Justice and the Pursuit of Decency* (1993), 62.

The second claim is similar in some respects. It is that society expects the police to combat crime with their hands tied behind their backs, or that society expects prosecutors to obtain convictions with one hand tied behind their backs. The precise formulation varies, but the target is always the 'restrictions' imposed, usually by the legislature but sometimes by the higher judiciary. The claim could be countered by means of the three arguments deployed above—the constitutional point, the values argument, and the question of evidence. However, another argument is worth raising here: the assumption that respecting the rights of suspects significantly diminishes the number of convictions and therefore the protection of the public and of victims. This is a complicated argument, requiring considerable space to develop and to rebut. Suffice it to say here that research suggests that the number of extra convictions likely to result from, say, abrogating the right to remain silent during police questioning, without adverse inferences being permitted, is relatively small; and that must be set against the possibility of more convictions of the innocent if the rule were changed.[104] The existing law appears to have a greater impact on police and prosecutors' perceptions than upon the outcome of cases.[105] This brings the discussion to the question of morale.

The third claim is that it is bad for police morale when the Crown Prosecution Service decides to drop a prosecution commenced by the police. Parallel claims are sometimes heard when a court gives a low sentence on conviction, and there is also the suggestion that one reason why station sergeants tend not to refuse charges from officers who bring in arrestees is that it might affect morale. Now as an empirical proposition this claim may well be correct. Such events may reduce police morale, as may new restrictions on their questioning of suspects, changes in their pay and conditions, and several other matters. The problem here is whether one should defer to the conservatism that underlies the morale of professions such as the police, a conservatism no doubt linked with a sturdy defence of the police mission discussed earlier. One reason for deferring to it would be that the mission of crime control is of supreme social importance and that it would be wrong to upset such a vital organization as the police. Alternatively, one could try to alter the culture that supports this version of the police mission, a culture that sees little reason for according rights to suspects. One justification for taking this course would be that the

---

[104] RCCJ Report, para. 4.22, recommending (by a majority) no change in the law, for this reason.

[105] See R. Leng, *The Right to Silence in Police Interrogation*, RCJ Research Study 10 (1993); McConville and Hodgson, *Custodial Legal Advice*.

democratic institutions have decided that there are other values worthy of respect.

9. Criminal Justice Reform through Ethics

Law enforcement agencies and the administrative of criminal justice are governed by masses of legislative rules, and yet it is common ground that there are wide areas of discretion and that there must continue to be some areas of discretion. The next step, at least for those who favour the principle of legality as a general principle,[106] is to attempt to structure discretion by the use of guidance and guidelines. Other common features of reform proposals are better training of criminal justice personnel and better lines of accountability. Measures of this kind, espoused in various forms by such politically disparate groups as the 1993 Royal Commission on Criminal Justice after their review of criminal justice processes and by Michael McConville, Andrew Sanders, and Roger Leng at the end of their sharply critical research report on police and prosecution services,[107] are now recognized to be far more promising than mere changes in legal rules. The reason for this is the strength of occupational cultures within such key agencies as the police, the prosecution service, the various regulatory inspectorates, defence solicitors, the criminal Bar, the Forensic Science Service, and so on. More has been said here about the occupational culture of the police, to some extent justifiably since they form the principal filter into the criminal justice system, but to some extent simply because there has been more research into the police. Since occupational cultures are so powerful, better understanding of their nature and their support systems requires further research into the professions.[108]

The importance of occupational cultures has often been stated, but the Royal Commission paid insufficient attention to them (despite some critical remarks on the culture of the criminal Bar and on overzealous police officers), and few have ventured to suggest what should be done about them. What is noticeable about at least some of the occupational cultures in criminal justice is that their concern is not simply to preserve established working practices or to defend traditional territories of influence, but also to see that 'justice' is done. This is the sense of mission. Everything turns, of course, on what one takes

---

[106] For discussion, see P. H. Robinson, 'Legality and Discretion in the Distribution of Criminal Sanctions', (1988) 25 *Harvard Journal on Legislation* 393.

[107] M. McConville, A. Sanders, and R. Leng, *The Case for the Prosecution* (1991), ch. 10.

[108] Cf. M. McConville and L. Bridges, *Standing Accused* (1994).

to be 'justice' in this context. We must refuse to accept references to 'the interests of justice', 'the public interest', and even (more emotively) 'the interests of victims'—unless it is carefully spelt out how exactly these rather sweeping claims have been arrived at. We need to identify the values that underlie such statements, and then consider what values should be recognized in criminal justice. This is where ethical values should be reasserted.

The criminal justice system has, as we stated earlier, a moral dimension other than the moral force of the law against those who do wrong. That moral dimension is that citizens who are suspected of or charged with offences must be dealt with in a way which respects their rights. There is good psychological evidence that procedural fairness is more important to many citizens that the outcomes of the procedures,[109] suggesting that some groups such as the police have misjudged the public mood on this issue. However, much more important is the principled proposition that fairness forms part of the integrity of the system, as well as being supported by the classical 'rule of law' virtues such as impartiality, equal treatment, and consistent application of the rules laid down. Of course there is room for controversy about the rights that should be recognized, as the extensive philosophical literature shows, but the existence of the European Convention on Human Rights enables some progress to be made. It may properly be seen as a basic specification of relevant ethical principles, although not an exhaustive one—it does not deal with victims, and says nothing about the ethical orientation of parties such as prosecutors, defence lawyers, or police officers. The European Convention may be seen as a higher law, standing above English legislation and case-law, although it is a form of positive law. It does not offer any clear theoretical basis for the rights it propounds, apart from a general reference in the Preamble to 'a common heritage of political traditions, ideals, freedom and the rule of law', but it can be regarded as an authoritative source of principles for legislators and judges. We then move to the political proposition that, once legislation has been enacted, it is not for any group of officials, however committed to advancing the 'public interest', to go behind it. What are needed, then, in terms of criminal justice reform, are some working formulations of ethical principles for professional groups within the system.

---

[109] T. Tyler, *Why People Obey the Law* (1990).

10. Codes of Ethics

This is the era of codes of professional ethics. Whilst the Bar's ethical code has been little changed for some years, the Law Society issued new guidelines for solicitors in police stations as recently as 1985. The police service is at an advanced stage of preparing its code of ethics, and the Crown Prosecution Service has issued a *Statement of Purpose and Values*.[110] These are welcome developments, although one must bear in mind that even so moderate a body as the Royal Commission remarks that it was 'struck by evidence of a disquieting lack of professional competence in many parts' of the criminal justice system.[111] Issuing a few codes of ethics will not necessarily bring changes of outlook and practice.

Codes of ethics must, however, play an important part in the dynamics of change. Although they tend to be addressed to individuals within each profession, they often form part of a package including 'mission statements' and 'declarations of purpose', thus recognizing that decision-making takes place within an organizational setting. A draft of the Police Service's *Statement of Ethical Principles* includes two principles that are particularly relevant to our discussion. The first is the duty to 'uphold fundamental human rights, treating every person as an individual and display respect and compassion towards them'; the second is the duty to 'act only within the law, in the understanding that I have no authority to depart from due legal process'. The first recognizes the idea of fundamental human rights, and the second confronts directly the cultural dispensation to bend rules 'in the interests of justice'. Apart from the obvious point that they would need to be harnessed to an effective system of accountability, it would be particularly important to promulgate the reasons behind the principles. Thus an essential part of training must be to convey the reasons why these principles are worth adhering to, whether by abstract instruction or by means of role-play exercises, debates, etc. This approach must be integrated into a programme for retraining personnel at all levels, from senior management down to new recruits. Otherwise, a statement of ethical principles would be a poor match for a well-entrenched occupational culture. The key questions must be addressed convincingly: why must I show respect towards someone who admits to a dreadful crime? If I feel that I can solve a difficult case by deviating from the rules, is it not in the interests of society that I should do so? Both the democratic argument and ethical principles should be elaborated in reply.

[110] Crown Prosecution Service, *Statement of Purpose and Values* (1993).
[111] RCCJ Report, para. 1.20.

Part of the framework of the Police and Criminal Evidence Act 1984 was to recognize, as not all European countries have done, the right of a suspect in a police station to consult with a lawyer and to have a lawyer present during questioning. This right will only be of proper benefit to suspects if their legal advisers give them due protection from unfair police practices. The Royal Commission regards as 'disturbing' the findings of researchers that competent legal advice is not always given and that legal advisers sometimes remain passive whilst police officers break the rules by indulging in oppressive, threatening, or insulting practices.[112] Many practical improvements are necessary here, but there are several other ethical problems for defence lawyers in an adversarial system.[113] Particularly acute are those where the lawyer is defending someone believed or known to be guilty who is pleading not guilty, and where there is the question of putting forward a witness strongly believed to be lying or of trying to discredit a witness strongly believed to be telling the truth.[114] It is here that the lawyer's 'principle of neutrality' and obligation to support the client's autonomy need to be considered in relation to the duty to the court.

The literature of English criminal procedure is replete with statements about the proper role of the prosecutor. In the nineteenth century it was said that the motivation of a prosecutor should be that of a Minister of Justice,[115] and this was elaborated by Sir Herbert Stephen when he wrote that the object of the prosecutor should be 'not to get a conviction, without qualification, but to get a conviction only if justice requires it'.[116] Christmas Humphreys, writing as Senior Crown Counsel, stated that 'the Crown is interested in justice; the defence in obtaining an acquittal within the limits of lawful procedure'.[117] The rhetoric of this position recognizes that crime control should not be regarded as the sole or dominant aim of the prosecutor, and that the concept of justice also includes recognition of certain rights of defendants and of victims.[118] The CPS *Statement of Purpose and Values* may be read as affirming these principles, since it refers to the importance

[112] Ibid., paras. 3.56–3.63.

[113] For general surveys, see David Luban, *The Good Lawyer* (1983), and J. G. Haber and B. H. Baumrin, 'The Moral Obligations of Lawyers', (1988) 1 *Canadian Journal of Law and Jurisprudence* 105.

[114] Cf. the discussions by Charles Fried, 'The Lawyer as Friend: The Moral Foundations of the Lawyer–Client Relation', (1976) 85 *Yale LJ* 1060.

[115] Crompton, J., in *Puddick* (1865) 1 F. & F. 497.

[116] H. Stephen, *The Conduct of an English Criminal Trial* (1926), 11.

[117] C. Humphreys, 'The Duties of Prosecuting Counsel', [1955] *Crim. LR* 739, at 741.

[118] Cf. D. M. Nissman and E. Hagen, *The Prosecution Function* (1982), 2: 'In pursuing his goal to seek justice, the prosecutor must punch through the tiresome criminal defender, whose goals are necessarily in conflict with the search for truth and justice.'

of treating victims with 'sensitivity and understanding' and commits the Service to 'treat all defendants fairly'. There is a little elaboration of the latter point,[119] but this particular document stops short of giving guidelines or even examples of practices this would favour or disfavour. Rapid progress will only be made when the values on which this approach rests are given due prominence, and are incorporated successfully into the training and retraining of personnel.[120]

Much more could be said about ethical principles for the Forensic Science Service,[121] about revisions of *Conduct and Etiquette at the Bar* to take account of changing conceptions of the rights of defendants and of victims,[122] and about codes of ethics for the many other professional groups operating within the criminal justice system, such as the Inland Revenue, Customs and Excise, the Serious Fraud Office, and the regulatory agencies. Indeed, the very diversity of the legislative frameworks and discretionary practices of these different agencies raises further issues. When one refers to 'the State' in the context of criminal justice, that entity acts in practice through these many different groups, each with their own objectives and cultures that may differ more or less from one another. Also, one might call into question the justification for having separate statements of ethical principles. At a fundamental level one might ask whether it is justifiable to speak of an ethical approach to criminal justice in a system that institutionalizes different approaches and different rights according to whether one's offence falls within the 'police' category or the 'regulatory' category, producing inequalities of treatment that are hard to defend.[123] There is a strong case for developing a statement of common ethical principles for those involved in the administration of criminal justice, to which further principles could be added for each particular agency or group. The task then would be one of persuasion.

---

[119] CPS, *Statement of Purpose and Values*, 8, 10; cf. also CPS, *Statement on the Treatment of Victims and Witnesses by the Crown Prosecution Service* (1993).

[120] One value that is stated explicitly is the principle of equality before the law: *Statement of Purpose and Values*, 8.

[121] RCCJ Report, paras. 9.34–9.36.

[122] Cf. ibid., ch. 8.

[123] Cf. e.g. A. Sanders, 'Class Bias in Prosecutions', (1985) 24 *Howard JCJ* 176, with the reference in J. Braithwaite, *Corporate Crime in the Pharmaceutical Industry* (1984), ch. 9, to the narrow concerns of 'liberal bleeding hearts'.

PART II

Particular Decisions

4

Investigating Crime

THE process of investigating crime, before a suspected offender is charged or summoned, is the subject of this chapter. The process varies between simple and complex cases, between police and non-police agencies. What remains fairly constant, however, is the high significance of judgements made at this early stage. As the case against a particular person begins to take shape, so (in most cases) does the investigator's belief that that person is guilty. Much as the system may provide for review of investigators' judgements—see, for example, Chapter 6 on prosecutorial review—the original file put together by the police will have a considerable hold. Prosecutors do not review two files, one for the prosecution and one for the defence. They are merely provided with the police file, and that will probably have been constructed in a way that is selective in what it includes and excludes, that interprets certain phenomena in accordance with the investigating officer's beliefs, and that tends to present the 'evidence' so as to support a particular conclusion. These are familiar aspects of arguing a case, whether in business, in a debate, in court, in the family, etc. One question is whether the concern of the police should be to argue a case, or rather to discover the truth about what happened. But that question should not be allowed to obscure the difficulty that what are presented as 'objective facts' may often incorporate an amount of subjective interpretation of which the investigator is unaware. Sometimes this is evident at the level of language (a police officer might say or write, 'X stole the money' rather than 'X took possession of the money'; the former implies a completed offence, the latter leaves open the mental element of dishonesty); on other occasions it may be concealed in the construction of the file.

So far as police investigations are concerned, the trend in recent years has been to increase the amount of formal regulation, largely through the Police and Criminal Evidence Act 1984 and its Codes of Practice. Behind these regulations lie various goals, as discussed in Chapters 2 and 3. They are not simply designed to improve the reliability of investigative practices, with a view to minimizing the number of mistakes and maximizing the pursuit of the truth. Some of the rules uphold certain rights of suspects and defendants, such as the right to legal advice. Others are mainly aimed at increasing accountability, although that can be linked ultimately to the protection of individuals from the wrongful or excessive use of official power. Rules of these kinds create a tension if it is assumed that the primary purpose of the police is to prevent and detect crime, since it is then a short step to regarding as obstructive those rules designed to uphold rights or to enhance accountability. The tension may sometimes be resolved, as we saw in Chapter 3, by indulging in unethical behaviour. Wide-ranging as the regulations flowing from the Police and Criminal Evidence Act are, they leave some unregulated discretion and, and more tellingly, leave room for the police to 'cover their backs'[1] by appearing to have complied with the formalities when they have not.

The first part of this chapter outlines some seventeen issues in the investigation of crime. Many of them concern the interviewing of suspects, others deal with questions from the tactics of entrapment to identification procedures. The aim is to convey a general impression of issues of principle and procedure in investigations, particularly by the police. The discussion is largely descriptive, though it then leads into a general discussion of more fundamental questions such as the right of silence, the use of confession evidence, the securing of suspects' rights, and remedies for non-compliance with the regulations.

1. Issues in Investigation

None of the seventeen issues will be discussed in full here. In respect of each one, the law and/or regulations will be described, research on practice will be noted, any sanctions for non-compliance will be mentioned, and there will be brief discussion of any relevant proposals from the 1993 Royal Commission on Criminal Justice. The concern is more with the general ethos and general problems of investigation than with a comprehensive or critical survey of the law and practice. However, one general point should be made about the Codes of Practice and the legal significance of any breach. The Court of Appeal has emphasized on several occasions that proof of breach of a Code of Practice does not lead automatically to exclusion of the evidence thereby obtained.[2] Much will depend on such matters of judgement as whether the breach is substantial, whether it had a significant effect on the defendant's conduct, whether it was deliberate or in good faith,

---

[1] A major practical concern, as identified by R. Reiner, *The Politics of the Police* (2nd edn., 1992), ch. 3.

[2] e.g. *Delaney* (1988) 88 Cr. App. R. 338, *Keenan* (1989) 90 Cr. App. R. 1.

and so forth. These judgements will be made in applying two provisions in the Police and Criminal Evidence Act 1984. The first is section 76 (2):

If, in any proceedings where the prosecution proposes to give in evidence a confession made by an accused person, it is represented to the court that the confession was or may have been obtained—

(a) by oppression of the person who made it; or
(b) in consequence of anything said or done which was likely, in the circumstances existing at the time, to render unreliable any confession which might be made by him in consequence thereof,

the court shall not allow the confession to be given in evidence against him except in so far as the prosecution proves to the court beyond reasonable doubt that the confession (notwithstanding that it may be true) was not obtained as aforesaid.

It will be seen that, if 'oppression' is proved, the court must exclude the resulting confession.[3] In other cases, the test is whether the circumstances and what was said or done were likely to render unreliable 'any confession which might be made by him', a hypothetical question that leaves room for evaluative judgements in the courts. However, confessions in general and breaches of the Codes of Practice in particular may also be brought within section 78 (1), which states:

In any proceedings the court may refuse to allow evidence on which the prosecution proposes to rely to be given if it appears to the court that, having regard to all the circumstances, including the circumstances in which the evidence was obtained, the admission of the evidence would have such an adverse effect on the fairness of the proceedings that the court ought not to admit it.

Although this section refers expressly to the circumstances in which the evidence was obtained, it also leaves the court with an evaluative judgement to make. It will be seen below that not all breaches of a Code of Practice result in exclusion.

1. *Entrapment*: the vast majority of offences coming to the notice of the police are reported by members of the public. Indeed, in a majority of cases the public also give information which leads the police to the suspect.[4] However, there are some forms of crime (notably drug dealing) of which the police cannot obtain much evidence without engaging in undercover operations. Police officers may themselves infiltrate groups as part of undercover operations, and the police may make use of informers—themselves often small-time criminals—in order to obtain information about offences and offenders. It can therefore be

[3] See *Fulling* [1987] 2 All ER 65.
[4] e.g. M. McConville, A. Sanders, and R. Leng, *The Case for the Prosecution* (1991), 19, who found that 70% of arrests stemmed from information from the public.

argued that informers and undercover activities are necessary for crime control, in the sense that they make a significant contribution to this goal that could not be achieved through ordinary methods of detection. But there is the important issue of safeguards: if the operations of the police or their informers instigate the commission of offences that would not otherwise have been committed, is this not unfair on the entrapped person? Is it right that the police should be able to tempt people into committing offences?

When the activities of informers came to the attention of the courts in a number of cases in the late 1960s, the issue was mainly one of ensuring that courts were told where one of the parties was an informer, particularly in cases where this might have a bearing on the legal elements in the offence.[5] The Home Office issued guidelines on this matter.[6] Subsequently, however, defence counsel pressed the issue of the impact of entrapment on the culpability of the defendant, and the question came before the House of Lords in *Sang* (1980).[7] The House upheld previous decisions to the effect that entrapment cannot be a defence to criminal liability, and then argued that it would be inconsistent to approve a discretion to exclude evidence obtained by entrapment, since this would often have the same practical effect as allowing a defence. So far as the court was concerned, mitigation of sentence and the disciplining of errant police officers were the most appropriate responses to clear instances of instigation. There is no shortage of examples of sentences being mitigated to reflect the possibility that the offence might not have taken place if there had been no entrapment,[8] although the courts have been unwilling to mitigate the sentence if it appears that the offence was substantially planned before or without the involvement of the informer.[9] Some would argue that mitigation of sentence is not a sufficient safeguard for people who are approached by undercover police officers and tempted into crime:[10] it fudges the question of whether this was really an example of the police creating a crime and a criminal, in which case there is a strong argument for a defence to liability, or was in fact a routine criminal transac-

---

[5] The leading case was *Birtles* (1969) 53 Cr. App. R. 469; cf. also *Macro* [1969] Crim. LR 205.

[6] Home Office Consolidated Circular to the Police on Crime and Kindred Matters (1969).

[7] [1980] AC 402; see J. D. Heydon, 'Entrapment and Unfairly Obtained Evidence in the House of Lords'. [1980] *Crim. LR* 129.

[8] e.g. *Underhill* (1979) 1 Cr. App. R. (S) 270, *Beaumont* (1987) 9 Cr. App. R. (S) 342, *Chapman and Denton* (1989) 11 Cr. App. R. (S) 222, *Perrin* (1992) 13 Cr. App. R. (S) 518.

[9] *Kelly and Holcroft* (1989) 11 Cr. App. R. (S) 127.

[10] A. Choo, *Abuse of Process and Judicial Stays of Criminal Proceedings* (1993), ch. 6; A. J. Ashworth, 'Entrapment', [1978] *Crim. LR* 137.

tion by the defendant which on this occasion happened to involve an informer or police officer. In many practical situations the line between encouraging the commission of an offence and 'stringing along' a person in order to obtain evidence may be gossamer thin, but it is highly significant in point of principle. Moreover, there is a powerful argument that law enforcement officers whose duty is to prevent crime should not be allowed to engage in the creation of crime and that, when they do so, it is inadequate simply to exclude evidence or to mitigate sentence. The courts should insist on the integrity of the criminal process by granting a judicial stay of the proceedings where the entrapper's activities have crossed the boundary of permissibility.[11]

Developments in the last few years have taken a different turn. The enactment of section 78 of the Police and Criminal Evidence Act 1984 has provided courts with a new statutory discretion to exclude evidence and a new opportunity to elaborate some guidance. In *Gill and Ranuana* (1989)[12] the Court of Appeal held that *Sang* does not preclude the exercise of the section 78 discretion in entrapment cases, although the speeches in *Sang* must be kept in mind. In the much-discussed case of *Christou and Wright* (1992)[13] the activity of the police officers in running a jeweller's shop in order to collect evidence against thieves and handlers was certainly a form of trick, but it cannot properly be described as entrapment because the conduct of the undercover officers was predominantly reactive and involved no instigation. They simply waited for customers to offer them stolen goods. The Court of Appeal held that the discretion under section 78 was available, but approved the trial judge's decision not to exercise it.[14] A similar conclusion had been reached some years earlier in *DPP* v. *Marshall and Downes* (1988),[15] where two undercover officers made 'test purchases' of liquor from an unlicensed vendor. Since the vendor was plainly offering the liquor for sale, it could hardly be said that the officers had instigated the commission of the offence.

The Court of Appeal has now given rounded consideration to the issues in *Smurthwaite and Gill* (1994),[16] two separate cases in which the defendants had sought the murder of a spouse by soliciting a person who turned out to be an undercover police officer. The court accepted that entrapment could be relevant to the exercise of the section 78

[11] Choo, *Abuse of Process*; see now *R.* v. *Horseferry Road Magistrates' Court, ex p. Bennett* [1993] 3 WLR 90, where the House of Lords went beyond *Sang* in holding that a prosecution may be stayed 'if it offends the court's sense of justice and propriety to be asked to try the accused in the circumstances of a particular case'.

[12] [1989] Crim. LR 358.

[13] (1992) 95 Cr. App. R. 264.

[14] See below, para. 12, on lies.

[15] [1988] Crim. LR 750.

[16] [1994] Crim. LR 53.

discretion, and it set out six considerations to be taken into account: whether the officer enticed the defendant to commit an offence that would not otherwise have been committed; what the nature of the entrapment was; whether the evidence related to a completed offence; whether the officer was mainly passive or active; whether there was a reliable record of events; and whether the officer had abused his role by acting as an interviewer. This decision may be seen as shifting the emphasis from entrapment as a concept towards an exercise of discretion that takes account more generally of the role of the police officer or informer.

Two issues need to be reaffirmed. First, individuals should be protected from the results of police officers or other *agents provocateurs* instigating offences: infiltrating a group once an offence has been planned or 'laid on' is a separate issue, as are the many questions about other covert investigative methods that do not infringe any recognized rights.[17] There is certainly a need for greater police accountability for investigative methods: the Metropolitan Police say that the activities of undercover officers are controlled in everyday policing by means of guidance based on a specially solicited counsel's opinion in 1986 and revised in the light of recent appellate decisions. This is printed in the police pocket book.[18] However, it would be better if the limits were set out plainly in a Code of Practice, for all to see. Second, there is the question of which remedy or sanction is appropriate if entrapment is established. The possibilities run from a full defence to liability or stay of proceedings for abuse of process, through exclusion of evidence to mitigation of sentence. If entrapment is defined in terms of instigation, the proper response in respect of the defendant is a complete defence or stay of proceedings. The question of police discipline is a separate matter.

2. *Interviewing victims*: in relation to the majority of crimes, which are reported to the police by members of the public, one of the first tasks is to obtain a statement from the victim. Where the alleged offence is a particularly sensitive one, such as a sexual assault or violent attack, the need to show due respect for the victim's feelings is obvious. About three-quarters of the victims of violent or sexual crimes participating in the survey by Shapland, Willmore, and Duff expressed satisfaction with the approach of the police, whereas some 6 per cent were not satisfied.[19] At that time, in the early 1980s, much publicity had

---

[17] See below, para. 12.
[18] Private communication from the Metropolitan Police.
[19] J. Shapland, J. Willmore, and P. Duff, *Victims in the Criminal Justice System* (1985), 34–5.

been given to the overbearing and disrespectful manner of some police officers when dealing with women who alleged they had been raped. In 1985 the Women's National Commission produced a report recommending changes of approach in the questioning of victims of rape and domestic violence,[20] including awareness training about the effects of victimization. It is often said that police practices now show greater respect for victims, following a circular of 1990,[21] but research on child victims by Morgan and Zedner casts doubt on this.[22] In over a third of their cases—mostly involving sexual abuse or assault, physical assault, or theft—dissatisfaction was expressed by children or parents about the police response to the complaint. This was a reaction to the whole investigation, but many were distinctly dissatisfied with the manner of police questioning. The majority of child victims of violence or sexual offences said they felt that the police did not believe their account,[23] although some police forces have set up specialist units for sexual abuse cases and the response of victims and their families was much more favourable here.[24] The Royal Commission noted the difficulties of interviewing victims and witnesses who may be in a distressed or vulnerable state, recommending improved police training and the adoption of the guidelines for rape and domestic violence cases in other cases too.[25] In so far as the police fail to measure up to these standards, it seems that the causes lie party in ignorance about the psychological state of the victims and the effect of their questioning, and partly in a desire to determine whether the victim would be a credible witness in court.[26] The latter point raises an awkward conflict between respect for the victim's feelings and the importance (for victims as well as defendants) of not proceeding to trial if the case lacks reasonable prospects of conviction.[27]

3. *Stop and search*: sections 1–3 of the Police and Criminal Evidence Act 1984 permit the police to stop and search a person when they have reasonable grounds for suspicion that articles unlawfully obtained or possessed are being carried. Code of Practice A sets out the procedure to be followed when exercising this statutory power. Official statistics show that the number of recorded stop-searches declined from 2

---

[20] For discussion of the report and its reception, see L. Smith, *Concerns about Rape*, HORS 106 (1989), 6–9; see also I. Blair, *Investigating Rape: A New Approach for the Police* (1985).

[21] Home Office Circular 60/1990 sets standards for the police approach to cases of domestic violence. See also House of Commons Home Affairs Committee, Third Report, Session 1992–3, *Domestic Violence* (1993), recommendations 3–10.

[22] J. Morgan and L. Zedner, *Child Victims* (1992), 96–105.   [23] Ibid. 101–2.

[24] Ibid. 80–1.   [25] RCCJ Report, Cm. 2263 (1993), para. 2.16.

[26] Morgan and Zedner, *Child Victims*, 102–4 and 122.

[27] See Ch. 6 on prosecutorial review.

million per annum to around 120,000 in 1989, but McConville, Sanders, and Leng argue that these figures give a false impression. They found that in practice the police tend to ask people's consent to search them. If they consent, the statutory power is not invoked and no formal record is necessary. If they refuse consent, the refusal is treated as grounds for reasonable suspicion, and the statutory power is then invoked.[28] The 1981 Royal Commission, when recommending the new powers, argued that 'there must be safeguards to protect members of the public from random, arbitrary and discriminatory searches',[29] but the above findings suggest that the various safeguards incorporated in Code of Practice A are only applicable in a minority of cases. One particular cause for concern is racial prejudice in stop-searches, where the evidence shows higher rates of stop for those of Afro-Caribbean origin than for whites, and higher rates for whites than for those of Asian origin.[30] Robert Reiner draws a careful distinction between discrimination and differentiation, arguing that some account must be taken of the different rate of involvement of certain groups in some forms of activity, and that discrimination occurs less frequently than would appear from the bald statistics.[31] None the less, there is a strong argument for reviewing police practice and the law so as to make a renewed attempt to implement the proposals of the 1981 Royal Commission.

4. *Arrest, charge, or summons*: section 24 of the Police and Criminal Evidence Act 1984 provides that a police officer may arrest any person whom he or she has reasonable grounds to suspect of having committed, committing, or being about to commit an arrestable offence. Arrest is not the only way of beginning an investigation into the involvement of a suspect, but it is the most coercive. The Royal Commission on Criminal Procedure, reporting in 1981, found that 'arrest represents a major disruption to a suspect's life', and that 'police officers are so involved with the process of arrest and detention that they fail at times to understand the sense of alarm and dismay felt by some of those who suffer such treatment'.[32] They recommended that the police should make greater use of the summons, and that arrest and the consequent detention should be confined to cases of necessity, for which they articulated five criteria.[33] The 1984 Act was intended to embody this approach, but research has found evidence of two police practices that effectively neutralize the intended reform. One is that detention follow-

---

[28] McConville, Sanders, and Leng, *The Case for the Prosecution*, 95.

[29] RCCP, *Report*, Cmd. 8092 (1981), para. 3.24.

[30] M. Fitzgerald, *Ethnic Minorities and the Criminal Justice System*, RCCJ Research Study 20 (1993), 14–16.

[31] Reiner, *Politics of the Police*, 156–70.   [32] RCCP Report, para. 3.75.

[33] Ibid., para. 3.76.

ing arrest seems to be authorized as a matter of routine and that there is no fresh application of the 'necessity principle' by the custody officer at the police station, as the 1981 Royal Commission had hoped. The other practice, less widespread but little less effective, is not to make an arrest but to rely on the 'voluntary' attendance of the suspect at a police station, circumscribed by various disincentives to leave.[34] The Royal Commission of 1993 fails to deal with these issues, leaving the police to continue their adaptive behaviour towards the provisions of the 1984 Act. It was probably naïve to think that the custody officer, a colleague of the arresting officers and receiving information only from arresting officers, could act as an independent arbiter on the necessity for detention. The result is that the custody record is meaningless on this issue, and that what Reiner describes as 'a central tenet of the highly practical culture of policing—that "you can't play it by the book"'[35] has once again asserted itself. It is quite wrong that the police should have been able to succeed in preventing 'mere' legislation from obstructing their established practices, and the Royal Commission should have made a fresh attempt to engineer change. However, in some cases of wrongful arrest there may be far-reaching consequences. In *Fennelley* (1989)[36] a Circuit Judge excluded evidence found in a search that followed an unlawful arrest, although it is not clear whether this view would be adopted widely. There is certainly the possibility of suing the police for damages for wrongful arrest.[37]

5. *Interviewing outside the police station*: it will be seen below that one of the great changes in police interrogation in the last ten years has been the advent of tape recording. However, the move towards tape recording has not been accompanied by restrictions on the use by the police, and in court, of unrecorded statements attributed to the defendant. Does this mean that the well-known practice of 'verballing' suspects, when the police attribute to them statements that they did not make, continues to flourish unchecked? Questioning was found to have taken place outside the police station in 10 per cent of cases in one study[38] and in 8 per cent in another study.[39] The 1993 Royal Commission is attracted by the idea of tape recording remarks by suspects outside police stations, whilst trying to ensure that any actual

[34] See generally I. McKenzie, R. Morgan, and R. Reiner, 'Helping the Police with their Inquiries', [1990] *Crim. LR* 22.

[35] Reiner, *Politics of the Police*, 107. [37] [1989] Crim. LR 142.

[37] R. Clayton and H. Tomlinson, *Civil Actions against the Police* (1987).

[38] D. Brown, T. Ellis, and K. Larcombe, *Changing the Code: Police Detention under the Revised PACE Codes of Practice*, HORS 129 (1993).

[39] S. Moston and G. Stephenson, *The Questioning and Interviewing of Suspects outside the Police Station*, RCCJ Research Study 22 (1993).

questioning is left until arrival at the police station. It expresses an interest in an experiment in which police officers carry tape recorders for use when remarks are likely to be made by suspects, and it recommends that a suspect should be invited to comment on any alleged confession when a recorded interview subsequently takes place at a police station.[40] What it fails to recommend, however, is that unrecorded remarks should be inadmissible in court. This leaves open the possibility of abuse, recognized even by the Royal Commission itself: 'it is difficult, if not impossible, to devise rules that ensure that those who are determined to evade those rules are prevented from doing so.'[41] In view of this, the proper course would have been to emphasize that there are safeguards for questioning (such as legal advice), that these apply only at the police station, that questioning should therefore take place only in a police station, and that remarks made spontaneously by a suspect outside the police station should only be admissible if recorded.

The courts are not able to make elaborate rules of this kind, but they have tended to give a broad interpretation to the term 'interview'. In *Absolam* (1989)[42] the word was said to encompass all questioning 'with a view to obtaining admissions on which proceedings can be founded', and in *Cox* (1993)[43] the Court of Appeal cast doubt on a previous decision that had purported to distinguish questioning designed to give the suspect an opportunity to offer an innocent explanation as falling outside the definition of an interview.[44] Behind these decisions lies an appreciation of the importance of ensuring that the protections in Code C are available in most cases where questions are asked, other than questions merely to establish identity.[45] In cases involving an element of entrapment, where the police have put questions without revealing that they are police officers investigating offences, the Court of Appeal has drawn a distinction between cases where this has been done in order to maintain the officers' cover (evidence not excluded)[46] and cases where the officers were really trying to question the suspect outside the requirements of the 1984 Act (evidence excluded).[47] The revised provision in paragraph 11.1 of Code C lists three limited cir-

[40] RCCJ Report, paras. 3.11–3.15.   [41] Ibid., para. 3.5.

[42] (1989) 88 Cr. App. R. 332; see also *Keenan* (1989) 90 Cr. App. R. 1 and *Matthews, Dennison and Voss* (1900) 91 Cr. App. R. 43.

[43] [1993] Crim. LR 382.

[44] *Maguire* (1989) 90 Cr. App. R. 115; this decision was also distinguished in *Weekes* [1993] Crim. LR 211, where the evidence was excluded.

[45] As the Court noted in *Cox*, n. 11A to Code C is most unclear in its terms. RCCJ Report, para. 3.10, calls for the note to be redrafted.

[46] *Christou and Wright* (1992) 95 Cr. App. R. 264.

[47] *Bryce* (1992) 95 Cr. App. R. 320.

cumstances in which it is permissible to question suspects outside a
police station: that should make it easier to identify breaches of the
Code in future, although even then the courts have not always
excluded the results of the questioning.[48] Parliament should avoid the
need for discretionary exclusion by declaring the principle that
unrecorded statements attributed to a defendant are inadmissible.

6. *Reading the defendant's rights*: paragraph 3.1 of Code C provides
that persons arriving at a police station under arrest or voluntarily must
be informed clearly of three rights—the right to have someone
informed of their arrest, the right to obtain independent legal advice
privately from a solicitor free of charge, and the right to consult the
Codes of Practice. Research findings appear to agree on two things.
First, custody officers are now performing their duty to inform suspects
more frequently and more fully than before 1991, although about one-
quarter of suspects are still not told everything that they should be
told.[49] And second, in a significant minority of cases the words are spoken in an unclear or unduly hurried fashion, and/or the police emphasize the possible problems of insisting on a solicitor (such as delay
before one arrives).[50] Some of these failures might stem from forgetful-
ness in the heat of the moment, but others suggest that the police
officers resent the 'rights' and think that lawyers would impede the
smooth progress of the investigation. Courts have excluded evidence in
cases where suspects have not been notified of their rights or have
been misinformed, and the Court of Appeal has upheld this
approach.[51] The Royal Commission pays little attention to the important ethical issues raised by attempts to persuade suspects not to exercise their rights, but recommends further testing of a new notice of
rights, intended to create a fuller understanding of what is being said.[52]

7. *Legal advice at the police station*: section 58 of the Police and
Criminal Evidence Act 1984 provides that 'a person arrested and held
in custody . . . shall be entitled, if he so requests, to consult a solicitor
privately at any time'. Paragraph 6 of Code C contains detailed

---

[48] Such as *Khan* [1993] Crim. LR 54, involving customs officers.

[49] Brown, Ellis, and Larcombe, *Changing the Code*; M. Zander and P. Henderson,
Crown Court Study RCCJ Research Study 19 (1993), 9.

[50] Brown, Ellis, and Larcombe, *Changing the Code*, about a quarter of cases; see also A.
Sanders and L. Bridges, 'Access to Legal Advice and Police Malpractice', [1990] *Crim. LR*
494 at 498, some 41% of cases; McConville, Sanders, and Leng, *Case for the Prosecution*,
47. Code C, para. 6.4, states: 'No attempt should be made to dissuade the suspect from
obtaining legal advice.'

[51] e.g. *Absolam* (1989) 88 Cr. App. R. 332, *Beycan* [1990] Crim. LR 185.

[52] RCCJ Report, para. 3.40, following I. Clare and G. Gudjonsson, *Devising and Piloting
an Experimental Version of the 'Notice to Detained Persons'*, RCCJ Research Study 7
(1993).

guidance on the presence and rights of legal advisers. The percentage of suspects requesting legal advice increased from 24 to 32 following the introduction of the revised Code in 1991.[53] This still leaves some two-thirds of suspects refusing 'the offer of a free gift',[54] in some cases because they see no reason to have it, in others because there would be a delay.[55] However, the proportion requesting legal advice is much higher in serious cases: some 66 per cent of those appearing in the Crown Court ask for a solicitor in the police station.[56] Research has called into question whether those who do request legal advice receive advice and support of the appropriate quality. Two studies have found that a majority of legal advisers attending police stations are not admitted solicitors but clerks or other staff.[57] Michael McConville and Jacqueline Hodgson found that when legal advisers arrive at the police station they have difficulty in ascertaining details of the allegations, and usually have nothing more than a hurried interview with their client.[58] Whether from inexperience or from lack of familiarity with the case or both, the advice given to suspects was variable in quality and the protection given to suspects during interviews was sometimes non-existent. McConville and Hodgson state that some advisers 'fail to protect clients from improper, inappropriate and irrelevant—but potentially damaging—questions';[59] John Baldwin argues that some legal advisers are, by their passivity during interviews, failing to safeguard their client's interests in the face of hostile or repetitive questioning.[60]

There are provisions in the 1984 Act for a senior officer to authorize delaying a detainee's exercise of the right to legal advice, where a serious arrestable offence is concerned and interference with the course of justice is thought likely.[61] The Court of Appeal has taken a strong view on this, requiring the police to give persuasive evidence of the existence of justifying circumstances, and the quashing of the conviction in

---

[53] Brown, Ellis, and Larcombe, *Changing the Code*.

[54] Sanders and Bridges, 'Access to Legal Advice', at 497.

[55] Zander and Henderson, *Crown Court Study*, 12, found that about half of those who declined legal advice thought that they could handle matters alone, and a further 13% wanted to avoid delay.

[56] Ibid. 10.

[57] J. Baldwin, *The Role of Legal Representatives at Police Stations*, RCCJ Research Study 3 (1992); M. McConville and J. Hodgson, *Custodial Legal Advice and the Right to Silence*, RCCJ Research Study 16 (1993).

[58] McConville and Hodgson, *Custodial Legal Advice*, ch. 4.

[59] Ibid.

[60] Baldwin, *Role of Legal Representatives*, 35; the Court of Appeal advanced similar criticisms in a case involving just such passivity by a legal adviser: *Glaves* [1993] Crim. LR 685. See also the case of the 'Cardiff Three', below, n. 84.

[61] PACE 1984, ss. 56 and 58.

Samuel (1988)[62] was a notable symbolic blow in favour of the right to legal advice. The Royal Commission focuses its concern on two matters, waiver of the right to legal advice and the quality of advice for those who request it. On waiver, it recommends recording on tape a suspect's reason for not wanting a lawyer, and offering those who decline a lawyer the opportunity to speak to a duty solicitor by telephone.[63] On quality, the Commission takes the point that some legal advisers advise silence because they have not been told enough about the case to give more constructive advice. The Commission recommends that legal advisers be given more information when they attend the police station, that Law Society guidance to solicitors at police stations be better known,[64] and that more attention be given to the training of legal advisers who are not solicitors.[65] This is particularly important in view of the extra significance sometimes accorded to interviews conducted in the presence of a legal adviser, a significance that is entirely misplaced if the legal adviser fails to protect the client.[66] The Commission grasps the need to educate the police about the proper role of the solicitor in the police station. The police may believe that they are acting in the public interest, but this may neglect the argument that it is in the public interest for suspects' rights to be honoured.

8. *An appropriate adult*: Code of Practice C provides that, if it is proposed to question a juvenile, mentally disordered, or mentally handicapped person, the police must inform an appropriate adult (e.g. parent, social worker) and ask him or her to come to the police station to see the person.[67] The appropriate adult is allowed to consult privately with the person and to be present during any interview, and these rights are additional to the normal right to legal advice. In practice it seems that the police sometimes fail to inform the juvenile of the right to legal advice until the appropriate adult arrives, so that the prospect of further delay leads to the waiver of the right to legal advice.[68] It seems that, as with adults, there are some interviews in which juveniles are 'harangued, belittled or indirectly threatened that they will not be left alone until either the police obtain irrefutable evidence or the suspect confesses', and where the parent, social worker,

---

[62] (1988) 87 Cr. App. R. 232; cf. *Alladice* (1988) 87 Cr. App. R. 380, where the Court advanced the same principle but upheld the conviction.

[63] RCCJ Report, paras. 3.48–3.49.

[64] See D. Roberts, 'Questioning the Suspect: The Solicitor's Role', [1993] *Crim. LR* 368.

[65] RCCJ Report, paras. 3.53–3.64.

[66] A point recognized by Lord Taylor, CJ, in *Miller* (below, n. 84).

[67] Code C, paras. 1 and 3.

[68] Brown, Ellis, and Larcombe, *Changing the Code*.

or legal adviser remains silent none the less.[69] The police also fail to recognize some suspects as mentally disordered, classifying as 'vulnerable' only about a quarter of those who actually are.[70] The Court of Appeal has been willing to exclude evidence arising from the questioning of juveniles and of the mentally disordered in the absence of an appropriate adult and to quash the resulting convictions.[71] The Royal Commission recognizes the many difficulties connected with 'appropriate adults' and proposes a review by a multi-disciplinary working party.[72] It also recommends that section 77 of the 1984 Act, on the inadmissibility of confessions made in the absence of an independent person, should be extended from the mentally handicapped to cover all mentally disordered suspects.[73] These are worthwhile steps but, once again, real progress depends on changes in the practices of the police and defence lawyers.

9. *Recording of interviews*: there is no statutory basis for the audio or video recording of interviews, but Code of Practice E now sets out guidance for recording. Little difficulty seems to be caused by audio recording itself: the problems are rather that the police choose to ask some questions outside the police station, as we saw in (5) above, and that there is a tendency to rely on police summaries (which are often defective) rather than to listen to the tapes themselves.[74] There have been several experiments with the video recording of police interviews, and two particular problems have emerged. One is that jurors and magistrates may attribute too much importance to the facial expressions of the interviewee, failing to understand the stresses and perhaps strangeness of the conditions.[75] The other is that the videotapes might appear to cover the whole interview, whereas there are documented examples of the police conducting other, off-the-record interviews in order to change the suspect's mind about certain things.[76] The Royal Commission recommends further experimentation and research on audio taping, and in order to reduce malpractice puts faith in its proposal that there should be a permanent camera in the custody suites of

[69] R. Evans, *The Conduct of Police Interviews with Juveniles*, RCCJ Research Study 8 (1993).

[70] G. Gudjonsson *et al.*, *Persons at Risk during Interviews in Police Custody: The Identification of Vulnerabilities*, RCCJ Research Study 12 (1993).

[71] e.g. *Everett* [1988] Crim. LR 826 (mentally handicapped adult); *Weekes* [1993] Crim. LR 211 (juvenile); *Glaves* [1993] Crim. LR 685 (juvenile).

[72] RCCJ Report, para. 3.86.

[73] Ibid., para. 4.40.

[74] J. Baldwin, *Preparing the Record of Taped Interviews*, RCCJ Research Study 2 (1992).

[75] See RCCJ Report, paras. 3.71–3.72.

[76] For details, see M. McConville, 'Videotaping Interrogations: Police Behaviour on and off Camera', [1992] *Crim. LR* 532.

police stations.[77] The role of the courts was chiefly to insist on contemporaneous records of interviews in the days before universal tape recording.[78] Their role in the future is likely to focus on the definition of an interview, since one of the results of the Royal Commission's proposal for cameras in custody suites may well be an increase in attempts to question suspects elsewhere.

10. *The conduct of interviews*: Code of Practice C contains not only guidance on the detention of persons in police stations and the rights to be accorded to them, but also guidance on when a suspect should be cautioned about his or her rights and on the conditions in which interviews should be held. Those conditions include heating, periods of rest, breaks for refreshment, and so on. The origins of the guidance lie in the Report of the 1981 Royal Commission: that Commission received considerable evidence on the psychological tactics and psychological effects of police interrogation,[79] but made no specific recommendations on the style of questioning.[80] In a similar vein, the 1993 Royal Commission emphasizes the benefits of better police training, 'instilling in officers a recognition that oppressive interviews are liable to be inaccurate. Fatigue is an important factor in increasing the suggestibility and the inaccuracy of a suspect's performance.'[81] The courts have frequently expressed disapproval of departures from Code C, but have rarely held that such departures justify the exclusion of the resulting evidence, taking the view that only serious misconduct is likely to have an adverse effect on the fairness of the proceedings (section 78 of the 1984 Act) or likely to render any subsequent confession unreliable (section 76 of the 1984 Act).[82]

The 1993 Royal Commission received much evidence, from its own research programme, of 'undue pressure amounting to bullying or harassment' by the police during interrogations.[83] One particular example that has become notorious is the tape recorded interrogation of the so-called Cardiff Three, involving repeated questions and assertions on the same point and described by the Lord Chief Justice as a

---

[77] RCCJ Report, paras. 3.72.

[78] e.g. *Delaney* (1988) 88 Cr. App. R. 338, *Keenan* (1989) 90 Cr. App. R. 1.

[79] Notably B. Irving and L. Hilgendorf, *Police Interrogation: The Psychological Approach*, RCCP Research Study 1 (1980).

[80] RCCP Report, para. 4.113.

[81] RCCJ Report, para. 2.24; this paragraph also contains a recommendation that Code C be revised.

[82] e.g. *Samuel* [1988] QB 615, *Alladice* (1988) 87 Cr. App. R. 380. For a detailed discussion see R. Pattenden, *Judicial Discretion and Criminal Litigation* (2nd edn., 1990), 264–91.

[83] RCCJ Report, para. 2.18; see Baldwin, *Role of Legal Representatives*; Evans, *Conduct of Police Interviews*; McConville and Hodgson, *Custodial Legal Advice*.

'travesty'.[84] Even when no such tactics are used, there is a tendency to proceed by means of suggestions and statements to which the suspect's assent is sought, an approach that may be pursued despite the suspect's silence.[85] The Royal Commission's response is to endorse a recent Home Office circular and new guide to interviewing, and to emphasize the need for better police training and supervision.[86] However, there is also a need to articulate clearly those approaches to questioning that are not acceptable: the Royal Commission accepts too readily the notion that there is 'no simple rule that applies to all police interviews',[87] when its own research demonstrates the need to be clearer about the boundaries of unacceptable conduct. The Court of Appeal has now shown a willingness to apply the concept of oppression to repetitive, hectoring questioning, thereby excluding the confession under section 76 (2) (*a*).[88] Lesser departures from the proper approach to questioning may justify exclusion under section 76 (2) (*b*) or section 78.[89]

11. *Confessions*: it has often been said that the police see the primary purpose of questioning as the obtaining of a confession, and this is perfectly natural. There are secondary purposes, such as the obtaining of criminal intelligence, but confessions and admissions are the goal. Much questioning is directed to this end, although it appears than in information-seeking approach is adopted more frequently with juveniles.[90] Some of the techniques of interviewing referred to in the previous paragraph may lead some suspects to confess when they have not committed the crime, simply as a reaction to the pressure placed upon them. The Royal Commission recognizes this as a possibility,[91] but, apart from the recommendations discussed in (10) above, its main concern is the use of confessions at trial. It rejects a rule allowing only tape recorded confessions into evidence, on the ground that 'spontaneous remarks uttered on arrest are often the most truthful', but is rather vague about the evidential use of remarks attributed to a defendant that he declines to repeat on tape at the police station.[92] It rejects a rule restricting admissibility to confessions made in the presence of a solicitor, probably rightly in view of the variable performance of legal

[84] *Paris, Abdullahi and Miller* (1993) 97 Cr. App. R. 99, discussed in Ch. 1.3.
[85] McConville, Sanders, and Leng, *Case for the Prosecution*, 60.
[86] RCCJ Report, para. 2.22.   [87] Ibid., para. 2.17.
[88] See the case of the 'Cardiff Three', above, n. 84.
[89] e.g. *Canale* (1990) 91 Cr. App. R. 1; *Weekes* [1993] Crim. LR 211.
[90] See Evans, *Conduct of Police Interviews*.
[91] RCCJ Report, para. 5.32, citing G. Gudjonsson, *The Psychology of Interrogations, Confessions and Testimony* (1992).
[92] RCCJ Report, para. 5.50.

advisers at police stations.[93] And it rejects (by a majority) a rule requiring supporting evidence before a confession is admitted into evidence, preferring instead a judicial warning of the great care needed before convicting on the evidence of a confession alone.[94] Much would then depend on the use by the courts of their discretion to exclude. Under the 1984 Act they have excluded confessions, not only applying the mandatory rule of section 76 (2) (*a*) when conduct amounting to 'oppression' has been found, but also using their discretion in cases where there have been serious and intentional breaches of the Codes of Practice.[95] They have continued to maintain that not every breach of the Codes justifies exclusion, and have favoured the disciplinary approach (was the police officer in bad faith?) rather than the protective approach (was the defendant prejudiced by the breach?). Unfortunately the Royal Commission has failed to give a firm lead on the subject of false confessions, recognizing the danger but rejecting any strong version of a corroboration rule.[96] These issues are taken further in Section 3 of this chapter.

12. *Telling lies*: lies told by the police or by the suspect may play a significant role in interrogations. If the police tell lies in order to mislead a suspect into confessing, the courts may well exclude the resulting confession. This was done in *Mason* (1987),[97] where the police told the suspect and his solicitor that his fingerprints had been found on incriminating evidence, when this was quite untrue. The Court of Appeal excluded the resulting confession under section 78 of the 1984 Act, stating that a deceit practised both on a suspect and on his solicitor would have an adverse effect on the fairness of the proceedings. However, this does not mean that the practising of any deceit during an investigation ought to lead to the exclusion of any resulting evidence. We have seen that in *Christou and Wright* (1992)[98] there was an element of deceit, in that the undercover police officers were running a jewellery shop in the hope that criminals would offer them stolen goods, but there was no particular lie or inducement. The Court of Appeal has held that the covert recording of conversations between two defendants placed in the same police cell is a passive deceit rather than an active lie,[99] but there are more doubtful cases in which the court has declined to overrule a trial judge's decision to admit evidence

[93] Ibid., para. 5.55; for the performance of legal advisers, see (7) above.
[94] RCCJ Report, paras. 5.85–5.87 and 5.77.
[95] e.g. *Doolan* [1988] Crim. LR 747, *Everett* [1988] Crim. LR 826.
[96] Cf. McConville and Hodgson, *Custodial Legal Advice.*
[97] (1988) 86 Cr. App. R. 349.   [98] [1992] Crim. LR 792, above, para. (1).
[99] *Bailey and Smith* [1993] Crim. LR 681.

obtained by subterfuge.[100] Where, on the other hand, it is the suspect
who tells lies, this may constitute weighty evidence for the prosecution.
In the leading case of *Lucas* (1981)[101] it was confirmed that lies can cor-
roborate elements of the case against a defendant, although the Court
of Appeal also stated that juries should be reminded that there may be
other reasons for telling lies, such as a desire to shield a third party. The
evidential significance of lies depends on the facts of the particular
case, and it seems that the trial judge has a discretion whether to caution the jury against assuming that lies show guilt.[102]

13. *Silence during questioning*: when reference is made to a defendant's 'right of silence' there is often a failure to distinguish between
silence in response to police questions and silence in court. The discussion here is confined to the right to remain silent when questioned out
of court: the right is not declared in any law or constitutional document
but, subject to a limited number of statutory exceptions, it can be
inferred from the long-established police caution ('you are not obliged
to say anything . . .') and from the rule that the prosecution may not
comment at the trial on the defendant's failure to answer questions at
an earlier stage.[103] At the doctrinal level the right to silence is closely
linked to the presumption of innocence.[104] At the practical level it has
been under strong challenge for over twenty years from the police and
others, who argue that it is an unfair impediment to proper investigation. The Royal Commission on Criminal Justice has examined the
issue again, drawing on a considerable body of recent research. It
seems that around 5 per cent of suspects decline to answer any questions at all during police interviews, and probably double that number
refuse to answer some questions.[105] It is often argued that the right of
silence is used as a shield by professional criminals: that claim has not
been made out, but it does appear that defendants in serious cases
tend to rely on silence more than others.[106] It appears that any link
between the exercise of the right to silence and the failure of prosecutions is not strong: Roger Leng found that the defendant's silence was a
prominent factor in only about 2 per cent of cases in which no action

[100] Especially close to the borderline is *Maclean and Kosten* [1993] Crim. LR 687.
[101] (1981) 73 Cr. App. R. 159, reaffirmed in *Goodway* [1993] Crim. LR 948.
[102] *Bey* [1993] Crim. LR 692.
[103] See A. A. S. Zuckerman, *The Principles of Criminal Evidence* (1989), ch. 15.
[104] See the discussion in s. 2 of this chapter.
[105] R. Leng, *The Right to Silence in Police Interrogation*, RCCJ Research Study 10 (1993).
Some studies found total silence (i.e. answering no questions at all) to be rare:
McConville and Hodgson, *Custodial Legal Advice*. Brown's survey found that silence is
more frequent in the Metropolitan Police District: RCCJ Report, para. 4.15.
[106] Zander and Henderson, *Crown Court Study*, 3.

was taken,[107] and Michael Zander and Paul Henderson found that defendants in the Crown Court who had exercised their right of silence were more likely to be convicted than those who had not exercised this right.[108]

There are long-standing exceptions to the right, in cases where a person is found in possession of recently stolen goods, or is being questioned by the Inland Revenue on tax matters. In 1967 Parliament introduced the requirement to give advance notice of an alibi defence (and in 1986 a requirement to give advance notice of expert evidence). In the Criminal Justice Act 1987 Parliament appeared to create a new exception in cases where a person is being questioned by the Serious Fraud Office, even to the extent of providing in section 2 (13) that failure to answer questions without reasonable cause constitutes an offence. However, the Royal Commission of 1993 followed its predecessor of 1981 in recommending no change in the right to remain silent during police questioning, accepting the argument that any change might result in more innocent defendants—particularly the 'less experienced and more vulnerable'—being convicted.[109] The matter is discussed further in Section 2 of this chapter.

14. *Search of premises*: the Police and Criminal Evidence Act 1984 contains various powers for the search of premises, apart from search under a warrant. Section 8 contains the principal powers for the grant of a search warrant by a magistrate. In other cases, section 18 empowers an officer to enter premises occupied or controlled by a person arrested for an arrestable offence, to search for evidence relating to that offence or a similar offence. Section 19 contains the companion power to seize evidence found on such premises. Section 32 (2) empowers an officer to enter premises where the arrestee was when or immediately before he was arrested, to search for evidence relating to the offence for which he was arrested. Code of Practice B regulates the conduct of such searches. In *Beckford* (1992)[110] the Court of Appeal held that the power under section 32 (2) should only be used in good faith, and not in order to search premises for other reasons. If the court finds that the search was unlawful it may decide to exercise its power to exclude any evidence thereby obtained under section 78 of the 1984 Act, although there are many decisions in which this step has not been taken and the unlawfulness of the search has been held to be a separate matter from the admissibility of the evidence.[111]

15. *Samples from the defendant*: Sections 61–5 of the Police and

---

[107] Leng, *The Right to Silence*, 27.
[108] Zander and Henderson, *Crown Court Study*, 4–6.
[109] RCCJ Report, para. 4.23.   [110] (1992) 94 Cr. App. R. 43.   [111] Ibid., at 50.

Criminal Evidence Act 1984 provide for the taking of fingerprints and bodily samples. In brief, non-intimate samples may be taken without the suspect's consent so long as a police officer of at least superintendent rank believes that the suspect is involved in a serious arrestable offence; intimate samples may only be taken if a police superintendent has such a belief and the suspect consents, although refusal of consent entitles the court to draw whatever inferences are proper.[112] There are some who argue that these provisions violate the right to silence or privilege against self-incrimination, but that depends on the strength of analogies between compelled speech and compelled yielding of samples.[113] As Wigmore pointed out, if a defendant refused to come to court on the basis that he did not wish to show his face to witnesses and jurors, we would surely waste little time in concluding that he should be compelled.[114] The argument is that compelling him or her to yield bodily samples, or at least threatening adverse inferences from refusal, may be displeasing for the defendant but cannot be connected with any right other than, perhaps, the right to privacy. The privacy claim relates not only to the procedure for taking certain samples (whether classified as intimate or not) but also to the subsequent use of the samples. The 1993 Royal Commission accepts several arguments from the police that the rules should be altered so that they are more favourable to them and to the prosecution. It recommends that saliva be reclassified as a non-intimate sample, to facilitate the taking of samples for DNA analysis; that the police be given the right to take samples of plucked hair, for the same reason; that dental impressions be brought within the Act, as intimate samples; and that the category of 'serious arrestable offences' be extended to include, for the purpose of sample-taking only, assault and burglary.[115] The Commission accepts some of the privacy arguments in relation to the analysis and subsequent use of samples, with its recommendation for an independent body to oversee DNA databanks, but includes neither analysis of nor reference to Article 8 of the European Convention.[116] Its discussion of these issues is extremely short on principle and, as Robert Reiner puts it bluntly, 'the section reads like the straightforward endorsement of a police shopping list'.[117]

[112] s. 62 (10) of the 1984 Act so provides.
[113] S. Easton, 'Bodily Samples and the Privilege against Self-Incrimination', [1991] *Crim. LR* 18.
[114] H. Wigmore, *Evidence* (McNaughten edn.), para. 2265, cited by Easton, 'Bodily Samples'.
[115] RCCJ Report, paras. 2.28–2.33.   [116] Ibid., paras. 2.36–2.38.
[117] R. Reiner, 'Investigative Powers and Safeguards for Suspects', [1993] *Crim. LR* 808, at 813.

16. *Expert evidence*: it seems that there is some kind of scientific evidence in about one-third of contested Crown Court cases. About one-half of such cases involve medical evidence of the victim's condition, and one-quarter relate to the analysis of drugs. Only the remaining quarter come within the field usually described as 'forensic', relating to fingerprints, blood samples, etc.[118] In some of these cases the Forensic Science Service carries out a number of tests. In the cases of the Maguire Seven, the Birmingham Six, and Judith Ward, the results of certain tests favourable to the defendants were not disclosed to the prosecution, let alone to the defence.[119] The Royal Commission accepts that the Forensic Science Service has become better regulated and more impartial since the 1970s when those cases were decided,[120] but one of its research studies found continuing evidence of an adversarial approach among some forensic scientists, excluding certain items from their reports and arguing that it is for the defence to expose the limitations of their findings.[121] The Commission's principal recommendation is for a Forensic Science Advisory Council to monitor performance and to formulate codes of practice for forensic scientists.[122] Among its other recommendations are greater defence rights in relation to scientific evidence possessed by the prosecution, and pre-trial conferences between prosecution and defence expert witnesses when both are to be called in a case.[123] Important as these recommendations are, they lack a certain sharpness. Stronger words should have been written about the adversarial tendency revealed by the research carried out for the Commission, and proper attention given to the notion of the Forensic Science Service as a trustee of samples and of findings of analysis. A major reorientation of ethics and attitudes seems to be required.

17. *Identification evidence*: cases of mistaken identification have been well documented over the years. The fragility of identification is widely recognized.[124] The Devlin Committee drew together various cases in which mistaken identification had occurred,[125] but the only official reaction to its report was a decision of the Court of Appeal requiring a special form of warning to be given in cases resting on evi-

---

[118] All statistics from Zander and Henderson, *Crown Court Study*, 84–5.
[119] See Ch. 1.3.   [120] RCCJ Reports, paras. 9.27 and 9.47.
[121] P. Roberts and C. Willmore, *The Role of Forensic Science Evidence in Criminal Proceedings*, RCCJ Research Study 11 (1993).
[122] RCCJ Report, paras. 9.33–9.35.
[123] Ibid., paras. 9.52 and 9.63.
[124] See e.g. E. Loftus, *Eyewitness Testimony* (1979), and S. Lloyd-Bostock and B. Clifford (eds.), *Evaluating Witness Evidence* (1983).
[125] Home Office, *Evidence of Identification in Criminal Cases* (1976).

dence of identification.[126] However, Code of Practice D now deals with 'The Identification of Persons by Police Officers'. It establishes that the four alternative methods of identification should be considered in order of priority in each case—(a) identification parade; (b) group identification; (c) video film; (d) confrontation. Failure to give proper consideration to each may result in unfairness to the suspect, and is therefore a ground for excluding the evidence under section 78 of the 1984 Act.[127] Code D also sets out rules for the conduct of identification parades and other procedures. There are several cases in which evidence has been excluded because of departures from the Code,[128] particularly where the breach was deliberate,[129] but the Court of Appeal has maintained that the fact of a breach is not sufficient. There appears to be a need for proof of unfairness, and, where the breach was minor or where it is established that the breach did not prejudice the suspect, the Court has been willing to admit the evidence.[130] What the decisions provide is considerable evidence of deviations from Code D, some deliberate, some apparently stemming from ignorance. Since it appears that identification evidence is of some importance in about one-quarter of contested cases,[131] not to mention those cases that end in a guilty plea for one reason or another, police practice in this area requires scrutiny. Courts operating months after the event are hardly the appropriate body. There is a need for greater accountability at the time, probably through the involvement of defence solicitors and of officers at a higher level of seniority.

2. Innocence and Silence

One of the fundamental principles discussed in Chapter 3 was the presumption of innocence. The link between the presumption and the right to remain silent during police questioning has been recognized many times, notably by the Royal Commission on Criminal Procedure in 1981[132] and by the European Court of Human Rights in 1993.[133] If there is to be a presumption that a person is innocent until proved guilty by the prosecution, there appears to be some inconsistency in

---

[126] *Turnbull* [1977] QB 224; see J. D. Jackson, 'The Insufficiency of Identification Evidence Based on Personal Impression', [1986] *Crim. LR* 203.

[127] e.g. *Gaynor* [1988] Crim. LR 242.

[128] e.g. *Gall* [1989] Crim. LR 745; *Finley* [1993] Crim. LR 50.

[129] *Nagah* [1991] Crim. LR 55.

[130] *Jones* [1992] Crim. LR 365 (breach minor); *Ryan* [1992] Crim. LR 187 (no prejudice apparent).

[131] Zander and Henderson, *Crown Court Study*, 92.

[132] RCCP Report, paras. 4.51–4.52.

[133] *Funke, Cremieux and Miailhe* v. *France* A. 256 (1993).

holding that the defendant can through his or her silence supply an element in that case. Whether this is a true or absolute inconsistency is for analysis elsewhere: because Parliament has introduced a few particular obligations on defendants to deliver records or submit to searches, it has been argued that to take the further step of requiring defendants to answer questions or to risk adverse inferences is 'incremental rather than fundamental'.[134] This seems less than persuasive. The Royal Commissions of both 1981 and 1993 took the 'middle line' that adverse inferences from silence would be permissible once the defendant has received full notice of the prosecution case and has declined to comment on it.[135] But both Royal Commissions argued that it would be inappropriate to permit adverse inferences to be drawn from silence in the face of police questioning, since the defendant is unlikely to know what evidence the police have and police stations are known to be perceived by many suspects as intimidating. The availability of legal advisers—who, as we have seen, are often not qualified lawyers—may not be sufficient to offset this disadvantage.

The right of silence at the police station does not derive strength merely from the presumption of innocence, but also from the privilege against self-incrimination and the right of privacy. There is no constitutional or statutory declaration of the privilege against self-incrimination in English law, but it has been recognized judicially in the House of Lords: 'The underlying rationale . . . is, in my view, now to be found in the maxim *nemo debet prodere se ipsum*, no one can be required to be his own betrayer or in its popular English mistranslation "the right to silence." '[136] Although spoken in a different context, these words recognize the place of the privilege against self-incrimination in the English criminal process. It can be justified by arguing that the State should not indulge in the unfairness of forcing on defendants a choice between speaking and convicting themselves out of their own mouths, or not speaking and being convicted by default. Whilst it should be said that most modern formulations make it clear that guilt is not the only thing that may be inferred from a person's failure to speak—other reasons, such as shame or shielding others from harm are often mentioned—it is believed that courts will often draw adverse inferences if invited to do so.

A third argument, based on privacy, has been developed by Dennis Galligan and receives support from Article 8 of the European

[134] D. Galligan, 'The Right to Silence Reconsidered', [1988] *CLP* at 88.
[135] For a thoughtful review of the debate until 1990, see S. Greer, 'The Right to Silence: A Review of the Current Debate', (1990) 53 *MLR* 709.
[136] *R.* v. *Sang* (1979) 69 Cr. App. R. 282, at 290 per Lord Diplock.

Convention: 'everyone has the right to respect for his private and family life, his home and his correspondence.' Galligan argues that the right not to be compelled to vouchsafe one's secrets is particularly important when the aim of questioning is to obtain evidence for use against the person. If the right of privacy is to have any meaning, then these are surely the cases in which it should be asserted. We should no more approve of the imposition of a requirement to answer questions, on pain of adverse inferences, than of the compulsory use of machines that can extract information directly from the human memory.[137] This rationale can claim to be more fundamental than the privilege against self-incrimination and the presumption of innocence, since it is directly connected with the concepts of personhood and respect for individual autonomy. However, Galligan recognizes that privacy cannot be regarded as an absolute right, although he argues strongly that the propriety of derogating from it cannot be left to the judgement of police officers and ought to be settled at the level of general policy.

A fourth argument starts from a factual rather than a theoretical proposition. It is that the balance of power in the pre-trial stages of the criminal process is so much in favour of the investigators that the right of silence is needed to protect suspects from being overborne. Among the evidence led in support of this are the findings on the psychological effects of police interrogation;[138] the finding that the police still sometimes fail to inform suspects of their full rights or, when they do give the information, convey it in a manner calculated to persuade them to waive some rights;[139] and the superior access of the police to forensic science laboratories and other expert services.[140] This is challenged by those who want to see the right of silence removed or curtailed. They argue that the spread of legal aid and duty solicitor schemes now puts suspects on a par with the police, and that the provisions for an 'appropriate adult' afford sufficient protection to vulnerable suspects. In favour of this reply are those cases in which a defendant arrives at a police station with his or her own solicitor, with the result that the constable questioning the suspect may feel under greater pressure than the suspect. This was the position described by Lawton, LJ, in the judgment in *Chandler*.[141] However, it is an unusual situation, and the implication that it is becoming the norm can be dispelled by the findings of research for the 1993 Royal Commission that many defen-

---

[137] Galligan, 'Right to Silence Reconsidered', 88–90.
[138] e.g. Irving and Hilgendorf, *Police Interrogation*, and Gudjonsson, *The Psychology of Interrogations*.
[139] See above, s. 1 (6).   [140] See above, s. 1 (16).
[141] (1976) 63 Cr. App. R. 1.

dants waive their right to a lawyer, that many 'legal advisers' are not legally qualified, and also that defence access to expert evidence is limited.[142]

The 1993 Royal Commission expresses its recommendations in terms of a 'balance' of practical considerations: the risk to innocent persons, especially those who are less experienced and more vulnerable, is such as to outweigh the probable increase in convictions of the guilty. Evidence of breaches of the PACE Codes of Practice by the police shows that they cannot be trusted to honour the compromise struck by the existing law under the Police and Criminal Evidence Act, and this tells against giving them more legal power in relation to suspects.[143] It should be noted, however, that this is merely a contingent argument, as was that advanced by the Royal Commission of 1981. Since it is not expressed as resting on any fundamental principles, it is an argument that could be rebutted if certain practices were altered. The conclusions of the majority of the 1981 Royal Commission are worth stating in full:

Quite apart from the psychological pressures that such a change [sc. abolishing the right of silence] would place upon some suspects it would . . . amount to requiring a person during investigation to answer questions based upon possibly unsubstantiated and unspecific allegations or suspicion, even though he is not required to do that at the trial. Such a change could be regarded as acceptable only if, at a minimum, the suspect were to be provided at all stages of the investigation with full knowledge of his rights, complete information about the evidence available to the police at the time, and an exact understanding of the consequences of silence.[144]

This shows recognition of the pressure on suspects in police custody. It also recognizes the dangers of allowing answers or non-answers to questions put by the police at that time to constitute evidence: much depends on the basis for and the form of the questions put, a point developed powerfully by Michael McConville and Jacqueline Hodgson in their research report for the 1993 Royal Commission.[145] But it still seems to suggest that there might be a regime under which silence at the stage of police questioning might fairly be regarded as providing evidence against a defendant.

The police have campaigned persistently for a change in this direction. Among their arguments, two stand out. One is that the existing system enables defendants to ambush the prosecution, by concealing their line of defence until the trial and thus leaving the police

---

[142] See above, s. 1 (7) and (16).   [143] RCCJ Report, para. 4.23.
[144] RCCP Report, para. 4.52.
[145] McConville and Hodgson, *Custodial Legal Advice*.

inadequate opportunity to verify its factual basis. This point was recognized by statute in 1967, when the Criminal Justice Act introduced a requirement on the defence to give notice of an alibi defence, so as to afford the police adequate time to check it; it was recognized again in the Police and Criminal Evidence Act 1984 in relation to expert evidence. However, the notion that the prosecution suffers greatly from ambushes at present has been questioned in research for the 1993 Royal Commission by Roger Leng, who points out that at most 5 per cent of contested trials involved a line of defence that could be described as an ambush, and that in some of these cases the surprise stemmed from a failure by the police to take a suspect's earlier explanation seriously enough to investigate it. Of the cases where the defence was known before the trial, Leng calculated that this advance notice assisted the prosecution in about one-fifth.[146] A second argument is that the change is particularly justified where a serious crime is being investigated. As with the alibi notice and advance notice of expert evidence, this is a point that has received some legislative recognition—in the provisions of the Criminal Justice Act 1987, which give the Director of the Serious Fraud Office the power to require any person under investigation (or other person who he has reason to believe has relevant knowledge) to provide information or specified documents, on pain of conviction for non-compliance. This provision is testimony to a haphazard approach by legislators, though perhaps encouraged on this occasion by the belief that persons charged with serious fraud will be fully advised by competent lawyers.[147] It does nothing to deal with the argument that offences that are serious for the community are also serious for the suspect/defendant, an argument canvassed extensively in Chapter 3.[148]

Against this is the argument of principle that the prosecution bears the burden of proof in criminal proceedings, and that a defendant's 'fault [is] not to be wrung out of himself, but rather discovered by other means, and other men'.[149] It is this principle that the European Court of Human Rights proclaimed in the *Funke* case: 'the special features of customs law . . . cannot justify such an infringement of the right of anyone "charged with a criminal offence", within the autonomous meaning of this expression in Article 6, to remain silent and not to contribute to incriminating himself.'[150] Another point about the possible abolition of the right of silence is that the permissible inferences from silence would need to be controlled carefully. There may be a tendency to

---

[146] Leng, *The Right to Silence.*   [147] Echoed by the RCCJ Report, para. 4.30.
[148] See Ch. 3.4.   [149] Blackstone, 4 *Bl. Comm.* 296.
[150] *Funke, Cremieux and Miailhe* v. *France* A. 256 (1993), para. 44,

assume that failure to mention a point constitutes strong evidence of guilt. The Home Office Working Group, reporting in 1989, suggested that any legislation should include guidelines on the factors to which a court should have regard when deciding on the proper inference, including any innocent explanation for the failure to mention the point earlier and whether it was reasonable not to disclose the matter at an earlier opportunity.[151]

The Government, nevertheless, has included several clauses restricting the right of silence in the Criminal Justice and Public Order Bill 1993–94. We have seen that two Royal Commissions have recommended no change at the stage of police investigation, but there is some support, even among some who have argued in favour of the right of silence, for what may be described as a middle way. Thus the two issues—whether to retain the right at the stage of police questioning, and whether to retain the right once the case comes to court[152]—do not exhaust the possibilities. The middle way is to argue that, once the prosecution case has crystallized and disclosure to the defence is required, the defence should be required to disclose the elements of its case to the prosecution. The 1993 Royal Commission recommends that, once primary prosecution disclosure has taken place,[153] the defence should be required to disclose the line of the defence, although not the names and addresses of witnesses. The proposal is therefore less than full-blooded:

In most cases disclosure of the defence should be a matter capable of being handled by the defendant's solicitor (in the same way that alibi notices are usually dealt with at present). Standard forms could be drawn up to cover the most common offences [?defences], with the solicitor having only to tick one or more of a list of possibilities, such as 'accident', 'self-defence', 'consent', 'no dishonest intent', 'no appropriation', 'abandoned goods', 'claim of right', 'mistaken identification' and so on. There will be complex cases which may require the assistance of counsel in formulating the defence.[154]

The supposed benefit is that the police will be able to explore the factual basis for the defence. The sanction is that the prosecution may invite the jury to draw adverse inferences from the failure to disclose a defence relied on subsequently at the trial, although the judge may prevent the prosecution from making a comment if it is decided that there are good reasons for departing from the disclosed line of defence.

[151] For discussion, see A. A. S. Zuckerman, 'Trial by Unfair Means: The Report of the Working Group on the Right of Silence', [1989] *Crim LR* 855.

[152] The word 'retain' is used here as shorthand: the various incursions into the right of silence were noted in para. 1 (13) above.

[153] For discussion, see J. Glynn, 'Disclosure', [1993] Crim. LR 841.

[154] RCCJ Report, para. 6.68; cf. also the Report of the Home Office Working Group on the Right of Silence (1989) for another hybrid approach.

This middle way meets most of the objections raised by the 1981 Royal Commission against abolishing the right of silence at the stage of police questioning. The prosecution case is known, legal advice should have been received, and the consequences of non-disclosure are plain. However, there remains the principled objection: that a requirement of defence disclosure goes against the presumption of innocence and the privilege against self-incrimination. The defendant is called upon to assist the prosecution, and to do so before the case has actually unfolded in court. Even if there are convincing arguments to justify the two existing requirements, relating to alibi notices and expert evidence, there is sufficient reason to overturn the general principle that a defendant is entitled to put the prosecution to proof and should not be required to do anything that amounts to self-incrimination. There may be many reasons for silence that are not at all incriminating—confusion about events, ignorance of the law, fear that they might express themselves too loosely, desire to protect family from embarrassment, and many others—and even to permit the drawing of an inference of guilt may go too far.[155] The reasons may be private ones, and there are arguments for respecting that privacy. There are also, as Michael Zander argues in his Dissent to the Report of the 1993 Royal Commission, several practical objections to the particular proposal.[156] A similar system for cases of serious fraud appears to have been ineffective in producing more pleas of guilty or more discontinued prosecutions, and the alibi notice procedure has been applied in a fairly lax manner. For reasons of both principle and practicality, then, both the abolition of the right of silence and the middle way based on defence disclosure before trial seem unsatisfactory and unacceptable. Instead, more should be done to ensure that there is proper guidance on and proper review of judicial comments on the failure of defendants to disclose a defence at an earlier stage. Otherwise there is a danger that the right of silence will be eroded stealthily, brick by brick, when it should be shored up.

3. Confessions and Innocence

The risk that some confessions may be untrue is now well known and was recognized expressly by the 1993 Royal Commission.[157] Indeed, it is a corollary of the proposition that there may be many reasons for

---

[155] *Gilbert* (1977) 66 Cr. App. R. 237, followed by the High Court of Australia in *Petty and Maiden* v. *R.* (1991) 65 ALJR 625; for reasons for remaining silent, see Greer, 'The Right to Silence', at 727.

[156] RCCJ Report, 221–3.   [157] Ibid., para. 4.32.

remaining silent that there may also be various reasons, other than guilt, for making a confession. The Royal Commission evidently thought—on the basis of what evidence it is not clear—that the risks are significantly lower when the confession is made to the police spontaneously and shortly after the alleged offence, before formal questioning at the police station has begun. It declined to recommend that such statements should be inadmissible in court when not mechanically recorded.[158] In respect of confessions made in the police station and tape recorded, the Royal Commission held that the balance of arguments was against requiring the presence of a solicitor as a precondition of admissibility and against a requirement that confessions be corroborated. Among the arguments against the latter requirement were that it would make a difference in only a small percentage of cases,[159] and that the trend is to move away from formal corroboration requirements.[160] The Commission concluded that it should be for the judge in each case to formulate an appropriate warning to give to the jury, pointing out the dangers of convicting in the absence of supporting evidence.[161] This is a welcome recognition of the problems of confession evidence, but it is not clear that it goes sufficiently far. Its basis is certainly insecure: the statement that the *Turnbull* warning in respect of identification evidence has worked well is supported by absolutely no empirical evidence. Moreover, the Commission makes much of the Law Commission's recommendation that the corroboration rules should be abolished in favour of greater judicial discretion on the form and timing of warnings—a recommendation that itself delivers a great part of the protection of rights to judicial discretion, with few apparent parameters.[162] Guidance and guidelines then become crucial instruments, and a satisfactory scientific basis for them becomes imperative.[163] These are matters far too important to be left to 'common sense'.

However, the focus should perhaps be more on the admissibility of

[158] Ibid., para. 4.50. Above, s. 1(5) and (9).

[159] Perhaps 5% of cases in which there was a confession, the Commission surmised at para. 4.69, interpreting evidence from M. McConville, *Corroboration and Confessions: The Impact of a Rule Requiring that no Conviction can be Sustained on the Basis of Confession Evidence Alone*, RCCJ Research Study 13 (1993).

[160] Cf. the decision of the High Court of Australia that confessions should be corroborated, taken against a somewhat different background (no tape recording, no lawyer present) in *McKinney and Judge* v. *R.* (1991) 65 ALJR 241. For general discussion, see R. Pattenden, 'Should Confessions be Corroborated?', (1991) 107 *LQR* 319.

[161] RCCJ Report, para, 4.77.

[162] Law Commission 102, *Criminal Law: Corroboration of Evidence in Criminal Trials* (1991), discussed at [1992] Crim. LR 1.

[163] See J. Jackson, 'The Evidence Provisions', [1993] *Crim. LR* 817, at 828.

confessions than upon their evidential value, once admitted. One might have greater confidence in a law that does not require confessions to be corroborated if one could be sure that the conditions in which confessions are made and recorded were properly regulated. The difficulty here is that the brief survey of seventeen requirements at the investigative stage of the criminal process revealed widespread departures from the rules and Code of Practice provisions. Even the presence of a tape recorder has failed to prevent egregious misconduct by investigating police officers in some cases,[164] and the various research studies for the 1993 Royal Commission confirm the incidence of 'rule-bending', which means depriving suspects of their rights. Several such cases have come to light and the Court of Appeal has often, but not always, quashed the ensuing convictions. In some cases the trial court will have ruled out a confession made following a clear breach of the rules. But it is not sufficient to rely on the courts to exclude such confessions, since the decision of the defence to challenge a confession might itself be influenced by other rules of evidence, such as the 'tit-for-tat' rule on cross-examination.[165] What is needed is a fresh approach to the task of investigation in general and of questioning in particular. This should be an ethical approach that starts from the proposition that it is in the public interest to accord the suspect his or her rights—that this is not an optional extra, let alone an impediment to justice, but part of justice. This concept of the ethical point of view was developed in Chapter 3, above. The Royal Commission does little more than endorse existing Home Office initiatives to improve 'interviewing skills',[166] when what is needed is a fundamental reappraisal that identifies and explains distorting or otherwise unacceptable practices. The aim should be to render the Codes of Practice much more specific by taking advantage of research findings on these matters.[167] Styles of questioning will become even more important if the Government's proposals to curtail the right of silence become law.

4. Accountability

A change in the police approach to investigation and to questioning should be accompanied by a change in the rules to which the police are subject. At present those rules are distributed between primary legisla-

[164] e.g. the case of the Cardiff Three, discussed in Ch. 1.3.
[165] For discussion, see Ch. 9 below and Zuckerman, *Principles of Criminal Evidence*, ch. 13.
[166] RCCJ Report, paras. 2.21–2.23.
[167] See A. A. S. Zuckerman, 'Miscarriage of Justice: A Root Treatment', [1992] *Crim. LR* 323, at 331–9; McConville and Hodgson, *Custodial Legal Advice*.

tion and the PACE Codes of Practice drawn up by the Home Office in consultation with other bodies, with some central but sensitive matters like restrictions on methods of undercover investigation (the entrapment problem) left entirely outside public regulation. The distribution of topics between primary legislation and Codes of Practice ought to be reviewed: the main principles and policies should be declared in the legislation, with the Codes refining and developing the practical details in accordance with those principles and policies. This is not the case with the Police and Criminal Evidence Act and its Codes, and there is a danger that topics appearing only in the Codes may be regarded as less important than those in primary legislation.

Once the rules are set out, and the police and other investigators suitably trained, there remains the question of enforcement of the rules. No police force, nor any other profession, can guarantee absolute observance of any set of rules. Certainly the police must do much more by way of supervision of junior officers, and the report of the 1993 Royal Commission contains a few recommendations of this kind.[168] But what ought to happen when a breach of the rules relating to the treatment of suspects is substantiated? There are three lines of answer to this question. The first is that there should be internal disciplinary procedures against the officer(s) concerned. An efficient mechanism for dealing with complaints against the police is needed in the first place. Then there should be a disciplinary procedure within the police that deals credibly with misconduct: the Royal Commission has some worthwhile recommendations on this point.[169]

The second approach considers the damage to the suspect or defendant. A person who has been wrongfully arrested or detained may (unusually) bring an action for habeas corpus to secure release, or may (less infrequently) pursue a civil action for damages against the police.[170] This is much more likely in the case of someone who has been released without charge or who has been acquitted at trial, although it is in theory no less possible if the defendant is convicted of the offence concerned.

Where there is a prosecution the third approach comes into view— whether to stay the prosecution, or to exclude the evidence tainted by police misconduct, or to mitigate sentence, or to regard the irregularity as irrelevant. As a basic proposition, the court should exclude the resulting evidence if the proper procedures were not followed. The main justification for this is that it is a method of ensuring that

---

[168] RCCJ Report, paras. 2.59 and 2.61.
[169] Ibid., para. 3.103; for comment, see Reiner, 'Investigative Powers', at 816.
[170] Clayton and Tomlinson, *Civil Actions against the Police*.

the defendant is not disadvantaged by the infringement of his or her rights. The evidence is tainted—the 'fruit of the poisoned tree'—and a court should not admit it. However, there may be a strong temptation for the court not to take this course when the evidence resulting from the breach appears cogent and central to the case. What, then, should be done?

The relevant provisions of English law were set out at the beginning of this chapter. In particular, section 78 of the Police and Criminal Evidence Act 1984 permits a court to exclude evidence when it was obtained in circumstances such that its admission would have an adverse effect on the fairness of the proceedings. The discretion has been exercised many times, but on what principles should courts exercise it? No clear pattern emerges from the decided cases. There are those who favour the 'judicial integrity' approach, arguing that a court would compromise the integrity of the criminal process if it acted on evidence obtained by means of a breach of the law. As we saw in Chapter 2, Adrian Zuckerman argues that convictions based on the fruits of torture 'would defeat the aims of the administration of justice'.[171] However, this approach may be interpreted so as to exclude too little or too much. The Supreme Court of the United States, which purported to adhere to it for many years, has shown that it is possible to interpret its forcefulness away by arguing that judicial integrity can also be served by ensuring that probative evidence is not excluded merely as a result of a procedural irregularity. Thus in *Stone* v. *Powell*[172] the court was able to conclude that 'while courts must ever be concerned with preserving the integrity of the judicial process, this concern has limited force as a justification for the exclusion of highly probative evidence'.[173] This may be seen as a reaction to the rule of mandatory exclusion that was proclaimed by the Supreme Court for many years, with any departure from proper procedure leading to the exclusion of the evidence. If, to return to the quotation from Zuckerman, 'the aims of the administration of justice' include adherence to all the rules introduced for the protection of suspects and defendants, does it not follow that for a court to condone *any* departure would be to defeat those aims?

A protective principle might forge a stronger link with the rights of suspects and defendants. The principle here would be that courts should exclude evidence where that is necessary to protect the defen-

[171] Zuckerman, *Principles of Criminal Evidence*, 303, quoted in Ch. 2 at n. 22.
[172] (1976) 428 US 465, at 485.
[173] To a similar effect, see J. Kaplan, 'The Limits of the Exclusionary Rule', (1974) 26 *Stanford LR* 1027, at 1036.

dant from suffering any disadvantage as a result of the deviation from proper procedures.[174] The key question, therefore, should be asked from the defendant's point of view: did the irregularity prejudice the defendant's case? On this approach some irregularities might be overlooked, if a court decided that there was no prejudice to the defendant. Others would lead to the exclusion of evidence. Indeed, it has been argued that the exclusion of the tainted evidence might be insufficient in some cases to protect the defendant from the results of investigative wrongdoing, where the investigators have obtained other sources of evidence in consequence of their wrongful conduct. This argument would lead to the wider use of the doctrine of abuse of process, so as to stay the prosecution rather than simply to remove one item of evidence from the trial.[175]

A clear demonstration of the effect of the protective principle is to contrast it with the so-called disciplinary principle—the idea that courts should exclude evidence that has been obtained by a departure from proper procedure, so as to discipline the police. The many doubts about this approach (whether it affects the police in any way, given the statistical rarity of exclusion) need not be canvassed here. The point is that, on a disciplinary approach, a court would be concerned chiefly with whether the wrongful behaviour was intentional or unwitting, and perhaps also whether the departure was gross or 'technical'. On a protective principle, the central question is whether the defendant was disadvantaged: the damage may be the same whether the breach was intentional or not, and perhaps even whether it was 'technical' or not. If statements of concern for defendants' rights are to be carried through into practice, the protective principle has both practical and symbolic importance. It is sad that the 1993 Royal Commission failed to build upon the work of its 1981 predecessor and to discuss the proper approach of the courts under section 78, leaving it to case-by-case and, not surprisingly, theoretically incoherent development by the appellate courts.

5. Conclusion

Many of the themes of this chapter will be revisited in Chapter 10 below. For the present, there is value in emphasizing that the discussion above does not merely have implications for the police. As has been mentioned before, the police have opened themselves up to far more research than others involved in the administration of criminal

[174] A. J. Ashworth, 'Excluding Evidence as Protecting Rights', [1977] Crim. LR 723.
[175] A. Choo, 'A Defence of Entrapment', (1990) 53 *MLR* 453.

justice. Thus, many of the points may apply with equal or only slightly less force to other investigative agencies, such as the Customs and Excise, the Inland Revenue, and many 'regulatory' agencies. Moreover, we have noted evidence from several sources that defence solicitors and 'legal representatives' do not always protect their clients as they should do. Prosecutors, expert witnesses, and judges are also implicated in some malfunctions of the system, as we saw in Chapter 1.

The first section of the chapter demonstrated the importance of ensuring that the early stages of a criminal investigation are carried out and recorded properly. Police questioning must be regulated more closely, and interrogation should not be used as the first step in an investigation. Both these matters will be particularly important if the right to silence is curtailed, as the Government proposes: the police should be encouraged to investigate and gather evidence before they question the suspect, rather than relying on questioning as the primary tool. However, there are also powerful issues of principle raised by the right of silence and the law relating to confessions. These should not be discarded merely for short-term political gain or to placate the police or prosecutors. The European Convention on Human Rights should be given greater prominence in the English debate, and it should be recognized that even the recommendations of the 1993 Royal Commission on these two key issues compromise principle to an unacceptable extent. To reinforce this point, the relevance to the ethical arguments developed in Chapter 3 must be reasserted: criminal justice should not be regarded as merely a matter of crime control, and the maintenance of police morale must be exposed as a poor reason for any particular policy.

5

Gatekeeping Decisions

THE concern of this chapter is with those decisions that determine whether or not a case enters the criminal justice system and, if so, what course it is set upon.

Out of all the criminal offences committed in any one year, only a very low proportion result in formal proceedings being taken against a suspect/defendant. The process of attrition, as it has come to be known, is gradual and substantial. Figures derived from the British Crime Survey, dealing with eight of the most frequently committed types of indictable offences, suggest that no more than 2 per cent result in a conviction.[1] Starting with those offences actually committed, around half of them are never reported to the police. Members of the public may choose not to report an offence because they think the police unable to help, because they regard the offence as too minor to report, because the offence is regarded as a private or domestic matter, because of fear of reprisals, or for other reasons. Of the 50 per cent that are reported to the police, a significant proportion are not recorded as crimes. A variety of reasons may come into play here: the offence may be attributed to a child below the age of criminal responsibility, or the police may not accept the victim's account, or the incident may have been resolved quickly and informally.[2] This reduces the number of offences remaining in the system to 30 per cent. The next difficulty is that only a proportion of recorded offences are 'cleared up', in the sense of being detected or otherwise resolved. In relation to the eight types of crime studied in the British Crime Survey, fewer than one-quarter are cleared up and this reduces the percentage remaining in the system from 30 to 7 per cent. Some of the offences that are cleared up result in nothing more than an informal warning or no further action at all, particularly when they are traced to young offenders. Thus only 3 per cent of the offences result in a formal caution or in

---

[1] G. C. Barclay (ed.), *Digest 2: Information on the Criminal Justice System in England and Wales* (1993), 29. The offences are criminal damage; thefts of a motor vehicle; theft from a motor vehicle (including attempts); bicycle theft; burglary; wounding; robbery; and theft from the person.

[2] For an outline of police recording practices, see P. Mayhew, D. Elliott, and L. Dowds, *The 1988 British Crime Survey*, HORS 111 (1989), 11.

prosecution. One-third of those are cautions, which are widely used for younger offenders, leaving some 2 per cent to be sentenced by the courts.

This startling rate of attrition does not apply equally to all crimes. Among those studied in the British Crime Survey, offences of wounding resulted in a much higher rate of court appearance. A higher proportion of recorded offences were cleared up and were then dealt with formally, so that 10 per cent of offenders were sentenced by the courts. (For homicide the percentage would be much higher still.) On the other hand, it is estimated that fewer than 1 per cent of offences of criminal damage came to court.

What are the implications of the rate of attrition? One is that it demonstrates the *naïveté* of expecting the sentences passed by the courts to act as a significant control on crime. Those sentences deal with a small proportion of offenders—although, for the most part, they will be the most serious offenders—and, even making allowances for the probability that the symbolic effect of those (few) sentences will be greater than their proportionate size, this suggests that a strategy for the prevention of crime should not place great emphasis on sentencing. This is not to deny that sometimes sentences may exert a specific and/or general deterrent effect, but it is to counsel caution against overestimating those effects in the context of low rates of reporting, detection, and so on. A second implication is that decisions taken by law enforcement agents have a considerable influence on the selection of cases that go forward into the criminal process. Their decisions have a qualitative as well as a quantitative effect: the offenders who find themselves convicted in court are not a random group of the totality of offenders, nor necessarily are they the most serious group. They are chosen, when others are not, for a variety of reasons that ought to be explored.

The focus of this chapter will be upon the decisions taken by the gatekeepers of the criminal process. The discussion of different types of gatekeeper will be less detailed than the extensive literature would permit, in order to facilitate the analysis of general issues. There will be some discussion of the police, of some regulatory bodies, and of the Serious Fraud Office as agencies that select for official action certain types of person or situation, a selection that may lead either to prosecution and trial or to a form of diversion. The first section looks at practices of reporting and enforcing. The second section considers the range of formal responses to those who are believed to be offenders. The third section looks in greater detail at the approach of some regulatory agencies and of the Serious Fraud Office. The fourth section focuses on police cautioning and related practices. The fifth section analyses the values behind some of the differing policies, and the sixth considers accountability.

1. Reporting and Enforcing

There is a real sense in which society is self-policing. The vast majority of offences are brought to the attention of the police by members of the public, and so the police operate in a reactive role. The decision to report probably means that the victim or witness expects something to be done about the offence. However, as we saw earlier, about one-half of the eight common types of offence studied in the British Crime Survey are not reported, and prominent among the reasons are a belief that the crime was insufficiently serious to report, and a belief that the police would not be able to do anything about it. The latter reason may betray a pessimism about police effectiveness rather than a genuine judgement that no formal response is necessary. In practice, however, many of these cases will also involve the first reason—that the formal invocation of law enforcement machinery is not really necessary. To that extent, then, members of the public may be said to filter out of the system, at the earliest stage, many non-serious offences. This might be regarded as a primitive example of proportionality at work: the idea that, in order to justify reporting an offence to the police or other relevant authority, it has to achieve a certain level of seriousness.

However, the notion of society as self-policing cannot be pressed too far. The police are not simply the agents of the public, reacting whenever requested and not otherwise. There are at least four respects in which the police or other agencies exert a powerful influence. First, we have seen that the police do not record as crimes all incidents that are reported to them as crimes. As many as two-fifths of all incidents reported as thefts, robberies, woundings, etc. are not recorded by the police as such.[3] Some of these incidents might be dealt with by invoking minor public order charges, such as breach of the peace, which are not recorded crimes. But many of them will not be recorded or will be 'no-crimed'. The result is that, although the police are largely dependent on the public to report offences, they do not always record what is reported. The police operate as a significant filter on public reports, and even though members of the public may want official action (and, implicitly, official recording of the offence), this may not be what occurs.

---

[3] *The 1988 British Crime Survey*, HORS 111 (1989), 70.

Secondly, the idea of society as self-policing does not account for the many offences, perhaps one-quarter of indictable crimes, that are discovered by the police themselves. Here the argument becomes complicated. Sometimes, when the police have a 'crack-down' on certain forms of offences, such as homosexual importuning or drug-dealing in a particular locality, this is a response to complaints from the public. Such cases may be regarded, partly at least, as examples of social self-policing. On the other hand there may be many cases in which the police themselves decide to have a 'campaign' against a particular form of offending: drug-dealing would be more likely to fall into this category, as would drink-driving. The police are operating proactively here, to some extent because the crimes are victimless and therefore there is no victim to make a complaint. In this context the patterns of law enforcement may largely reflect the availability of police officers and the preferences of those in operational control: the police can only mount 'proactive' campaigns if they are not overwhelmed by the 'reactive' demands of crimes reported to them, and when they do adopt a proactive strategy there may be a choice of what type of offence to target.[4] No doubt those preferences will be connected to the concerns of the media and of influential members of the public, as well as to the views of police officers. The same might be said of the regulatory agencies concerned with trading standards, environment, health and safety at work, pollution, and so on. What they hear about the concerns of the media and influential people may have some effect on their enforcement policies, but they may also have their own priorities in the light of the need to allocate their limited resources. It would certainly be wrong to suggest that regulatory agencies tend simply to react to information supplied by members of the public.

A third difficulty with the idea of society as self-policing is that this overlooks, or at least over-simplifies, the nature of the police function. Thus far we have referred to police work as if its focus is enforcing the law by catching criminals, whether as a result of prompting by a member of the public or as a result of a police campaign. Research shows that these kinds of activity do not dominate everyday policing. Much of what the police do is to perform a kind of service function, attending to a wide range of incidents that require something to be done about them—from road accidents and rowdy parties to stray cattle and barking dogs. Into all these situations the police officer brings authority and

---

[4] Some police forces have special squads to target certain kinds of crime such as drugs and pornography that are thought to require proactive methods: see the research by M. Maguire and C. Norris, *The Conduct and Supervision of Criminal Investigations*, RCCJ Research Study 5 (1992).

the ability to draw upon coercive powers if needed. These powers become even more prominent when there is thought to be a risk of public disorder—for example, at a demonstration or march, at a football match, and during other local disturbances. These are the occasions on which the function of the police as maintainers of order comes to the fore. Whether the police use their coercive powers depends on a number of contingencies. If there is a genuine threat to good order they may intervene to make one or more arrests. Studies of police behaviour have long maintained that a police officer is more likely to arrest and charge someone who threatens the officer's authority by means of insults or failure to comply with the officer's commands or requests.[5] This forms part of the working culture of the police, discussed in Chapter 3.[6] Significant as that proposition is in explaining some of the people who come to be arrested and charged, it should not be allowed to overshadow the probability that some people clearly threaten to cause public disorder and should therefore be prevented from going further.[7] In other words, the use of arrest and criminal charges by the police in incidents thought to threaten good order is likely to be an amalgam of some clearly justifiable cases and others that turn more on the disposition, pride, or self-image of particular officers. Any description that ignores one or the other lacks realism. Both types of case show the criminal law as a resource for the police, however. The notion that Parliament makes the laws and the police then enforce them finds no echo here. The police manage situations so as to maintain order, using the offences in the Police Act 1964 and the Public Order Act 1986 as resources to draw upon, to be invoked against those who threaten the police conception of what constitutes good order and how it should be achieved.

It might be added that this aspect of police work has its parallels in the work of some regulatory agencies. Their primary concern, too, can be described as prevention and the maintenance of a conception of good order. This may indicate a form of negotiated compliance: not immediate compliance with the letter of the law, but evidence of efforts by the offending company or individual to move towards compliance to an extent that the inspector regards as reasonable. Coercive powers are available in reserve and, since these often take the form of strict liability offences (albeit with various defences often available),[8] they may be invoked readily if this is decided to be appropriate.

---

[5] The classic study is that by E. Bittner, 'The Police on Skid Row: A Study in Peacekeeping', (1967) *American Sociological Review*, 32.

[6] See Ch. 3.6.   [7] See R. Reiner, *The Politics of the Police* (2nd edn., 1992), 212.

[8] Cf. L. H. Leigh, *Strict and Vicarious Liability* (1982).

This leads on to the fourth difficulty with the idea of society as self-policing: that some regulatory agencies operate in fields that lie remote from popular consciousness. Much of the work done by the inspectorates of pollution and health and safety at work is of this nature: of course the public makes occasional demands in relation to notorious incidents, but much of their work lies outside popular notions of crime prevention. The Serious Fraud Office has a higher profile, not merely because it has brought a few well-publicized prosecutions of prominent businessmen, but also because the present minimum of frauds it will investigate is £5 million.[9] It may make its own decisions to investigate a company or an individual, or may accept a reference from the Department of Trade and Industry, the police, or another agency. A good example of lower profile law enforcement, away from popular consciousness, would be insider dealing on the Stock Market: there are agencies charged with the detection of offences of insider dealing[10] and, apart from the debate about their effectiveness, it is apparent that they operate in a sphere with which most people are unfamiliar. Indeed, it seems likely that popular conceptions of crime and criminality are somewhat traditional in nature, and that the media either reflect or cause this by showing little interest in 'modern' forms of criminality.[11] Thus the legislature is ahead of public opinion in enacting a fairly wide range of offences covering activities that lie well outside conventional ideas of crime. This argument must be interpreted carefully. It is not being maintained that the law or its enforcers deal even-handedly with conduct of equivalent social gravity. The point is that there is some law enforcement, mostly by regulatory agencies, that appears to be largely independent of the concerns of many members of the public.

This general survey suggests that society or the community is self-policing only to an extent. Most decisions not to report an offence to the police mean that the offence never comes to light and there is no prospect of the offender being charged and prosecuted to conviction. To that considerable extent, society does police itself. However, we have noted also the influence of the agencies of law enforcement and their own policies, which may be shaped to some extent but not entirely by public expectations and concerns. Later in this chapter we shall look further into the factors that determine the approaches of the police and of other law enforcement agencies. For the present, two

---

[9] Serious Fraud Office, *Annual Report, 1992–93*, 8–9.

[10] Department of Trade and Industry, in conjunction with the Securities Investment Board.

[11] Cf. S. Box, *Power, Crime and Mystification* (1983).

final points may be made. First, it is evident that the criminal law in action does not correspond with the criminal law on the statute books. The body of criminal legislation cannot be placed over social behaviour like a template, in the expectation that there will be a 'fit' with the actuality of law enforcement. Secondly, the considerable element of discretion in the decision to invoke the criminal law makes it important to scrutinize the reasons why the police and the regulatory agencies decide to proceed against some people and not against others.

2. The Range of Formal Responses

The criminal law provides the framework for formal responses to alleged law-breaking, and yet we have already seen that it sometimes functions merely as a resource to be invoked in situations where this is thought necessary so as to maintain order. Discretion appears to be a key element in what actually happens. Two methods of proceeding have long been available to the police—arrest and summons. The 1981 Royal Commission found that the police used arrest more than was necessary for effective law enforcement, and failed to take account of the fact that 'arrest represents a major disruption of the suspect's life'.[12] Following the Commission proposals, the Police and Criminal Evidence Act 1984 includes not only the requirement that persons only be arrested on reasonable suspicion, but also introduces a category of 'arrestable offences' and provides that an arrested person should not be detained at a police station unless that is necessary for various reasons. However, the 'necessity' principle appears to have been emptied of practical significance by the routine approval of detention by custody officers at police stations[13]—another example of the strength of police culture, in neutralizing inconvenient rules and supporting rather than reviewing the judgement of other (though often junior) officers. Historically the choice of arrest rather than summons made it less likely that the defendant would be cautioned and more likely that there would be a prosecution, since cases for caution had to be referred to a senior officer whereas decisions to arrest were rarely reviewed.[14] However, the recent encouragement from the Home Office to increase the proportionate use of cautions may have led to changes here.

Whether the police choose to proceed by arrest of by summons, the

---

[12] Royal Commission on Criminal Procedure, *Report*, Cmnd. 8092 (1981), para. 3.75.

[13] I. McKenzie, R. Morgan, and R. Reiner, 'Helping the Police with their Inquiries: The Necessity Principle and Voluntary Attendance at the Police Station', [1990] *Crim. LR* 22.

[14] A. Sanders, 'The Prosecution Process', in D. Moxon (ed.), *Managing Criminal Justice* (1985), at 66–73.

crucial question is what may happen next. In many European systems of law there is a doctrinal contrast between the principle of compulsory prosecution (sometimes called the principle of legality) and the principle of expediency (sometimes called the opportunity principle). Many systems, such as the German and the Austrian, have placed great emphasis on the principle of compulsory prosecution. This may be said to promote the principles of legality and equal treatment, to prevent political interference with the process of justice, and also to heighten general deterrence.[15] In theory all those who commit offences are brought before the courts for an open determination of guilt and (if convicted) for sentencing, and there is no broad discretionary power to avoid prosecution—which might lead to local variations, allegations of political motivation, or the undermining of law by expediency. If the administration of the criminal law produces unjust results, it is for the legislature to amend it and not for prosecutors to make their own policies. Thus section 152 of the German Code of Criminal Procedure requires the public prosecutor to bring a prosecution in respect of all punishable conduct, to the extent that there is sufficient evidence. In practice, of course, there are various exceptions to this, including section 153a, which allows conditional termination of proceedings.[16] There are financial pressures towards the streamlining of criminal justice systems, as well as an increasing realization that prosecution and sentence in court are stressful for the participants and are not necessarily more effective (in terms of reconviction rates) than forms of diversion. The Council of Europe has developed this theme in its recommendations for the simplification of criminal justice.[17]

The number of exceptions to the principle of compulsory prosecution might be thought to support an argument that systems such as the German are really little different from the English. The one proclaims a principle of compulsory prosecution and then derogates from it in several ways, whereas the other recognizes from the outset that prosecution policy must be a question of expediency.[18] However, there is good reason to retain some respect for the principle of compulsory prosecution because of the values (the principles of legality and equal treat-

[15] See e.g. J. Herrmann, 'The Rule of Compulsory Prosecution and the Scope of Prosecutorial Discretion in Germany', (1974) 41 *U. Chi. LR* 468, at 470; P. J. P. Tak, *The Legal Scope of Non-prosecution in Europe* (1986), 27.
[16] Herrmann, 'Rule of Compulsory Prosecution'; J. Langbein, 'Controlling Prosecutorial Discretion in Germany', (1974) 41 *U. Chi. LR* 439; J. Herrmann, 'Bargaining Justice: A Bargain for German Criminal Justice?', (1992) 53 *U. Pittsburgh LR* 755.
[17] Council of Europe, *The Simplification of Criminal Justice*, Recommendation R (87) 18 (1987).
[18] Cf. H. Jung, 'Criminal Justice: A European Perspective', [1993] *Crim. LR* 237, at 241.

ment) it upholds, even though in Germany the prosecutor enjoys wide discretion in practice. In the heavily pragmatic English system the values and principles have little recognition, even as starting-points. In England and Wales the police have at least five alternative forms of formal response to a case in which there is sufficient evidence that a person has committed an offence. *First*, they may decide to take no further action. This course should be taken where there is insufficient evidence, but our discussion here is limited to cases where there is sufficient evidence that the defendant has committed a crime. Even in some such cases the police may decide to take no further action because, for example, the offender is very young and the offence non-serious. A *second* alternative is an informal warning or caution, given by a police officer in circumstances where a formal caution is considered unnecessary or inappropriate. Motorists sometimes benefit from informal warnings of this kind. A *third* alternative is the formal police caution. The police should only offer to caution an offender when there is sufficient evidence to prosecute: this is a caution for an offence, and should be distinguished from informal cautions or warnings administered by individual officers. The formal police caution is usually given to the offender by a senior officer in uniform at a police station.[19] There is no legislative basis for the practice of cautioning, but cautions should be recorded by the police and disclosed to the court in an antecedents statement when relevant.[20] We shall see that the recent policy has been to increase the use of cautions, and in some areas these cautions are combined with obligations under a concept called 'caution plus'. The *fourth* alternative, available only in some areas, is to refer the case to a mediation scheme. There are only sixteen of these in England and Wales, mostly dealing with juveniles on a reference from a juvenile liaison panel. The details vary, but they depend on the willingness of the victim to meet the offender or, in some schemes, to allow a mediator to act as go-between. The outcome is likely to be an agreement involving a promise of reparation by the offender. This may not prevent prosecution, but may be drawn to the court's attention. The *fifth* course is to prosecute, and it is this alternative alone that results in the defendant being processed through one or more of the decision-making stages discussed in this book. Whilst decisions to take no further action or to give a formal caution have the effect of diverting the offender from the

---

[19] Home Office Circular 59/1990, *The Cautioning of Offenders*, annex B, para. 5. There is also the possibility of an 'instant caution', administered very soon after the offence but only where all the conditions for a formal caution are fulfilled. Instant cautions will not be discussed here.

[20] Ibid., para. 6.

criminal process, the decision to prosecute is the first step on what may become a long road.

The various regulatory agencies have somewhat different powers from the police. They may take no further action. Many of them have the power to issue a warning notice, requiring the addressee to rectify the defects that have led to the commission of the offence. Some agencies, notably the Inland Revenue, have the power to require compounded penalties as an alternative to prosecution. This means that a person may be required to pay, say, twice the underpaid tax under threat of being prosecuted otherwise. This approach is open to relatively few agencies, however. The bringing of a criminal prosecution remains the ultimate sanction. As we shall see, the tendency is for regulatory agencies to regard this as a last resort, whilst the police have tended to use it more widely and more routinely.

Many systems of law include some schemes whereby the police or the prosecution can ask for the payment of money instead of prosecution. In the Netherlands there is the 'transaction', whereby the public prosecutor may nominate a sum of money for a non-serious offence and if the offender pays it the right to prosecute is extinguished. In Germany the prosecutor may offer to terminate proceedings for a misdemeanour on condition that the accused agrees to pay a sum of money to a charity or to the State.[21] Prosecutor fines have also been introduced in Scotland.[22] There is no equivalent of these schemes in England, although there is the fixed penalty notice that, for a large number of traffic offences, may be issued to an offender.[23] Payment of a fixed penalty is the equivalent of a sentence, and a conviction is recorded. In this respect it differs from the Dutch, German, and Scottish schemes, but in one important respect it is the same. All of them allow the defendant the alternative of contesting guilt in court, by declining to accept the official offer and leaving the authorities to prosecute. This is in accordance with the European Convention on Human Rights, Article 6 (1) of which has been interpreted so as to require the possibility of recourse to a court for a person who contests the decision to impose a penalty.[24]

---

[21] Herrmann, 'Bargaining Justice', at 757–60.

[22] P. Duff and K. Meechan, 'The Prosecutor Fine', [1992] *Crim. LR* 22; P. Duff, 'The Prosecutor Fine and Social Control', (1993) 33 *BJ Crim.* 481.

[23] For discussion, see A. J. Turner, 'The New Fixed Penalty System', [1986] *Crim. LR* 782.

[24] *Le Compte, Van Leuven and De Meyere* A. 43 (1981) 23; *De Weer* A. 35 (1980) 23.

3. The Selectivity of Regulatory Agencies

The regulatory agencies enjoy a wide discretion in deciding how often and in which cases to prosecute. In their 1980 survey, Lidstone, Hogg, and Sutcliffe found that most non-police agencies regarded criminal prosecution as a last resort, and sought to enforce compliance by other, less formal methods as far as possible.[25] Cranston's research into consumer protection departments found that prosecution is usually regarded as a last resort, after informal settlements and warnings.[26] A similar finding emerges from the study of the Pollution Inspectorate by Richardson, Ogus, and Burrows,[27] from the research by Hawkins into environmental health officers,[28] and from the research by Hutter into the approaches of the Factory Inspectorate, the Industrial Air Pollution Inspectorate, and environmental health officers.[29]

The usual way to characterize the approach of the various regulatory agencies is to suggest that they follow a 'compliance strategy' or 'accommodative approach', as distinct from a 'deterrence' or 'sanctioning' strategy.[30] The former, 'prosecution as a last resort' approach is shared by most of these agencies, but the degree of their commitment to it may differ. Indeed, Hutter has argued that there is a considerable difference between those agencies that adopt a 'persuasive' version of the compliance strategy and those that adopt what she terms the 'insistent' version. The Industrial Air Pollution Inspectorate has openly committed itself to the persuasive strategy: 'discussion, persuasion and co-operation leading to mutually agreed solutions, are preferred to coercion.'[31] This approach has as long a history as the inspectorate itself, and has sometimes been likened to education rather than policing. It is worth pointing out, however, that the legislation governing air pollution requires companies to adopt the 'best practicable means', a statutory framework that almost encourages negotiated standards. By way of contrast, the Factory Inspectorate has long been characterized by some ambivalence towards prosecution, with significant groups advocating greater use of this approach. As a whole the inspectorate favours compliance over the use of formal

---

[25] K. Lidstone, R. Hogg, and F. Sutcliffe, *Prosecutions by Private Individuals and Non-police Agencies*, RCCP Research Study 10 (1980).

[26] R. Cranston, *Regulating Business* (1979), 107 and 168.

[27] G. Richardson, A. Ogus, and P. Burrows, *Policing Pollution* (1982).

[28] K. Hawkins, *Environment and Enforcement* (1984).

[29] B. Hutter, *The Reasonable Arm of the Law?* (1988).

[30] See the classic essay by A. Reiss, 'Selecting Strategies of Social Control over Organisational Life', in K. Hawkins and J. Thomas (eds.), *Enforcing Regulation* (1984).

[31] Quoted by B. Hutter, 'Variations in Regulatory Enforcement Styles', (1989) 11 *Law and Policy* 153, at 161, from the 1981 Annual Report of the Inspectorate.

sanctions, but there is a much readier resort to oral and written advice and even to improvement notices. Hutter found that inspectors tend to speak of prosecution more frequently, even though they resort to it fairly rarely. In her research among environmental health officers there were also divergences, with some areas tending to resort to prosecution more frequently than others.[32]

It is therefore as well to bear in mind that, not only may the regulatory agencies differ among themselves in their degree of commitment to a compliance strategy, but different local departments may take somewhat different approaches. This may depend on the organizational structure: typically, environmental health officers could not prosecute unless this was approved by a committee of the local council. The resources available to the agency may also influence their enforcement style; this may independently have effects on enforcement policy, inasmuch as there is likely to be more negotiation if inspectors visit company officials more frequently and therefore get to know them more fully. Most agencies, however, respond firmly to incidents that attract considerable publicity, such as a accident at work that causes several deaths or injuries, or an outbreak of food poisoning.[33] Another factor that can lead to prosecution, even under the 'last resort' approach, would be the failure to respond to warnings, advice, or improvement notices.[34]

These variations are of much less significance than the considerable difference in approach between most regulatory agencies and the police. The breadth of discretion under the law is equally great, but there are divergent traditions. It would be too simple to suggest that the police resort to prosecution more frequently because they deal with more serious offences: a more sophisticated analysis would show that some of the offences with which the regulatory agencies deal can be regarded as more serious than many of the small thefts and handlings that the police routinely prosecute. The almost educational spirit in which some inspectorates were founded still dominates their approach, with an understanding of the difficulties faced by employers in finding the money for improvements in safety at a time of economic recession. This leads to awkward questions about social justice and, ultimately, about the aims of law enforcement. The contrast is rendered more complex by the co-option of the police into an approach to juvenile crime that relies on warnings rather than prosecutions: it is to the impact of cautioning, in respect of both juveniles and older offenders, that we now turn.

---

[32] Hutter, 'Variations', 158–9.   [33] Ibid. 165–6.
[34] G. Richardson, 'Strict Liability for Regulatory Crime', [1987] *Crim. LR* 295, at 301.

4. The Selectivity of the Police

Once the police have sufficient evidence against an offender, they have in theory all the alternatives set out in Section 3 above. They may take no further action, give an informal warning, administer a formal caution, or decide on a prosecution. Only the last alternative is open to review, by the Crown Prosecution Service. All the lesser alternatives have the effect of diverting the case from the criminal justice system, except in those rare cases where a private prosecution is brought, and there is no external review of those decisions. The Home Office made several attempts, in circulars in 1983, 1985, and 1990, to persuade the police to increase diversion and to reduce the proportionate use of prosecutions. These have had considerable success, particularly in respect of juveniles. The cautioning rate for males under 17 rose from 55 per cent in 1984 to 76 per cent in 1991, and for females under 17 from 79 to 90 per cent. For adult males the cautioning rose from 5 per cent in 1984 to 18 per cent in 1991, and for adult females from 14 to 40 per cent.[35] The circular of 1990 states 'that the courts should only be used as a last resort, particularly for juveniles and young adults'.[36] However, as we shall see, this use of the 'last resort' principle has rather different implications from its use by the regulatory agencies.

1. *The formal principles*: the principles on which the police should take their gatekeeping decisions are set out as 'National Standards' in Home Office Circular 59/1990. This document has no legal significance; indeed, police cautioning is almost entirely a set of extra-legal practices. The National Standards do not explicitly lay down an order of preference: although it is stated that 'where the criteria for cautioning are met' there should be 'a presumption in favour of not prosecuting', it is merely mentioned that the Standards are not 'intended to inhibit the police practice of taking action short of a formal caution'.[37] It is unfortunate that there is no clear commitment to the principle of minimum intervention: this could have been achieved, as in respect of identification procedures, by presenting the four alternatives in their preferred order of use.[38]

The National Standards reaffirm that a formal caution should not be

[35] *Criminal Statistics, England and Wales* (1986 and 1991), table 5.5. The 1986 figures for adults are for those aged 17 and over, whereas the 1991 figure for adults is for those aged 21 and over; in fact this understates the magnitude of the increase.

[36] Home Office Circular 59/1990, para. 7.

[37] *The Cautioning of Offenders*, annex B, notes 3D and 1B.

[38] Home Office, *Police and Criminal Evidence Act 1984, Codes of Practice* (2nd edn., 1991), Code D. ch. 2.

offered unless there is sufficient evidence to prosecute, the offender admits the offence, and the offender gives informed consent. When those requirements are fulfilled, the key issue is then one of 'public interest'. Paragraph 5 of the National Standards lists five factors to be taken into account:

(*a*) the nature of the offence;
(*b*) the likely penalty if convicted in court;
(*c*) the offender's age and state of health;
(*d*) the offender's previous criminal history;
(*e*) the offender's attitude to the offence.

The decision to caution is a dispositive decision, analogous to sentencing in some of its principles and effects. The seriousness of the offence is a major factor, with some offences being regarded as too serious for cautioning even where the offender fulfils conditions (*c*), (*d*), (*e*), or indeed all of them. On the other hand, less serious offences may result in a caution even though the offender cannot be brought within (*c*), (*d*), or (*e*). The reference in (*b*) to the likely penalty may be treated as a yardstick of seriousness: if a court would be likely to give nothing more than a discharge or perhaps a small fine, that may indicate that the nature of the offence is insufficiently serious for prosecution.

The National Standards state clearly that a previous conviction or caution does not rule out a subsequent caution if other factors suggest that it might be suitable, 'such as an appreciable lapse of time since the last offence, whether the more recent offence and the previous offences are different in character and seriousness, and the effects of a previous caution on the pattern of offending'.[39] The criteria here bear some similarity to those for the sentencing of offenders with previous convictions, in that they do not accept as inevitable the notion of harsher responses to successive offences and emphasize the importance of considering the circumstances of each offence.[40]

The relevance of factor (*e*) is more debatable. It includes 'the wilfulness with which it was committed', which is clearly related to the question of culpability. Deliberate acts are usually more serious than 'spur of the moment' excesses. It also includes 'a practical demonstration of regret such as apologising to the victim and/or offering to put matters right as far as he is able'.[41] The difficulty here is that wealthy offenders

[39] Home Office, *Police and Criminal Evidence Act 1984, Codes of Practice* (2nd edn., 1991), annex B, note 3E.
[40] Cf. A. Ashworth, *Sentencing and Criminal Justice* (1992), ch. 6; compare *The Cautioning of Offenders*, para. 8, which warns against the 'inappropriate use of cautioning, especially repeat cautioning'.
[41] *The Cautioning of Offenders*, note 3F.

might be able to buy themselves out of prosecution by offering payments to their victims, whereas impecunious offenders cannot. The law of sentencing contains clear declarations of principle against such inequality,[42] but the National Standards for Cautioning contain none. Moreover, the difficulties go further than this. Only a court can order an offender to pay compensation to the victim, and so one effect of a decision to caution is that there can be no legal framework for the payment of compensation to the victim. The National Standards refer obliquely to 'the possibility of the court's awarding compensation' as being a 'major determining factor' in bringing a prosecution in some cases[43]—presumably, even though a caution would be indicated by the other criteria—yet it is also stated that 'a prosecution should not be brought simply as a means of obtaining redress and the police should fully explain to the victim that the award of compensation is entirely a matter of discretion for the court'.[44] Once again, the introduction of victim-related considerations has produced confused guidance, without assuring that those who cause injury, loss, or damage are ordered to compensate their victims. However, a few local schemes appear to have accommodated both offenders and victims to a reasonable degree of satisfaction.[45]

The clearest and best-established reason for cautioning is where the offender is very young, or elderly, or suffering from ill health. Reference has already been made to the increasingly high probability that a juvenile offender will be cautioned rather than prosecuted: the younger the offender, the higher the probability of a caution. Elderly offenders are also quite likely to receive a caution, often for theft from a shop. Where an offender is suffering from mental disorder or a severe physical illness, this also militates in favour of a caution. The rationale behind this category has never been made clear. The link with culpability is rather uncertain, although it can be maintained that those who are very young or mentally disordered are less to blame than others. The same could be said of some elderly offenders. However, there is considerable support for the rehabilitative argument that the process of prosecution, conviction, and sentence may cause stigma and otherwise be less effective in turning a young offender away from crime than a caution. In the case of young offenders this approach merges into the argument that

[42] See Ashworth, *Sentencing and Criminal Justice*, ch. 7.

[43] *The Cautioning of Offenders*, annex B, note 4C; note 4B mentions that it may be proper to prosecute in order to protect a victim from further attention from the offender.

[44] Ibid., para. 6; the latter statement is wrong, since courts are required to consider making a compensation order and to give reasons if they do not do so in an appropriate case: Criminal Justice Act 1988, s. 104.

[45] M. Cavadino and J. Dignan, *The Penal System: An Introduction* (1992), 185–6.

sentences may have a harsher impact on certain types of offender, and therefore that a lesser response would be appropriate in order to preserve proportionality. This is perhaps uppermost in cases of elderly offenders. It therefore appears that three rationales—culpability as an element of seriousness, rehabilitation, and equality of impact—may support this ground for cautioning. The National Standards, without explicitly stating a rationale, may draw promiscuously on all three.

2. *For and against cautioning*: why has there been such a strong movement towards cautioning in recent years? The National Standards begin by stating three purposes of cautions:

(*a*) to deal quickly and simply with less serious offenders;
(*b*) to divert them from the criminal courts;
(*c*) to reduce the chances of their reoffending.

The first purpose refers to proportionality, implying that quicker and simpler responses are more appropriate for less serious offences. However, the undertones of economics are also evident here, and the words 'and more cheaply' are implicit. The same undertones might be detected beneath the second purpose, although that might also be seen as a gesture towards the principle of minimum intervention.[46] The third purpose makes a bold claim about effectiveness. Statistics show that some 13 per cent of those cautioned in 1985 were convicted of a further offence within two years. Some four-fifths of those cautioned had no previous caution or conviction, and for this group the conviction rate was 10 per cent. For young adults, many of whom had a previous caution or conviction, the conviction rate was higher at 19 per cent.[47] However, the overall reconviction rate of 13 per cent is considerably lower than the reconviction rate of those sentenced in courts, which is 29 per cent for those without any previous convictions.[48] It could be commented that any such comparison is flawed because the court group is likely to have a higher proportion of people with previous cautions, who are more likely to be reconvicted anyway. A small matched study of juveniles by Mott suggests that those cautioned are still less likely to reoffend than those sentenced in court.[49] However,

[46] Properly speaking, diversion from the criminal courts cannot be a 'purpose' of cautioning. It is simply its effect. A 'purpose' would offer a reason why offenders should be diverted in this way.

[47] 'The Criminal Histories of those Cautioned in 1985 and 1988', *Home Office Statistical Bulletin*, 20/92.

[48] G. J. O. Phillpotts and L. B. Lancucki, *Previous Convictions, Sentence and Reconviction*, HORS 53 (1979), 16. This study had a longer follow-up period of six years, but it is known that most reconvictions occur early in the period.

[49] J. Mott, 'Police Decisions for Dealing with Juvenile Offenders', (1983) 23 *BJ Crim.* 249.

those who adopt the principle of minimum intervention do not need to establish that cautions are more effective, in terms of reconvictions. It is sufficient to argue that they have not been shown to be less effective than conviction and sentence.

What are the disadvantages of cautioning? Three possible disadvantages merit brief discussion—the danger of net-widening, pressure on defendants to admit to offences, and unfairness to victims. Net-widening is the process of using a new measure, not (or not only) to encompass the target group of offenders who would otherwise have been prosecuted, but also to drag into the net people who might otherwise have benefited from a lesser response. This danger was pointed out to the police in the 1985 circular, and there is little evidence that the considerable increases in cautioning during the 1980s have been achieved through any significant net-widening.[50] Whilst there may be some cases of this kind, the figures suggest a genuine transfer of offenders away from prosecution towards cautioning. In respect of juveniles, many areas have developed the practice of referring cases either to a juvenile bureau or to some multi-agency team, for an opinion on the most suitable response to the offence and offender. Arrangements differ locally, so that in some areas cases are not referred if they are obviously so serious that a charge is appropriate or obviously so minor that a formal caution would be unnecessary.[51]

The offer of a caution may put pressure on a suspect to admit an offence when it is not clear that he or she committed it. If the suspect denies knowledge of a certain fact, he or she might wish to decline a caution and have the point adjudicated in court; and yet the disincentives to taking that course are so great (delay, risk of not being believed, risk of conviction) that acceptance of the caution is likely. The National Standards state that 'a caution will not be appropriate where a person does not make a clear and reliable admission of the offence',[52] but there is the additional problem that the police may not fully understand the relevant law, such as the mental element required for the crime or the possible defences.[53] In effect, whenever a person knows or believes that there will be a choice between accepting a caution and risking a prosecution, there is bound to be pressure to accept the caution. The disadvantages of this must be minimized by ensuring, as far

[50] M. McMahon, 'Net-Widening: Vagaries in the Use of a Concept', (1990) 30 *BJ Crim.* 121.

[51] For one example, the Kent arrangements for reference to a Juvenile Offender Liaison Team, see S. Uglow *et al.*, 'Cautioning Juveniles: Multi-agency Impotence', [1992] *Crim. LR* 632.

[52] *The Cautioning of Offenders*, annex B, note 2B.

[53] A. Sanders, 'The Limits to Diversion from Prosecution', (1988) 28 *BJ Crim.* 513.

as possible, that cautions are only offered if the conditions are strictly met. This would require far greater supervision within the police, or the provision of legal advice, or the transfer of the function to the CPS.

Unfairness to victims is an ingrained problem of the trend towards greater cautioning. The statistics show that since 1988 an ever-higher proportion of convicted offenders is being ordered to pay compensation to victims, and yet those statistics must be read in the context of the increased percentage of offenders who are cautioned rather than prosecuted. Thus in 1991 fewer offenders were ordered to pay compensation by criminal courts than in 1981, some 112,800 compared with 129,400.[54] Of course some offenders will have made voluntary payments to their victims, but the National Standards emphasize that 'under no circumstances should police officers become involved in negotiating or awarding reparation or compensation'.[55] The result is that in some cases a police decision to caution, made on the merits of the case, will mean that the victim's chance of receiving compensation is destroyed. Some ambiguity about this in the National Standards was noted earlier,[56] but this is an awkward practical problem for any system with some commitment to victims. Courts are required to reduce a compensation order so as to take account of the means of the offender: the police could not be expected to make inquiries of this kind, even if they were permitted to involve themselves in drawing up agreements. Such agreements would not be binding unless a new legal framework were devised, but 'caution plus' schemes are now in use in several areas. What success can be claimed for them is unclear.

3. *The practical implementation of National Standards*: it is too early to be confident about the effect of the 1990 National Standards. Their expressed aim was to foster greater consistency, but it was stated that some of the awkward issues about repeat cautions and victims' rights should be decided locally through a 'force policy statement' on cautioning.[57] For some years different forces have had varying arrangements in relation to juveniles. The inter-agency approach has now gained the ascendancy. Some areas have juvenile bureaux, where members of the different agencies are located and deal with referred cases. Others have an inter-agency panel or other liaison arrangement, to meet from time to time to discuss cases. Whichever approach is adopted, the police tend to refer cautionable cases, having already weeded out some that require no further action and others that are so serious as to require prosecution. The bureau or panel will then refer

---

[54] *Criminal Statistics, England and Wales* (1991), table 7.24.
[55] *The Cautioning of Offenders*, annex B, note 4c.
[56] See n. 45 above, and text thereat.   [57] *The Cautioning of Offenders*, para. 9.

the case back to the police with a recommendation, and the police take the final decision. The Home Office expressed a wish that the inter-agency approach should be extended to young adult offenders, but progress in this direction has been slow. For juveniles the approach has been influenced by the obligation on the juvenile court (and still retained for the youth court) to have regard to the welfare of the offender.[58]

Although cautioning for juveniles is a fairly long-established practice, there has been and continues to be a different approach taken in different areas, resulting in the claim of 'justice by geography' rather than justice according to the seriousness of the offence. The 1991 statistics show a national average of 76 per cent for the cautioning of juvenile males, but this masks a variation between 90 per cent in Kent and 60 per cent in Avon and Somerset. Two points may be made about these variations. First, when variable cautioning rates were studied by Evans and Wilkinson in the period 1985–90, they found that there were substantial variations within police force areas, not merely between forces.[59] This shows that cautioning had been left largely to local divisional policy, and one of the aims of the new National Standards is to ensure that every police force should produce a 'force policy statement on cautioning', after appropriate consultation with the Crown Prosecution Service, Probation Service, and social services.[60] This initiative is to be supported by systematic monitoring, but it should be noted that the framework is still not national. The police force is the unit, and in respect of juveniles there may be different local consultation requirements. However, the recent reorganization of the CPS into only thirteen areas may have the effect of bringing about greater uniformity of approach in neighbouring police forces, since two or more of the forty-one police areas will fall within each CPS area. Secondly, it might be argued that much of the variation in cautioning rates among police forces is attributable not to differing policies but to different mixes of cases. Since cautioning is much used for first offenders, the proportion of first offenders coming to police attention is highly likely to affect the cautioning rate. Evans and Wilkinson found that the percentage of first offenders did differ significantly among areas (from 46 to 64 per cent) and that it was related to the juvenile cautioning rate in the ten forces studied. However, they also found that further variation in cautioning was not explained by the different offence-mix: much

[58] Children and Young Persons Act 1933, s. 44.
[59] R. Evans and C. Wilkinson, 'Variations in Police Cautioning Policy and Practice in England and Wales', (1990) 29 *Howard JCJ* 155.
[60] *The Cautioning of Offenders*, para. 9.

cautioning is for shoplifting, but it appeared that forces adopted differing policies towards this.[61] One of the conclusions of this study was that cautioning guidelines tend to say little about the most crucial factor in practice—the type and seriousness of the offence. This abstentionist tradition has been continued in the National Standards,[62] and since those Standards leave the formulation of policy to local police forces (in consultation with other local agencies), the opportunity for justice by geography remains.

All of this, however, is to assume that the written guidelines are faithfully translated into practice. McConville, Sanders, and Leng, on the basis of their research in the late 1980s, have argued that the reality is quite different: the cautioning guidelines are so broadly worded that they can easily be used by the police to justify decisions taken on other grounds.[63] These other grounds are likely to reflect the working practices and concerns of the police. They give examples of a case being prosecuted in response to the insistence of a local business, even though it fell within the cautioning guidelines, and of another case resulting in a caution when (as a theft in breach of trust) it fell squarely within the prosecution category. Whether matters have improved since the late 1980s is unclear: Evens and Wilkinson found that some police forces had not even reflected the 1985 guidelines in their standing orders, although it seems likely that the 1990 circular will have achieved a wider effect. However, we noted that those guidelines are often unspecific on the crucial factor of 'type and seriousness of offence', allowing just the leeway to which McConville, Sanders, and Leng draw attention. The study by Evans of attempts to introduce new guidance for the cautioning of young adults in two London police divisions shows once again that it is attitudes and working philosophies rather than written rules that tend to determine outcomes.[64] A 'Caution Consideration Chart' was introduced, but it tended to be used in some police stations as a resource, to legitimate decisions taken by the custody officer on other grounds. Sometimes, too, victims' views were similarly manipulated, being ignored when inconvenient and cited when they supported a decision already taken. Overall, the proba-

[61] *The Cautioning of Offenders*, 160–3.
[62] There is a related issue, on which much could be written, about whether prosecution and cautioning policy in respect of specific offences should be published, lest it spreads a belief in immunity and impunity. This is less of a problem with guidance that refers to culpability-related factors (e.g. mental disorder, dying relative). The presumption in favour of cautioning juvenile first offenders is on the borderline.
[63] M. McConville, A. Sanders, and R. Leng, *The Case for the Prosecution* (1991), 122 and ch. 6 generally.
[64] R. Evans, 'Evaluating Young Adult Diversion Schemes in the Metropolitan Police District', [1993] *Crim. LR* 490.

bility is that some decisions result from a simple following of the guidelines, whereas others are motivated more by the 'moral character' of the offender or victim or by concerns related to the police mission.[65] It might also be observed that the police will some times take a decision that might be justifiable on the limited information available but that might cease to be justifiable when more information comes to light. Some of the 'public interest' criteria for not prosecuting depend on matters extraneous to the offence, of which the police may have no knowledge.[66]

The Government has recently signified its desire that cautioning should be used less frequently. In a consultation paper, the Home Secretary raises a number of issues, such as the use of cautions for 'serious' offences and, more particularly, repeat cautions.[67] In the context of the more repressive approach to crime advocated by some politicians and journalists, even relatively small amendments to the National Standards may result in significant changes of practice. The system may lose both in proportionality and in effectiveness.

5. Accountability

It is apparent from the discussion of the gatekeeping practices of the police and of regulatory agencies that discretion is the dominant characteristic. There is little law in these areas, and what law there is aims merely to facilitate rather than to direct. Guidelines have been created, but these are so generally phrased and so lightly enforced that their impact is muted. To what extent, if at all, are these decision-makers accountable? The question has to be answered on two different levels: accountability for general policy, and accountability for individual decisions.

It is not clear to what extent the various regulatory agencies are accountable for their policies. We saw that the Factories Inspectorate and the Air Pollution Inspectorate have long had different policies in respect of prosecution, but is there any higher agency that can point to these divergent traditions and ask for justifications? It appears not. The enforcement practices of the Inland Revenue and the Customs and Excise were examined by the Keith Committee in 1983,[68] and their frequent use of compounded penalties was commended as 'swift and economical', but on a continuing basis the only vestige of accountability is

[65] See above, Ch. 3.6. [66] See the discussion of PICA schemes below, Ch. 6.3.
[67] *The Times*, 29 Oct. 1993.
[68] Report of the Interdepartmental Committee, The Enforcement of Revenue Legislation (chairman: Lord Keith), Cmnd. 8822 (1983).

the submission to Parliament of an annual report. For almost all regulatory agencies this is the only means of being called to account for policy.

With the police there is a much greater appearance of accountability, since there are now 'National Standards for Cautioning'. Yet those National Standards are supported merely by a Home Office circular, the terms of which were agreed with the Association of Chief Police Officers and the Crown Prosecution Service. No doubt the terms of the circular will be used as a basis for inspections by Her Majesty's Inspector of Constabulary. No doubt, also, there are possible financial implications for refusal to comply. However, as far as the law is concerned the Chief Constable of each area is solely responsible for decisions on law enforcement in that area. Since the Court of Appeal has held that 'No Minister of the Crown can tell him that he must or must not prosecute this man or that one',[69] the National Standards cannot be binding in law. The 1993 Royal Commission has recommended:

that police cautioning should be governed by statute, under which national guidelines, drawn up in consultation with the CPS and the police service among others, should be laid down in regulations. These regulations should also govern the keeping of records of cautions so that information about whether a suspect has been cautioned can easily be transferred between police forces.[70]

To give statutory authority for police cautions would be an worthwhile step, as would an efficient system of record-keeping. National guidelines, however, we already have. The key question is whether any newly drafted guidelines would be different and, if so, in what way. The Royal Commission gives no hint of whether it considered the existing National Standards and found them wanting in any respect: the discussion above has identified some respects in which improvement is needed. Nor does the Royal Commission deal with the problem of accountability: how would the new regulations be enforced? The National Standards of 1990 were to be supported by the monitoring of cautioning practice within each police force. If that monitoring yields reliable information about local practices, sharper questions about policy variations are likely to be raised. The frequent refrain of the individual decision-maker—'it all depends on the facts of the case'—can be shown to have its limitations if monitoring confirms that many cases fall into the same legal or other category.

Accountability for individual decisions depends largely on the inter-

[69] R. v. *Metropolitan Police Commissioner, ex p. Blackburn (No. 1)* [1968] 2 QB 118, per Lord Denning, MR.
[70] RCCJ, *Report*, Cm. 2263 (1993), para 5.57.

nal structure of the agency. Within the police, there may be local police traditions or cultures that lead to variation in interpretation, even if there is a clear force policy.[71] It is a well-known characteristic of the police that the amount of supervision of constables is not great, and that they have much *de facto* discretion.[72] Historically this has not been true of cautioning decisions, since cases for caution have tended to be referred to inspector level for approval. This is not always so, now that cautioning is becoming a more widespread practice, but it remains true that a key stage is when a constable brings into a police station someone who has just been arrested. The station sergeant has to decide whether or not to accept the charge. The constable may press for the person to be charged, making it into an issue of support or non-support for another officer, and the sergeant may not have sufficient information on 'public interest' factors to be able to resist this even if this were thought advisable. Thus any policy of increasing the use of cautions is far more likely to succeed if there is force-wide commitment to its objectives; if there is not, aspects of the occupational culture are likely to overshadow it in practice. If in a particular case a person is charged, despite falling within one of the categories for cautioning outlined in the National Standards, it seems that judicial review may be possible but that this would be judicial review of the Crown Prosecution Service if they decide to continue the prosecution rather than discontinuing it. This, the Divisional Court held,[73] is because the police are merely the initiators of proceedings, and the 'last and decisive word' on the issue now lies with the Crown Prosecution Service. The CPS would take this decision within the framework of the *Code for Crown Prosecutors* (to be discussed in the next chapter), which is similar in terms to the National Standards. A decision to continue the prosecution would be reviewable in the case of a juvenile and, although one court held that judicial review is 'unlikely to be available' if the decision concerns an adult, that decision now seems to have been superseded.[74] What of the reverse situation, where the police decide to caution an

[71] For a recent example, in relation to the cautioning of young adults, see the comparison between two police divisions by Evans, 'Evaluating Young Adult Diversion Schemes', 490.

[72] e.g. Maguire and Norris, *Conduct and Supervision*; B. Irving and C. Dunnighan, *Human Factors in the Quality Control of CID Investigations*, RCCJ Research Study 21 (1993).

[73] In *R. v. Chief Constable of Kent et al., ex p. L.* (1991) 93 Cr. App. R. 416, per Watkins, LJ, at 426. Cf. *R. v. Croydon Justices, ex p. Dean* [1993] Crim. LR 759, dealing with an offence which may only be prosecuted with the consent of the Director of Public Prosecutions, where the CPS have the 'last word' on prosecuting.

[74] Compare *Ex p. L.*, at 428, with the judgement of Stuart-Smith, LJ, in *R. v. Inland Revenue Commissioner, ex p. Mead* [1993] 1 All ER 772, at 780.

offender and the victim or another interested person can demonstrate that the case does not fall within the National Standards? Apart from the possibility of a private prosecution, an action for judicial review of the police decision might be brought. This is a matter on which the police have the 'last and decisive word', since such a case would never reach the CPS. If the decision could be shown to be *Wednesbury* unreasonable,[75] judicial review could be expected to succeed, whether the case concerns a juvenile or an adult.[76]

As for the regulatory agencies, the research often suggests that there are variations in the local culture of different parts of a single agency— one familiar finding is a divergence of approach between rural areas and urban areas. The accountability of the individual inspector may depend on how paperwork is completed and how thoroughly it is supervised. Good training and retraining may be important factors, but on the other hand these have to fight against any local culture, financial pressures, and other countervailing forces. However, an individual decision to prosecute or not to prosecute is unlikely to be reviewed, within most agencies, unless it is a case of particular sensitivity to which the attention of senior officials has been drawn. Judicial review of a decision to prosecute or not to prosecute would be available in theory, since most of these agencies have the 'last and decisive word' within their own sphere of operation, but the reluctance of the Divisional Court in the *Kent* case to introduce judicial review into prosecution decisions may prove not to have been displaced by the greater willingness of the court in *Mead*.[77]

These uncertainties in the formal avenues of accountability assume greater significance when the consequences of the decisions are recalled. If a case is not prosecuted by the police, but is dealt with by caution or no formal action, this is the end of the process. The only way to revive the case is by means of a private prosecution: those are rare, and the immense investment of time and money needed to mount such a prosecution means that it cannot realistically be termed a method of accountability. If the decision is in favour of prosecution, the case then goes to the Crown Prosecution Service, which has powers of discontinuance: the extent to which they are exercised is discussed in the next chapter.

---

[75] The reference is to the test in the leading case of *Associated Provincial Picture Houses Ltd.* v. *Wednesbury Corporation* [1948] 1 KB 223.

[76] See *General Council of the Bar, ex p. Percival* [1990] 3 All ER 137, discussed by C. Hilson, 'Discretion to Prosecute and Judicial Review', [1993] *Crim. LR* 639.

[77] See above, nn. 73–4.

6. Values and Principles

The stages of decision-making discussed here raise several questions of value that need further discussion. Is equality of treatment ensured? Are the interests of victims properly respected? Are the rights of defendants respected? Is there too great a sacrifice of crime control? How might the difficulties be dealt with?

1. *Equality of treatment*: in the previous section we saw that the due execution of stated policies is not *ensured* by the law because legal accountability is rather sketchy in this sphere. The practice of cautioning and almost all other forms of diversion have no statutory basis: they operate in a world where there is little law, save at the extremes, and considerable discretion. Decisions are taken in private, without argument and without reasons needing to be given. Even if the recommendation of the 1993 Royal Commission is implemented, the new statutory basis will not deal with the problems of cautioning unless accompanied by clearer guidelines and better channels of accountability, and will not deal with the regulatory agencies at all.

The predominance of discretion might be regarded as a contradiction of the principle of equality before the law and equal treatment. In many European countries, the considerable weight given to the principle of compulsory prosecution shows awareness of the values at stake. It is true that most countries do not regard this as an absolute principle, and in recent years have sought to allow scope to the principle of expediency whereby certain cases are diverted from the courts, usually by prosecutors. But these can be regarded as circumscribed exceptions to the principle that criminal justice should be dispensed in open court, after a full consideration of the issues, with reasons given. Whilst these values are usually compromised in some way,[78] there is surely good reason to ensure that they are expressed and are accorded some respect. The decisions in this chapter are decisions that may profoundly affect the course of a suspect/offender's life, since prosecution itself may be highly significant for the defendant in terms of anxiety and stress, damage to reputation, and possible loss of employment. If discretion is to be bestowed on certain authorities, it should be carefully structured so as to achieve desired policies and properly controlled through channels of accountability. The few laconic remarks of the 1993 Royal Commission on this question are most unsatisfactory.[79]

---

[78] In many Continental systems the court proceedings amount to little more than confirmation of what is in the dossier, with the real decisions have been taken earlier by the public prosecutor and others. See e.g. H. Lensing and L. Rayar, 'Notes on Criminal Procedure in the Netherlands', [1992] *Crim. LR* 623.   [79] RCCJ Report, para. 5.59.

Cautioning practices and diversion generally do seem to accord favourable treatment to vulnerable groups such as the young and the mentally disturbed. Policies in respect of juveniles have been strongly in favour of cautioning and against prosecution throughout the last decade, although we have seen that some retrenchment of policy is likely. The diversion of the mentally disturbed is a well-established practice, although it has been argued that the ready referral of mentally disturbed suspects to the mental health services and hospitals may sometimes be a disproportionately severe response, or may deprive them of rights they would have if prosecuted, or both.[80]

Apart from particularly vulnerable groups, does the system ensure equality of treatment? One obvious problem is the difference of approach to 'police' matters and to spheres of conduct that are regulated by the various non-police agencies. Companies, wealthy offenders, and middle-class offenders are more often dealt with by regulatory agencies whereas the more disadvantaged members of society are more likely to find their conduct defined as a police matter. The different approaches are then likely to result in more frequent prosecution of the disadvantaged than the advantaged for offences that may be no different in terms of seriousness. Norval Morris and Michael Tonry might adapt their argument on sentencing, to the effect that it is wrong to insist on equality if it means equality of misery.[81] The effect of this would be to allow middle-class or white-collar offenders to benefit from diversion and other alternatives to prosecution, even though lower-class or blue-collar offenders were processed in the 'normal' way, since to assimilate the treatment of the former group to that of the latter would increase the overall suffering. On a principle of parsimony, minimum intervention may thus be given higher priority than equality of treatment. However, the factual basis for this is the assumption that there is no practical way of extending forms of diversion to lower-class offenders who commit 'police' crimes. This is quite unsubstantiated. Thus, even without attacking their order of priorities, it can be argued that there is a need to devise further forms of diversion that can be operated swiftly for large numbers of small-time offenders.

A second problem of equality of treatment concerns racial discrimination. Several studies suggest that there is some discrimination against Afro-Caribbeans in respect of decisions to prosecute or caution. For example, Tony Jefferson and Monica Walker found that Asians were much more likely to be cautioned than any others, but that Afro-

---

[80] D. Carson, 'Prosecuting People with Mental Handicaps', [1989] *Crim. LR* 87.
[81] N. Morris and M. Tonry, *Between Prison and Probation* (1990).

Caribbeans were less likely than whites to receive a caution.[82] The Commission for Racial Equality monitored the cautioning of juveniles in seven police forces and found that Afro-Caribbeans were more likely to be referred for prosecution than whites.[83] It seems likely that part of the difference in prosecution rates revealed by these studies would disappear of account were taken of whether the individual was willing to admit the offence: more Afro-Caribbeans decline to admit the allegations against them, which removes their eligibility for a caution.[84] However, this certainly does not eliminate the differences found, and there remains cause for concern about differential responses. The principle of equality of treatment, enshrined in Article 14 of the European Convention on Human Rights, seems to be being breached.

A third problem is posed by the differential cautioning rates for females, which are much higher than those for men—in 1991, 90 per cent for juvenile girls compared with 76 per cent for juvenile boys, and 40 per cent for women compared with 18 per cent for men. The face-value interpretation would be that females are receiving unduly favourable treatment, but this fails to take account of the probability that offences of different types and different levels of seriousness would be found in the different groups. Relatively little research into the differences has been reported, but the literature on the sentencing of women suggests that the impression of overall leniency might disappear on further inspection and might also conceal some groups of women who are prosecuted when a man might be cautioned.[85]

2. *Victims' rights*: are the existing arrangements for diversion, dominated by the police caution, effective in securing the rights of victims? There is a small number of mediation schemes that may assist victims in coming to terms with the offence and in securing compensation from the offender. However, there remain doubts about whether these schemes are truly for the benefit of victims, especially if participation is likely to gain mitigation of sentence for the offender.[86] As for formal police cautions, these appear inadequate for the purpose of ensuring that victims receive compensation. The National Standards refer to the view of the victims as a factor in the decision whether or not to caution,

[82] T. Jefferson and M. Walker, 'Ethnic Minorities in the Criminal Justice System', [1992] *Crim. LR* 83, at 88.

[83] Commission for Racial Equality, *Juvenile Cautioning: Ethnic Monitoring in Practice* (1992).

[84] M. Fitzgerald, *Ethnic Minorities and the Criminal Justice System*, RCCJ Research Study 20 (1993), 18.

[85] For a survey of an analogous field, see A. Morris, 'Sex and Sentencing', [1988] *Crim. LR* 163.

[86] Cf. R. Young, 'Reparation as Mitigation', [1989] *Crim. LR* 463.

but this procedural involvement is surely far less appropriate and far less important than ensuring the payment of some compensation. In theory there is no reason why the offer of a formal caution, extra-statutory as it is, should not be made conditional on the payment of compensation to the victim. This might well achieve some of the aims of 'caution plus' schemes and, whilst the 1993 Royal Commission recommends further experiments in using the Probation Service to combine cautions with co-operation in treatment programmes, it is unfortunate that it failed to examine the possibility of incorporating victim compensation when proposing the introduction of prosecutor fines.[87] In some of those European countries that have a system of conditional non-prosecution or conditional waiver of prosecution, this is a possibility.[88] However, the introduction of conditional non-prosecution linked to the payment of compensation would raise some practical problems. It is not clear how the amount of the compensation would be settled, nor whether it might be reduced if the offender were impecunious. It would be important to ensure that such a system did not enable wealthy offenders to buy themselves out of prosecution: there would need to be proper guidelines for the use of this alternative to prosecution. The Crown Prosecution Service, as a quasi-judicial body,[89] would be more appropriate than the police for administering such a system, in view of its overall responsibility for prosecution policy.

One question that remains open is whether a form of mediation should be *offered* to offenders and their victims. It is easier to give a positive response to this question than to determine exactly how the outcome of such mediation should relate to the formal criminal process. Since the participation of victims in such schemes must remain voluntary, it seems wrong that the victim's decision to participate or not should influence the way in which the criminal justice system responds to the offence. There are signs, however, that such schemes can operate by way of diversion without prejudicing the interests of victims.[90]

3. *Defendants' rights*: one common feature of diversion schemes is that the defendant can decline the offer made by the police or prosecution if guilt is disputed, leaving them to prosecute in court and have the matter decided there. Whilst this is sufficient to comply with the

[87] RCCJ Report, comparing para. 5.60 with para. 5.62.
[88] Tak, *Legal Scope of Non-prosecution*.
[89] In many European countries prosecutors are, constitutionally, part of the judicial branch.
[90] See Cavadino and Dignan, *The Penal System*, 186, reporting on a Northamptonshire scheme.

European Convention on Human Rights,[91] it none the less leaves to the defendant a choice that is not without pressure. There is a strong incentive to take an offer that dispenses with prosecution in court, especially if (as with cautioning in England and Wales) no formal conditions can be attached. However, a formal caution will be recorded and may be cited to a court in any proceedings for future offences. If the defendant disputes criminal liability and refuses the offer, the police may drop the case or may decide to prosecute. The latter course is likely to cause considerable inconvenience, pressure, or even stress to the defendant. This is why even an innocent person may decide, on balance, to accept a caution—even for something that the police could not, in the event, have proved.

Two possible means of preventing such injustices may be mentioned. First, decisions on cautioning could be transferred from the police to the Crown Prosecution Service, with a view to ensuring that a caution is offered only in cases where the evidence really does fulfil the appropriate legal criteria. Second, there could be a provision for access to legal advice before deciding whether or not to accept a caution. The second is important if cautioning decisions are to remain in the hands of the police, but it would be desirable to introduce both safeguards. No doubt these would slow down the system, and would therefore be resisted as making it more expensive and more 'inefficient'. But the transfer of power to the Crown Prosecution Service can be supported independently, as we shall see, and the provision for legal advice is necessary to deal with that minority of cases in which defendants may be materially disadvantaged by the present arrangements.

4. *Crime control*: one of the objections frequently raised against forms of diversion is that they undermine crime prevention, simply because many offenders do not take them seriously. It is not uncommon to hear anecdotes about offenders, often young, who express themselves as if they have a 'licence to offend' because they know that nothing worse than a caution will result. There are at least two points to set against such anecdotes. The first is that the reconviction figures for persons cautioned in England are not only lower than those for persons prosecuted but also, at 13 per cent, relatively low in any event—certainly low enough to suggest that the anecdotes apply to a small minority. The second point is that the anecdote does not compare the effects of cautions with the effects of conviction and sentence, notably the stigma and labelling that may result. This argument is all the more important for young offenders, where the law still requires courts (and,

---

[91] See above, n. 24.

implicitly, all those dealing with juvenile offenders) to have regard to the welfare of the child or young person.[92] In many areas, as we have seen, there is a corporate approach to decision-making for juveniles that is intended to ensure that the claims of welfare and of punishment are given appropriate weight.[93] The particular local arrangements may, of course, result in more emphasis being placed on one or the other, often depending on the deference shown by the local police towards the juvenile liaison scheme or other body. As far as the law is concerned, there is no 'right' balance because the welfare principle stands alongside the principle of proportionality enshrined in the Criminal Justice Act 1991, with no official attempt at reconciliation or priority. This is unsatisfactory, but it does mean that the possibility of diversion from prosecution, by cautioning or other means, ensures that both purposes remain in play. If the anecdote were followed and diversion were to cease, it seems likely that the system would achieve no greater crime prevention overall, and it would be more expensive and slower.

Two issues should not be overlooked, however. One is whether the move towards police cautions in recent years, particularly for juveniles, has an effect on the way in which they perceive the criminal law. There are those that argue that extensive cautioning may undermine what moral restraints exist, by fostering the notion that offences can be committed with impunity. The suggestion remains unproved, but its closeness to the foundations of social order requires it to be kept firmly in view. It appears to have informed that policy change in the Netherlands in 1990 towards increasing the proportion of cases that resulted in some formal action by the authorities,[94] and it is a prominent factor in the recent 'toughening' of cautioning policy proposed by the Home Secretary.[95] The second issue is the rights of victims. An offender should be required to do something to make good any loss or damage inflicted: it will rarely be possible for young offenders to do this by paying money (unless the parents are able to pay), but some other form of reparation may be possible. For older offenders, however, the payment of compensation should be a primary feature of diversion, as argued above. Many questions of detail would need to be resolved, but the principle of compensation to victims from offenders should be respected. This is a major failing of the existing English arrangements.

---

[92] Children and Young Persons Act 1933, s. 44.

[93] Cf. J. Pratt, 'Corporatism: The Third Model of Juvenile Justice', (1989) 29 *BJ Crim.* 236.

[94] Ministry of Justice, *Law in Motion* (1990), 40–1.

[95] See n. 67 above and accompanying text.

7. Conclusions

There are good arguments in favour of the diversion of non-serious offenders from the criminal courts, but this should be done at the least possible cost to the rights of victims and of defendants. It is quite proper that the prospect of saving time and money should lead policy-makers to expand diversion, not least because prosecuting offenders is not necessarily more effective in terms of reconviction rates. But the attraction of schemes of diversion should not be allowed to obscure the principles of criminal justice outlined in Chapter 3. Quite apart from the strong criticism of the English cautioning system that it fails to respect victims' rights to compensation, decisions on caution, prosecution, or no further action are left to the police, without meaningful review or accountability, particularly when a caution is offered. There is even less accountability in respect of the practices of the so-called regulatory agencies.

The existing system encourages the police to caution certain offenders, but does not provide sources of information on the factors necessary for a caution. The Crown Prosecution Service benefits from information from PICA schemes in some areas, when reassessing the public interest in prosecution.[96] The police service have to assemble the information for themselves, unless the case involves a juvenile and there is multi-agency co-operation. On the other hand, active defence solicitors will often draw the attention of the police or the CPS to factors in a case that might justify cautioning rather than prosecution. The police also lack expertise on legal issues relevant to guilt, although they can consult the CPS for advice. The recommendation of the 1993 Royal Commission in favour of prosecutor fines seems likely only to confuse the picture. It raises awkward questions about strategies for diversion. First there are several questions about the role of prosecutor fines. Are they to be treated as more severe than cautions, and therefore to be used for more serious cases or for people who have already been cautioned? How can the extraordinary failure to consider, let alone to give priority to, victim compensation be explained? Would prosecutor fines be used chiefly for 'victimless' crimes such as public order offences? In Scotland, prosecutor fines do not require an admission of guilt and are not recorded, unlike cautions in England: can these differences be justified? A second issue is the division of responsibilities between the police and the CPS. Hitherto the CPS have not been directly involved in diversion: even in the few cases that have been remitted to the police at

---

[96] See RCCJ Report, para. 5.61, and Ch. 4 below, p. 000.

the stage of prosecutorial review, this has been in the form of a request to the police to caution the offender. The CPS are not involved themselves. If prosecutor fines were introduced, two agencies would be able to divert offenders. Would the police refer cases to the CPS for prosecutor fines? If so, which cases?

These questions revive the proposal of Andrew Sanders that diversion decisions should be placed in the hands of a single agency, and that that agency should be the CPS.[97] The benefits of this might be greater consistency in the exercise of discretion, once the appropriate criteria had been decided upon, and a fuller separation of the investigative function from the prosecutorial and dispositive. The police would be reduced to the role of investigators, with most of the significant decisions on whether and how to proceed transferred to another agency. Against this might be ranged the long-standing experience of the police in decision-making of this kind, combined with their involvement in some schemes for diversion; the CPS are relatively inexperienced in this kind of decision-making, but if this argument is always given weight the CPS will of course remain inexperienced. They could be trained. More to the point is whether the CPS would welcome these wider responsibilities and would adapt to them, and whether they could find suitable staff to take on decision-making of this kind. Other more pragmatic considerations would be the cost of transferring these decisions to the CPS (more staff for the CPS, but perhaps more paperwork for the police, thereby minimizing any staff reductions there), and historically the considerable power of the police lobby. The CPS remains the least powerful public prosecution service in Europe. Assessing its performance and its suitability for further tasks remains difficult, as the Royal Commission of 1993 itself found.[98]

Apart from the future role of the CPS there are the more general issues about social justice, touched on in various places above. If it is accepted that the criminal justice system should respond to alleged offenders in a way that is consistent according to the amount of harm done and their culpability, then this principle should be considered across the boundaries between the many different enforcement agencies. Why should there be differences in response to someone who pollutes a river, someone who defrauds the Inland Revenue, someone who fails to take proper precautions for the safety of employees, someone who steals property from another, someone who sells unsound meat, and so on? One reply is that it is impossible to compare the relative seriousness of these different offences, and hence each of them must

---

[97] A. Sanders, 'The Limits of Diversion from Prosecution', (1988) 28 *BJ Crim.* 513.
[98] RCCJ, cf. para. 5.9 (optimistic) with para. 6.12 (pessimistic).

be viewed in its separate context. But that is a stalling reply, using the well-known difficulties of settling on criteria of offence-seriousness as an excuse for avoiding the broader questions of social justice that arise when relatively poor and powerless people are prosecuted whereas the better-connected are enabled to pay their way out of trouble without the stigma of a criminal conviction.[99] The Royal Commission does not accept Levi's suggestion that regulatory mechanisms be used quite widely in fraud cases,[100] but it does recommend that some fraud cases and some of those handled by the Securities and Investments Board might receive different treatment:

Where the offence is of a technical nature, there has been no specific loss or risk to any member of the public (or if there has, where restitution can be made), and the predominant issues relates to the protection of the integrity of the markets rather than to serious dishonesty as such, then it may be that regulatory action is both appropriate and sufficient.[101]

The Commission insists that the penalties 'must be sufficiently severe that it could not be alleged that so-called "white-collar crime" was being more leniently handled than other equivalent offences'. That recognizes the point of principle,[102] in terms of consistent treatment, but hardly deals with it in a manner that convinces across the spectrum of crimes. Another example comes from HM Customs and Excise, which in 1990 introduced procedures to streamline the seizure, compounding, and restoration of non-drugs goods smuggled in at Manchester airport:

For all smuggling offences involving revenue charges of up to £100, offenders were offered the choice of court proceedings or payment of a single sum which combined the compounded penalty and the restoration charge. Most offenders accepted. A parallel experiment under which credit cards could be used as a means of payment (even of fines) undoubtedly helped the success of the scheme. The number of offenders opting to appear in court did not increase.[103]

The questions of social justice raised by this are self-evident: those who smuggle modest amounts can avoid prosecution on payment, whereas those who commit ordinary thefts and deceptions of similar amounts

---

[99] Cf. S. Uglow, 'Defrauding the Public Purse', [1984] *Crim. LR* 128; A. Sanders, 'Class Bias in Prosecutions', (1985) 24 *Howard JCJ* 176.

[100] M. Levi, *The Investigation, Prosecution and Trial of Serious Fraud*, RCCJ Research Study 14 (1993).

[101] RCCJ Report, para. 7.63.

[102] The RCCP Report, para. 7.43, also raised the possibility of dealing with more regulatory and revenue cases outside the criminal process, without canvassing the issues of principle.

[103] *81st Report of the Commissioners of Her Majesty's Customs and Excise*, Cm. 1223 (1990), para. 7.7.

may be prosecuted (without option) or may receive a caution (without payment). What is necessary is a thorough review of the prosecution policies of the various regulatory agencies. At present there is virtually no accountability, and certainly no overall accountability to a single body that can oversee consistency in matters of prosecution. It is one thing to argue that the different contexts in which some agencies work make different approaches appropriate. It is quite another thing to argue that there should be no attempt at a common starting-point, and no concern with broader issues of social justice and the apparent unfairness of these differing arrangements.

The best way forward is to take two steps simultaneously. First, there should be experiments with the use of conditional non-prosecution (conditional on the payment of compensation, usually) as an alternative to cautioning. These experiments would require the involvement of the police and the CPS in co-operation. Second, there should be an urgent review of the justifications for different responses to different kinds of law-breaking. For too long the assumptions behind the policies of the Inland Revenue, the Customs and Excise, the various regulatory agencies, and the police have remained without thorough re-examination.[104] The principle of legality should be reconsidered: do the volume and variety of diversion decisions tend to undermine the rule of law, and would it not be more appropriate to decriminalize certain conduct or to regulate it to some non-criminal category? The principle of equality of treatment ought also to be taken more seriously, which means that further steps should be taken to combat racial discrimination and to ensure that there is no discrimination according to class or social status in matters as serious as prosecution.

[104] Cf. the Report of the Interdepartmental Committee, *The Enforcement of Revenue Legislation*; A. Ashworth, 'Prosecution, Police and Public: A Guide to Good Gatekeeping?', (1984) 23 *Howard JCJ* 65; Sanders, 'Class Bias in Prosecutions', 176.

6

Prosecutorial Review

ONCE a case against a person has been put together by the police or other investigatory agency, and that person has been charged or summoned, the next step should be prosecutorial review—that is, the review of the case by a legally trained prosecutor. This is one of the main functions of the Crown Prosecution Service in England and Wales. As we will see, the CPS has a number of statutory obligations, but it operates largely in a sphere of discretion. It may create its own policies, and its prosecutors exercise considerable discretion in their day-to-day decisions. Its functions concern almost exclusively prosecutions initiated by the police. The other agencies that bring prosecutions, discussed in the previous chapter, tend to prosecute their own cases. We will see that, once again, this raises questions about equality of treatment.

This chapter begins with a brief description of the Crown Prosecution Service, considering its practices in relation to evidential sufficiency and the public interest. The approach of the regulatory agencies is then compared. After that, there is consideration of the role of the victim, and of accountability for prosecutorial decisions. The chapter concludes with a discussion of policy-making within the CPS and of the ethics of prosecution.

1. The Crown Prosecution Service

Prosecution arrangements in England and Wales were altered in the mid-1980s. Until then there were three principal prosecuting agencies. The police brought most prosecutions and, whilst many police forces had developed or begun to develop a prosecuting solicitors' department, it was the police who took most of the decisions since the prosecuting solicitors were in their employ. The Director of Public Prosecutions had a small department in London, dealing with all murder prosecutions, and with a spread of other cases concerned with such matters as national security, public figures, and alleged offences by police officers. And then, thirdly, there were the various agencies such as the Inland Revenue, the Post Office, the Health and Safety Executive (including the Factory Inspectorate), the Pollution Inspectorate, local authorities (including, for example, their environmental health officers), and so forth. For convenience these will be referred to as the 'regulatory agencies', although this is certainly not intended to suggest that the offences with which they are concerned are non-serious.

The Royal Commission on Criminal Procedure, reporting in 1981, had relatively little to say about the regulatory agencies, but it did take the view that the police should not be so heavily involved in prosecution policy. It rejected the full separation of investigative and prosecutorial functions that obtains in many other jurisdictions, and decided to leave in the hands of the police the initial decision whether or not to prosecute. It favoured an independent prosecution service to review decisions to prosecute, applying a higher evidential standard than that hitherto adopted by the police. A primary reason for introducing independent legal review was to prevent weak cases from being prosecuted: in earlier years this had been the function of committal proceedings before examining magistrates, but since the requirement of committal proceedings was abolished in 1967, there had been no control on the quality of cases going to the Crown Court except in the small minority in which either the defence or the prosecution opted for a full committal.

The 1981 Royal Commission recommended a prosecution service based on the principles adopted by the Director of Public Prosecutions.[1] After considerable debate,[2] the Prosecution of Offences Act 1985 became law. The Act creates a Crown Prosecution Service, headed by the Director of Public Prosecutions and formally accountable to the Attorney-General. The new service has a duty to take over all prosecutions instituted by the police (except for certain minor offences), and has a power to take over other prosecutions. The CPS has therefore been accorded a status independent of the police. Section 10 of the Prosecution of Offences Act 1985 lays upon it the duty to publish a *Code for Crown Prosecutors* and to report annually to Parliament on its work and the use of its powers. Notable among these is its power to discontinue prosecutions in the magistrates' courts.[3] However, unlike public prosecution systems in many other jurisdictions, it was not given powers to institute proceedings itself, to direct the police to investigate any matter, or to put questions to any person.[4]

---

[1] RCCP, *Report*, Cmnd 8092 (1981), ch. 7.

[2] See in particular the Government's White Paper, *An Independent Prosecution Service for England and Wales*, Cmnd. 9074 (1983).

[3] s. 23 of the Prosecution of Offences Act 1985.

[4] See F. Bennion, 'The Crown Prosecution Service', [1986] *Crim. LR* 4.

As we will see below, its powers might be enlarged slightly if the recommendations of the 1993 Royal Commission are implemented.

In its early days the CPS was widely criticized. The Royal Commission on Criminal Justice observes that 'it appears to have been hastily conceived and inadequately resourced'.[5] Recruitment is now reported to be much improved, and reliance on non-CPS 'agents' (i.e. solicitors in private practice, and barristers) to carry out prosecuting work in the magistrates' courts is being reduced from one-third towards the 10 per cent of cases that is considered reasonable.[6] A particular source of tension between the CPS and the police has been the preparation and delivery of files on cases: the Working Group on Pre-Trial Issues has formulated some working rules on the different types of file required and the recommended contents of the various files, with national guidelines on the time of delivery, and these are now being put into effect.[7] The CPS has recently undergone an internal restructuring, reducing the number of its areas from thirty-one to thirteen, but the effects of these changes remain to be evaluated.

2. Evidential Sufficiency

It is wrong for a person to be prosecuted if the evidence is insufficient. The essence of the wrongness lies in the protection of the innocent: if this principle is taken seriously, it should mean not merely that innocent people are not convicted, but also that innocent people should not be prosecuted. The reasons for this may be found in the dictum that 'the process is the punishment':[8] being prosecuted is an inconvenience at least, often a source of profound worry, and sometimes a considerable expense, and it may also lead to an element of stigma and loss of social esteem. The homely phrase, 'no smoke without fire' might well be applied. There are therefore sound moral reasons for not prosecuting someone against whom the evidence is insufficient. There are also good economic reasons: it is a waste of police time in compiling a full file on the case, of prosecution time in reviewing the case, and of court time in dealing with the case. It is therefore desirable in general that weak cases should be eliminated as early as possible, and it was for this purpose that the Royal Commission on Criminal Procedure recommended the introduction of a public prosecution service to provide independent review.

[5] RCCJ, *Report*, Cm. 2263 (1993), para. 5.7.   [6] Ibid., para. 5.7.
[7] Working Group on Pre-Trial Issues, *Action Plan* (2nd edn., Feb. 1993), Recommendations 1–22 and pp. 41–7.
[8] M. Feeley, *The Process is the Punishment* (1979), 200.

There are at least three major issues to be discussed before the principle of evidential sufficiency can be translated into practice. One is the test of sufficiency—what should it be? Closely intertwined with this is the second—should the test vary according to the stage the case has reached? And third, how can prosecutors be expected to assess cases on the basis of a written file? In discussing these issues, it must constantly be borne in mind that evidential sufficiency is only one of the factors relevant in prosecutions. Another is the lawfulness of the prosecution in procedural terms—have the appropriate formalities been completed? Have the time-limits been observed? Has there been a previous prosecution arising out of the incident, so as to raise considerations of double jeopardy?[9] A further factor is the policy of diversion, discussed in the previous chapter in the context of the cautioning of offenders. Thus, even if a case satisfies the test of evidential sufficiency, there may be strong reasons of public policy or, as it is termed in England and Wales, 'public interest' in favour of dealing with the case by means other than prosecution. In practice questions of evidential sufficiency and public interest often interact, but for clarity of exposition this part of the chapter is devoted chiefly to evidential sufficiency, and the issue of 'public interest' is left over until the following part.

(a) Formulating the Test of Evidential Sufficiency

Until the early 1980s the test that the police were said to apply in deciding whether the evidence was strong enough for prosecution was the 'prima facie test': is there 'evidence on the basis of which, if it were accepted, a reasonable jury or magistrates' court would be justified in convicting'?[10] This often seemed to mean that as long as there was some evidence on the main points that need to be proved the defendant ought to be brought to court to answer the charge. The test made no explicit reference to probable lines of defence, nor to the strength and credibility of the evidence. In his submission to the 1981 Royal Commission on Criminal Procedure, the then Director of Public Prosecutions denounced this test as inadequate: it was wrong, he argued, that a person could be prosecuted when an acquittal was more likely than a conviction, and the minimum standard should require that conviction is more probable than acquittal.[11] The Director's approach was commended by the Royal Commission on the basis that a lower standard would be 'both unfair to the accused and a waste of

---

[9] See the discussion below, in the context of accountability.
[10] RCCP Report, para. 8.8.
[11] Reproduced in RCCP, vol. ii: *The Law and the Procedure* (1981), app. 25.

the restricted resources of the criminal justice system'.[12] The new test was incorporated into the Attorney-General's *Criteria for Prosecution*, issued to the police in 1983. These guidelines stated that there should be no prosecution unless there were a 'reasonable prospect of conviction'. At the time this was colloquially known as the '51 per cent' test. The wording was subsequently revised, so that the first edition of the *Code for Crown Prosecutors* in 1986 referred to a 'realistic prospect of conviction', a test that remains unchanged today.

Paragraph 4 of the *Code for Crown Prosecutors* requires the Crown Prosecutor to be satisfied that there is 'admissible, substantial and reliable evidence' against the accused. As a first step towards determining the prospects of conviction, the prosecutor should be satisfied that 'there is no realistic expectation of an ordered acquittal or a successful submission in the magistrates' court of no case to answer'. The prosecutor is enjoined to have regard to 'any lines of defence which are plainly open to, or have been indicated by, the accused'. Paragraph 5 states some thirteen factors that might be relevant in evaluating the evidence, and paragraph 6 urges the prosecutor to draw on experience in assessing the likelihood of conviction.

What is the legal basis for the 'realistic prospects' test, and what are its theoretical justifications? It is clearly predictive in nature: it requires the prosecutor to assess whether, on the evidence likely to be given at the trial, a conviction is more probable than an acquittal. This includes matters such as the admissibility of the evidence and the likely defence. Beyond that, some of the key points are debatable. What amounts to a 'realistic prospect'? In linguistic terms it is not clear that this means anything more than 'reasonable prospects', which was interpreted to mean a 51 per cent probability. If the new words were intended to impose a higher standard, they do not do so clearly and unambiguously. The reference to realism seems to require the prosecutor to consider such practical matters as whether the trial will be summary or on indictment, whether certain types of case are generally easier or more difficult to bring to a conviction, and whether the courts in a particular area are known to be especially favourable or unfavourable towards certain types of case, of defendant, or of evidence. On this interpretation, a prosecutor might apply a lower standard if the case is to be heard in a magistrates' court than if it is to be heard in the Crown Court, for magistrates' courts are widely thought to be more favourable to the prosecution and certainly have a higher conviction rate.[13] A

[12] RCCP, Report, para. 8.9.
[13] Acquittal rates of 30% in magistrates' courts and 57% in the Crown Court were found in a study by J. Vennard, 'The Outcome of Contested Trials', in D. Moxon (ed.),

prosecutor in one part of the country might likewise apply a lower or higher standard if it is believed that local juries are particularly reluctant to accept police evidence, or that local magistrates appear unusually ready to convict New Age travellers. If the 'realistic prospects' test is truly predictive, judgements of this kind must be made.

Is it right that prosecutors should defer to the apparent vagaries of the courts? Much depends on the significance attributed to the local and lay element in criminal justice. Some, particularly the supporters of the jury as an institution, set great store by lay tribunals as bastions against oppression and in favour of 'common sense'. Presumably they are willing to accept inconsistencies or even consistent misapplications of the law as the price to be paid for juries in the Crown Court—and perhaps also for a lay magistracy, although there are far more critics of the representativeness of the magistracy.[14] In order to sustain the opposite ('intrinsic merits') view, one would need to establish that professionally trained prosecutors are better able to judge the strength of evidence and to apply the law to it faithfully. On this basis, one would presumably suggest that prosecutors should exercise the function of keeping cases away from the lay tribunal when they judge that the evidence is insufficient, even though they think that the tribunal might well convict, and correspondingly that prosecutors should persevere with a case when they believe that the evidence is sufficient, even though they recognize that the local court is unlikely to convict. Thus on the predictive view the disposition of the local courts sets the standard, whereas on the 'intrinsic merits' view it is a legal standard applied by various prosecutors to case files that determines decisions.

Those who believe in the supreme importance of lay adjudications would favour the predictive view. One legal difficulty, however, is that there is the possibility of the defendant appealing against a Crown Court conviction. At present the Court of Appeal has the power to quash a conviction if it is considered 'unsafe or unsatisfactory', a formula interpreted by the Court as requiring it to quash where it has a 'lurking doubt'.[15] However, the Court has been fairly reluctant to quash jury verdicts, even though there has been a slight increase in the use of this power in the last few years.[16] The 1993 Royal Commission on Criminal Justice proposes that the Court should quash a conviction

Managing Criminal Justice (1985); for the views of defendants and their lawyers, see D. Riley and J. Vennard, *Triable-Either-Way Cases: Crown Court or Magistrates' Courts*, HORS 98 (1988), and C. Hedderman and D. Moxon, *Magistrates' Court or Crown Court? Mode of Trial Decisions and Sentencing*, HORS 125 (1992), 20.

[14] See J. Spencer, *Jackson's Machinery of Justice* (8th edn., 1989), ch. IV.
[15] Criminal Appeal Act 1968, s. 2 (1) (*a*), as interpreted in *Cooper* [1969] 1 QB 267.
[16] K. Malleson, *Review of the Appeal Process*, RCCJ Research Study 17 (1993).

whenever it concludes that the verdict 'is or may be unsafe', even though the jury heard all the relevant evidence and there was no irregularity at the trial.[17] The relevance of this is that, if the predictive approach to prosecutorial review is followed to its logical conclusion, prosecutors should drop weak cases even if they do think that a local jury will convict, if they are further satisfied that such a verdict would be so unsafe that it might be successfully appealed. Now this formulation relies on a further prediction of how the Court of Appeal will exercise its powers and, although successful appeals on this ground are rare now, the Royal Commission's report may induce a change of attitude. If so, that might bring outcomes under the predictive approach closer to those on the 'intrinsic merits' approach, although cases in which local courts are prone to acquit despite strong evidence would not be affected by Court of Appeal changes, since jury acquittals are not appealable.[18]

Fidelity to law might favour the 'intrinsic merits' approach, since one might doubt whether there could be sufficient reason why a local bench or justices' clerk, or the juries of a particular neighbourhood, should be allowed to disregard the law of the country as a whole. Accordingly the American Bar Association's principle is that: 'In cases which involve a serious threat to the community, the prosecutor should not be deterred from prosecution by the fact that in his jurisdiction juries have tended to acquit persons accused of the particular kind of criminal act in question.'[19] However, this view places great weight upon the judgement of prosecutors. The sufficiency of evidence must be judged on the basis of a file, without hearing the witnesses in court, and often without knowing exactly what form the defence will take.[20] It must then be an assessment of the proper reaction of a reasonable jury or bench of magistrates, correctly directed on the law, including the rules on the burden of proof. This approach turns on the conscientious application of abstract standards rather than on a prediction. It involves the prosecutor in deciding how jurors ought to view the evidence if they apply the correct legal tests, and that will involve an assessment of the strength of the evidence on file and the application of the legal test (proof beyond reasonable doubt) to it. Experience of how courts actually take their decisions would not determine these judgements, since the prosecutor would be engaged in the clinical

---

[17] RCCJ Report, para. 10.46.

[18] The Royal Commission gives brief consideration to appeals against acquittals, but is generally against them: ibid. paras. 10.72–10.76.

[19] ABA, *Standards Relating to the Prosecution Function* (2nd edn., 1980), 3–3.9.

[20] Cf. RCCJ Report, para. 6.59, discussed in Ch. 4.2, above, recommending a limited form of defence disclosure.

application of a legal standard. Whilst there are few benchmarks against which to test any particular assessment, the prospect is that if the task is properly executed it should avoid a number of wrongful convictions. Some may contend that this arrogates too much power to prosecutors, placing them above juries and magistrates. The reply that judges are empowered to withdraw cases from juries may be thought unconvincing, since judges exercise this power after hearing at least some evidence in court, and often after hearing submissions from counsel, whereas prosecutors would be preventing such cases from ever coming to court. This, however, is the whole purpose of prosecutorial review—to weed out at an early stage cases that are unlikely to succeed[21] (or ought not to succeed). It is one thing to suggest that some 2,000 Crown Prosecutors with variable experience are unlikely to be able to perform this task consistently and reliably. It is quite another thing to argue that prosecutors ought not to filter out cases so as to prevent some miscarriages of justice from taking place.

A third alternative would be to require prosecutors to do no more than predict the reaction of a judge or bench of magistrates to the prosecution case. Thus Graham Mansfield and Jill Peay suggest that a prosecution should only be brought and continued if there is 'no rational expectation of a directed acquittal'.[22] The concept of 'rational expectation' is vague on the crucial question of probabilities, yielding no more precise a quantification than 'reasonable' or 'realistic'. But the idea of focusing on the judge's decision, on a submission of no case, does at least connect the prosecutor's test with an established legal test within the trial process. This argument would gain in attraction if the *Galbraith* test[23] were to be overturned. At present a judge should not accede to a submission of no case if the strength or weakness of the prosecution case depends on the view to be taken of a witness's reliability. This means that a judge may have to allow a case to go to the jury, even though he or she is convinced that it would be unsafe to convict on the prosecution evidence—the test that the Court of Appeal should later apply in deciding whether to uphold or quash the conviction. This anomaly has been criticized many times,[24] and the Royal Commission recommends the reversal of *Galbraith* so that a case may be stopped if the judge 'takes the view that the prosecution evidence is demonstrably unsafe or unsatisfactory or too weak to be allowed to go

[21] Home Office, *An Independent Prosecution Service*, 14.

[22] G. Manfield and J. Peay, *The Director of Public Prosecutions* (1985), 54.

[23] *Galbraith* (1981) 73 Cr. App. R. 124.

[24] See Manfield and Peay, *The Director of Public Prosecutions*, 16–21; B. Block, C. Corbett, and J. Peay, *Ordered and Directed Acquittals in the Crown Court*, RCCJ Research Study 15 (1993), 9–10.

to the jury'.[25] This recommendation may be interpreted as a blow against the supreme importance of the jury and in favour of the prevention of miscarriages of justice. The effect would be to align the third alternative with the second if *Galbraith* were reversed; at present, the third alternative is distinct, because *Galbraith* established a lower threshold for allowing a case to go to the jury.

Thus far the discussion has focused on differences between levels of tribunal (Crown Court, magistrates' court) and on local differences in propensity to convict or acquit. It is also worth mentioning differences according to types of case. For example, it is well known that it is difficult to obtain convictions of police officers charged with forms of assault (and, some would argue, generally difficult to persuade juries to convict police officers).[26] How should the CPS react to this? If they adopt a predictive approach, they should presumably discontinue any prosecution of a police officer that does not rely on highly cogent evidence. This may be seen as applying a higher test, or it may be argued that attainment of the 'realistic prospects' test takes far more evidence in this type of case. If, however, the 'intrinsic merits' approach is adopted, a uniform standard would be applied to all cases, irrespective of the varying practices of the courts. Both approaches may bring politically unwelcome consequences: the predictive approach would lead to the discontinuance of many cases against police officers, which might damage public confidence in the system if interpreted as showing favour to the police, whereas the 'intrinsic merits' approach could be expected to lead to many acquittals of police officers, which might damage public confidence if interpreted as showing a lack of competence in the prosecution service.

These remarks about public confidence lead to a final point in this part of the discussion. Some public criticism of the CPS has alleged or implied that the criminal justice system is being undermined by the dropping of so many cases. The foundations of this view probably lie in the concept of a trial as a public exercise in communication.[27] The suggestion then would be that the best arrangement, from the public's point of view, is to bring to court all cases in which there is prima-facie evidence that the defendant committed the crime charged. This would have the benefit of allowing matters to be aired in a public forum: it is far better for the victim, the accused, and the public at large that the

[25] RCCJ Report, para. 4.41.
[26] See Mansfield and Peay, *The Director of Public Prosecutions*, 200 and n. 13; cf. G. Williams, 'Letting off the Guilty and Prosecuting the Innocent', [1985] *Crim. LR* 115; with P. Worboys, 'Convicting the Right Persons on the Right Evidence', [1985] *Crim. LR* 764.
[27] See generally R. A. Duff, *Trials and Punishments* (1986).

matter is resolved in the open rather than behind the closed doors of the CPS offices, with all the suspicion and misunderstandings that might create. This coincides fairly closely with the understanding of the principle of legality in continental Europe.[28] However, several countries now allow wide exceptions to the principle. There is a need to justify inflicting on victims the anxiety and stresses of giving evidence in court if there is no more prospect of a conviction than an acquittal. The same applies to inflicting on defendants the anxiety and other costs of being prosecuted in such circumstances. There is also a need to justify the economic cost of trying more cases, especially disputed ones. If they are cases that the judge or magistrates should dismiss anyway, does the social and communicative function of trials really constitute sufficient reason to bring them to court? Surely the way forward is to encourage the CPS to give reasons for dropping cases which are properly linked to the *Code for Crown Prosecutors*, and to take particular care in ensuring that victims, the police, and (where appropriate) the public at large receive proper explanations.[29]

(b) Evidential Sufficiency and the Stages of the Criminal Process

The *Code for Crown Prosecutors* states a single test of evidential sufficiency: whether there is a 'realistic prospect of conviction'. This suggests that prosecutors are expected to apply the same standard from the first moment when a case file comes into their possession until just before the trial. Immediately a difficulty is apparent. In many cases prosecutors receive a file for the first time just before remand proceedings are due to begin. This may be the morning after an arrest: the police may believe that they have sufficient evidence to charge the defendant,[30] they keep him in custody overnight, and he appears at court the next morning. Is the prosecutor expected to examine the file to see whether, at that stage, the weight of the evidence is sufficient to yield a realistic prospect of conviction? It is easy to see that this will often be difficult in practice. There will be the pressure of other cases to be dealt with—even under the recommended practice, which is that

[28] See the discussion in Ch. 5.2.

[29] See the Working Group on Pre-Trial Issues, *Action Plan*, 11, and now the Crown Prosecution Service, *Statement of Purpose and Values* (1993), 9–11, committing the CPS to giving fuller information about its policies.

[30] Under the PACE, Code of Practice C states that an investigating officer should bring a suspect before a custody officer if he or she believes that there is sufficient evidence for a prosecution to succeed. The PACE imposes a limit of six hours on police questioning, but provides that the police may request certain extensions in limited circumstances: s. 41.

the police should have the papers in the hands of prosecutors at least one hour before proceedings begin.[31] There will rarely be time to listen to any tapes of interviews, and so the police summary will dominate. Moreover, the police may not yet have been able to trace all the witnesses; a forensic report may be awaited, etc. However, the question of principle is whether it is right to apply the same test at this stage and, indeed, at all the stages.

There can be little doubt that a case file may change its complexion and its strength between the initial charge and the day of the trial. Perhaps there should be a series of different tests of evidential sufficiency, based on the purpose and significance of each decision. This may be particularly appropriate at the stage of remand: a defendant is at risk of losing at least one week's liberty and possibly three weeks' liberty, that time probably to be spent in an overcrowded local prison with poor facilities, away from family, friends, employment (if any), and without unrestricted access to legal advisers. One week's remand in custody is a serious deprivation, and it should not be inflicted unless there are good grounds. As we shall see in Chapter 7, a magistrates' court must determine whether remand in custody is justifiable, and one of the considerations deemed relevant by the law is the strength of the evidence. Yet magistrates rarely inquire into the strength of the prosecution evidence, let alone the defence case: they tend to take it on trust from the prosecutor, even when remanding in custody. In many cases the prosecutor may take it on trust from the police. This is unsatisfactory: it reduces prosecutorial review and judicial scrutiny to almost vanishing point.

The serious consequences of the remand decision make it imperative that there be some review of the quantum of evidence at this stage. Should it be the 'realistic prospect of conviction' test? How could anyone tell, at this early stage, whether the prospect is realistic? The evidence may be incomplete, the line of defence unknown, and so on. That test is simply inappropriate, and if it is the test that now governs prosecutors they must be ignoring it or misapplying it in some cases. Apart from the problem of time pressures before the remand court sits to hear 'overnight' cases, the question of principle concerns the test to be applied in such a review. If there is little sense in referring to the prospects of conviction at this stage, to what should the reference be at the first remand? The obvious answer is, 'sufficient incriminating evidence to justify a remand in custody', but that hardly moves the argument forwards. Would it be appropriate to have a test of 'evidence

<hr>

[31] Working Group on Pre-Trial Issues, *Action Plan*, Recommendation 9, p. 39.

sufficient, if given in court and not contradicted, to justify the case being left to the jury or heard in full by a magistrates' court'? The middle clause of this proposed test confines the prosecutor's attention to the case for the prosecution, and that is a weakness. If the defendant has a plausible defence (e.g. self-defence), would it not be right for the prosecutor to take it into account and wrong for a defendant to be at risk of a custodial remand? Surely the answer should be in the affirmative. And yet what is known about the investigation methods of the police and the composition of files tends to suggest that little prominence is typically given to the line of defence, let alone to evidence that favours it, since the primary concern is to construct a winning case.[32] Unless the defendant or his advocate presses the matter, the prosecutor may sometimes learn little about the probable line of defence. The case file itself may be scrutinized in respect of the elements of the crime charged, but the production of some evidence may have to be taken largely on trust at this stage. This is hardly satisfactory, particularly if the defendant's liberty (i.e. remand in custody) is at stake.

At a second remand, which may be up to three weeks later, matters may be different. A defendant in custody is entitled to expect release if the police have still not traced a key witness, for example, but a more formidable problem is presented by delays in the arrival of a laboratory report. If this concerns an item vital to the strength of the case, such as a DNA sample, should the prosecutor continue to make representations to the court in favour of custody, on the basis of the strength of the evidence? In practice the prosecutor may be influenced by such matters as whether or not the defendant has previous convictions, and by other circumstantial elements of the case. If the charge is a very serious one, such as rape or wounding, does that tilt the balance in favour of public protection or should it strengthen the need to respect the defendant's rights? The temptation to jump to the former conclusion was criticized in Chapter 3, above.[33] To be remanded in custody for a very serious offence is a great slur, quite apart from the deprivations of custody. Yet, as we will see in Chapter 7 below, the question of protecting past and possible future victims must be confronted.

A fresh way of dealing with these difficult and sensitive decisions must be found. One approach would be to alter the procedures rather than the substantive criteria, by introducing increasing accountability. The law might require, at least before a second or subsequent remand hearing of a case in which evidence was still awaited, and especially in custody cases, that the case be reviewed by a Branch Crown Prosecutor

---

[32] M. McConville, A. Sanders, and R. Leng, *The Case for the Prosecution* (1991), 76.
[33] Ch. 3.4.

or someone of similar rank. It might be preferable, alternatively or additionally, to require a limited amount of prosecution disclosure so as to enable a meaningful defence challenge in court. When, eventually, the full file is passed by the police to the Crown Prosecution Service, the 'realistic prospect' test or its successor must be applied. However, what may appear to be a realistic prospect at this stage may change subsequently. If 'full committal' proceedings take place, whether at the request of one side or the other, the prosecutor may learn more about the witnesses and the strength of the case. Even if the magistrates decide to commit the defendant for trial, the prosecutor may take the view that there is not a realistic prospect of conviction. Because the test for committal for trial is lower than the evidential test applied by prosecutors,[34] a prosecutor might decide that the case should be dropped even though it has been committed for trial. There is only the power to do this before the magistrates announce their intention to commit the case for trial: after that, the prosecutor has no power to drop it until the day of the trial, when no evidence may be offered.[35] If weaknesses become apparent, why should discontinuance of the case be delayed?

There are two ways of dealing with this. One is to abolish committal proceedings, as the Royal Commission on Criminal Justice recommends.[36] They are cumbersome, and are not necessarily the most effective way of challenging the decision to prosecute. The Royal Commission proposes that most cases should be committed on the papers, as now, but that it should be open to the defence to submit that there is no case to answer. In these circumstances a decision should be made on the papers (i.e. without hearing witnesses) by a stipendiary magistrate in either-way cases or by a Crown Court judge in indictable cases.[37] The efficacy of this filter remains to be tested, but at least it preserves the principle that a decision to proceed against a person should be open to challenge, thereby reaffirming the importance of keeping weak cases out of court and of not putting defendants through the anxiety of a trial without good reason. Another, independent, way of dealing with the problem of the prosecutor's limited powers would

[34] Magistrates may commit a case for trial if there is evidence on all the essential elements, and it is not so unreliable that no reasonable tribunal could safely conflict on it: see the Practice Direction at [1962] 1 All ER 448. For discussion of this Direction in relation to the *Galbraith* test, see Mansfield and Peay, *The Director of Public Prosecutions*, 18–23.

[35] See the criticism of this anomaly by B. Block, C. Corbett, and J. Peay, 'Ordered and Directed Acquittals in the Crown Court: A Time of Change?', [1993] *Crim. LR* 95.

[36] RCCJ Report, para. 6.26; the same recommendation was made by the RCCP Report and the Fraud Trials Committee, *Report* (1986).

[37] RCCJ Report, para. 6.27–6.29.

be to extend those powers. In their research report for the Royal Commission, Block, Corbett, and Peay found that cases which appeared watertight at committal might become unsafe subsequently.[38] All that the prosecutor can do is to wait for the trial and then inform the judge that no evidence is being offered against the defendant; the judge is then bound to instruct the jury to acquit.[39] They proposed that the CPS should be empowered to discontinue a case at any time until the beginning of a Crown Court trial, and the Royal Commission recommends this.[40]

At or just before a Crown Court trial, the prosecution can expect to receive advice from counsel. The findings of Block, Corbett, and Peay from the 100 cases they studied led them to criticize the performance of counsel. In only eighteen of the cases did counsel offer advice to the CPS before trial (usually, to discontinue or to seek further evidence), and in eight of these cases the advice was either incomplete or inadequate, neglecting weaknesses that were soon spotted by others.[41] In many other cases counsel failed to offer any advice, even though the judge directed an acquittal and a CPS assessor, reviewing the case as part of the research, regarded its weaknesses as foreseeable.[42] The Royal Commission recommends changes in the system of allocation of briefs within chambers, so as to ensure that counsel receive briefs in good time and may discharge the duty to advise the CPS on the case before it reaches court.[43] In view of the criminal Bar's culture of last-minute preparation, it will take a considerable change of attitude to bring about genuine improvements in this sphere.

(c) The Assessment of Files by Prosecutors

Those who have conducted research into the prosecution system report that prosecutors place heavy reliance on the police—both explicitly, when deciding on the likelihood that a witness will 'come up to proof' in court and say what is already in the written statement, and implicitly, in that case files are constructed by the police and therefore

[38] Block, Corbett, and Peay, *Ordered and Directed Acquittals*, 76.
[39] *Grafton* (1993) 96 Cr. App. R. 156.
[40] RCCJ Report, para. 5.37. It should be added that the principle of continuous review of cases works both ways: 'if a case is stopped because of insufficient evidence, but further significant evidence becomes available at a later date, it is sometimes possible for the police (or other investigating body) to resubmit the case for us to consider again.' Crown Prosecution Service, *Statement of Purpose and Values*, 6.
[41] Block, Corbett, and Peay, *Ordered and Directed Acquittals*, 37–9.
[42] Ibid. 678–70.
[43] RCCJ Report, para. 5.39.

some elements may be emphasized and others omitted.[44] The English prosecutor has no power to order the police to interview different people, or to ask further questions of the defendant or other witnesses. The CPS may put a request to the police for further investigations, but it seems that in the past this has sometimes been a source of friction between the two organizations. The Royal Commission recommends that there be a formal system of consultation at a high level, to resolve disagreements of this kind.[45]

The Director of Public Prosecutions has a statutory function of giving advice to police forces, as he or she considers appropriate, on matters relating to criminal offences.[46] In practice it is the police who take the initiative. Research undertaken in the early days of the CPS found that the police asked for prior advice in only fifty-one out of 711 cases.[47] Recent research suggests that the police ask the CPS for prior advice in an average of 4 per cent of cases, chiefly in order to resolve doubts about the sufficiency of evidence.[48] However, practices vary and in some areas advice is sought in as many as 14 per cent of cases. The Royal Commission proposes the formulation of guidelines to ensure that advice is sought consistently in certain types of case, particularly those that are serious, complex, or sensitive.[49]

How reliable are prosecutors at assessing whether or not cases will succeed? This question cannot be answered unless there is an agreed criterion of success. One possible criterion would be the discontinuance rate—arguing that the more cases the CPS discontinue, the better they are doing their job. The rate appears to have risen in the years since the introduction of the CPS, and in 1992-3 stood at 13.5 per cent:[50] this included cases withdrawn at the Crown Court on the day of the hearing, but most of these would be cases at magistrates' courts discontinued under the statutory powers in section 23 of the Prosecution of Offences Act 1985. However, research has also found that very few cases are discontinued before there has been a court hearing: most are discontinued at the second or a subsequent hearing, and many others between first and second court appearances.[51] The Royal Commission recommends that the CPS should ensure that cases are discontinued as early as possible.[52] It would be dangerous, none

[44] Mansfield and Peay, *The Director of Public Prosecutions*, 87–91; McConville, Sanders, and Leng, *Case for the Prosecution*, 76.
[45] RCCJ Report, para. 5.26.   [46] Prosecution of Offences Act 1985, s. 3 (2).
[47] McConville, Sanders, and Leng, *Case for the Prosecution*, ch. 7.
[48] Research by Moxon and Crisp, reported in RCCJ Report, para. 5.17.
[49] Ibid., para. 5.18.
[50] Crown Prosecution Service, *Annual Report 1992–93*, 18.
[51] Moxon and Crisp, quoted by RCCJ Report, para. 5.34.   [52] Ibid., para. 3.35.

the less, to accept the discontinuance rate as a barometer of CPS effectiveness. Cases may be discontinued on either evidential or 'public interest' grounds, and in both cases the police may begin to anticipate CPS decisions and drop cases themselves—what point is there in preparing all the papers if the CPS appear likely to discontinue it? Indeed, if the CPS are used more frequently for advice prior to charge, the rate for discontinuance on evidential grounds should be very low indeed. The same should apply to discontinuance on 'public interest' grounds, since the police cautioning criteria mirror those in the *Code for Crown Prosecutors*.

Another possible criterion of CPS success might be the overall acquittal rate. However, not merely is it difficult to predict the persuasiveness of the evidence given in court and the response of the jury or magistrates to it, but there may be limited knowledge of the defence case. Unless there is some system of defence disclosure, such as that recommended by the Royal Commission,[53] the prosecution will lack the information needed to assess this aspect of the case. If the predictive approach to the sufficiency of evidence is adopted, prosecutors would be expected to take some account of the known propensities of local juries or magistrates. If the 'intrinsic merits' approach is adopted, it would be quite wrong to assess CPS performance by the numbers of jury acquittals.

The criterion of success most frequently adopted is the proportion of acquittals by judge (as distinct from jury) in the Crown Court. If a case is withdrawn from the jury by the judge, this may be taken to suggest that the case should not have been allowed to proceed so far. The argument here, however, is rather involved and ultimately unconvincing. In the first place, the category of 'acquittals by judge' includes both directed acquittals (where the judge rules that the prosecution has failed to establish a case to answer) and ordered acquittals (where the prosecution decides to offer no evidence against the accused). It is debatable whether ordered acquittals are properly regarded as failures of the prosecution. Many of them stem from a reassessment of the case by CPS or counsel, resulting in a decision that the evidence is insufficient to justify pursuing it. This may be regarded as good prosecutorial practice: as the *Code for Crown Prosecutors* puts it, 'it is important that cases be kept under continuous review, not least because the emergence of evidence or information previously unknown to the Crown Prosecutor may sometimes cast doubt on the propriety of the initial decision to proceed'.[54] In some cases it is arguable that the

[53] Moxon and Crisp, quoted by RCCJ Report, para. 6.59; discussed in Ch. 4.2, above.
[54] *Code for Crown Prosecutors* (1992), para. 10.

case ought to have been discontinued earlier,[55] but, as we have seen, the law does not now permit a prosecutor to discontinue between committal for trial and the beginning of a Crown Court trial. These are therefore cases of prosecutorial success rather than failure. Other cases may be discontinued, not because of any inherent weakness, but simply because a key witness fails to turn up at the trial (and, in some cases, the judge declines an adjournment).[56] It is doubtful whether these should be regarded as either successes or failures.[57] Finally, about one-fifth of ordered acquittals are instigated by judges who, having read the papers, inform prosecuting counsel that it is unwise to proceed.[58] The CPS cannot claim credit for discontinuing those cases.

There might seem to be a much stronger argument in favour of regarding cases which end in a directed acquittal as prosecutorial features. After all, the judge is directing the jury, at the close of the prosecution case or even before, that the evidence is so weak that 'a jury properly directed could not properly convict on it'.[59] However, researchers have argued that some of these cases are prosecutorial failures and others are not. To be more precise, some were foreseeable and therefore should have been foreseen. Others were unforeseeable and ought not to be regarded as failures. Block, Corbett, and Peay examined 100 cases in which an acquittal was either ordered or directed. On their assessment,

although fewer than half of ordered acquittals were considered definitely or possibly foreseeable, three quarters of directed acquittals were so classified. This supports our view, derived from the study, that directed acquittals result largely from weak cases that should have been discontinued, whereas ordered acquittals result largely from unforeseeable circumstances.[60]

Noting the qualification in the word 'largely', these findings confirm that in general the weak cases ought to have been recognized earlier. The Crown Court study for the Royal Commission tends to support the findings.[61] However, as McConville, Sanders, and Leng argue, some cases that are so weak as to justify dropping are pursued in order to

[55] See generally the research of Block, Corbett, and Peay, *Ordered and Directed Acquittals*, 6–7.

[56] Ibid. 76; see also A. Sanders, 'Personal Violence and Public Order: The Prosecution of Domestic Violence in England and Wales', (1988) 16 *International Journal of the Sociology of Law* 359, at 369.

[57] RCCJ Report, para. 6.32, makes proposals to avoid this.

[58] Block, Corbett, and Peay, *Ordered and Directed Acquittals*, 39–40.

[59] *Galbraith* (1981) 73 Cr. App. R. 124, at 127.

[60] Block, Corbett, and Peay, 'Ordered and Directed Acquittals' 100.

[61] M. Zander and P. Henderson, *Crown Court Study*, RCCJ Research Study 19 (1993), 184–8.

placate the police, and a few of them go through all the stages and result in a conviction—apparently vindicating the idea of 'running' a doubtful case.[62] In truth these cases merely go to show the limited predictability of trial by jury. Just as some strong cases may be thrown out by juries, so some weak cases may be accepted by juries. Sometimes the explanation will lie in the apparent cogency of the evidence as it comes out in court, and sometimes the mood and disposition of the jurors will make the difference.

There is therefore no clear benchmark of the success or failure of prosecutorial predictions. The proportion of all acquittals that are ordered or directed by judges increased from 42 per cent in 1980 to 58 per cent in 1990, and in 1990 over two-thirds of those were ordered acquittals compared with one-half in 1980.[63] Whether this reflects on the effectiveness of the Crown Prosecution Service, and if so exactly how, is difficult to determine. Moreover, the rates have always varied considerably from circuit to circuit. Research suggests that dispassionate scrutineers could identify weak cases among those that ended in an acquittal by judge (some 22 per cent in the survey by Block, Corbett, and Peay were regarded as foreseeably flawed in the opinion of a trained prosecutor).[64] It seems likely that prosecutors tend to continue these cases through a mixture of inertia, lack of alternative information, lack of competence, and a desire not to be seen as letting the police down. The power of the police over the information on which the CPS must base their prosecutorial review brings them considerable influence. By including some matters, excluding others, and using certain phraseology, the police can exert some more or less subtle control.[65] Even without such selectivity, prosecutors are reliant on the police for assessments of the credibility of key witnesses, since the police will have questioned them whereas the prosecutor will have only the papers (and, possibly, a tape recording).[66] In their study of child victims, Jane Morgan and Lucia Zedner found that: 'prosecutors rely heavily on the expertise of the specialist police officers who interview children alleging abuse to provide an indication of the child's credibility as a witness.'[67] Similar reliance is recognized by the CPS in its state-

---

[62] McConville, Sanders, and Leng, *Case for the Prosecution*, ch. 8.
[63] Block, Corbett, and Peay, *Ordered and Directed Acquittals*, 12.
[64] Block, Corbett, and Peay, 'Ordered and Directed Acquittals', 105.
[65] McConville, Sanders, and Leng, *Case for the Prosecution*, ch. 7.
[66] The Royal Commission of 1993 recommends that 'the CPS lawyers handling the case should meet victims and key witnesses before the trial whenever there is particular reason for checking any part of the evidence they are likely to give': RCCJ Report, para. 5.49.
[67] J. Morgan and L. Zedner, *Child Victims* (1992), 122.

ment of policy on 'Domestic Violence'.[68] In addition, prosecutorial inertia, or 'prosecution momentum', is a phenomenon well documented by researchers: once a case has been charged in a particular way, the tendency is to let it run as it stands, even though the prosecutor might have taken a different approach if dealing with the case afresh.[69] This may be one aspect of police–prosecutor relations in the hybrid English system, and another example of the CPS not wishing to be seen to let the police down. This would be a natural, if not entirely professional, response to the necessity to work closely with others whose esteem and co-operation is desired for other decisions in the process.[70]

In the work of the Serious Fraud Office the pressures are likely to be somewhat different. The SFO has its own investigators and its own lawyers, and may be said to be in a much more dominant position *vis-à-vis* the police than the CPS is. On the other hand its record of successful prosecutions is not high, and Michael Levi argues that many prosecutions go ahead despite foreseeable weaknesses in the case.[71] Greater judicial involvement before the commencement of the trial, and better debriefing after trials so as to learn the lessons of acquittals, are among the measures he proposes.

3. The Public Interest

No similar survey of decision-making by the various regulatory agencies has been carried out, although at least one of them (the Post Office) was stated to be using the 'reasonable prospects of conviction' test rather than the 'prima-facie evidence' test even before the Attorney-General's Guidelines on prosecution were issued in 1983.[72] What is most evident about these agencies, as we saw in the previous chapter, is that many of them tend to have a rather different conception of the public interest from that apparently held, at least formerly,

---

[68] 'A Statement of Prosecution Policy: Domestic Violence' (CPS, 1993), annexed to the Government Reply to the Third Report from the Home Affairs Committee, Session 1992–3, *Domestic Violence* (1993), 18–23.

[69] Mansfield and Peay, *The Director of Public Relations*, 47–8, 87; McConville, Sanders, and Leng, *Case for the Prosecution*, 142 and ch. 7 generally. The Royal Commission considered whether this might be avoided by requiring the police to consult the CPS before laying any charges, but regarded this as too cumbersome: RCCJ Report, para. 5.21.

[70] Cf. K. Hawkins, 'The Use of Legal Discretion', in K. Hawkins (ed.), *The Uses of Discretion* (1992), 29.

[71] M. Levi, *The Investigation, Prosecution and Trial of Serious Fraud*, RCCJ Research Study 14 (1993).

[72] See K. W. Lidstone, R. Hogg, and F. Sutcliffe, *Prosecution by Private Individuals and Non-police Agencies*, RCCP Research Study 10 (1981), 49.

by the police and prosecutors. For many agencies, the primary goal is to secure compliance with the standards laid down by law. This might take time to achieve, and the approach may be termed accommodative or conciliatory—using persuasion, education, and negotiation as the principal methods, and leaving the power to prosecute as a background threat which is rarely invoked.[73]

This is not the fundamental orientation of the Crown Prosecution Service, save in respect of juveniles.[74] It is noticeable that paragraph 7 of the *Code for Crown Prosecutors* is phrased so as to suggest that a prosecution should only be brought if 'the public interest requires' it, and that the bulk of paragraph 8 outlines factors that tend against prosecution. However, the opening section of paragraph 8 now elaborates some factors in favour of prosecution, bringing the Code more into line with reality.[75] The general principle is that 'the graver the offence, the less likelihood there will be that the public interest will allow of a disposal less than prosecution'. Paragraph 8 goes on to identify two of the factors that have a bearing on the gravity of an offence. One is 'where the victim has suffered significant harm or loss',[76] and the other is that 'a clear racial motivation will be regarded as an aggravating factor'. The range of aggravating factors should be as wide here as it is at the sentencing stage, including such matters as offences against the elderly, offences against the very young, offences against the police and others executing official duties, offences committed in breach of trust, and so forth.[77] Later in paragraph 8 comes a definite statement on one class of offence: 'sexual assaults upon children should always be regarded seriously, as should offences against adults, such as rape, which amount to gross personal violation.'

The rest of paragraph 8 lists factors that tend against prosecution. Several of the provisions seem to be related to the notion of proportionality, since they refer to types of case in which prosecution and sentence might be an inappropriately severe response to the offence

[73] For general discussions, see A. Reiss, 'Selecting Strategies of Social Control over Organisational Life', in K. Hawkins and J. Thomas (eds.), *Enforcing Regulation* (1984); G. Richardson, 'Strict Liability for Regulatory Crime: The Empirical Research', [1987] *Crim. LR* 295; B. Hutter, 'Variations in Regulatory Enforcement Styles', (1989) 11 *Law and Policy* 153.

[74] Cf. *Code for Crown Prosecutors*, para. 21: 'The objective should be to divert juveniles from court wherever possible.'

[75] This is evident in the latest issue of the Code, dated Jan. 1992, and should be compared with the version issued when the Service began in 1986.

[76] It is not clear whether this is merely a statement of the obvious, or whether it is connected with the point that, unless a prosecution is brought, no enforceable compensation order can be made. See above, Ch. 5.4.

[77] For discussion, see A. Ashworth, *Sentencing and Criminal Justice* (1992), ch. 5.

committed. Where the offence is so minor that a court is only likely to impose 'a purely nominal penalty', prosecution might not be 'in the public interest'.[78] What sentences should be regarded as 'purely nominal' is not clear, but presumably an absolute discharge, conditional discharge, or bind-over would fall within this description, as might small fines. These would be cases in which the harmfulness of the conduct was relatively low. There would also be cases where the offender's culpability was low, including some cases where the offender is elderly or suffering from mental illness. These, then, are cases lying towards the foot of any scale of offence-seriousness. The argument is that many of them do not warrant the bringing of formal proceedings, and might be dealt with more appropriately by a police caution, an informal warning, or no action at all. The theory of desert or proportionality,[79] combined with the established finding that the process of being prosecuted may itself involve inconvenience, anxiety, or pain,[80] supports the proposition that a line should be drawn beneath which prosecution as a response is disproportionately strong.

In practice, the positioning of the line appears to be influenced by matters such as expenditure constraints and beliefs in effectiveness. This is evident from the statement in paragraph 8 (i) of the Code that prosecutors should 'weigh the likely penalty with the likely length and cost of proceedings'. This means, in effect, that non-serious cases should not be allowed to proceed in the Crown Court, where trial by judge and jury costs a great deal of public money. At present the law allows any person charged with theft to elect to go for trial in the Crown Court, no matter how low the value of the goods allegedly stolen.[81] Thus a person charged with theft of goods worth £10, and who is prosecuted rather than cautioned (perhaps because of the number of previous convictions), may choose Crown Court trial. The prosecutor, applying the Code, would then reassess the decision to prosecute. If it seemed likely that the penalty would be fairly low, the case should be dropped. But if it seemed likely that the court would regard the case as serious enough for a community sentence or even a custodial sentence, the case might be pursued.

The wording of the Code is predictive, referring here and elsewhere to the 'likely' penalty on conviction. In this respect, then, the Code is not uncertain as between a predictive and an 'intrinsic merits'

[78] *Code for Crown Prosecutors*, para. 8 (i).

[79] For discussion of that theory, see A. von Hirsch, *Censure and Sanctions* (1993) and, more briefly, A. von Hirsch and A. Ashworth, *Principled Sentencing* (1993), ch. 4.

[80] Feeley, *The Process is the Punishment*; M. McConville and J. Baldwin, *Prosecution, Courts and Conviction* (1981), 48-50, 69–71; RCCP Report, para. 8.7.

[81] For discussion, see Ch. 8.4, below.

approach: prosecutors are expected to concern themselves with what the courts in their area are likely to do in practice. Prosecutors are not being encouraged to apply the law of sentencing themselves, to determine what penalty ought to be given by the court, and then to decide whether or not to discontinue. The 'intrinsic merits' approach would certainly be more difficult to apply in this sphere. For many of these crimes in the middle and lower ranges there are few guidelines or other parameters for sentencing, and English prosecutors are less experienced in sentencing matters than on evidential sufficiency. On the other hand, such is the local variation in the use of sentencing powers[82] that there is good reason to strive for greater consistency. A difficulty with both the predictive and the 'intrinsic merits' approaches is that prosecutors may lack the necessary information. If only the police file is available to the prosecutor, this may not deal with various factors likely to be raised in mitigation of sentence. The police may not only regard this as none of their concern, but the gathering of such information may require extra time and effort. Sometimes a defence solicitor may contact the CPS with information that might lead to a decision to discontinue. One formal initiative has been the creation of Public Interest Case Assessment units in certain areas, staffed by probation officers. The aim is to select cases where there might be personal or other circumstances that might justify the discontinuance of a prosecution on 'public interest' grounds, and to seek information that could assist the Crown Prosecution Service in taking their decisions.[83] These schemes are in their infancy and have yet to be evaluated, but they stem from the important point that decisions on certain factors cannot be taken properly in the absence of information about those factors.

Among the other matters stated by the Code to be relevant to decisions not to prosecute are mitigating factors that do not bear on the seriousness of the offence. There are factors personal to the offender which make it likely that prosecution and conviction will have a disproportionately severe effect: old age, youth (not merely juveniles but also young adults), infirmity, mental disorder, and cases where there is 'a medical report to the effect that the strain of criminal proceedings may lead to a considerable worsening of the accused's mental health'.[84] The justification for tipping the scales against prosecution in these cases is presumably some notion of equality of impact, at least to the extent

[82] See now Home Office, *Cost of Proceedings* (1993).

[83] See A. J. Brown and D. Crisp, 'Diverting Cases from Prosecution in the Public Interest', (1992) 32 *Home Office Research Bulletin* 7.

[84] Para. 8 (v) of the *Code for Crown Prosecutors* (Jan. 1992) includes detailed guidance on how to deal with such cases.

that it would be unfair to continue with a prosecution if that would have an impact on the particular offender far greater than is warranted by the offence.[85] However, the Code also provides that the scales would be tipped in favour of prosecution if the offence 'is of such gravity that it is impossible to overlook'. A similar approach is taken to 'stale' offences, committed more than three years before the probable date of trial: stale offences might not be worth prosecuting, particularly if the defendant has not contributed to the delay, but graver allegations make this factor less powerful. Paragraph 8 of the Code also refers to the relevance of the victim's wishes, an issue discussed separately in Section 4 below.

Research into decision-making by the Crown Prosecution Service raises questions about the effective pursuit of the Code's principles. Thus, in their research in the early years of the Crown Prosecution Service, McConville, Sanders, and Leng found little evidence of any reconsideration of police decisions to prosecute, except in fixed categories of case such as 'shoplifting cases [involving] people over 65 and menopausal women'.[86] The earlier conclusion of Sanders, on the basis of his research in the prosecuting solicitors' departments of some police forces before the advent of the CPS, had been that the then guidelines for prosecutors were being used as flexible tools to justify decisions based on other operational grounds.[87] McConville, Sanders, and Leng go further and suggest that the CPS have been willing to persevere with some prosecutions that ought to be dropped on 'public interest' grounds, simply in order to placate certain victims such as local businesses.[88] However, a more recent survey by Moxon and Crisp suggests that, of the national average of 11 per cent of cases discontinued, about one-third are discontinued on 'public interest' grounds. Of these, nearly one-half are discontinued because the offence is thought to be trivial or a nominal penalty seems likely. The complainant's reluctance to proceed accounts for 13 per cent, and mental illness or stress for a further 10 per cent.[89] In a high proportion of cases the evidential and 'public interest' grounds may interact and, for example, there may be a greater willingness to drop fairly minor cases whereas more serious charges might be pursued despite some weakness in the evidence. Also critical to decision-making is the flow of information,

---

[85] For discussion of this principle in sentencing, see Ashworth, *Sentencing and Criminal Justice*, 134–47 and 179–82.

[86] McConville, Sanders, and Leng, *Case for the Prosecution*, ch. 7.

[87] A. Sanders, 'Prosecution Decisions and the Attorney-General's Guidelines', [1985] *Crim. LR* 4, at 17.

[88] McConville, Sanders, and Leng, *Case for the Prosecution*, 114.

[89] As reported by RCCJ Report, para. 5.36.

and the introduction of some PICA schemes shows a realization that some of the information needed for these decisions is unlikely to be found in case files.

If it is true that the CPS are discontinuing more cases on 'public interest' grounds, what does this say about their relationship with the police? The criteria for police cautioning are intended to be closely similar to those in the *Code for Crown Prosecutors*. It could therefore be argued that many of the discontinued cases should already have been cautioned by the police, and that they are 'police failures' rather than 'CPS successes'. The trend is too recent to have been examined by research, but it raises intriguing possibilities. Few police officers are likely to want to do all the paperwork for a case file if they believe that it is likely to be discontinued when the CPS see it, and one might therefore expect the discontinuance rate to decrease once the police have the measure of CPS practices—assuming that those practices are consistent, and are not resented by the police.

A related question concerns the rate at which the courts give absolute and conditional discharges: since these might be regarded as nominal measures, one might expect the percentage to have declined in the years since the introduction of the Crown Prosecution Service, as more and more cases are discontinued on public interest grounds. The statistics show that the opposite has happened: between 1986 and 1991 the percentage of indictable offences resulting in a discharge (either absolute or conditional) increased for all age-groups, an example being the rises from 10 to 12 per cent for adult males and from 24 to 28 per cent for adult females.[90] Again, the interpretation of this trend is not straightforward. It may simply reflect sentencing constraints felt by the courts, for example the view that discharges have to be granted to certain offenders because no other suitable measure is available. In theory, however, since the *Code for Crown Prosecutors* urges the discontinuance of cases likely to result merely in a nominal measure, the CPS should adjust its practices accordingly.

This discussion of the role of the Crown Prosecution Service in terms of prosecutorial review cannot, it seems, be transferred directly to the role of the regulatory agencies. They bring relatively few prosecutions, and it is assumed that considerations of public interest have already been taken into account by the reluctance to prosecute save in clear and necessary cases. However, those who have conducted research into these agencies have pointed out that some prosecutions are brought readily, in response to a single incident that has received pub-

---

[90] *Criminal Statistics of England and Wales* (1991), table 7.7.

licity (perhaps through deaths, serious injuries, or an outbreak of food poisoning) and that has revealed failure to comply with legal standards. Such prosecutions could be examples of a form of 'public interest' reasoning hinted at above: that, where serious harm has resulted, it is important to have a public airing of the issues and a decision taken in a public forum about the appropriate disposal of the case. On the other hand, they also demonstrate the danger of identifying the 'public interest' too closely with newsworthiness. One consequence could be 'that safety matters are given disproportionate attention at the expense of occupational health problems, where deaths may in fact be far more numerous'.[91] This bring back into focus the general question of equality of response to similarly harmful and culpable conduct, pointing out that the question is raised not just by the different practices of the police and regulatory agencies but also by practices within regulatory agencies.

4. The Role of the Victim

What role victims actually play in prosecutorial review is not clear. Crown Prosecutors are unlikely to meet victims as part of the review process, and are therefore reliant on what is contained in the papers. There are research findings from the early years of the CPS suggesting that they are willing to defer to the wishes of 'important' victims such as local businesses, at least to the extent of not discontinuing cases that appear to fulfil the criteria.[92] Recent research by Moxon and Crisp shows that some 13 per cent of discontinuances were attributable to the victim's reluctance to proceed—which usually makes it difficult to pursue the case, since the victim's evidence is likely to be crucial—and that a further 6 per cent of discontinuances stemmed from the offender's agreement to compensate the victim.[93] There are no recent findings on the point raised by McConville, Sanders, and Leng—whether cases that ought to be discontinued are continued if there is pressure from an important victim to carry on.

What role for the victim is recognized in the *Code for Crown Prosecutors*? Paragraph 8 now begins with the statement that 'although the public interest will be the paramount consideration, the interests of the victim are an important factor in determining the balance of the

---

[91] Hawkins, 'The Use of Legal Discretion', at 37, referring to K. Hawkins, 'FATCATS and Prosecution in a Regulatory Agency: A Footnote on the Social Construction of Risk', (1989) 11 *Law and Policy* 370.

[92] See McConville, Sanders, and Leng, *Case for the Prosecution*, 114.

[93] As reported in RCCJ Report, para. 4.36.

public interest and should be taken into account'. This enigmatic statement refers to 'interests', not 'wishes'. A later section suggests that, if
the complainant no longer wants the case to be pursued, this should
tell in favour of discontinuing it 'unless either there is suspicion that
the change of heart was actuated by fear or the offence was of some
gravity'.[94] In practice, many such decisions are often taken on evidential grounds: without the victim's evidence, the case will not pass the
sufficiency test. But the wording of the Code suggests that the victim's
wish to see the case discontinued should be relevant in its own right.
This raises questions about the difference between the public interest
and the individual victim's interest. The reverse situation, where the
victim wants a prosecution but the prosecutor takes the view that this
would not be in the public interest (for one of the foregoing reasons), is
not dealt with. The Code does state that Crown Prosecutors 'should
strive to ensure that the spirit of the Home Office Cautioning
Guidelines is observed', but those guidelines give no clear indication of
how this kind of problem should be resolved. The general approach
is that, whilst account should be taken of any views expressed by the
victim, 'the general public interest must continue to prevail'.[95] A recent
declaration by the CPS includes several commitments to assist victims,
but asserts that it 'has to take decisions reflecting the overall public
interest rather than the particular interests of any one person.
Nevertheless, the interests of the victim are very important when we
make decisions.'[96]

What ought to be the role of victims in prosecutorial review? In
theory their role should be the same here as in the original decision to
prosecute. The proper approach is to distinguish between criminal and
civil proceedings. Civil proceedings are brought by individuals to seek
damages (or an injunction) from a person who has wronged them. The
plaintiff may decide whether or not to commence the action and
whether or not to drop it. Criminal proceedings are brought on behalf
of the Crown, with a view to convicting guilty defendants and rendering them liable to be sentenced. Prosecutions are a matter of public
interest, and it would be wrong to allow the disposal of a defendant's
case to depend on whether the victim is vengeful or forgiving. This is
not to say that all matters relating to the individual victim are therefore
irrelevant. Clearly it is right that the criminal process should offer

[94] Para. 8 (vii).
[95] Home Office Circular 59/1990, *The Cautioning of Offenders*, para. 6; cf. annex B,
para. 4.
[96] Crown Prosecution Service, *Statement on the Treatment of Victims and Witnesses by
the Crown Prosecution Service* (1993), para. 5.

protection from danger where this is possible, and prosecutors must bear this in mind at remand proceedings.[97] It is also right that the criminal process should not deprive victims of the possibility of having an enforceable compensation order made in their favour, a particularly troublesome point at present.[98] There is the further practical point that a prosecution can rarely be successful if the victim decides that he or she is unwilling to give evidence, unless a guilty plea has already been intimated. But, apart from these issues, the general principle is that prosecution policy should be consistent among defendants, following guidelines rather than following the desires of individual victims. It is a function of the State, preliminary to the exercise of the coercive power to punish, and should therefore deal comparably with those whose offences are similar in terms of harm and culpability.

The spheres in which improvements are still required, despite the Government's publication of its *Victim's Charter* in 1990, are information for victims about the progress of the case and proper facilities at court. These points were made many times during the 1980s,[99] but change has been fairly slow. It is the responsibility of the police to communicate with victims about the progress of the case, but it seems that the police perform this function less effectively as the case proceeds to trial.[100] The Royal Commission on Criminal Justice proposes that the CPS should communicate directly with the victim when decisions have been taken, in advance of the date for trial, either to drop the case or to proceed on lesser or fewer charges.[101] The Royal Commission also recommends that the Bar's Code of Conduct be amended so as to allow victims and other prosecution witnesses to meet with counsel before the case: this could be of considerable benefit to the victims and witnesses, and might assist counsel in the presentation of the case.[102] In the last few years the 'Victim in Court' project has been developed by Victim Support, using volunteers to help familiarize victims with the

[97] RCCJ Report, para. 5.48; see now the CPS *Statement on the Treatment of Victims* (1993), paras. 8 and 14, not quite meeting this point.

[98] See Ch. 5.4.

[99] e.g. J. Shapland, J. Willmore, and P. Duff, *Victims in the Criminal Justice System* (1985), J. Shapland and D. Cohen, 'Facilities for Victims: The Role of the Police and the Courts', [1987] *Crim. LR* 28; Home Office Circular 20/1988.

[100] See Morgan and Zedner, *Child Victims*, 106–7. Cf. the suggestion of T. Newburn and S. Merry, *Keeping in Touch: Police–Victim Communication in Two Areas*, HORS 116 (1990), that victims should be encouraged to telephone the police, and that the police should have reliable arrangements for responding informatively to these calls.

[101] RCCJ Report, para. 4.47. See also the House of Commons Home Affairs Committee, *Domestic Violence* (1993), Recommendation 20, 'that the CPS make particular efforts to explain their actions to victims when charges are downgraded'.

[102] RCCJ Report, para. 4.52.

layout and procedure of the court.[103] The Home Secretary has announced that the Government accepts all these recommendations relating to victims.[104] Whilst these innovations go well beyond prosecutorial review, they bear on the general orientation and functions of the Crown Prosecution Service, as the CPS has recognized in its *Statement on the Treatment of Victims and Witnesses by the Crown Prosecution Service* (1993).

5. Delay

Delay in the conclusion of criminal proceedings can work to the disadvantage of either party: witnesses may forget or become unavailable, prolonged anxiety may be caused to the defendant, and the public impact of the trial may be diluted by its distance from the events to which it relates. In some cases the prosecution may cause delays, whether through incompetence or neglect. Reasons of this kind presumably underlie the provisions against delay in the European Convention on Human Rights.[105] However, there are also cases in which delay may work in favour of the defence, if it is prosecution witnesses that are likely to forget their story, or if there is enough time for the defendant to become established in a more settled or 'respectable' way of life. This means that there is also a public interest in securing trial without delay. Thus delays should be minimized, whether they are attributable to defence tactics or to prosecution indiscipline.

In order to achieve this, however, it is necessary to arrive at a definition of delay. There must be some lapse of time between arrest, first court appearance, and final disposal: the question concerns what is reasonable and what is unreasonable. To determine this one has to set periods of time as the norm for certain stages in the process of a case. This may be accomplished by comparisons of the time taken in different parts of the country at similar stages of the process, with due regard to variations in types of case.[106] Some relevant national guidelines have been promulgated by the Working Group on Pre-Trial Issues,[107] and the Efficiency Commission is also studying the possibilities for reducing delay.

Section 22 of the Prosecution of Offences Act 1985 empowers the

---

[103] See P. Rock, *The Social World of an English Crown Court* (1993).

[104] Speech of Rt. Hon. Michael Howard to the Conservative Party Conference, reported in *The Times*, 26 Sept. 1993

[105] See above, Ch. 3.3.11.

[106] P. Morgan and J. Vennard, *Pre-trial Delay: The Implications of Time Limits*, HORS 110 (1989); see also Council of Europe, *Delays in Criminal Justice System* (1992).

[107] *Action Plan*, 41–7.

Secretary of State to make regulations on time-limits for the maximum time taken by the prosecution at certain stages when a defendant is on remand in custody. Failure to comply with a time-limit results in the defendant being treated as if acquitted, but there is provision for the prosecution to apply for an extension. The court should only grant this if satisfied that 'there is good and sufficient cause for doing so' and that 'the prosecution has acted with all due expedition'. The Divisional Court has had many opportunities to review the application of these tests.[108] Quite apart from the time-limits applicable in custody cases, delay in bringing any case to court may also be challenged through the doctrine of abuse of process. In the leading decision in *Attorney-General's Reference (No. 1 of 1990)*,[109] Lord Lane, CJ, held that proceedings may be stayed for unjustifiable delay, but only in exceptional circumstances. No stay should be granted if there has been fault by the defendant or if the delay stems from the complexity of the case, and generally fault should be shown on the part of the prosecution. The defendant must also show that he or she would suffer serious prejudice to the extent that a fair trial could no longer take place. This decision constitutes a narrowing of the previous jurisprudence.[110]

The decision on this Attorney-General's Reference is also notable for the respondent's reliance on Magna Carta, clause 29 of which guarantees that 'we will not deny, or defer, to any man, either justice or right'. The Court of Appeal held that deferment must connote wrongful delay or deferment, and therefore saw no need to discuss the argument further on the facts of the Reference. The argument has been considered fully in the High Court of Australia, where the conclusion was that clause 29 cannot be used as a basis for a right to speedy trial.[111]

6. Accountability

To what authorities and to what extent are prosecutors accountable? The absence of clear and effective lines of accountability for many regulatory agencies was discussed in the previous chapter.[112] The focus here will be chiefly upon the Crown Prosecution Service, in the context of prosecutorial review.

---

[108] See A. Choo, *Abuse of Process and Judicial Stays of Criminal Proceedings* (1993), 48–9.

[109] [1992] 1 QB 630.

[110] A. Choo, 'Delay and Abuse of Process', (1992) 108 *LQR* 565.

[111] *Jago* v. *District Court (NSW)* (1989) 63 AJLR 640, discussed by R. G. Fox, 'Jago's Case: Delay, Unfairness and Abuse of Process in the High Court of Australia', [1990] *Crim. LR* 552.

[112] See Ch. 5.4, above.

1. *Accountability to Parliament*: the CPS is organized hierarchically, with local branches, regional areas, and a headquarters. Internal lines of accountability end with the Director of Public Prosecutions. He or she is answerable to the Attorney-General, who has ministerial responsibility for the general policies pursued by the CPS but not in respect of decisions taken in individual cases. As we saw earlier,[113] the Prosecution of Offences Act 1985 imposes on the Director a statutory responsibility to issue a code, and to report annually to Parliament. There is no accountability to Parliament for decisions in individual cases, but it is the practice of Members of Parliament to refer to the Director of Public Prosecutions individual cases brought to their attention by constituents or others. The Director will usually reply by letter, giving some reason for the decision (often, a decision to discontinue a prosecution). The CPS is also open to scrutiny by the Home Affairs Committee of the House of Commons[114] and by the Audit Commission.[115]

2. *Accountability to the courts*: for some years the courts have expressed a willingness to review certain prosecution decisions, and recent years have seen striking developments.[116] It was established in the first *Blackburn* case[117] that the courts would be prepared judicially to review a general policy not to prosecute for certain classes of offence, for example, all thefts with a value below £100. In the third *Blackburn* case[118] Lord Denning, MR, suggested that the courts would also be prepared to review an individual decision not to prosecute, and this dictum has received recent judicial support.[119] The primary basis for judicial review would be that either the policy or the individual decision was unreasonable in a *Wednesbury* sense, that is, was such that no reasonable prosecuting authority would have adopted the policy or taken the decision.[120] It seems that few people who feel aggrieved at a decision not to prosecute embark on judicial review: the Government dismissed the idea of appealing to a magistrates' court for

[113] See above, s.1.
[114] The Committee last inquired into the CPS in 1990: House of Commons Home Affairs Committee, *Crown Prosecution Service*, Fourth Report, Session 1989–90.
[115] See Audit Commission, *Review of the Crown Prosecution Service*, National Audit Office (1989).
[116] See C. Hilson, 'Discretion to Prosecute and Judicial Review', [1993] *Crim. LR* 639; a subsequent decision of importance is *R.* v. *Croydon Justices, ex p. Dean* [1993] 3 All ER 129.
[117] *R.* v. *Metropolitan Police Commissioner, ex p. Blackburn* [1968] 2 QB 118.
[118] *R.* v. *Metropolitan Police Commissioner, ex p. Blackburn (No. 3)* [1973] 1 QB 241.
[119] *R.* v. *General Council of the Bar, ex p. Percival* [1990] 3 All ER 137.
[120] The scope of the leading case of *Associated Provincial Picture Houses* v. *Wednesbury Corporation* [1948] 1 KB 223 is discussed by P. P. Craig, *Administrative Law* (2nd edn., 1989), 281–305.

review of a decision not to prosecute,[121] and preferred to allow continued reliance on the power to bring a private prosecution. This requires considerable strength and persistence, usually from the victim or victim's family, but there are examples of such prosecutions succeeding.[122]

Would it be possible to obtain judicial review of a decision *to* prosecute that was thought unfair? The Divisional Court took this step, with great caution, in *R. v. Chief Constable of Kent and another, ex part L.* (1991).[123] The court accepted that an individual decision to prosecute could be subject to judicial review if it was clearly contrary to a settled policy of the Director of Public Prosecutions, i.e. the *Code for Crown Prosecutors*. However, the particular case involved a juvenile, and the court was careful to confine its remarks to cases involving juveniles, where there is a strong public policy of avoiding court appearances. Notwithstanding this caution, Stuart-Smith, LJ, in the Divisional Court in *R. v. Inland Revenue Commissioners, ex parte Mead* (1993)[124] accepted that judicial review of a decision to prosecute would also be possible where the applicant was an adult; the other member of the court, Popplewell, J., disagreed with this. Stuart-Smith, LJ, expressed the opinion that successful review would be less likely for adults since the public policy in favour of diversion is less strong than for juveniles. However, the *Code for Crown Prosecutors* contains a number of clear policies in respect of adult offenders, and it seems perfectly possible that a decision to continue the prosecution of an adult despite that person's age or the staleness of the offence might result in judicial review. The *Mead* case involved the Inland Revenue Commissioners, and this shows that judicial review of decisions taken by other prosecuting authorities would be available if they had declared criteria for prosecution that were sufficiently detailed. Judicial review of decisions to prosecute would be based either on the failure to follow a declared policy, or on the failure to take account of a relevant consideration in reaching the decision.

The doctrine of abuse of process has been invoked against prosecutors in recent years in two main classes of case.[125] First, the court may exercise its power to stay proceedings if there has been delay in the

---

[121] Home Office, *An Independent Prosecution Service.*

[122] Perhaps the most remarkable in recent years is the case that became *Attorney-General's Reference (No. 3 of 1989)* (1990) 90 Cr. App. R. 358, in which the CPS had declined to prosecute for a more serious offence than careless driving.

[123] (1991) 93 Cr. App. R. 416; see the discussion by S. Uglow *et al.*, 'Cautioning Juveniles: Multi-agency Impotence', [1992] *Crim. LR* 632.

[124] [1993] 1 All ER 772.

[125] For detailed analysis, see Choo, *Abuse of Process*, chs. 1 and 2.

bringing of proceedings that would seriously prejudice the fairness of the trial. The effects of delay are well known, and the European Convention holds that there must be trial 'within a reasonable time'.[126] In the leading case of *Attorney-General's Reference (No. 1 of 1990)*,[127] discussed in Section 5 above, the Court of Appeal emphasized that stays of proceedings on grounds of delay would be exceptional, especially if there were no fault on the part of the prosecution. The second class of case is where the defendant is being placed in double jeopardy by the present proceedings, having already been acquitted or convicted on substantially the same facts.[128] However, the Divisional Court has stated that the doctrine of abuse of process is not limited to these two classes of case. In *R. v. Croydon Justices, ex parte Dean* (1993)[129] the police had told a young man who was a fringe participant in a major crime that he would not be prosecuted if he gave evidence against the major participants. However, he was subsequently prosecuted for the crime of assisting offenders, one of the few offences for which the decision to prosecute lies with the CPS rather than the police. The Divisional Court stayed the prosecution, accepting that there had been an abuse of process stemming from the promise of non-prosecution given by the police, even though the police did not have the power to prosecute for this offence. At the very least, this decision suggests that the boundaries of the doctrine of abuse of process have not yet been reached.

These increases in the accountability of prosecutors may be welcomed as supplying the necessary counterbalance to the considerable discretion that exists in the sphere of prosecutorial review. State officials and others are entrusted with great power over the lives of citizens, and the exercise of this power should be open to scrutiny on grounds of fairness. Whether judicial review is the most suitable approach, and whether the three doctrines considered—*Wednesbury* unreasonableness, failure to apply a stated policy, and abuse of process—cover the ground adequately and appropriately is a subject for continuing inquiry.

7. Prosecutorial Ethics

In its present form the *Code for Crown Prosecutors* says nothing about the ethical orientation of prosecutors. No doubt each Crown Prosecutor,

---

[126] See Ch. 3.3.11; cf. also para. 8 (3) of the *Code for Crown Prosecutors* relating to 'stale offences', discussed above, s. 3.

[127] (1992) 95 Cr. App. R. 296.

[128] The leading case is *Connelly* v. *DPP* [1964] AC 1254.   [129] [1993] 3 All ER 129.

as a solicitor or barrister, would claim to be governed by the ethical code of the relevant professional organization. But there is a need to settle the distinctive ethical principles on which the CPS should operate.

In Chapter 3 we reviewed the various formulations of the prosecutor's role, as a kind of 'Minister of Justice' concerned with obtaining convictions without unfairness to defendants.[130] The role has been expressed similarly in the US Supreme Court: the prosecutor

is in a peculiar and very definite sense the servant of the law, the twofold aim of which is that guilt shall not escape or innocence suffer . . . It is as much his duty to refrain from improper methods calculated to produce a wrongful conviction as it is to use every legitimate means to bring about a just one.[131]

The importance of these statements lies in their endorsement of the argument, developed in Chapter 3 above, that the protection of rights should be regarded as part of the law, and not as standing in opposition to the proper role of police or prosecutors. Whilst it is true that defence lawyers have the primary task of securing the defendant's rights, prosecutors should neither indulge in nor condone unlawful or unethical practices. They should show no less respect for fairness, as embodied in principles such as those developed in Chapter 3, than for the obtaining of convictions of the guilty. The CPS has recently stated that 'we will do everything in our power to ensure that all defendants are dealt with fairly, and if a case proceeds, that they have a fair trial'.[132]

What are the implications of these fine words for practice? One obvious implication concerns the bringing of prosecutions based on tainted investigative procedures. If the CPS discover that evidence has been obtained in breach of the PACE Codes or other rules, should they 'let the court decide' on admissibility or discontinue the case themselves? The answer to the question can be fudged in part by stating that there will be some cases where no breach is apparent on the file, and others where the breach or its significance leave room for doubt which is properly settled in court. But even the most casual reading of appellate decisions in the last seven years shows that many prosecutions have been brought in cases of manifest departure from central provisions of the Codes of Practice. This suggests that there is no ethical insistence on respect for fair procedures. A first step, therefore, would be to introduce an ethical statement that is not only general in its import but also accompanied by specific examples of the kinds of situation that might

[130] See above, pp. 87–8.

[131] *Berger* v. *United States* (1935) 294 US 78, at 88 per Sutherland, J.

[132] CPS, *Statement of Purpose and Values*, 10; cf. also, at 8: 'Our decisions are informed by, but independent of, the police. This process acts as an important safeguard for the suspect.'

demand a principled approach. The second step is to convince Crown Prosecutors that the ethical statement is well founded and ought to be followed, and to dispel the rival notions of 'crime control' and 'prosecuting with one hand tied behind one's back'.[133]

8. Policy-Making on Prosecutions

Statements of policy should deal appropriately with vulnerable groups. One such issue is decisions to prosecute the mentally disordered and mentally disturbed.[134] The *Code for Crown Prosecutors* contains considerable guidance on this, but practices could be improved.[135] A further such issue is the effect of race. This is not addressed directly in the *Code for Crown Prosecutors*, but is the subject of commitments made in the *Statement of Purpose and Values*. The statement itself declares that 'our decisions will be independent of bias and discrimination', and the document later subscribes to the principle of equality before the law. Among the details is a commitment not to be 'improperly influenced by the sex, ethnic or national origin, religious belief, political association or sexual orientation of the victim, witness or defendant'.[136] Since there is some evidence of a belief that racial factors do enter into some decisions to prosecute,[137] this calls for particular vigilance on the part of the CPS to use the power of discontinuance to counteract any tendency to prosecute in cases that should result in a caution.

It was argued above that prosecutors should adopt the 'intrinsic merits' approach when reviewing cases with a view to continuing or discontinuing them. This means, for example, that prosecutors should not continue a weak case simply because local juries are known to convict in such cases on relatively little evidence, and that they should be prepared to discontinue a weak case even though the defendant has intimated a willingness to plead guilty in the magistrates' court. Such decisions must be explained clearly but carefully to the general public. They also call for considerable independence of mind, born of thorough training and adequate experience, and it is not known how widespread this is in the CPS. There have been constant worries about the independence of the CPS since its introduction. McConville,

---

[133] See above, Ch. 3.8.

[134] Cf. D. Carson, 'Prosecuting People with Mental Handicaps', [1989] *Crim. LR* 87, arguing that current policy may sometimes result in a loss of safeguards for the patient.

[135] NACRO Mental Health Advisory Committee, *Diverting Mentally Disturbed Offenders from Prosecution*, Policy Paper 2 (1993).

[136] *Statement of Purpose and Values*, 3 and 8.

[137] M. Fitzgerald, *Ethnic Minorities and the Criminal Justice System*, RCCJ Research Study 20 (1993), 17–19.

Sanders, and Leng, on the basis of research carried out in the early years, concluded that the CPS prosecuted in the police's interest rather than in the public interest, substantially doubting whether there was much independent review of case files.[138] Even the House of Commons Home Affairs Committee, which insisted that the CPS should act independently and be seen to do so, succumbed to the temptation of urging the CPS to 'act co-operatively with the police' in supporting local policing initiatives.[139] Whilst this would not necessarily compromise independence, one should recognize that prosecution decisions are taken not in a laboratory atmosphere but in a working context that brings the CPS into contact with the police, with victims, and with magistrates. Although the emphasis in this chapter has been upon criteria and guidelines, any attempt to explain practical decision-making must take account of the organizational and operational contexts in which the decisions tend to be made.[140] What pressures are placed on decision-makers within the CPS? What is thought to please one's superiors in the CPS? What in fact gains promotion within the CPS? How important are good working relations with the police, and how do most Crown Prosecutors think that good relations can be achieved? Questions of this kind do not remove the need to establish guidelines on policy matters, but they emphasize the need to ensure that the declared policies are put into practice—what is stated in the CPS *Manuals* (which are confidential and which most Crown Prosecutors would consult rather than the Code), and how if at all do managers within the CPS ensure that the declared policies are followed?

These are questions for research to answer. There are also questions of policy about the responsibilities of the CPS. At the end of the last chapter, the possibility of conferring on the CPS overall responsibility for prosecutions and diversion was considered. At present the police possess both a dispositive function (decisions on cautioning) and a prosecutorial function (decisions on charging). These are more in the nature of judicial or quasi-judicial functions than tasks for investigators. Should not England and Wales move towards the separation of investigative from these other functions that obtains, more or less, in almost all other European jurisdictions? The 1981 Royal Commission was concerned:

to secure that after a clearly defined point during the preparation of a case for trial and during its presentation at trial someone with legal qualifications

---

[138] McConville, Sanders, and Leng, *Case for the Prosecution*, ch. 10.

[139] House of Commons Home Affairs Committee, Session 1989–90, *The Crown Prosecution Service*, HC 118 (1990), para. 27.

[140] See Hawkins, 'The Use of Legal Discretion'.

makes the variety of decisions necessary to ensure that only properly selected, prepared and presented cases come before the court for disposal; and to do that without diminishing the quality of police investigation and preliminary case preparation and without increasing delays.[141]

That Royal Commission decided not to overthrow the whole of previous practice and instead proposed that the decision to charge be left in the hands of the police, bringing in the CPS at the subsequent stage. Any change now would necessitate major reorganization of the police and the CPS, but the arguments for separating the investigative and prosecutorial functions considered by the 1981 Royal Commission tell in favour of change. No doubt the police would wish to keep their existing power. No doubt the economic argument, based on the cost of change, would be pressed hard. No doubt there would be much discussion of the shortcomings, real and alleged, in the performance of the CPS in its existing tasks—a matter on which independent research is urgently needed.

The 1993 Royal Commission has made no recommendations for structural change of this kind. This is a matter for regret, but presumably it decided not to examine these issues in depth.[142] Its most far-reaching recommendation in this sphere is that the CPS be given the power to impose prosecutor fines, adapting the Scottish model.[143] Whatever the merits of this proposal in isolation, it raises many questions about the division of responsibilities for diversion that are not tackled in the Commission's Report, thus leaving even greater confusion in this area. The elementary question of the relationship between cautioning and prosecutor fines is not put, let alone answered. The proposition that a single agency should deal with dispositive decisions is not properly considered. There would, of course, be problems of ensuring that such decisions are taken on the basis of sufficient information from the various sources, but that is a consequential rather than a fundamental issue. Taken together with the 1993 Royal Commission's curt dismissal of the proposal that the CPS should decide on the mode of trial of offences triable either way[144]—a proposal that also reflects the Scottish system—it seems that the path of reform is blocked either by a lack of confidence in the CPS or by the power of the police or by a combination of the two.

[141] RCCP, *Report*, para. 7.6.
[142] There is brief mention in RCCJ Report, paras. 5.56–5.59.
[143] Ibid., paras. 5.62 and 5.63.
[144] Ibid., para. 6.12: it 'would not be acceptable here at least for the time being'.

7

Remands before Trial

THE bail/custody decision raises some of the most acute conflicts in the whole criminal process. On the one hand there is the defendant's interest in remaining at liberty until the trial has taken place. On the other hand there is a public interest in obtaining protection from crime. Some practitioners, politicians, and others have concluded that the way to deal with this conflict is in each case to balance the defendant's rights with the interests of society. However, the vague notion of 'balancing' that is usually advanced in this context is manifestly inadequate. No judgement of balance can be properly reached until there is a clear appreciation of what rights defendants (and actual or potential victims) have at this stage, and fuller analysis of the content and legitimacy of the claimed public interests. It will be evident during the course of this chapter that there is a wide range of relevant considerations, combined with a dearth of practical information at some crucial stages. The view might well be taken that no set of rules and exceptions could be framed to deal satisfactorily with all or even most cases— unless the rule itself contained several value-judgements which were left for interpretation in the courts. That remains for discussion. But the issues are too important to leave to wide expanses of little-regulated discretion, whether in the hands of police officers, magistrates, or judges. The focus in this chapter will be on the issues of principle raised by the law and practice.[1]

Questions of remand on bail or in custody arise at various stages in the criminal process. First, there is the question of police bail. Section 38 of the Police and Criminal Evidence Act 1984 provides, in outline, that where a person is charged with an offence, the custody officer should order his release pending the court appearance unless there are reasonable grounds for believing that the defendant will fail to appear in court, will interfere with witnesses or with the investigation of the offence, or will cause physical injury or loss or damage to property. Second, there is the decision on remand between the first and the final court appearance. Third, there is the question of remand pending an

[1] For a full account of the law and practice, see Paul Cavadino and Bryan Gibson, *Bail: The Law, Best Practice and the Debate* (1993).

appeal against verdict or sentence, which is the subject of a Practice Direction.[2] And fourth, there is the question of remand after conviction and before sentence is passed, for example in order to allow time for the preparation of a report on the defendant. In order to keep the discussion within reasonable bounds, the third and fourth decisions will not be discussed here, and there will be only a few references to police bail. The principal focus is upon the court's decision whether to remand on bail or in custody between first appearance and trial.

1. Remands and Rights

What rights of a defendant are at stake here? The fundamental right of an innocent person not to be convicted is not called directly into question by a custodial remand, but the principle that the criminal process should cause the minimum of inconvenience to suspects and defendants is central. Custodial remands take away liberty. Indeed, one of the reasons why the right not to be wrongly convicted is described as fundamental is the value of liberty. The significance of taking it away is heightened when it is connected to the presumption of innocence: since we are discussing remands before trial, there has been no conviction and the defendant is entitled to be presumed innocent unless and until it is proved otherwise at a trial. As we have seen in Chapter 3, Article 6 (2) of the European Convention on Human Rights affirms the presumption of innocence, Article 5 (1) (c) provides that a person may be deprived of liberty on reasonable suspicion for the purpose of bringing him or her before a court, and Article 5 (3) provides that such a person should be brought promptly before a court and entitled to trial within a reasonable time or to release pending trial.[3]

It is quite wrong that anyone, including agents of law enforcement, should be able to make an arrest, bring a charge, and then, without proving that charge in court, secure the immediate detention of the defendant. Detention without trial is widely regarded as an incident of totalitarianism, or at least an expedient to be contemplated only in an extreme kind of national emergency. It therefore follows that any argument for depriving unconvicted individuals of their liberty in civil society ought to have peculiar strength. Indeed, that point is reinforced when one considers the potential consequences for the defendant of a loss of liberty before trial—not just the deprivation of freedom to live a normal

---

[2] *Practice Direction: Bail Pending Appeal* [1983] 1 WLR 1292.

[3] J. E. S. Fawcett, *Application of the European Convention on Human Rights* (2nd edn., 1987) argues that there is a need for some redrafting of the various parts of Art. 5 in order to clarify the principles relevant to remand pending trial (p. 88).

life, often compounded by incarceration under the worst conditions in the prison system, but also restricted ability to prepare a defence to the charge, loss of job, strain on family relations and friendships, and often appearance in court in a deteriorated or demoralized condition. The higher rates of suicide and self-injury for unconvicted rather than convicted prisoners may have much to do with these adversities.[4]

No doubt it was considerations of this kind that led the Supreme Court of the United States to declare:

this traditional right to freedom before conviction permits the unhampered preparation of a defence and serves to prevent the infliction of punishment prior to conviction. Unless this right to bail before trial is preserved, the presumption of innocence, secured only after centuries of struggle, would lose its meaning.[5]

Yet this statement introduces another concept that needs careful inquiry. If remands in custody are to be permitted at all, can they fairly be described as 'the infliction of punishment'? From time to time it has been alleged that courts have indulged in 'punitive remands', remanding a person in custody when it is known full well that a custodial sentence would not be appropriate on conviction.[6] Remand for those reasons is plainly an abuse. But even in cases where the remand is not punitive, the hardship inflicted on the defendant is undeniable. However, definitions of punishment invariably link the element of hard treatment to conviction of an offence by a court.[7] Remand in custody inflicts hardship, as might a dog-bite or a falling tree in a storm, but it cannot be regarded as punishment. Yet custodial remands do differ in one marked respect from natural disasters: they are intentionally inflicted by a court as a result of a hearing.

The US Supreme Court rejected a challenge to the Bail Reform Act of 1984, which allows a judicial officer to authorize pre-trial detention if there is clear and convincing evidence that 'no condition or combination of conditions of pre-trial release will reasonably assure the safety of any other person and the community'. Rejecting the argument that the statute was unconstitutional because it imposed punishment before trial, the majority held that a statute on pre-trial detention is 'regulatory, not penal'.[8] The minority retorted that this approach

---

[4] A. Liebling and H. Krarup, *Suicide Attempts and Self-Injury in Male Prisons* (1993), 52.

[5] Per Vinson, CJ, in *Stack* v. *Boyle* (1951) 342 US 1, at 4.

[6] See e.g. the warning of Lord Hailsham, LC, against punitive remands in 1971—[1972] *Magistrate* 21.

[7] The classic definition is that of H. L. A. Hart, *Punishment and Responsibility* (1968), 5.

[8] *United States* v. *Salerno* (1987) 481 US 739. For an accessible discussion, see Lord Windlesham, 'Punishment and Prevention: The Inappropriate Prisoners', [1988] *Crim. LR* 140, at 143–5.

'merely redefine[s] any measure which is claimed to be punishment as "regulation" and, magically, the Constitution no longer prohibits its imposition'.[9] The reply scores a debating point, but leaves open the justifications for the detention of the mentally disordered, of persons subject to quarantine, of illegal immigrants pending deportation, etc. There surely are circumstances in which the State is justified in depriving a person of liberty even though that person has not been convicted of an offence—indeed, is not even suspected of one. Is there not some analogy between the main grounds for custodial remand and those other types of case?[10]

The first of the three main grounds for refusing bail is that otherwise the defendant is unlikely to stand trial: there is thought to be a significant risk of absconding. The use of the term 'risk' shows that this is a predictive judgment, but so presumably are those that lead to the detention of certain mentally disordered people, illegal immigrants, etc. One central question concerns the relative social importance of ensuring that persons charged with offences attend their trial on the due date. Presumably the police could be dispatched to arrest someone who failed to attend without offering a reasonable excuse, but there might be a greater anxiety over certain defendants who seem likely to flee the country or to hide themselves away. In all cases, the relevant questions concern the evidence of probability on the particular facts, the seriousness of the offence charged (to be set against the risk of the defendant's non-attendance), the possibility of imposing conditions or taking sureties, and thus the degree of risk that must be attained before liberty is taken away. Without concluding this line of argument, one might say that there would be no justification for ordering the detention of persons charged with drunkenness offences simply because they seemed likely to wander off, since the offence is so minor that the public interest in their trial is fairly small; but that there might be ample justification if the defendant were charged with major offences (e.g. violence or serious fraud) and had on previous occasions failed to attend trial.

The second main ground is the probability of committing offences if granted bail. Again, this is a question of risk and prediction. It is often asserted that there is a public interest in ensuring that people already charged with an offence do not commit offences during the period before their trial. The exact basis for this is unclear. Is it that the State is somehow responsible for the conduct of persons who have been

---

[9] *United States* v. *Salerno*, at 760, per Marshall and Brennan, JJ.

[10] Cf. L. M. Natali and E. D. Ohlbaum, 'Redrafting the Due Process Model: The Preventive Detention Blueprint', (1989) 62 *Temple LR* 1225, at 1237–8.

charged but not yet tried, perhaps because it is the slowness of the machinery of criminal justice that creates the opportunities? Otherwise, in what way do remandees differ from, say, people with previous convictions who are walking the streets? Surely it cannot be that anyone who has been charged may be presumed guilty, and for that reason may just as well be likely to commit a further offence if left at large before the formal trial: that would contradict the presumption of innocence. A further possibility, raised by the recent enactment of a statutory provision requiring courts to treat the fact that an offence was committed on bail as an aggravating factor in sentencing,[11] is that the period between charge and trial is regarded as a period of special trust, which the 'bail-breaking' offender breaches. Yet this does not explain why the period on bail should be so regarded: is it the idea of State responsibility again or, if not, is there some reason why the defendant should have greater obligations at this time than, say, immediately after the conclusion of a sentence? The latter reason suggests that defendants who are released on bail are granted a privilege that they should not abuse, but if the presumption of innocence and the right to liberty are valued, it is wrong to describe this as a privilege. Questions of this kind are rarely confronted, but it seems clear that considerable significance is attributed to the mere fact that a person has been charged. Some might say that this is no 'mere fact' if a person has already confessed guilt and indicated an intention to plead guilty; but certain well-publicized cases of miscarriage of justice suggest that it would be unwise to build too much on those foundations. It might also be argued that the laying of a charge ought to be attributed significance now that there is a national system of trained prosecutors; but that overlooks the probability that there may have been no real prosecutorial review of the case file at the first remand hearing, and not until some weeks have elapsed since the original charge may the prosecutor be confident that there is a 'realistic prospect of conviction'.[12] The arguments here, then, are much weaker than is commonly supposed.

The third ground is the probability that the defendant might interfere with witnesses or otherwise obstruct the course of justice if released on bail. In some instances the defendant may have been involved in such incidents before, but this ground is of particular importance to the protection of people who have already been victimized. Where a defendant has uttered threats against that person or the court has heard other convincing reasons why the victim fears attack,

---

[11] Criminal Justice Act 1993, s. 66 (6), substituting s. 29 (2) of the Criminal Justice Act 1991.

[12] See the discussion in Ch. 6.2, above.

and a non-custodial remand is unlikely to provide sufficient protection, custody may be justified. This is a particular problem in domestic violence cases.[13] Threats weaken the presumption of innocence and, if it appears to be a choice between the defendant's liberty or the victim's freedom from probable harm, a court may be justified in choosing the latter and ordering a remand in custody. Threats and interference may regarded as attempts to undermine the integrity of the criminal trial, and incarceration may be justified as the only way of protecting the process.

All three grounds for the refusal of bail turn on questions of predicted risk. Risk consists of the probability of an offence being committed if the defendant is granted bail, and the seriousness of any likely offence. A low probability of a very serious offence ought to have more weight than a high probability of a minor offence. Indeed, for non-serious offences, custodial remands should simply be ruled out. If the alleged offence is serious, and if the court is satisfied that there is sufficient evidential basis for the charge and that there is a substantial risk of an offence if the person is released on bail (whether with or without conditions), there might be grounds for deprivation of liberty before trial. Where the line should be drawn between serious and non-serious is a matter to be taken up at the end of the chapter. The purpose of this introduction is merely to demonstrate the social importance of the issues in bail/custody matters.

2. The Law Relating to Remands

Both in England and Wales and in the United States the law relating to remands has developed in two distinct phases. The first phase in both countries focused chiefly on the problem of securing the attendance of the defendant at the trial. In *Robinson* (1854), Coleridge, J., held that this was the sole point to which the magistrates should give attention.[14] In *Rose* (1898),[15] Lord Russell stated that 'it cannot be too strongly impressed on the magistracy that bail is not to be withheld as a punishment but that the requirements as to bail are merely to secure the attendance of the prisoner at his trial'. It was not until the 1940s and 1950s that the English courts, with Lord Goddard as Lord Chief Justice,

---

[13] House of Commons Home Affairs Committee, Third Report Session 1992–3, *Domestic Violence* (1993), and the Government's Reply, *Domestic Violence*, Cm. 2269 (1993), paras. 45 and 69.

[14] (1854) 23 LJQB 286. For summaries of the history, see A. K. Bottomley, 'The Granting of Bail: Principles and Practice', (1968) 31 MLR 40, and N. Corre, *Bail in Criminal Proceedings* (1990), pp. ix–xiv.

[15] (1898) 78 LT 119.

began to establish that an alternative ground for remanding in custody is that the defendant is likely to commit an offence if granted bail.[16] The Home Office took the unusual step of circulating to all magistrates the text of Lord Goddard's remarks in *Wharton* (1955).[17] Statutory confirmation came in the provisions of the Criminal Justice Act 1967, an Act which also introduced the possibility of granting conditional bail.

Two similar phases can be discerned in the American law. Until the 1960s the law and practice tended to concentrate on the problem of securing the attendance of defendants at trial: surveys showed that courts were mostly using financial bonds (sureties) as the means to this end, and that the result was the pre-trial imprisonment of people too poor to raise the money for such a bond.[18] Congress passed the Federal Bail Reform Act in 1966, legislating for 'release on recognisance' rather than financial bonds as the normal pre-trial order.[19] The second phase was marked by a growing anxiety about the commission of offences by people on bail, a concern that culminated in Congress passing the Bail Reform Act of 1984. Although the Act contains a number of procedural safeguards, its main provision is, as we have seen, based on a prediction of future danger.[20] Many other jurisdictions seem to have arrived at positions broadly similar to the English and American, although the provision in the Canadian Criminal Code still maintains that the primary ground for refusing bail is to secure attendance at the trial. However, the secondary ground (to be considered if the primary ground is inapplicable) refers to 'the protection or safety of the public'.[21]

The relevant law for England and Wales is now contained chiefly in the Bail Act 1976, as amended. In essence, a court has four main alternatives: release on unconditional bail, release on conditional bail, release on bail subject to a surety or security, and remand in custody.

[16] See *Phillips* (1947) 32 Cr. App. R. 47; *Pegg* [1955] Crim. LR 308 (the court also mentioning that D had no answer to the charge); *Wharton* [1955] Crim. LR 565 ('unless the justices felt real doubt as to the result of the case, men with bad criminal records should not be granted bail'); *Gentry* [1956] Crim. LR 120 (same policy reiterated).

[17] This was pointed out by Bottomley, 'The Granting of Bail', at 52.

[18] See C. Foote, 'Compelling Appearance in Court: Administration of Bail in Philadelphia', (1954) 102 *U. Pa. LR* 1031, and, on the subsequent research by the Vera Institute that led to the change in federal law, D. J. Freed and P. Wald, *Bail in the United States* (1964).

[19] For a general outline, see P. R. Jones and J. S. Goldkamp, 'Judicial Guidelines for Pre-trial Release: Research and Policy Developments in the United States', (1991) 30 *Howard JCJ* 140.

[20] See n. 13 above and accompanying text.

[21] N. Padfield, 'The Right to Bail: A Canadian Perspective', [1993] *Crim. LR* 510, discussing the provision and its interpretation in the Canadian Supreme Court.

Little needs to be said about unconditional bail. As for conditional bail, the Act makes provision for this in section 3 (6). It appears that around one-quarter of defendants granted bail are placed under conditions, some negative (e.g. not going within a specified distance of a certain place) and some positive (e.g. reporting periodically at a police station, living at a certain address).[22] The Act also provides that a court may, subject to certain restrictions, require a surety to secure the defendant's attendance at court. It may also require a defendant to give security for surrender to custody before release on bail.[23] The danger with financial conditions, as the American experience shows, is that they may tend to exclude the less well-off from bail, and there is English evidence to suggest that some remands in custody occur because the levels of surety set by the courts are unrealistic.[24] This is quite wrong, being unfair discrimination against people of modest means.

The centrepiece of the Act is section 4, which proclaims what has been described as a general right to bail or a presumption in favour of bail. Thus section 4 (1) provides that 'a person to whom this section applies shall be granted bail except as provided in Schedule 1 to this Act'. Paragraphs 2 to 6 of part I of that Schedule[25] list a number of 'exceptions to the right to bail', including custodial remands for the defendant's own protection and (more doubtfully) custodial remands because the court does not yet have sufficient information to take a decision on bail. The main provision is paragraph 2, which must be quoted in full:

The defendant need not be granted bail if the court is satisfied that there are substantial grounds for believing that the defendant, if released on bail (whether subject to conditions or not), would—

(a) fail to surrender to custody, or
(b) commit an offence while on bail, or
(c) interfere with witnesses or otherwise obstruct the course of justice, whether in relation to himself or any other person.

These three grounds correspond broadly with those subsequently incorporated in the Bail Reform Act of 1984 in the United States.[26] The

[22] Bail Act 1976, Schedule 1, pt. I, para. 8, and Corre, *Bail in Criminal Proceedings*, 14–29.
[23] For further details, see Cavadino and Gibson, *Bail*, 40–6.
[24] Ibid. 170, proposing a legislative provision to require courts to take account of defendants' means and social background.
[25] Pt. II of the Schedule deals separately with non-imprisonable offences, which will not be discussed here.
[26] i.e. serious risk that the defendant will flee or will obstruct justice, or where the case involves a crime of violence (very broadly defined), a major drug offence, or any crime punishable by life imprisonment, or where the case involves a felony charge against someone previously convicted of two offences in the above categories.

Schedule to the English Act goes on to set out various considerations to which regard should be had when taking bail/custody decisions. Among those is 'the defendant's record as respect the fulfilment of his obligations under previous grants of bail in criminal proceedings', a matter plainly relevant when the court is considering exception (a) to the right to bail.

Another consideration is 'the character, antecedents, associations and community ties of the defendant'. Community ties may be relevant to the probability that a defendant will attend his trial (exception (a)), since it may be argued that a person who is homeless or in temporary accommodation is more likely to abscond than someone with a permanent address (and a family) in the locality. However, it has been urged repeatedly that homelessness should not lead to a custodial remand without thorough exploration of other alternatives.[27] The 'character and antecedents' of the offender may give grounds for a prediction of whether he or she is likely to offend if given bail: exception (b). This question has attracted surprisingly little legal analysis or empirical inquiry. One oft-quoted statement is that of Atkinson, J., in the Court of Criminal Appeal in *Phillips* (1947),[28] where he warned courts against granting bail to defendants with a 'record of housebreaking', and added that 'in 19 out of 20 cases it is a mistake [to] release young housebreakers on bail'. Statistical studies suggest that this is a considerable exaggeration.[29]

A further consideration listed in paragraph 9 is 'the nature and seriousness of the offence or default (and the probable method of dealing with the offender for it)'. There is nineteenth-century authority for the view that the seriousness of the offence may have a bearing on the probability of D absconding—the more serious the offence, the greater the incentive to abscond.[30] Again, its statistical basis is untested, and might of its nature be difficult to test. Another interpretation is that this consideration is intended to relate to exception (b), the likelihood of D committing offences if released on bail. In fact it exposes a defect in the wording of exception (b), which nowhere mentions the seriousness of any offences that might be committed. On the face of the Act, and the exceptions to bail that it enumerates, the probability of further shoplifting offences could justify a custodial remand. For paragraph 9 to mention the probable sentence is insufficient, since the exceptions

[27] See e.g. Home Office Circular 155/1975, *Bail Procedures.*
[28] (1947) 32 Cr. App. R. 47.
[29] See the discussion of Patricia Morgan's work below, n. 52 and accompanying text.
[30] See the remarks of Coleridge, J., in *Scaife* (1841) 10 LJMC 144 and later in *Robinson* (1854) 23 LJQB 286.

to bail in the Act fail to make any reference to that at all. The probable sentence would be relevant if exception (*b*) referred to the likelihood of committing a *serious* offence whilst on bail, as does the new provision on custodial remands of juveniles,[31] but it does not do so.

3. The Treatment of Unconvicted Defendants

The vast majority of cases in magistrates' courts do not involve any remand of the defendant, whether on bail or in custody. In 1989 some 94 per cent of summary motoring offences were dealt with on first appearance, as were some 86 per cent of summary non-motoring offences and even 42 per cent of indictable offences.[32] Many of the last category would have been proceeded against by way of summons, which means that they do not appear in court the day after arrest (since there has been no arrest) and instead appear for the first time on an arranged date. However, our main concern here lies with those who are remanded by magistrates. In 1989 the overwhelming majority of remanded defendants whose cases were ultimately dealt with in a mag- istrates' court were remanded on bail—87 per cent of the indictable cases, 93 per cent of the summary non-motoring cases, and 95 per cent of the summary motoring cases.[33] Among those committed for trial to the Crown Court, however, the bail rate was lower at 79 per cent in 1989. Thus some 21 per cent of persons committed to the Crown Court are committed in custody. It should be noted, however, that all those figures are national averages. Research by Jones (1985) revealed wide variations in the use of custodial remands by courts in different areas, with Bedfordshire (7 per cent), Gwent (8 per cent), Merseyside, and the Metropolitan Police District (both 12 per cent) among the lowest, and with a group of predominantly rural areas having the highest custody rates (North Yorkshire 37 per cent, Dorset 31 per cent, Wiltshire and Devon and Cornwall both 29 per cent).[34]

Before commenting on these figures, it is worth considering the posi- tion in the prisons. In 1975, the year before the effect of the Home Office circular and the enactment of the Bail Act, some 53,000 persons were received into prison on remand. By 1978 the figure had declined

---

[31] One of the conditions in s. 62 of the Criminal Justice Act 1991 is that only a custodial remand 'would be adequate to protect the public from serious harm from him'.

[32] *Criminal Statistics, England and Wales* (1989), table 8.4.

[33] Ibid., table 8.5.

[34] P. Jones, 'Remand Decisions at Magistrates' Courts', in D. Moxon (ed.), *Managing Criminal Justice* (1985); see also M. Winfield, *Lacking Conviction: The Remand System in England and Wales* (1984).

sharply to 40,000, presumably as a result of the new approach to bail, but it began to rise thereafter and reached nearly 60,000 by 1987. Even more significant was the rise in the average numbers of remand prisoners in prison at any one time, from some 3,500 in 1975 to over 9,000 in 1987—an increase of some 175 per cent, far in excess of the rise in numbers received into prison on remand. The explanation for this is not far to seek: the average number of days spent in prison awaiting trial increased from 25 days in 1975 to 56 days by 1987. In other words, it is not so much that more people were being remanded in custody (although this is true), but rather that those remanded in custody were having to wait longer for their trials.

In terms of prison management, the burgeoning remand population in the 1980s caused considerable difficulties. Much public discussion at the time assumed that the problems of prison overcrowding stemmed chiefly from the numbers being sentenced to imprisonment. In fact, between 1975 and 1987, whilst the remand population increased by 175 per cent, the sentenced prison population increased by only 11 per cent. Of course these figures do not tell the whole story,[35] but what they do demonstrate is that remand prisoners have become far more of a problem for the prisons. A group that constituted a mere 8 per cent of the prison population in 1975 came to constitute some 22 per cent of the prison population in the late 1980s.[36] In principle they have to be held apart from sentenced prisoners, and have to be kept in establishments close to their homes. The result has been further overcrowding, with prisoners who have not yet been tried experiencing the most deplorable conditions in the English prison system. Remand prisoners were centrally involved in the disturbances at Strangeways and other prisons in 1990, and a substantial part of the Woolf Report is devoted to this problem.[37] Moreover some defendants, at times over 1,000, have spent several days in police cells on remand because the prisons are too full—in conditions with facilities for washing and exercise well

[35] In particular, the sentenced population was always far larger in total (increasing from 33,733 to 37,531 between 1975 and 1987), and would have been larger still if the Government had not altered the rules of eligibility for remission and parole during the 1980s: see A. Ashworth, *Sentencing and Criminal Justice* (1992), 233–5. No such direct method of controlling numbers was available in respect of the remand population.

[36] In international terms this percentage appears to be rather low. The proportion is much higher in some other European countries where waiting times for trials tend to be longer. In the United States some 57% of adults in jail in 1982 were unconvicted: M. R. Gottfredson and D. M. Gottfredson, *Decision-Making in Criminal Justice: Toward the Rational Exercise of Discretion* (1988), 81.

[37] *Prison Disturbances April 1990: Report of an Inquiry by Rt. Hon. Lord Justice Woolf and His Honour Judge Stephen Tumim*, Cm. 1456 (1991), particularly ch. 10.

below those even in the prisons.[38] Whatever happened between the mid-1970s and the mid-1980s had the effect of worsening the lot of those persons remanded in custody before trial.

What did happen? One explanation for the steep rise in the numbers of remand prisoners during these years has now gained wide acceptance.[39] The key factor seems to have been a sharp increase in the numbers of offences committed to the Crown Court for trial. Thus between 1979 and 1986 the number of persons charged with offences triable either way who were committed for Crown Court trial went from 55,000 to 81,000, almost a 50 per cent increase. Home Office research suggests that this does not reflect a general increase in the numbers of such offences being prosecuted.[40] The cause appears to have been an increased tendency among magistrates to commit to the Crown Court cases of burglary, theft, and handling. Defendants do have a right to elect trial for these offences, and some two-fifths of committals result from such elections. But the majority of the cases reach the Crown Court as a result of magistrates' decisions rather than defendants' elections. It seems that the judiciary, in particular local judges, may have exerted considerable influence on the numbers of cases committed to the Crown Court through their exhortations to magistrates.[41] This may have combined with the influence of the local police, who presented cases in most remand courts until the advent of the Crown Prosecution Service in 1986. Research by Jones shows that, although rates of custodial remand varied considerably across the country, there was usually a 90 per cent concordance between police decisions on bail or custody before court appearance and magistrates' decisions at the first court appearance.[42]

The sequence of events may therefore have been as follows. Judges formed the opinion that too many burglaries and other crimes were being dealt with by magistrates when they should have been committed to the Crown Court. Magistrates were advised by judges to commit more of these cases for trial, and responded. The police too wanted to see more of these cases go to the Crown Court, and regarded them as serious enough for custodial remands. The proportion of persons committed to the Crown Court in custody also rose slightly (from 19 per

[38] R. Morgan and S. Jones, 'Bail or Jail?', in E. Stockdale and S. Casale (eds.), *Criminal Justice under Stress* (1992).
[39] The leading article is by Rod Morgan, 'Remands in Custody: Problems and Prospects', [1989] *Crim. LR* 481.
[40] R. Pearce, *Waiting for Crown Court Trial: The Remand Population* (1987).
[41] D. Riley and J. Vennard, *Triable-Either-Way Cases: Crown Court or Magistrates' Courts?*, HORS 98 (1988), discussed in Ch. 8 below.
[42] Jones, 'Remand Decisions', at 113.

cent in 1979 to 22 per cent in 1987), but the real increase was in the total numbers committed. As a result, waiting times for Crown Court trials lengthened, even though new courtrooms were built. Remand prisoners therefore spent longer in custody awaiting trial, and that in turn exacerbated the problem of prison overcrowding, worsening the conditions in which remand prisoners were held.

This explanation certainly does not imply that a particular group, such as the judiciary or the police, is 'to blame'. The early stages of the explanation are distinctly less concrete than the latter parts. Even if the increased rate of committals by magistrates does reflect judicial advice—and that needs to be substantiated on a national level[43]—there may have been good reasons for that advice. For example, it might be argued that in the 1970s some magistrates tended to undervalue the seriousness of burglary in a dwelling, treating it as a property offence without sufficient regard to the psychological effects which sometimes result. A logical response to the publication of criminological research on the point in the early 1980s[44] might well have been to treat burglary more seriously by committing more cases to the Crown Court. Some may scoff at the notion that criminological research had any influence at all on the judiciary, and may prefer to speculate that there was greater general awareness of the after-effects of burglary. It might be the case that there were more serious burglaries being prosecuted than hitherto.[45] This chapter of history remains to be written, and should include an assessment of the drafting and practical effect of the National Mode of Trial Guidelines.[46] What cannot be denied is that between 1975 and 1987 defendants who were refused bail suffered increasingly greater deprivations, in terms of the average length of pre-trial detention in the poorest prison conditions, and that the risk of defendants being refused bail varied widely in different parts of the country.

The proportion of untried prisoners subsequently acquitted or not proceeded against is around 14 per cent.[47] The loss of liberty in these cases is particularly hard on the individuals concerned. Yet it can be

[43] The influence of the local liaison judges in Leicestershire and Northamptonshire is fairly clear from Riley and Vennard's research (*Triable-Either-Way Cases*).

[44] M. Maguire, 'The Impact of Burglary upon victims', (1980) 20 *BJ Crim.* 261; M. Maguire, *Burglary in a Dwelling* (1982).

[45] The hypothesis that the nature of particular crimes is becoming more serious as time goes by was tested in relation to the crime of rape by Home Office researchers. Comparing the features of rapes in 1973 and 1985, they found that there were some aggravating features of the offences that showed a modest increase, but that the primary difference was the courts in 1985 viewed rape as far more serious than courts in 1973: C. Lloyd and R. Walmsley, *Changes in Rape Offences and Sentencing* (1989).

[46] (1991) 92 Cr. App. R. 143, on which see Ch. 8 below.

[47] Morgan and Jones, 'Bail or Jail?', at 38.

argued that these are not necessarily cases of malfunction in the criminal justice system: if a conscientious judgement was made about the probability that, if not remanded in custody, they would fail to attend trial, commit offences whilst on bail, or interfere with witnesses, none of those matters bears directly on the probability of conviction. It is true that paragraph 9 of Schedule 1 to the Bail Act states that the strength of the evidence should be considered, but it is by no means clear which exception to the right to bail it relates to, and in many cases the court may find it difficult to assess the strength of the evidence at a remand hearing. The European Convention on Human Rights states, in Article 5 (5), that 'everyone who has been the victim of arrest or detention in contravention of the provisions of this Article shall have an enforceable right to compensation'. Again, this cannot apply literally if there was reasonable suspicion and if a court ordered the pre-trial detention. But several European countries provide State compensation for those acquitted after a custodial remand, and this is logical since the remand could only be justified on the ground that it was in the public interest.

This, therefore, is an area in which considerable improvement is needed. First, the need to assess the strength of the evidence before ordering a custodial remand should be stated in the law. The practical problems of doing so are acute, particularly at the first remand when inquiries may be incomplete and forensic reports awaited, but it is contrary to principle to detain anyone against whom the evidence remains sketchy. Second, there should be a system of compensation for those acquitted after a custodial remand.

4. The Treatment of Victims and Potential Victims

This is a provocative heading, intended to raise starkly the question whether the public in general or victims in particular have received any benefit from having larger numbers of defendants in custody at any one time. It would be almost impossible to trace any effects on the crime rate, largely because (1) the 'crime rate' is itself an elusive phenomenon which even surveys of victims (which are more complete than official records) have difficulty in charting,[48] and (2) even if we had a reliable measure of the number of crimes committed each year, it would necessarily be a product of several interacting influences, and it would rarely be possible to attribute particular trends to particular causes. But the question can be approached from other angles. One is

[48] See e.g. P. Mayhew and N. A. Maung, *Surveying Crime: Findings from the 1992 British Crime Survey* (1992).

to inquire into the volume of offences committed by persons who have been granted bail, perhaps with a view to suggesting that either too few people or the wrong people are remanded in custody. Another is to inquire into the proportion of those remanded in custody who are subsequently given non-custodial sentences, with a view to suggesting that it was unnecessary to order their pre-trial detention to secure public protection.

The most direct sense of public protection is to protect someone who has been threatened with violence by the defendant, or who has a well-grounded fear of violence. Such issues may arise in neighbourhood disputes or intra-family offences. If the court is satisfied that the only way to remove the threat of violence is to remand the defendant in custody, then this should be done, for the reasons outlined earlier. However, only recently has a prosecution right of appeal been introduced: the prosecution may appeal against a decision to grant bail to someone charged with an offence punishable with a maximum sentence of at least five years.[49]

Turning to public protection in a more general sense, let us begin by considering possible bail failures. Of those granted bail in any year, some 5 per cent fail to appear on the date set for their trial.[50] These may be regarded as wrong decisions in the sense that the court evidently thought that there were no substantial grounds for believing that they would fail to surrender to custody. However, no such grounds may have been apparent at the time, and in any event the courts could be said to have decided correctly in 95 per cent of cases. It is not known whether the small percentage of absconders have any features in common which might be used as as basis for prediction.

Of greater public concern are those defendants remanded on bail who are found to have committed offences during the period of remand. A Home Office survey in 1978 suggested that offences on bail are committed by about 7 per cent of those remanded to appear in a magistrates' court and about 9 per cent of those remanded to appear in the Crown Court.[51] During 1992 there was increased public anxiety about offending by defendants, often young men, who had been released on bail. Senior police officers made statements which suggested that the situation was becoming intolerable, in that a small number of people on bail were responsible for a large number of offences being committed. From a study of the statistics on which these claims were based, Patricia Morgan argued that there had been

[49] Bail (Amendment) Act 1993, discussed below, s. 7.
[50] *Criminal Statistics* (1989, table 8.10).
[51] Home Office, *Report of the Working Group on Magistrates' Courts* (1982).

little change in the rate of offending on bail since the earlier Home Office survey.[52] Depending on the definition and the counting rules, the figure was in the range from 10 to 12 per cent, although it could become 17 per cent if offences resulting in a caution and offences taken into consideration were included. The rise from 9 per cent in 1978 to 10 to 12 per cent in 1992 is not negligible, but one finding of the earlier Home Office research is that offending on bail became more likely, the longer the period of remand.[53] If that is so, then it is hardly surprising that offences have increased as waiting times have lengthened. Morgan also showed the difficulty of using the statistics as a basis for prediction: whilst the figures for the Metropolitan Police area showed that the offending rate was 18 per cent in cases where the police had opposed bail compared with 9 per cent in other cases, this still suggests that 82 per cent of these police objections to bail proved to be unduly cautious.[54]

The statistics show that the people most likely to offend on bail are those charged with theft of or from a vehicle (23 per cent) or with burglary (20 per cent), particularly those in the 17–20 age-group. If public protection is to be an important purpose of the bail/custody decision, then it needs to be asked whether we can predict with sufficient accuracy which offenders are more likely to offend on bail than not. If we could do so, the next question would be whether their offences would be so serious that only custody could be justified for them, to adopt the wording of section 1 of the Criminal Justice Act 1991. If not, then it would be necessary to devise an order that could be made in bail cases which would impose some obligations on the defendant. A measure of public protection might be possible without custody, through various community schemes. A determination to increase the number of people remanded in custody might not bring any noticeable difference in offending whilst on bail unless it were targeted on the right people. However, the Association of Chief Police Officers and the Government, in statements in early 1992, seemed to argue not in favour of remanding more people in custody but in favour of remanding the right people. What they failed to make clear was the criterion to be applied in practice.[55]

Having considered the failure of remands on bail, we should now

---

[52] P. M. Morgan, *Offending while on Bail: A Survey of Recent Studies* (1992).

[53] Discussed in Home Office, *Report of the Working Group on Magistrates' Courts*.

[54] A similar finding emerged from the 1978 Home Office survey, some three-quarters of those granted bail in the face of police objections completing their remand period without any recorded offending.

[55] For discussion, see Morgan and Jones 'Bail or Jail?' 41–4, and NACRO, *Legislation on Bail: What should be Done?* (1992).

turn to the failures of remands in custody. Is it necessary to remand so many people in custody for so long, as a measure of public protection? There are immediate difficulties with the concept of public protection here. One might say that the public is protected if the commission of any crime is avoided by means of a custodial remand, whether that crime is minor in nature or not. On this view, remands in custody of persons with a record of shop thefts might might be justified as protecting the public. To defeat that proposition, it must be argued either (1) that public protection is not an absolute value but rather a benefit to be weighed against disbenefits such as increased costs of imprisonment and increased incursions on the liberty of defendants, or (2) that the concept of public protection ought to be confined (in this context as in sentencing) to the protection of the public from violent or sexual offences of a serious nature.[56] This argument will be taken up in the concluding part of the chapter.

For the mean time we will interpret the concept of public protection in a functional sense, asking what percentage of defendants remanded in custody were subsequently given their liberty when sentenced. The assumption here is that, if custody is thought unnecessary at the sentencing stage, then a custodial remand can hardly have been necessary to protect the public. The 1985 statistics show that some five-sixths of those committed in custody for Crown Court trial were convicted and received custodial sentences. The figures for magistrates' courts were significantly less satisfactory: of 20,000 people remanded in custody before trial in a magistrates' court, 10,000 were convicted and given a non-custodial sentence, a further 2,500 were acquitted, and some 7,600 were convicted and received a custodial sentence.[57] The face-value interpretation of these figures is that only two-fifths of those remanded in custody to appear in magistrates' courts can conceivably be described as people from whom the public needs protection. Is this the correct interpretation?

At least three lines of argument cast doubt on this. The first is the one that most sentencers hasten to offer: that a court passing sentence must recognize the fact that the offender has already spent time in custody, and that a court may properly take this into account and impose a non-custodial sentence in a case where, if there had been no custodial remand, it would probably have imposed custody. The magistrates

[56] The new sentencing law provides some definitions of these terms: see Criminal Justice Act 1991, ss. 1 (2) (b), 2 (2) (b), and 31. See also above, n. 26 and accompanying text.

[57] 'The Use of Custodial Remand by the Courts 1980 to 1986', *Home Office Statistical Bulletin*, 7/87 (1987), para. 26.

who pass sentence will rarely be the same individuals who refused bail and ordered the custodial remand, so the sentencing decision will be taken entirely *de novo*. There can be no objection to the court taking account of what has already happened: indeed, this may allow the court to adopt a more constructive approach than it might otherwise have felt able to do, by making a community order rather than imposing a custodial sentence. The implication of this argument is that the imposition of a non-custodial sentence does not necessarily suggest that the custodial remand was wrong, since in many cases if there had not been a custodial remand there would have bene a custodial sentence. In theory this argument seems plausible. It is difficult, however, to determine how much substance it has in practice, since no research has been carried out into the reasoning of magistrates when sentencing offenders who have been in custody on remand. No one knows what proportion of the cases resulting in a non-custodial sentence are a response to the custodial remand, and what proportion imply that there need have been no custodial remand in the first place.

Moreover, this first argument may prove rather more than was intended. If it is true that sentencers tend to take account of the fact that an offender has spent time in custody on remand, it may be the case that some of those given custodial sentences are sentenced in that way simply so as to facilitate their immediate release. If the court learns that an offender has been in prison for two months awaiting trial, it may feel that he or she has already been punished quite sufficiently for the offence, and may therefore impose a sentence of four months' imprisonment so as to ensure immediate release.[58] Otherwise, the court might have chosen a suspended sentence or a community service order as a suitable sentence. It is not known how many courts would react in this way—some might grant a conditional discharge or other sentence in these circumstances. But the point is that the numbers of people remanded in custody who are subsequently given *custodial* sentences by magistrates' courts may also include some cases (we know not how many) where the court would not have imposed custody if there had been no custodial remand. To take the further step and assert that the numbers of those given non-custodial sentences who would have received custody but for the custodial remand are far greater than the numbers of those given custodial sentences who would have received non-custodial sentences but for the custodial

---

[58] This is said to be the approach of some courts in other European countries: see e.g. W. Heinz, 'The Problems of Imprisonment', in R. Hood (ed.), *Crime and Criminal Policy in Europe: Proceedings of a European Colloquium* (1989).

remand is to advance into the realms of speculation. The proportions are not known.

A second argument against taking the figures at face value is that the criteria for granting or withholding bail are not directly related to the probability of a custodial sentence. The three criteria in paragraph 2 of the Schedule to the Bail Act focus only on the period between first court appearance and trial. It is true that paragraph 9 of that Schedule suggests that courts should also have regard to 'the nature and serious-ness of the offence and the probable method of dealing with the offender for it', but, as argued above, this does not match any of the substantive criteria. Moreover, many remands in custody are not based on this ground. Where a defendant is remanded in custody because there are substantial grounds for believing that otherwise he or she may not attend the trial, or for believing that otherwise witnesses might be threatened, these reasons have nothing to do with the likely sen-tence in the case. The statistics are not sharp enough to determine to relative proportions of cases: in the Home Office's 1978 survey, the probability of committing an offence was given as a reason in 63 per cent of cases, and the probability of the defendant absconding was given as a reason in 51 per cent of cases. Exactly how many cases depended only on one or the other reason is unclear, but some evi-dently bear no relationship to the probability of a custodial sentence on conviction.

A third argument, arising from the provisions of the Criminal Justice Act 1991, is that there is now a clear disjunction between remand crite-ria and sentencing criteria. The 1991 Act states that a court may only impose a custodial sentence if it is of opinion either that the offence(s) are so serious that only a custodial sentence can be justified, or that (where the offence is a violent or sexual offence) only a custodial sen-tence would be adequate to protect the public from serious harm.[59] No such restrictions are to be found in the Bail Act,[60] and the gap between the two statutes is only narrowed slightly by the provisions of the Criminal Justice Act 1993 on previous convictions and multiple offences.

Consideration of the three lines of argument against a face-value interpretation of the statistics on trial and sentence therefore demon-strates a pervasive uncertainty about the use of bail and of remands in custody. We lack the detailed research necessary to establish which explanations account for what percentage of cases. What does seem to

[59] For analysis, see Ashworth, *Sentencing and Criminal Justice*, 228–31 and 163–7.
[60] Although there are some similar restrictions in respect of juvenile remands: see n. 31 above.

be clear, however, is that the terms of the law on remands ought to be re-examined. It must be decided whether the strength of the case against a defendant ought to be a factor. It must also be decided whether the probable penalty, if the defendant is convicted as charged, ought to be a factor. If either answer is affirmative, the factor must be integrated with the legal criteria for granting and refusing bail—and not left floating freely, as the Schedule to the Bail Act leaves matters now. If dangerousness is to be a criterion, some guidance on types and seriousness of probable conduct must be formulated. Any reform should also address the question of the information on which magistrates may be expected to reach such a decision. Without information, or with information only from one source, decisions may fail to give proper weight to all relevant issues. This calls into question the procedure for taking remand decisions: how can their promptness be preserved whilst their information base is broadened?

5. Procedural Justice and Remand Hearings

We now move on to consider four aspects of procedure relevant to the fairness of remand hearings—the speed of such hearings, the problem of obtaining information, the limitations on fresh argument at subsequent hearings, and appeals.

1. *Speed and delay*: in the 1960s and early 1970s it was the police who dominated remand hearings. A frequent argument was that the defendant should be remanded in custody so that the police could pursue further inquiries, and courts responded to this. The Bail Act 1976 removed this as a reason for refusing bail, but until the mid-1980s almost all remand hearings involved representations from a police officer. The officer would inform the magistrates of any police objections to bail, and then there would be an opportunity for the defendant or (if represented) his solicitor to make representations. Several studies had suggested that the police exerted considerable influence on the outcome of these proceedings, with magistrates following their suggestions in the vast majority of cases.[61] In 1986 the Crown Prosecution Service took over the task of staffing the remand courts, and it was thought that one result would be that greater attention would be paid to the legal criteria in the Bail Act than to the convenience of the police (who might wish to make further inquiries with the defendant 'out of the way'). However, Stone found that there had been no significant

---

[61] See A. K. Bottomley, *Decisions in the Penal Process* (1973).

change in the substance of the representations made to magistrates.[62] This is hardly surprising, for in practice the Crown Prosecutor is likely to receive a large pile of case files on arrival at work in the morning (consisting of 'overnight arrests' by the police) and will have to present these cases to the court that very morning. In those circumstances the most likely course of events is for the prosecutor to rely on the notes appended by the police to each file. Prior to the remand hearing there is unlikely to be much time for a detached review of the nature of the case, as we saw in Chapter 6, and it cannot realistically be expected that the evidential test for bringing a prosecution will be met at the first (or even second) remand hearing. During the hearing, speed seems to be of the essence. In their study of a remand court in Cardiff in 1981, Doherty and East found that cases were processed in court with great rapidity, the clerk setting the tone by rattling through the necessary words. Even in cases where defendants were remanded in custody, some 38 per cent were concluded within two minutes and 87 per cent within ten minutes.[63] No doubt some of the former were remands of persons already in prison, whereas most of those taking longer than ten minutes were probably first hearings; no doubt, also, matters have improved in many courts. Nevertheless, it is important to signal the full seriousness of taking away liberty, and to insist on an inquiry as searching as is feasible at that stage.

People who work in the courts may argue that speed is essential: it is in the defendant's interest to have the question of remand dealt with at the earliest opportunity, and magistrates often have large numbers of cases to hear. But these arguments sometimes divert attention away from the issues at stake. For example, courts may not have sufficient information relating to each of the three criteria in the Bail Act—the probability of absconding, the probability of offending, and the probability of interfering with witnesses. The defendant may be unrepresented, or even if legally represented, the solicitor may have had little time to make background inquiries that address the relevant statutory criteria. We have seen that the Schedule to the Bail Act permits a court to remand a person in custody because there is insufficient information to reach a decision. In principle this is an unsatisfactory state of affairs, and two improvements must be made. First, the Schedule should be amended to ensure that a court should first consider conditional bail, and that if this is not suitable it should order the minimum remand period that is feasible (i.e. not seven days routinely, but no

---

[62] C. Stone, *Bail Information for the Crown Prosecution Service* (1988).
[63] C. Doherty and R. East, 'Bail Decisions in Magistrates' Courts' (1985) 25 *BJ Crim.* 251; cf. A. Hucklesby, 'Unnecessary Legislative Changes', (1993) 143 *NLJ* 233.

more than two or three days unless there are special circumstances). Second, there should be greater funding for bail information schemes, described below, which may both avoid unnecessary custodial remands and enable magistrates to take better-informed decisions.

2. *Bail information schemes*: the problem of obtaining relevant and verified information for remand courts has been recognized for some time. The Vera Institute of Justice began programmes in the United States in the early 1960s, aimed at supplying courts with some objective data on which they could base their decisions, in particular data about the defendant's 'community ties'.[64] This theme was much discussed in England and Wales in the mid-1970s, when bail reform was under consideration, but the innovative Home Office circular on bail in 1975 did no more than state that the Government would be 'grateful' if courts and the Probation Service would 'consider the introduction' of schemes to gather information on community ties for presentation to remand courts. Such schemes as were set up in the mid-1970s were short-lived, apparently because of lack of funds and waning enthusiasm,[65] but the idea behind them was revived in the late 1980s. The Home Office circular of 1988 referred again to the importance of information,[66] but most of the pioneering work in this revival was carried out by the London office of the Vera Institute of Justice.[67] Bail information schemes now appear to be gaining acceptance in the English system. Some of the schemes are based in prisons, helping with information for those already remanded in custody, but the vast majority of schemes operate at magistrates' courts.[68] A probation officer is installed as a bail information officer, with the task of obtaining (and, so far as possible, verifying by telephone) information on an address at which the defendant could stay, on employment, on family ties, etc. The information has to be gathered quickly, usually on the morning of the first remand hearing, but there seems to be general satisfaction with the reliability of the information obtained.[69] In those cases where the defendant seems in danger of being remanded in custody largely because of the absence of an address to stay at, the bail information officer may need to make an attempt to find a place in a bail hostel. This may take time, and may require a case to be put back in the list for hearing.

[64] Jones and Goldkamp, 'Judicial Guidelines', 140–4.
[65] C. Lloyd, *Bail Information Schemes: Practice and Effect*, Home Office RPU Paper 69 (1992).
[66] Home Office Circular 25/1988, *Bail*, para. 5.   [67] Stone, 'Bail Information'.
[68] See Lloyd, 'Bail Information Schemes'.
[69] HM Inspectorate of Probation, *Bail Information: Report of a Thematic Inspection in 1992* (1993).

One feature of the current schemes in England and Wales is that the information is not presented directly to the court. The reasoning is that courts might assume that, if no information had been prepared in a case (because the schemes are inevitably selective), there was nothing favourable to say. The American experience, however, is that involving the courts in the introduction and organization of the schemes is an important element in gaining acceptance for them.[70] In England the information is usually made available both to the Crown Prosecution Service and to the defence. Research suggests that in some areas the CPS treat it as an important component in their decision-making, whereas in other areas they regard it as primarily relevant for the defence rather than the prosecution.[71] The latter point is perhaps understandable, because bail information schemes only transmit information favourable to the defendant,[72] but the ethics of prosecuting suggest that Crown Prosecutors should be equally interested in information that leads them not to make representations against the grant of bail. The task of the CPS should not be simply to advance the police view, or to put forward a 'modified police view', but to take a broader 'Minister of Justice' approach.[73] It is unfortunate that the *Code for Crown Prosecutors* says nothing about bail applications.

Bail information schemes seem likely to make some difference in practice.[74] However, their limited bearing on remand decisions should not be overlooked. Their primary relevance is to the first ground for refusing bail, that the defendant is likely to abscond and not attend the trial. Information about 'community ties' might show that he is less likely to abscond. A place at a bail hostel will ensure accommodation for the period before trial. If by these means we can avoid putting people in prison simply to ensure that they attend their trial, this would be a great advance. But it remains the case that the reason behind the majority of decisions to remand in custody is the second statutory ground, the likelihood that the defendant would commit an offence whilst on bail. Bail information schemes are not concerned principally with this ground or this group of defendants, and are therefore unlikely to have much effect on large numbers of cases.

3. *Fresh argument*: the procedural rules surrounding applications for bail also raise important issues. In *Nottingham Justices, ex parte Davies* (1981),[75] the Divisional Court held that the justices were right to adopt

---

[70] Jones and Goldkamp, 'Judicial Guidelines'.
[71] Lloyd, 'Bail Information Schemes'.
[72] See the discussion by Cavadino and Gibson, *Bail*, 98–100.
[73] See Ch. 3.10, above.   [74] Lloyd, 'Bail Information Schemes'.
[75] [1981] QB 38.

a policy of not reconsidering a remand decision unless the defence could show a change of circumstances or adduce new considerations. Although in many cases it is possible for a defendant denied bail to appeal to the Crown Court, the practical effect of the *Nottingham Justices* ruling was that many defendants did not apply for bail at the first hearing, so as to enable a full argument to be put together by defence lawyers in time for the second hearing. Otherwise there was a risk that a denial of bail after one argued application would preclude argument at subsequent hearing unless a change of circumstances could be shown. Brink and Stone found that between a half and three-quarters of all those remanded in custody at their first appearance had not asked for bail—exposing at once the extraordinary power of a single Divisional Court ruling, and its potential for injustice.[76] Perhaps in response to Brink and Stone's research, the Government promoted what became section 154 of the Criminal Justice Act 1988, which took effect as an amendment to Schedule 1 of the 1976 Act. Paragraph 2 states that: 'At the first hearing after that at which the court decided not to grant the defendant bail he may support an application for bail with any argument as to fact or law that he desires (whether or not he has advanced that argument previously).' After that, a court is not bound to hear arguments that it has heard previously. The intention was widely thought to be to allow defendants 'two bites at the cherry', in other words two argued applications for bail. Yet on one reading the new law merely confirms the *Nottingham Justices* decision: if no application was made on the first occasion and the second one was argued, only new arguments could be raised at the third hearing. The first hearing counts even if no application for bail was made, on this view. Thus defendants have been freed to apply for bail at their first hearing, since they know that they will always have an opportunity to argue for bail fully again on their second appearance, but it remains unclear whether they are entitled to two argued applications, or only to two hearings of any kind. This is regrettable.

4. *Appeals and reapplications*: when a court refuses bail or attaches conditions to it, there is an obligation to state the ground(s) on which the court relies and to give reasons for bringing the case within that ground.[77] If the charge is murder or attempted murder, manslaughter, or rape or attempted rape, a court which grants bail in the face of representations by the prosecution must give reasons for doing so.[78] A defendant who is refused bail by a magistrates' court may make a

---

[76] B. Brink and C. Stone, 'Defendants who do not Ask for Bail', [1988] *Crim.LR* 152.
[77] Bail Act 1976, s. 5 (3).
[78] Criminal Justice Act 1988, s. 153, amending Schedule 1 of the Bail Act.

reapplication to a judge in chambers. Correspondingly, the Bail (Amendment) Act 1993 grants the prosecution the power to appeal to a judge against the grant of bail by a magistrates' court in the face of representations by the prosecution, so long as the charge relates to an offence punishable with five years' imprisonment or more, or is an offence of taking a conveyance without authority or aggravated vehicle-taking. This new power has been criticized, persuasively on the ground that the reference to the offences of taking cars is a political response to a 'moral panic' but unconvincingly on the ground that it is wider than the prosecution's powers in relation to allegedly lenient sentences.[79] In principle, the power constitutes a fair and proper counterbalance to the defence right of reapplication, unless it comes to be used oppressively. The case for allowing decisions for and against bail to be appealable is one of natural justice. The argument for restricting the court's powers to grant bail to persons accused of certain offences trades on political popularity and 'public opinion' as constructed by the media, to the neglect of the presumption of innocence and a principled examination of the issues.[80]

6. Equal Treatment in Remand Decisions

To what extent do remand decisions appear to discriminate against certain sections of the population? To what extent do they fail to recognize the special needs of certain groups? These questions warrant considerable discussion in their own right, and it is possible only to give some general indications here.

The findings of research into the impact of *race* on remand decisions prompt questions about discrimination. In his study of over 3,000 cases Roger Hood found that a higher proportion of defendants from an Afro-Caribbean background (26 per cent) than whites (20 per cent) were remanded in custody pending trial and that, even after taking account of variations in the key facts of individual cases, some apparent discrimination remained.[81] The average number of *females* in prison on remand almost doubled between 1978 and 1988, but has decreased significantly since then. None the less, some 6,000 females are remanded in custody each year. Since women tend to be convicted

[79] See Cavadino and Gibson, *Bail*, 162–5.

[80] Powers in the Criminal Justice and Public Order Bill 1994 will prevent bail being granted to persons charged with murder, attempted murder, manslaughter, rape, or attempted rape, if they already have one conviction for such an offence.

[81] R. Hood, *Race and Sentencing* (1992), 146–50; see generally M. Fitzgerald, *Ethnic Minorities and the Criminal Justice System*, RCCJ Research Study 20 (1993), 19–21.

of less serious offences than men, this total needs careful scrutiny: some of the women will be charged with drug-smuggling offences which might result in substantial prison sentences, but others may be repeat small-time property offenders. The Holloway prison bail unit may have improved conditions,[82] but the most significant problems stem from court decisions. Research by Mary Eaton follows other research in suggesting that women who do not occupy the traditional role of wife and mother are at greater risk of custodial remand, and goes on to suggest that the control exerted by family life on women may, in effect, be treated as 'comparable to that offered by the prison system' when considering whether or not to remand a female defendant in custody.[83] Thus the apparently benevolent emphasis on a defendant's 'community ties' may have disturbing implications for women in differing situations.

Special arrangements for the remand of *mentally disordered defendants* were introduced by the Mental Health Act 1983. However, the power to remand defendants to hospital for a psychiatric report, rather than to prison, appears not to have been widely used. Courts still remand defendants to prison for reports in larger numbers. A further power to remand defendants to hospital for treatment has hardly been used at all.[84] The Reed Committee has now recommended the broadening of these statutory powers, together with restrictions on the power of courts to remand defendants to prison for the primary purpose of medical assessment.[85] Until then, many persons suffering from mental disorder may still be remanded to prison, where conditions are likely to be unsuitable. The suggestion of Paul Cavadino and Bryan Gibson for a new statutory requirement on remand courts to consider 'the state of the physical and mental health of the defendant and the likely effect upon this of a remand in custody' has much to commend it.[86]

There are also special arrangements for the remand of *juvenile* defendants. In essence, the court has three alternatives if it decides not to remand a juvenile on bail: remand to local authority accommodation, remand to local authority accommodation with conditions

---

[82] See Cavadino and Gibson, *Bail*, 102–4.

[83] M. Eaton, 'The Question of Bail', in P. Carlen and A. Worrall (eds.), *Gender, Crime and Justice* (1987), 95, at 107; the previous research cited is that by D. Farrington and A. Morris, 'Sex, Sentencing and Reconvictions', (1983) 23 *BJ Crim*. 229.

[84] P. Fennell, 'Diversion of Mentally Disordered Offenders from Custody', [1991] *Crim. LR* 333, at 337–40.

[85] Department of Health and Home Office, *Review of Health and Social Services for Mentally Disordered Offenders and Others Requiring Similar Services*, Cm. 2088 (1992).

[86] Cavadino and Gibson, *Bail*, 166.

attached, and remand to a prison or remand centre.[87] The last-mentioned alternative is hedged about with restrictions to ensure that the power is only used for sexual, violent, or other serious charges, for juveniles who have absconded persistently from local authority accommodation and have committed a serious offence whilst unlawfully at large, and for those in respect of whom only a custodial remand is adequate to protect the public from serious harm.[88] Despite these restrictions, it appears that this new power has been used in significantly more cases than the previous power.[89] This is worrying, since it is so widely accepted that Prison Service establishments are not suited to the care of the young that the 1991 Act makes provision for the ultimate abolition of these remands for defendants aged under 17. The present powers are said to be 'transitional'.

7. Reducing the Problems

In the concluding part of this chapter there will be further discussion of the justifications for depriving individuals of their liberty before trial, and the length of that deprivation. Here, some ways of dealing with the problem of unnecessary custodial remands will be outlined briefly—bail hostels, electronic monitoring, time-limits for prosecution, and new arrangements to determine mode of trial. The contribution of bail information schemes has already been discussed.

1. *Bail hostels*: we have seen that one of the main problems is ensuring that defendants attend their trials. To imprison someone simply in order to secure this result is to adopt an extremely strong measure, and facilities for placing defendants in hostels have therefore been developed. At the end of 1991 there were 559 places in bail hostels in England and Wales, plus 1,782 places in joint probation/bail hostels, and the Government is committed to providing more places.[90] Since many defendants will spend weeks rather than months in these hostels, their contribution in relieving the prisons is probably much greater than those figures suggest. However, one abiding difficulty with any such measure of 'diversion from custody' is whether courts might not be using bail hostels for defendants who would not have been sent to prison if bail hostels had not existed. Hostels do impose restrictions on liberty, and there is some research suggesting that such a 'malfunction' exists in relation to their use.[91]

---

[87] For fuller discussion, see ibid. 135–8 and 210–13.
[88] Criminal Justice Act 1991, s. 62.   [89] Cavadino and Gibson, *Bail*, 141–3.
[90] House of Commons Written Answer, 8 July 1992, Mr Michael Jack.
[91] H. Lewis and G. Mair, *Bail and Probation Work, ii: The Use of London Probation Bail Hostels for Bailees*, Home Office Research and Planning Unit Paper 50 (1989).

2. *Electronic monitoring*: another expedient, which might succeed both in ensuring that a defendant attends trial and in preventing (or at least detecting) the commission of offences during the period before trial, would be to introduce the electronic monitoring of defendants thought to be at risk. Once again this might be contemplated as a means of 'diversion from custody', by identifying people who might otherwise be remanded in custody but for whom the machinery of 'tagging' might allow them to be returned to the community. There was a field trial at three courts in 1989: in fact, the courts seemed reluctant to use this alternative, and out of the fifty defendants for whom electronic monitoring was used there were eighteen breaches of conditions and eleven offences committed.[92] Although the researchers found that courts were using it only for defendants who would otherwise have been remanded in custody (i.e. no evidence of the expected 'malfunction'), the low usage and apparently high failure rate have meant that little has been heard of this alternative in recent years. There are strong ethical objections to electronic monitoring, on the grounds that it is degrading and an invasion of privacy.[93] However, in the 1991 National Prison Survey, some 82 per cent of those remanded in custody who had heard of electronic monitoring said that they would have preferred it to prison.[94]

3. *Time-limits*: since 1987 there have been limits on the length of time that a person may be kept in custody before trial. It is not proposed to enter into the details of the limits here,[95] since they appear not to have exerted any significant influence on waiting times so far, chiefly because courts have often acceded to prosecution requests for extensions. However, the use of time-limits is one strategy for controlling the duration of pre-trial remands in custody, as has also been recognized in the United States.[96] There are now sufficient decisions of the Divisional Court on what constitutes a 'good and sufficient cause' for extending the law to provide the foundation for clearer and tighter guidelines.

4. *Mode of trial*: it was observed earlier that one reason for the steep increase in the number of persons in custody awaiting trial during the

[92] G. Mair and C. Nee, *Electronic Monitoring: The Trials and their Results*, HORS 120 (1990).

[93] For discussion, see Ashworth, *Sentencing and Criminal Justice*, 265–6.

[94] R. Walmsley *et al.*, *The National Prison Survey 1991: Main Findings*, HORS 128 (1992), 55.

[95] See Cavadino and Gibson, *Bail*, 50–4, summarizing the case-law, and P. Henderson, *Monitoring Time Limits on Custodial Remands*, Home Office Research and Planning Unit Paper 69 (1991).

[96] See generally J. Vennard, 'Court Delay and Speedy Trial Provisions', [1985] *Crim. LR* 73.

1980s was the higher proportion of defendants committed for trial to the Crown Court. Waiting times for Crown Court trials have always been longer than those for the magistrates' courts, and the increase in committals has made them longer still. The National Mode of Trial Guidelines were introduced in 1990, and the proposals of the Royal Commission on Criminal Justice are discussed in Chapter 8 below. Whether there will be a reduction in the proportion of either-way offences committed to the Crown Court for trial, particularly those committed by decision of the magistrates themselves, remains in doubt.

8. Conclusions

To deprive someone of liberty before trial and conviction is prima facie an incursion into that individual's rights, and in principle any burden on an individual at this stage (let alone the deprivation of liberty) needs to be justified.[97] The only way to construct a justification for doing so is to argue that either there is a distinct risk to the rights of another citizen, or there are overwhelming reasons of public interest. A distinct risk to the rights of another citizen might arise if the defendant had already been charged with assaulting a person and there was evidence to suggest a risk of further violence. Alternatively it might arise where there is reason to believe that the defendant will threaten a witness. It might also be said to arise where there is a risk of the defendant committing offences if granted bail, since many offences infringe the rights of individuals. On this last point, however, it is important to be more specific about the kinds of rights to be violated. Since the issue is whether or not the deprivation of liberty before trial an be justified, and since we are discussing probabilities rather than the certainty of infringing another's rights, this ought to be confined to crimes of a particular level of seriousness—that is, at least those crimes likely in themselves to lead to a custodial sentence for the perpetrator.

The second possible justification refers to overwhelming reasons of public interest. One of these might be the public interest in ensuring that defendants who have been charged attend their trials. Although it would be difficult to deny some such interest, it is questionable whether it is strong enough to justify taking away a person's liberty, particularly when absconding is not a certainty but a greater or lesser probability. This is, *par excellence*, a sphere in which non-custodial methods of securing attendance should be developed. It may be argued

[97] R. A. Duff, *Trials and Punishments* (1986), 140, arguing that in principle custodial remands are utterly inconsistent with respect for individual citizens as rational agents.

that the public interest in ensuring that someone is tried becomes greater as the crime charged becomes more serious, and so the seriousness of the charge should be a relevant factor. Once again, however, a court should surely satisfy itself that the Crown Prosecution Service believes that there is sufficient evidence to continue with the charge (recognizing the practical difficulties of this).[98] Moreover, the court should satisfy itself that the offence as alleged is 'worth imprisonment', before there is any question of imprisoning someone so as to ensure that the trial takes place. Expressed in the form that the court should have regard to the punishment to be expected on the basis of the available evidence, this principle would ensure a proper sense of proportion on pre-trial detention.[99]

Another form of public interest may be that of minimizing the number of offences committed by persons on bail. The foundations of this interest were discussed critically in section 1 of this chapter, but the recent enactment of a provision requiring courts to treat offending on bail as an aggravating factor in sentencing demonstrates the political force of this concern.[100] It is particularly strong when there is reason to believe that a defendant has already committed one serious offence and is likely to commit others. It should therefore be insisted that, before a custodial remand is ordered, the prosecution set out the main elements of their case, so that the court can be satisfied (so far as is possible at this early stage) that there is cogent evidence against the defendant. That would also provide some kind of safeguard against the detention of someone likely to be acquitted. There should be a similar safeguard against the detention of someone unlikely to be given a custodial sentence for the offence(s) alleged, as stated in the previous paragraph. It should also be shown that it is more likely than not that this defendant will commit an offence likely to result in imprisonment if granted bail: this requires database for the prediction of offending, the like of which appears not to exist in England and Wales. There is a database for the probability of keeping the conditions of parole if released from prison, and there are some data on the probability of certain offenders committing so-called 'dangerous' offences. But here, unlike the United States,[101] there is no database that can be used to predict offending, let alone serious offending, whilst on bail. The

[98] See Ch. 6.2 above.
[99] See the judgment of the Bundesgerichthof in Germany to this effect, quoted at length by Fawcett, *Application of the European Convention*, 111–13.
[100] Criminal Justice Act 1993, s. 66 (6), substituting s. 29 (2) of the Criminal Justice Act 1991.
[101] See J. Goldkamp and M. R. Gottfredson, *Policy Guidelines for Bail: An Exercise in Court Reform* (1985), based on research in Philadelphia courts.

American research by Goldkamp and Gottfredson does contain some useful pointers—for example, that reoffending and non-appearance at trial are highly correlated so that to predict one is usually to predict the other; and that bailees are more likely to offend the longer the period awaiting trial[102]—but it remains true that the numbers of false positives would be high. The scattered research in England suggests the same, as we saw above: it is easy to say that people charged with taking cars are the group most likely to offend on bail, but most of them are not in fact detected in law-breaking whilst on bail. It is easy to claim that courts should have greater regard to objections to bail advanced by the police, but the vast majority of those to whom the court grants bail in the face of police objections are not detected in law-breaking whilst on bail.[103] As Gottfredson and Gottfredson remark, referring to several pieces of American research, 'the results of these studies cast serious doubt on current abilities to predict with great accuracy the statistically rare events of failure to appear at trial and pre-trial crime'.[104]

None of these observations breaks new ground, and yet their significance for bail has been accorded little attention. Thousands of people are being deprived of their liberty every year on the basis of predictions. These have no statistical foundation, and all the criminological evidence in analogous fields points to the likelihood of considerable over-prediction. Even if it were emphasized that the primary concern is to prevent the commission of *serious* crimes in the period between arrest and trial, that does not make the problem any easier. Serious crimes are harder to predict than law-breaking in general, and the rate of false positives may well be very high. The only possible justification here is that, where the crime is so serious that a substantial custodial sentence is likely to result, pre-trial imprisonment is less of an unwarranted imposition on the guilty (but not the innocent) defendant.[105]

Several points emerge from the foregoing. First, bail/custody decisions are generally predictive, and the evidence for making these predictions is rarely strong. That counsels great caution. Second, much turns on the seriousness of the charge. Rather than simply stating that courts should 'balance' this factor against others, more attention should be paid to the deep significance of depriving someone of liberty and to the probability of a prison sentence being imposed if the facts

[102] Ibid.   [103] See above, n. 54 and accompanying text.
[104] Gottfredson and Gottfredson, *Decision-Making in Criminal Justice*, 93.
[105] This is not to overlook the disadvantages of custodial remands mentioned at the beginning of the chapter—the poor prison conditions, the effect on a person's morale and physical appearance, the inhibitions of preparing the defence, etc.

alleged are proved. That requires the court to make a prediction of a
different kind, but one that should be possible if there is coherent guidance on sentencing. This leads on to the third factor, which is the need
for cogent evidence of guilt before a person is remanded in custody.
Such a requirement is likely to cause considerable difficulties in practice: can the police or prosecution be expected to marshall their evidence quickly? To what extent should account be taken of the probable
line of defence, and the evidence for it? If both these hurdles could be
surmounted, would not a decision to remand in custody tend to create
a presumption of guilt when the case subsequently comes to trial—and
unfairly so, since any previous determination will have incorporated
few safeguards?

These uncertainties have not prevented the Government from
putting before Parliament proposals to 'toughen' the laws on bail.[106]
Whilst the proposed power for the police to impose conditions when
granting police bail is to be welcomed in so far as it removes the stark
choice between custody and unconditional bail, the proposal to restrict
the grant of bail to a person charged with an offence whilst on bail on
another charge raises many of the problems discussed above. In this
climate it is essential to reassert fundamental principles: there should
be a strong presumption in favour of liberty; this ought not to be displaced unless the court is satisfied that there is sufficient evidence to
continue with the charge, a test which should become stricter as time
progresses and should require careful judgements by the Crown
Prosecution Service; the charge, if proved at the trial, should be likely to
result in the imposition of a custodial sentence; and, even in such
cases, the presumption ought not to be displaced unless remand in
custody is necessary because either (1) the defendant appears unlikely
to attend the trial and that non-custodial measures such as the imposition of conditions or the taking of sureties appear unlikely to be successful in securing his or her attendance; even if the court is satisfied
on that ground, it should consider whether the defendant might be
remanded to a bail hostel rather than to prison; or (2) the defendant
appears likely to commit an offence serious enough for custody if
granted bail, whether subject to conditions or not;[107] or (3) the defendant appears likely to threaten witnesses or otherwise to interfere with
the course of justice.[108]

[106] Criminal Justice and Public Order Bill, 1994.
[107] It should be noted that French law has a presumption in favour of custody where
the alleged offence is a *crime* rather than a mere *délit*: L. Leigh and L. Zedner, *A Report on
the Administration of Criminal Justice in the Pre-trial Phase in France and Germany*,
RCCJ Research Study 1 (1992), 23.
[108] Cf. the Canadian provision discussed by Padfield, 'The Right to Bail', 510, which

In order to translate the principles into practice, some thought should be devoted to the idea of developing bail guidelines as a basis for magistrates' decision-making and training. Guidelines have been introduced in Philadelphia with a measure of success.[109] One precondition would be thorough research into the characteristics of remand cases, their disposal at present, and the subsequent conduct of remandees. This would provide the necessary database. Guidelines would then be constructed, and it would remain necessary to insist on improvements in the availability of information relating to defendants. It would remain open to courts to depart from the guidelines on giving reasons, but this would surely be a more sensitive approach to the problems of remand decisions than legislative restrictions.

In those cases where a custodial remand is held to be necessary for one of the reasons above, efforts must be made to keep its duration to a minimum. The question of unnecessary delay in bringing cases to court must be reconsidered at the highest level—not merely because people who should have the benefit of the presumption of innocence are losing days, weeks, and months of their lives, but also because longer waiting times in prison cost the State money. Time-limits and their exceptions should be tightened, and there should be fresh consideration of the need for twenty-eight-day remands in some cases. For those who are remanded in custody, the conditions in which they are held must be improved urgently. Lord Windelesham has argued powerfully for the separate treatment of individuals on remand,[110] and the Woolf Report placed particular emphasis on this,[111] resulting in a Prison Service statement of principles on unconvicted prisoners in 1992. Further attention must also be given to the creation of a new middle path between custodial remand and conditional bail. This might take the form of release upon undertakings, with properly funded supervision from the Probation Service. If successful, it could avoid loss of liberty and show proper respect for the rights of defendants and victims.

refers only to 'the commission of an offence' without any express reference to seriousness, although it does use the phrase 'necessary in the public interest or for the protection or safety of the public'.

[109] Gottfredson and Gottfredson, *Decision-Making in Criminal Justice*, 105–10.
[110] Windlesham, 'Punishment and Prevention', 140.
[111] See Morgan and Jones, 'Bail or Jail?'

8

Mode of Trial

THIS chapter deals with decisions on mode of trial. In England and Wales criminal cases may be tried either at the Crown Court or in a magistrates' court, depending on the legal classification of the offence and sometimes also on the decision of a magistrates' court or of the defendant. The choice of mode of trial has a number of possible implications—the length of delay before trial, the probability and duration of remand in custody, anxiety for defendants, the probability of acquittal, the severity of sentence if convicted, the cost to the public, etc. Decisions on mode of trial can be influenced or even controlled through the charging and discontinuance practices of the prosecution, but one of the central recommendations in the report of the Royal Commission on Criminal Justice raises again the question whether and to what extent defendants can be said to have a right to trial by jury.

The chapter begins with an outline of the existing statutory framework. We then turn to the operation of the system in practice, considering decisions by defendants and decisions by magistrates. The powers of the Crown Prosecution Service are then discussed, before going on to examine some key issues of policy and principle relating to mode of trial. The implications of the present system and the proposed reform are considered in respect of victims and of certain ethnic minorities, and the recommendations of the 1993 Royal Commission are appraised.

1. The Statutory Framework

English law divides offences into three categories.[1] The first consists of offences triable only on indictment. Among these are the most serious offences in the criminal calendar, such as murder, manslaughter, rape, and wounding with intent, together with a number of other offences such as blackmail. These offences are triable only in the Crown Court: if the case is contested, trial is by judge and jury. The third category

[1] The law is contained in pt. II of the Criminal Law Act 1977. Those statutory provisions resulted from the recommendations of the James Committee, some of which are discussed in s. 3 of this chapter.

consists of offences triable summarily only. Among these are the least serious types of offence, such as non-payment of the television licence fee and many road traffic offences. These offences are triable only in a magistrates' court, and trial is usually by a bench of lay magistrates advised by a clerk.[2]

It is the second category of offences that gives rise to most discussion. These are offences 'triable either way', that is, they may be tried in the Crown Court or at a magistrates' court. Broadly speaking, this category includes offences of intermediate seriousness or of variable seriousness. It includes several of the most frequently committed offences, such as theft, handling stolen goods, obtaining by deception, and burglary. The procedure here is that the mode of trial must be decided in a magistrates' court. In the first place, the law confers on the magistrates the power to decide whether the case should be tried summarily or should be committed to the Crown Court for trial. Among the circumstances that the statute directs them to consider are the nature of the case, whether the circumstances of the offence give it a serious character, and whether the sentencing powers of a magistrates' court would be adequate. Before taking their decision, the magistrates must invite the prosecution and the defence to make representations on mode of trial. If the magistrates decide that the case ought to be committed to the Crown Court for trial, the next step would be to hold committal proceedings in order to determine whether there is sufficient evidence for the case to be committed for trial.[3] If, on the other hand, the magistrates decide that the case is suitable for summary trial, they must then ask the defendant whether he or she consents to summary trial or wishes to elect trial in the Crown Court. At present the defendant has an absolute right to elect Crown Court trial for all either-way offences, but, as we shall see, its abolition has been recommended by the Royal Commission on Criminal Justice.

2. Mode of Trial Decisions in Practice

In 1991 some 490,000 persons were prosecuted for offences that were triable either way or on indictment only (the latter group probably amounts to fewer than 20,000). Some 80,000 of the either-way cases were committed for trial to the Crown Court, which means that

[2] There is also a relatively small number of stipendiary magistrates, who are legally qualified and sit alone, usually in the courts of large urban areas. See further *Emmins on Criminal Procedure* (5th edn. by J. Sprack, 1992), 171–2.

[3] These will not be discussed here. In practice, the vast majority of committals are now 'paper committals', not challenged by the defence and not requiring a court hearing of any kind. For further discussion, see ibid., ch. 4.

five-sixths of the total were tried in the magistrates' courts.[4] In general, therefore, the vast majority of mode of trial decisions are in favour of trial in the magistrates' court. Looked at from the Crown Court, however, around four-fifths of its case-load consists of cases triable either way. Some three-fifths of these cases are committed because of decisions taken by magistrates, with elections by defendants forming around two-fifths. These figures show that most of the defendants who could choose Crown Court trial do not do so, chiefly because they intend to plead guilty. None the less, the Crown Court is overflowing with cases, and it is hardly surprising that there has been considerable pressure, for reasons of economy and management, to reduce the numbers of either-way cases going there. The first step is to inquire why those defendants who choose the Crown Court do so, and why magistrates' courts commit even larger numbers to the Crown Court.

(a) Decisions by Defendants

At least four major research studies in the last twenty years have inquired into the reasons why many defendants who could have their cases tried in a magistrates' court choose to go to the Crown Court.[5] The substance of their findings is strikingly similar, although both Gregory and Bottoms and McClean found a significant minority of defendants who seemed not properly to have appreciated the choice they had made.[6] The main finding is that those defendants and their advisers who choose Crown Court trial seem to lack confidence in the quality of magistrates' justice. They seem to believe that magistrates' courts favour the prosecution unduly, and that the Crown Court offers a fairer and fuller hearing with a higher chance of acquittal. Indeed, in Hedderman and Moxon's sample some 69 per cent of defendants and 81 per cent of solicitors gave the higher chance of acquittal as a reason.[7] In Riley and Vennard's study the reason given most frequently by defendants who chose the Crown Court was 'previous experience with the courts', a reason not developed by the authors but which may well reflect perceptions of fairness and of acquittal rates.[8] All the

[4] Home Office Statistical Bulletin 30/92, *Court Proceedings in 1991* (1992).

[5] A. E. Bottoms and J. D. McClean, *Defendants in the Criminal Process* (1976); J. Gregory, *Crown Court or Magistrates' Court?* (1976); D. Riley and J. Vennard, *Triable-Either-Way Cases: Crown Court or Magistrates' Court?*, HORS 98 (1988); C. Hedderman and D. Moxon, *Magistrates' Court or Crown Court? Mode of Trial Decisions and Sentencing*, HORS 125 (1992).

[6] Gregory, *Crown Court*, 10; Bottoms and McClean, *Defendants in the Criminal Process*, 84–5.   [7] Hedderman and Moxon, *Magistrates' Court*, 20.

[8] Riley and Vennard, *Triable-Either-Way Cases*, 17; cf. also Hedderman and Moxon, *Magistrates' Court*, 22.

studies show that most of those who intend to plead not guilty choose to be tried in the Crown Court, whereas most of those who intend to plead guilty consent to summary trial if it is offered.

These trends in practice may appear to reflect rational choices. A person who intends to plead not guilty to one or more charges will naturally wish to maximize the probability of acquittal. The acquittal rate in the magistrates' courts has been found to be about half that in the Crown Court, some 30 per cent compared with 57 per cent.[9] The rationality of choosing the Crown Court should not, however, be assessed on this basis alone. Consider, for example, the minority of defendants who intend to plead not guilty and yet who consent to trial by magistrates—about one-quarter of the defendants in Riley and Vennard's study who intended to plead not guilty.[10] Predominant among their reasons were the avoidance of delay and the chance of a lighter sentence if convicted. These reasons, if borne out by experience, might well be taken to outweigh the higher probability of acquittal offered by Crown Court trial. In fact, experience supports both reasons. Delays in bringing cases to trial are much shorter for trials in magistrates' courts than for the Crown Court trials.[11] A recent study suggests that sentences in the Crown Court for triable-either-way cases are some seven times as severe as they are for comparable cases sentenced by magistrates—custody is three times more likely, and custodial sentences are more than twice the length on average.[12]

This analysis might suggest that, from the defendant's point of view, decisions on mode of trial have an element of roulette. The defendant who opts for the Crown Court gambles on an acquittal, knowing that the delay will be longer and knowing that if the gamble fails the sentence is likely to be far more severe than in a magistrates' court. The defendant who consents to summary trial knows that the chances of acquittal are lower, but has the consolation that the process will be over more quickly and that the sentence will not be as severe. However, the research indicates that the reality is even more complex, since at least five further factors come into play. The first is that many defendants who elect trial in the Crown Court are unaware of the large differences in sentence severity between the Crown Court and magistrates' courts.[13] Indeed, 59 per cent of defendants and 38 per cent of solicitors in Hedderman and Moxon's sample expressed the belief that the

[9] J. Vennard, 'The Outcome of Contested Trials', in D. Moxon (ed.), *Managing Criminal Justice* (1985), at 131.

[10] Ibid. 16–17.   [11] *Criminal Statistics, England and Wales* (1991), ch. 8.

[12] Hedderman and Moxon, *Magistrates' Court*, 36–7.

[13] It is also likely that many of those who consent to summary trial do not realize how favourable to them the difference in sentence is likely to be.

sentence would be lighter in the Crown Court,[14] a belief which in general is false. Almost one-half of those defendants also said afterwards that they thought one benefit had been a lighter sentence, but what they probably meant by this was that a guilty plea in the Crown Court had secured for them a lighter sentence than they might otherwise have received there.[15] In so far as they believed that the sentence was lighter than magistrates would have given, the belief was a false one.

A second factor is that defendants committed for trial in custody may benefit from more congenial prison conditions for a longer period. Those conditions include the probability of being held close to home (facilitating more frequent visits from family and friends, and better access for lawyers), the right to wear one's own clothes, more money to spend, etc. The recommendations of the Woolf Inquiry to improve prison conditions for prisoners held on remand may well strengthen these advantages.[16] However, they can only be described as 'benefits' or 'advantages' if the defendant thinks it certain or highly likely that the Crown Court will impose a substantial custodial sentence—of such a length that the defendant's period on remand does not mean that he or she spends longer inside than is necessary in order to serve the sentence,[17] and certainly longer than a magistrates' court could have imposed.[18]

The third factor that renders these decisions more complex is that, although most of the defendants who intend to plead not guilty opt for Crown Court trial, some two-thirds of those who do so actually change their plea to guilty before the trial comes on.[19] This means that they choose Crown Court trial in order to obtain the benefits of a 'fuller and fairer' hearing and an increased probability of acquittal, only to forgo those benefits in the end. Most of those who change their plea to guilty do so on the day of the trial, almost invariably in response to legal advice and frequently, one assumes, as part of a bargain.[20] Questions of plea bargaining are discussed fully in Chapter 9 below.

[14] Hedderman and Moxon, *Magistrates' Court*, 20.   [15] Ibid. 25–6.

[16] *Prison Disturbances April 1990: Report of an Inquiry by the Rt. Hon. Lord Justice Woolf and His Honour Judge Stephen Tumim*, Cm. 1456 (1991), ch. 10, discussed above in Ch. 7.3.

[17] For example, a sentence of eight months' imprisonment means four months in prison followed by conditional release for four months; if, therefore, the defendant spent longer than four months on remand in custody, there would be no 'benefit' because he or she would have been deprived of liberty for a longer time than necessary.

[18] Although in this calculation the possibility of magistrates committing the offender to the Crown Court for sentence should be borne in mind.

[19] Riley and Vennard, *Triable-Either-Way Cases*, 19; see also Hedderman and Moxon, *Magistrates' Court*, 22–4.

[20] Hedderman and Moxon, *Magistrates' Court*, 23, found that 29% of those who changed their plea did so in exchange for the prosecution dropping or reducing one or more charges.

Connected with change of plea may be a fourth factor: almost a half of all defendants and solicitors interviewed in Hedderman and Moxon's study said that one reason for electing trial was to obtain more information about the prosecution case.[21] This is a reason for electing trial which the Government attempted to overcome in the mid-1980s by making advance disclosure of the prosecution case available for all either-way cases, irrespective of mode of trial.[22] However, it has remained true that the disclosure obtained after electing Crown Court trial tends to be more informative than the summaries available for the magistrates' courts, although changes are now in hand.[23] Whilst it may be doubted whether a desire for disclosure would ever be a sufficient reason for electing Crown Court trial, it seems that it is a significant element in some decisions, probably on legal advice. What that disclosure reveals may, in turn, tend to produce some of the changes of plea from not guilty to guilty in the Crown Court.

This leads on to the fifth factor, the legal advice itself. Whilst it is undoubtedly correct, as a matter of law and practice, for counsel to advise the defendant about the sentencing discount for pleading guilty in the Crown Court, the result is still that on average sentences received by defendants in the Crown Court are seven times as severe as those in magistrates' courts for comparable cases. This turns the attention to the advice given to defendants before they make their decision on mode of trial. About three-quarters of solicitors in Riley and Vennard's study offered advice to their clients on mode of trial, and it seems that that advice usually accorded with the defendant's own preference. 'Only 6 out of 98 defendants initially favouring the magistrates' court were advised to elect, while 23 of the 156 intending to opt for the Crown Court were advised to consent to summary trial.'[24] Solicitors' views on the advantages of the two modes of trial were similar to those of defendants, and it is possible that they too underestimate the high risks of electing trial in the Crown Court. They may underestimate the numbers who subsequently change their plea to guilty, and they may underestimate the much greater severity of Crown Court sentences. Otherwise, it might be argued, they would do their clients a greater service by advising strongly against election in more cases. However, even

[21] Ibid. 20.
[22] See F. Feeney, 'Advance Disclosure of the Prosecution Case', in Moxon (ed.), *Managing Criminal Justice*, and J. Baldwin and A. Mulvaney, 'Advance Disclosure in the Magistrates' Courts: How Useful are the Prosecution Summaries?', [1987] *Crim. LR* 805.
[23] Criminal Justice Consultative Council, *Mode of Trial Decisions and Sentencing* (1993), 17.
[24] Riley and Vennard, *Triable-Either-Way Cases*, 18.

this line of argument has its practical drawbacks.[25] When the case is tried summarily, magistrates' powers to commit the defendant to the Crown Court for sentence are substantial, and so there remains the possibility that the case may reach the higher court anyway.[26]

(b) Decisions by Magistrates

Magistrates may take a decision on mode of trial only after giving the prosecution and the defence an opportunity to make representations. In fewer than one-half of cases in Riley and Vennard's study where the defendant was legally represented did the defence make any submissions on mode of trial.[27] Since the defendant has an absolute right to elect Crown Court trial, the defence has no need to make representations in favour of this: the defendant will have the opportunity to make that election. But where the defence preferred summary trial and made representations in its favour, whilst the prosecution argued in favour of committal to the Crown Court, the magistrates accepted the prosecution's view in twenty-seven of the twenty-nine cases. Indeed, in Riley and Vennard's study some 96 per cent of magistrates' decisions were consistent with the prosecutor's representations.[28]

One possible explanation for this high degree of concordance is that the magistrates were failing to exercise independent judgement, and were simply accepting the prosecution's view almost every time. Another possible explanation is that prosecutors and magistrates were independently applying the same criteria, and usually came to the same conclusion. This has certainly been the formal position since the National Mode of Trial Guidelines were announced in 1991.[29] However, the problem with this explanation is that there have been long-standing local differences. The rates of committal to the Crown Court varied widely between the two areas studied by Riley and Vennard: almost two-thirds of the either-way cases at the Leicester and

---

[25] It also has one defect of principle, i.e. that it may lead a solicitor to say things which put pressure on an innocent person to plead guilty, even if the solicitor expressly disavowed that intention. See further Ch. 9.7.

[26] See s. 38 of the Magistrates' Courts Act 1980, as substituted by s. 25 of the Criminal Justice Act 1991, further amended by s. 66 of the Criminal Justice Act 1993. The previous law allowed magistrates to commit to the Crown Court for sentence only where the offender's previous record indicated the desirability of a longer sentence.

[27] Riley and Vennard, *Triable-Either-Way Cases*, 12.   [28] Ibid. 11.

[29] The *Code for Crown Prosecutors* (1992) states that 'the aim of the Crown Prosecutor in making representations as to venue should be to assist the Court in its exercise of judicial discretion' according to the guidelines (para. 18). The prosecutor may, however, consider the effect of delay, so as to avoid additional cost and possible adverse effect on witnesses (para. 19).

Northampton Crown Courts had been committed by magistrates, compared with fewer than one-third of either-way cases at the Newcastle and Durham Crown Courts. For the most numerous offences, theft and handling, some 52 per cent of cases had been committed by magistrates in Leicestershire and Northamptonshire, compared with a mere 20 per cent in Northumbria and Durham.[30] These figures show that magistrates and prosecutors may be applying the same criteria in each area, but that these were certainly not national criteria, such as those formerly set out in the *Code for Crown Prosecutors*. What had happened was that the liaison judges in Leicestershire and Northamptonshire had drawn up guidance for 'their' magistrates,[31] and the Crown Prosecution Service had adapted its practices accordingly. Figures from the survey by Hedderman and Moxon show that local variations were also evident in 1990, with magistrates declining jurisdiction in 5 per cent of either-way cases at Cardiff, 14 per cent at nearby Newport, and 18 per cent at Camberwell Green, London.[32] Whilst that study also shows that there is a general relationship between magistrates' decisions and the seriousness of offences, it is clear that different thresholds of seriousness for committal to the Crown Court operate in different localities.

It seems likely that there is an element of what might be termed 'adaptive behaviour'—prosecutors appear to shape their representations to magistrates' practice, perhaps in order not to lose the respect of the court by making 'unrealistic' representations. The Criminal Justice Consultative Council acknowledges that 'local cultures might build up and Crown Prosecutors in framing advice might be influenced by the informal policy of the local bench'.[33] The Council raises some poignant questions about local policies:[34] it is doubtful whether many of these policies could survive scrutiny from the national point of view, but the resilience of local cultures will make this an interesting challenge for the Council's ability to bring about change.

One factor that magistrates should take into account when deciding on mode of trial, according to section 19 (3) of the Magistrates' Courts Act 1980, is whether the maximum penalty they have power to impose would be adequate. The survey by Hedderman and Moxon showed that, of the cases sent to the Crown Court by magistrates, over two-thirds received sentences that lay within the powers of the magistrates'

[30] Ibid. 9–10.

[31] Liaison judges have no statutory or other authority to do so, but their views tend to be followed because they operate at a higher level in the criminal justice system than lay magistrates. See further A. Ashworth, *Sentencing and Criminal Justice* (1992), 51–2.

[32] Hedderman and Moxon, *Magistrates' Court*, 12.

[33] *Mode of Trial Decisions and Sentencing*, 8.   [34] Ibid. 10 and 20.

court.[35] This seems to suggest either that magistrates do not regard this as the most important factor, or that magistrates have insufficient information on which to base an accurate prediction of sentence. The latter is probably true, in that magistrates are not told about previous convictions at a mode of trial hearing, and may assume either that the defendant has them or that the prosecution is representing in favour of Crown Court trial because it knows of them. Mitigating factors are unlikely to come out fully at this stage, and no pre-sentence report is likely to be available. However, a more persuasive explanation is that the likely penalty has not been regarded as a sufficiently powerful reason to override some local policies or traditions, such as the policy of committing all residential burglaries to the Crown Court irrespective of the particular facts.[36] More attention to likely penalty could reduce the number of cases committed to the Crown Court for trial, provided that magistrates had the necessary information on seriousness of offence and personal mitigation.

3. Prosecutorial Powers and Mode of Trial

Whilst English prosecutors do not have the right to determine the level of court in which a case is tried, it is evident that in many cases they have considerable power *de facto*. A concordance rate of 96 per cent between magistrates' decisions and prosecution representations could include a number of cases where prosecutors are merely trying to anticipate magistrates' decisions rather than influence them, but the likelihood is that magistrates are (at least sometimes) influenced by what prosecutors say. However, English prosecutors have more subtle ways of influencing mode of trial, through decisions on the charge(s) to be brought in a particular case. If the prosecutor wishes a case to be heard in the Crown Court, the way to ensure this is to bring a charge that is triable only on indictment. If, on the other hand, a prosecutor wishes a case to be dealt with in a magistrates' court, the way to ensure this is to bring a charge that is triable summarily only.

Of course it would be wrong to suggest that prosecutors have a completely free hand in this matter. Much depends on the nature of the defendant's conduct and the availability of offences that are summary only or (perhaps less easy) indictable only. The criminal law does not offer great choice in some spheres. Much may also depend on the charge originally laid, usually by the police: the Crown Prosecution

---

[35] Hedderman and Moxon, *Magistrates' Court*, ch. 4.
[36] Referred to by the Criminal Justice Consultative Council, *Mode of Trial Decisions and Sentencing*, 10.

Service might continue with an either-way charge in order to avoid dis-appointment to the police and a possible deterioration in working arrangements, even if the case could have been dealt with adequately at a magistrates' court.[37] We have seen, in Chapter 6, that the Crown Prosecution Service has wide powers to drop cases, including the statutory power to discontinue prosecutions in the magistrates' courts, under section 23 of the Prosecution of Offences Act 1985, and a power to drop cases when they are called on at the Crown Court.[38]

Discontinuance can be followed by recharging, where appropriate. The relevant guidance would then be paragraph 12 (iii) of the *Code for Crown Prosecutors*, stating that the charges 'should adequately reflect the gravity of the defendant's conduct', should 'normally be the most serious revealed by the evidence', but may be less than the most serious so long as the court's sentencing powers remain adequate. This may be taken to suggest that the Crown Prosecution Service may prefer a summary-only charge, even though the facts disclose a more serious offence, where speed of trial is important and where magistrates' sentencing powers seem adequate. Presumably the Service's *Manuals*, which are protected by the Official Secrets Acts, give further guidance on this question.

Why might the prosecution wish to ensure that a case is tried in a magistrates' court? This question has been discussed by appellate courts in cases where prosecutors have dropped more serious charges in order to ensure summary trial, and where defendants have challenged the decision by seeking to invoke the doctrine of abuse of process.[39] In *Ramsgate Justices, ex parte Warren et al.* (1981)[40] the defendants were charged with various either-way offences as a result of disturbances on the sea-front at Ramsgate. When the defendants elected trial in the Crown Court, the police dropped the either-way charges and instead charged each defendant with a summary offence. In *Canterbury and St Augustine's Justices, ex parte Klisiak* (1981)[41] the defendant was charged with criminal damage at a public house to the value of £414. At this time persons charged with criminal damage had a right to elect Crown Court trial if the damage was valued at more than £200. Klisiak elected trial. The police subsequently wrote to the defendant's solicitors informing them of an intention to amend the charge to

[37] See M. McConville, A. Sanders, and R. Leng, *The Case for the Prosecution* (1991), 141–6.
[38] Discussed in Ch. 6.2 and 6.3, above.
[39] See generally A. Choo, *Abuse of Process and Judicial Stays of Criminal Proceedings* (1993).
[40] (1981) 72 Cr. App. R. 250.   [41] Ibid.

damage valued at £155, adding that this, 'as you of course will realise, precludes this case from a Crown Court hearing'.

Declining to accept the submission that the prosecutor's conduct in either case amounted to an abuse of process, Lord Lane, CJ, in the Divisional Court, placed great weight on the fact that the prosecutors could have chosen to prefer the lower charges at the outset. 'It seems to me that to achieve this same result by the procedural course which, in fact, was adopted, cannot be said to have been oppressive or unjust or any abuse of the processes of the court.' He added that there may be good reasons for choosing a lesser charge—e.g. speed of trial, sufficiency of proof, and trial summarily rather than on indictment, perhaps in order to deal swiftly with disorder such as sea-front disturbances during the summer holiday period. Lord Lane added that 'it is, however, to be hoped that, where proper, the lesser charge will be preferred at the outset'.[42]

This judgment has acquired great respect. The criteria in paragraph 12 of the *Code for Crown Prosecutors* are taken directly from it. Yet Lord Lane's discussion of the applicants' main point is unconvincing. He referred to the contention that, when the prosecution reduces the charges from either-way to summary offences, 'the defendant may thereby lose his right to trial by jury if, indeed, it is, on balance, properly to be described as a loss at all'. Lord Lane plainly thought that to speak of losing a right was a ridiculous analysis:

what the prosecution have done is to lower the nature of the case against the defendant and the possible consequential penalties. We have a Gilbertian result here of applicants complaining that they are now charged with lesser offences than those which they originally had to face.[43]

The allusion to comic opera misses the point. It is not so much that the defendants were complaining that they were likely to receive lower sentences: that would indeed be a nonsensical attitude. Surely their complaint was that they were being deprived of Crown Court trial and the higher chances of acquittal. After all, these are the reasons why most of the defendants electing trial in the Crown Court do so,[44] and the acquittal statistics certainly favour Crown Court trial.[45] As the James Committee recognized:

What matters to them is the fact of conviction or acquittal. Except in the most serious cases, where the defendant knows that if convicted he will receive a

---

[42] (1981) 72 Cr. App. R. at 261.   [43] Ibid., at 259.
[44] See n. 7 above and accompanying text.
[45] See n. 9 above and accompanying text.

substantial sentence of imprisonment, loss of reputation or loss of livelihood rather than the possible sentence may well be what is uppermost in his mind.[46]

Of course it is fair to say that such a defendant would probably receive a higher sentence if convicted in the Crown Court, but the Lord Chief Justice's reasoning in the *Canterbury* and *Ramsgate* cases overlooks the prior question of conviction or acquittal. The same reasoning was adopted by Leggatt, J., in the Divisional Court in *Liverpool Stipendiary Magistrate, ex parte Ellison* (1989).[47]

In the *Liverpool* case, Bingham, LJ, did warn against a prosecutor 'manipulating or using the procedures of the court in order to oppress or unfairly to prejudice a defendant before the court'. The position seems to be that a prosecutor can amend the charges so long as the charge remains an appropriate one on the facts, and so long as there is no bad faith on the part of the prosecutor or unfairness or prejudice to the defendant. The issue of prejudice raises deep questions concerning the nature of the defendant's rights. Since English law does confer on defendants an absolute right to elect Crown Court trial for either-way offences, at what stage does that right crystallize? One difference between the three cases is that in the *Ramsgate* and *Canterbury* cases the magistrates had already held the proceedings for the determination of mode of trial and the defendants had exercised their right to elect trial on indictment, whereas in the *Liverpool* case the charge was amended before the mode of trial decision had been taken. Leggatt, J., in the *Liverpool* case seemed not to make this distinction when he opined that 'to speak of depriving the applicant of his right to trial by jury is . . . only a pejorative way of making the point that on the reduction of the charge he ceased to be confronted by a charge sufficiently serious to warrant trial by jury'. He also stated that 'until the more serious charge in this case was withdrawn, the applicant enjoyed such a prospective right [to trial by jury], but in relation to the less serious charge he did not'.[48] On the facts of the *Liverpool* case it would be difficult to argue that any substantive right had yet vested in the defendant—both for the principled reason that no election had been made, and for the pragmatic reason that this might otherwise inhibit the prosecution from amending the charges where a review of the evidence or a change in circumstances rendered this advisable. However, once the magistrates have held proceedings for the determination of mode of

---

[46] James Committee, *The Distribution of Criminal Business between the Crown Court and Magistrates' Courts*, Cmnd. 6323 (1975), para. 59; see also para. 142 on the reasons for electing Crown Court trial in drunk driving cases in the 1970s.
[47] [1990] RTR 220.					[48] Ibid., at 226.

trial, one might maintain that the right has vested, and therefore any change should require the defendant's consent.

How far the pragmatic reason should be given weight in cases where the defendant has already elected trial on indictment is a difficult matter. In the *Canterbury* case the matter was clouded: the original charge related to property valued at £414 but the prosecution maintained that they then found that they had insufficient evidence of the damage to certain items. If this was true, then the defendant could hardly claim even an embryonic right to elect trial in respect of damage that he could not be proved to have caused. But the suspicion in the *Canterbury* case is that the explanation of 'insufficiency of evidence' may have been a device used to ensure that the case did not go to the Crown Court. The point is therefore reduced to one of the prosecutor's motivation. The *Ramsgate* case raises another difficulty. It seems that one reason for preferring summary charges was to ensure that the cases were dealt with more quickly (Crown Court waiting times tend to be longer) in the hope of achieving a deterrent effect during the summer holiday season. Could it be said that that deprives the defendant of an embryonic right? Is the reason given not a proper prosecutorial argument?

These arguments suggest that two questions should be kept distinct. One is the question of proper and improper reasons for prosecutors preferring certain charges. The basic proposition is that the charge should be the one that relates most closely to the facts that the prosecutor has a reasonable prospect of proving. Then there is a need for guidance on the broad range of the reasons for departing from this: among the proper reasons might be the need for expedition in dealing with the case, the effect on certain witnesses, and whether the magistrates' sentencing powers for a lesser offence would be adequate; one improper reason might be the improved chances of obtaining a conviction in the magistrates' court. Some such reasons should be stated in guidelines (although these could not be exhaustive), and a system of accountability should be put in place, since these decisions have significant consequences for defendants. A more focused doctrine of abuse of process might be a suitable way of enforcing accountability,[49] but the primary approach would be to articulate clear guidance for prosecutors.

The second question is that of timing, within the present system which grants defendants a right to elect. Whilst it is right that there should be continuing review of case files by prosecutors, it is surely

---

[49] See the discussion of accountability in Ch. 6.6, above.

wrong that a change of mind by the prosecution after a defendant has elected trial on an either-way charge should be allowed to remove the case to the magistrates' court, if the defendant is unwilling to agree to that course. This creates a difficulty, since it was argued in Chapter 6 above that the prosecution should have the right to drop a case (and, therefore, to reduce the charge) at any time until the start of the Crown Court trial. Sensible as this is as a matter of prosecution policy, it creates a conflict in cases where the defendant has already elected Crown Court trial. There is a difference between preferring a lesser charge originally, for acceptable reasons as set out in guidelines, and preferring a lesser charge after mode of trial proceedings, for whatever reasons. This difference was recognized in *Brooks* (1985),[50] where the Court of Appeal held that the prosecutor had abused the process of the court by bringing a charge of an indictable-only offence after mode of trial proceedings in which the magistrates did not follow the prosecutor's representations and declined to commit the defendant for trial on an either-way charge. O'Connor, LJ, held that the prosecutor's decision effectively amounted to overruling or usurping the decision of the magistrates.[51] The same reasoning ought to apply, *pari passu*, to decisions taken by prosecutors after the defendant has exercised the right to elect trial on indictment.

As it has been argued above that the proper exercise of prosecutors' powers may turn on motivation, can a similar argument be applied to defendants and their rights? We have seen that defendants occasionally elect trial on indictment in order to postpone the time of their conviction, perhaps to gain the privileges of a remand prisoner for a longer time if they believe a custodial sentence to be inevitable. Recent research shows that this strategy carries a high risk, since custodial sentences in the Crown Court are two-and-a-half times as long on average as those in magistrates' courts, although some of these defendants would in any event be committed for sentence to the Crown Court.[52] But it can be argued that this use of the right of election is improper, in that it bears no relation to the reason for granting the right. The James Committee mentioned elections made on the advice of a legal adviser, chiefly (although not explicitly) to obtain higher fees for that legal adviser.[53] Such elections would also be improper, though the

[50] [1985] Crim. LR 385.
[51] Cf. *R.* v. *Redbridge Justices and Fox, ex p. Whitehouse* (1992) 156 JPR 293, where Neill, LJ, held that there might be circumstances in which it might not be an abuse of process for a prosecutor to prefer a higher charge after the completion of mode of trial proceedings in court (at 300).
[52] See above, n. 12 and accompanying text.
[53] James Report, para. 52, '. . . neither proved nor disproved . . .'

impropriety stems from the defence lawyer rather than from the defendant. The most contestable category is that of guilty defendants who elect Crown Court trial in the hope of taking advantage of the tendency of juries to acquit: is this legitimate or not?

4. Policies Relevant to Mode of Trial Decisions

For at least twenty years governments have been concerned about mode of trial decisions. Most of this concern seems to have had far more to do with public expenditure and the staffing of the courts than with issues of principle. The report of the Royal Commission on Criminal Justice, to be discussed below, seems preoccupied by policy but does refer to some questions of principle. The purpose of this section is to identify and discuss the issues of policy raised by the existing law and proposals for change. Issues of principle will mostly be left over to the following section.

Most systems of criminal justice have at least two levels of court, one dealing with the less serious cases and one dealing with the more serious cases. The way in which offences are defined for the purposes of criminal liability may not yield distinctions that are suitable for allocating cases to one mode of trial rather than the other. At the extremes there may be some classes of crime so serious that only trials in a higher court would be appropriate, and some classes of offence so minor that only trial in a lower court would be appropriate. However, to define these categories it is necessary to mark boundaries, and there may be some offences that do not fit easily into either class. For example, a single offence of robbery may cover everything from a full-scale armed robbery down to a push in order to snatch a purse. The least serious variety might be suitable for the lower criminal courts, whereas other varieties should be tried on indictment. One possible solution would be to create an intermediate category of offences that may be tried either in the lower or in the higher courts, according to the circumstances. This is not the only solution: if prosecutors were given the absolute right to specify the mode of trial, no statutory division of offences might be needed, and only the sentencing powers of lower courts would restrict choices. However, the importance of these decisions would make it necessary to create some structures of guidance and accountability, probably through the drafting of guidelines with the possibility of judicial review to challenge departures. If, on the other hand, the idea of creating an intermediate category were pursued, three questions would arise: according to what criteria should the lower boundary of the class of offences triable only in higher courts be set? according to what criteria should the upper boundary of the class of offences triable only in the lower courts be set? in the intermediate class, who should choose whether the case is tried in the lower or higher courts?

These decisions must also be set in their policy context. Among the relevant considerations, in terms of government policy, are likely to be the relative cost of proceedings, the availability of judicial officers, and the availability of courtrooms in the higher and lower courts. If there were little difference in these spheres, the choices might be made on 'pure' criminal justice grounds. However, in England and Wales as in many other countries, the differences in public expenditure are considerable. In 1988–9 the average cost of a contested case at the Crown Court was £3,100, compared with £295 in a magistrates' court; the average costs of the prosecution were £460 and £50 respectively.[54] These differences, together with the related costs of legal aid for defendants, provide governments with powerful reasons for trying to minimize the number of Crown Court trials by encouraging, or legislating for, the trial of more cases in the magistrates' courts.

There is also a strong link between mode of trial decisions and pre-trial remands in custody. When the steep rise in the remand population in prisons in the 1980s was investigated, it was found that it was associated with a sharp increase in the numbers of defendants being committed for trial in the Crown Court. Between 1979 and 1986 the number of either-way cases committed to the Crown Court increased by nearly one-half, from 55,000 to 81,000. In addition to this, a somewhat higher percentage of these defendants were remanded in custody (a rise from 17 to 22 per cent). And waiting times for Crown Court trials, always longer than for magistrates' courts, lengthened further.[55] The result is that more people are spending longer periods of time in prison before they have been tried. The causes seem to lie in a greater propensity among magistrates to commit cases for trial, particularly burglary, theft, and handling.[56] Some of that increase may be attributable to the local guidelines laid down by liaison judges in certain areas, as discussed above. The consequences of overcrowding in the local prisons helped to draw attention to the importance of mode of trial decisions. The two principal policy responses were the reclassification of four offences from triable either way to triable summarily only, accomplished in the Criminal Justice Act 1988, and the National Mode of Trial

[54] Hedderman and Moxon, *Magistrates' Court*, 38.
[55] R. Morgan, 'Remands in Custody: Problems and Prospects', [1989] *Crim. LR* 481, at 483.
[56] R. Pearce, *Waiting for Crown Court Trial: The Remand Population* (1987).

Guidelines, issued as a Practice Direction by the Lord Chief Justice in 1990.[57]

Despite the diversion of some cases from the Crown Court, the Government remained concerned about the economic and managerial consequences of the numbers of people going for Crown Court trial on either-way charges. The Royal Commission on Criminal Justice, appointed in the wake of notorious miscarriages of justice, received much evidence in favour of altering the system for determining mode of trial, and decided to make recommendations. Their proposed system would have two main steps. If the prosecution and the defendant could reach agreement on the mode of trial of an either-way charge, that would be legally binding. If they disagreed, the magistrates would decide. The defendant's existing right to elect would be removed.[58]

The starting-point is that the numbers going to the Crown Court should be reduced. This is a bureaucratic concern, but the research findings lend it some support from the points of view of both the system and the defendant. The present system is malfunctioning, the Commission holds, because 'magistrates send for trial a large number of cases that they could try themselves [sc. because their sentencing powers are adequate]; while defendants opt for trial on the basis that they are going to plead not guilty but then usually plead guilty'.[59] The Commission rejects the approach of reclassifying more offences as triable summarily only because it would be difficult to draw suitable distinctions, especially in theft according to value.[60] The Commission considers three arguments against its proposal to abolish the defendant's right to jury trial.[61] First, there is the argument that jury trial is fairer than trial by magistrates. The Commission replies that it does not think the relative fairness of the modes of trial should be crucial, and that in any event magistrates should be trusted and that there is an avenue for appeal against conviction and/or sentence. This is an inadequate reply: fairness should be of high importance. The Commission cites some findings from the research by Hedderman and Moxon, but it ought also to heed the findings of the slightly earlier research by Riley and Vennard and show far more concern about defendants' and solicitors' conceptions of the inadequacies of summary trial.[62] Before magistrates' courts are entrusted with more contested cases, we must be assured that they are properly equipped to deal with them fairly. They must be able to set aside the court time to try these cases, bearing in

---

[57] (1991) 92 Cr. App. R. 143, discussed below.
[58] RCCJ, *Report*, Cm. 2263 (1993), para. 6.13.
[60] Ibid., para. 6.16; see further below.
[62] Riley and Vennard, *Triable-Either-Way Cases*.

[59] Ibid., para. 6.12.
[61] Ibid., paras. 6.17 and 6.18.

mind the other commitments of lay magistrates, and they must be better trained in the evaluation of evidence. The belief that magistrates are
too ready to accept police evidence and too anxious to dispose of cases
quickly is so widespread that, at least so that justice appears to be
done, this should be tackled through large-scale training and reorientation.

The second counter-argument considered by the Commission is that
defendants should be able to choose jury trial because it offers a better
chance of acquittal. This is countered by saying that defendants do not
have the right to choose the judge who will give them the most lenient
sentence. It is a poor response that avoids the question whether the
acquittal rates of juries are not more accurate than the conviction rates
of magistrates. Whereas the first argument concerned the relative fairness of the trials themselves, this focuses on the results. The Commission's reply fails to meet the point that we are dealing here, not with
the variations of individual courts or judges, but with what appears to
be a systematic tendency of one level of court to convict at a higher rate
than the other.

The third counter-argument appears to be the strongest but may
turn out to be the weakest. The Commission accepts that jury trial has
'long been regarded as appropriate for cases involving' loss of reputation. Critics would regard this as a strong argument in favour of the
defendant's right to elect, but the Commission sees it merely as one
consideration among several:

it should only be one of the factors to be taken into account and will often be
relevant only to first offenders. In our view, in either way offences the decision
as to the mode of trial should rest on a variety of relevant factors including the
gravity of the offence, the past record if any of the defendant, the complexity of
the case, and its likely effect on the defendant (including the likely sentence) if
there is a conviction.[63]

The Commission's scheme would allow the defendant to put forward
these and other considerations to the magistrates. What the
Commission fails to explore are the ways in which different benches
would be likely to respond to such arguments. Local variations in committal rates to the Crown Court are well known and, as we have seen,
even the Criminal Justice Consultative Council has commented on the
strength of 'local cultures'. Neither a statutory list of relevant considerations, as envisaged by the Commission, nor a set of National Mode of
Trial Guidelines seems likely to alter local patterns, especially if it is
suspected that the only reason why the Government wishes to have

[63] RCCJ Report, para. 6.18.

more cases heard by magistrates is to save money. Far more details of the decision procedures need to be worked out if a legislative scheme based on discretion is not to degenerate into a plethora of separate local cultures in which prosecutors and magistrates, but not defendants, collude.

5. Questions of Principle

Preliminary discussion of the Royal Commission's proposals has brought to light some of the issues of principle relevant to decisions on mode of trial. The Royal Commission quite properly challenges the so-called 'right to jury trial': any thorough inquiry should refuse to accept the labelling of something as a 'right' until the case has been made out. The alleged right to be tried by twelve of one's peers is not mentioned in the European Convention on Human Rights or similar documents. It is difficult to regard it as a constitutional right, since Magna Carta is vague and the Scots have never known such a right.[64] Is it merely a historical curiosity of the English system, or are there strong arguments of principle in its favour? Three issues are selected for brief discussion here—the benefits of jury trial, the right to jury trial, and the criteria for allocating cases to one or other mode of trial.

1. *The benefits of jury trial*: these benefits can only be considered thoroughly in comparison with the benefits of alternative modes of trial. Some research findings that compare the opinions of defendants and their solicitors on jury trial and trial by magistrates were given earlier.[65] They are strongly favourable to Crown Court trial in terms of the fairness of its procedure. The impression given is that the Crown Court looks into cases more thoroughly and allows more time for putting the case and examining the evidence, whereas magistrates' courts operate at too great a speed and tend to give undue weight to the word of police witnesses. These are mere opinions, although they have been reaffirmed by all research projects on the point. One undoubted benefit of jury trial for defendants, as explained earlier, is the higher probability of acquittal (57 per cent compared with 30 per cent). This does not establish that Crown Court trials reach correct verdicts more frequently than magistrates. The explanation for the higher acquittal rate could be that juries are often more gullible than magistrates, particularly when their members are relatively new to the courts; or in some cases juries could be unduly sceptical of police evidence. It is not

---

[64] See P. Darbyshire, 'The Lamp that Shows that Freedom Lives: Is it Worth the Candle?', [1991] *Crim. LR*, at 742–3.

known which mode of trial is a more 'accurate' tribunal in terms of rectitude of decision-making, but it is known which favours the defence and which favours the prosecution.

Other benefits have been claimed for jury trial, but some of these owe more to rhetoric than to careful analysis. It is sometimes argued that juries operate as a defence against the oppressive use of State power. This may be supported by reference to acquittals in a few famous trials, notably that of Clive Ponting in 1985, but sceptics point out that there are plenty of trials (e.g. the Guildford Four, the Birmingham Six) in which juries have not performed this function.[66] It is also argued that juries can go against the strict letter of the law and apply 'jury equity' where the situation seems to call for it. Again, there may be some examples of this, but it is hard to say exactly what this 'equity' stems from in the cases where it is exercised—an assertion that Parliament was wrong, proper or improper sympathy for the defendant, or an award for the oratory or even the charm of counsel in the case.[67] In any event, jury acquittals are unaccompanied by reasons, and in general one can only speculate about their basis. Certain other benefits claimed for jury trials are even more doubtful: proponents often point to the randomness of juries, overlooking the fact that this can lead to particular juries being grossly unrepresentative.[68] The arguments about the jury are many and complex, and will not be taken further here.[69] Suffice it to say that there is a death of hard evidence about the way in which English juries operate, as the Royal Commission recognized and lamented,[70] and that the most important fact is that juries acquit defendants at trials more frequently than magistrates do.

2. *The foundations of the right to jury trial*: although the use of the term 'right' in this context is time-honoured, it is doubtful how far such a notion can be used as a basis for arguing that more or fewer offences should be triable by jury. For a long time some cases have been triable only before magistrates, and there are no voices heard in favour of jury trial for every offence created by the law. Moreover some cases are triable only in the Crown Court and, as Darbyshire argues, to regard those as cases in which the defendant has a right to jury trial is to glorify the compulsion that exists: the defendant cannot choose any other mode

---

[65] See above, nn. 7–11 and accompanying text.

[66] See Darbyshire, 'The Lamp that Shows that Freedom Lives', at 747.

[67] Ibid. 750–1.

[68] Ibid. 744–5; cf. the new data in M. Zander and P. Henderson, *Crown Court Study*, RCCH Research Study 19 (1993), ch. 8.

[69] See further the essays in M. Findlay and P. Duff (eds.), *The Jury under Attack* (1988).

[70] RCCJ Report, para. 1.8; cf. the questions asked of individual jurors in the survey by Zander and Henderson, *Crown Court Study*, ch. 8.

of trial (unlike, for example, in the United States, where defendants can choose trial by judge alone).[71] Indeed, some would say that it is inaccurate to use the term 'right' for something that a person cannot decide to accept or waive.[72] In his criticism of the Royal Commission's proposals, Lord Taylor was careful to refer to 'our culture and the *perception* of many that trial by jury is a fundamental right.[73] For which offences of intermediate gravity, if any, can this properly be described as a right?

It is not difficult to find a historical answer to the question. Defendants in many cases have had the right to choose jury trial for over a century. The James Committee found great support among defendants for this right, and went so far as to conclude that 'there is a real danger that the total removal of the present right of election would undermine the trust and support which the criminal justice system at present commands among the general public'.[74] Whether the last few words would be true of the present day, following the notorious 'miscarriage of justice' cases, may be doubted; but the overall sentiments might still find favour if careful research on the point were undertaken. The James Committee did consider two alternatives. They held that the power should not be given to the prosecution, as it is in Scotland, because England and Wales had no public prosecutor system and it would be wrong 'for the authority that has investigated the offence, apprehended the accused and decided what offence should be charged to decide also the mode of trial'.[75] Since then the Crown Prosecution Service has been introduced, but the 1993 Royal Commission simply states that to give the power to the Crown Prosecution Service 'would not be acceptable here at least for the time being'.[76] This presumably means that there is not yet thought to be sufficient confidence in the work of the CPS.

It is evident from the *Canterbury, Ramsgate,* and *Liverpool* cases[77] that there are occasions when prosecutors have firm views on where the case should be tried, and that those views may differ from the defendant's. Since magistrates tend to acquit less frequently than juries, prosecutors might be expected to push more cases—or the more doubtful cases—into the lower courts. This would be welcome to the Government for the policy reasons elaborated above, but what of a defendant's right? The basis for asserting that could only be that cer-

---

[71] Darbyshire, 'The Lamp that Shows that Freedom Live', 743–4.
[72] J. Feinberg, 'In Defence of Moral Rights', (1992) 12 *Oxford JLS* 149, at 155.
[73] Lord Taylor, 'Criminal Justice after the Royal Commission', *The Times*, 28 July 1993.
[74] James Report, para. 60.   [75] Ibid., para. 48.
[76] RCCJ Report, para. 6.12.   [77] See above, nn. 40, 42, and 47.

tain types of case (serious, complex) ought to have a fuller examination than magistrates' courts can provide; that seriousness should be assessed from the defendant's point of view, since it is his or her future that is in question; and that others such as courts and prosecutors could not be trusted to take this decision from the defendant's point of view, since they have other concerns about speed and cost (and for the prosecutor, probably, winning).[78]

3. *Criteria for allocating cases to one or other mode of trial*: the general method by which the James Committee constructed its recommendations on the classification of offences was to consider sentence levels. If most of those dealt with at the Crown Court received sentences within the powers of magistrates, then the offence would generally be made summary only. This was the approach with drunk driving, which has been triable only in magistrates' courts since 1977.[79] In earlier years these charges had been a fertile field for oratory by defence counsel, addressed to the sympathies of jurors who might themselves have committed the offence, and for the exploitation of 'technicalities' in the law. The Committee hoped that the result of making the offence triable summarily only would be to increase the proportion of guilty pleas, and this seems to have happened. In some other respects, however, the Committee's views have not be followed. For example, they recommended that driving whilst disqualified needed the sterner hand of the Crown Court, but in 1988 this was made summary only. They also recommended that assaulting a police officer, one of the rare offences prior to 1977 that was triable on indictment at the instance only of the prosecution, should become triable either way. However, they recognized that this might cause a great increase in Crown Court trials, and in the event the Government avoided this consequence by reducing the maximum penalty and making the offence triable summarily only. This illustrates one element of compromise in these decisions—that maximum penalties tend to be reduced when offences are made triable summarily only—but it is an element that tells against those who maintain their innocence. As with the 'Gilbertian' argument above, some defendants want a better chance of acquittal rather than a lesser penalty if convicted.

In 1988 Parliament passed a Criminal Justice Act which reduced four offences to the 'summary only' category—driving whilst disqualified, taking a car without the owner's consent, common assault, and criminal damage to a value less than £2,000. The effect of this was to reduce

---

[78] Cf. the discussion of prosecutorial ethics in Ch. 6.7.
[79] Criminal Law Act 1977, pt. ii, applying James Report, paras. 146–8.

the work-load of the Crown Court by around 6 per cent.[80] In addition, a working party was set up to draft guidelines for mode of trial decisions. A Practice Note issued by the Divisional Court, under the authority of the Lord Chief Justice, sets out 'National Mode of Trial Guidelines'.[81] The expressed purpose 'is to provide guidance not direction'. Presumably another purpose is to do this on a national basis, and to move away from the local variations revealed by the research. The guidelines recall the criteria in the Magistrates' Courts Act, and then add that 'either way offences should be tried summarily unless the court considers that a particular case has one or more of the features set out and that its sentencing powers are insufficient'. The guidelines then proceed to identify certain features of each of some twelve common either-way offences that may render that offence serious enough to be committed for trial. It is not yet known whether these guidelines have had any effect in practice and, if so, what that effect has been. They are, however, objective criteria (though fairly general and lacking detail) which, if applied in the right spirit and without corruption by local policies, might lead magistrates to accept jurisdiction in more cases. This does not necessarily mean that all those cases would then be tried by magistrates, since the defendant retains the right to elect. The question whether that is justifiable remains.

The most awkward type of case to allocate is the small-value theft, deception, or handling. The James Committee grasped this nettle and decided to recommend that they should become triable summarily only. They accepted the argument that the value of the property stolen is not always a good guide to the seriousness of an offence, but concluded that in most cases it would be. They accepted the argument that to draw a monetary line would lead to some invidious distinctions, but pointed out that many other European. American, and Commonwealth jurisdictions have two or more offences of theft divided in monetary terms. They also accepted that a minor theft charge might have a major bearing on a defendant's career, but argued that many other stigmatic offences are triable only summarily (e.g. indecent exposure, soliciting, evasion of public transport fares). Their conclusion was that it is in the wider public interest to reserve the relatively scarce resource of trial on indictment for cases more serious than minor thefts and minor offences of damage.[82]

Their recommendations on minor damage were accepted and have been expanded to the extent that now any offence of damage valued at less than £2,000 is triable only in a magistrates' court. But the

---

[80] *Criminal Statistics, England and Wales* (1989), para. 6.12.
[81] (1991) 92 Cr. App. R. 142.   [82] James Report, paras. 78 ff.

recommendation on minor thefts had only a short-lived effect. The Government included a provision in its Criminal Justice Bill 1976–7 that would have made thefts of property valued at under £20 triable summarily only, but parliamentary opposition led to its withdrawal.[83] Members of Parliament made much of the link between dishonesty, career, and jury trial. Magistrates' courts were simply not thought adequate to the task of evaluating the evidence and applying the law in a case on which a respectable person's career hangs.

The subject reappeared in a Consultation Paper issued by the Government in 1986, where a compromise proposal was aired. This was to create a presumption that offences of dishonesty involving property less than a specified sum be tried summarily only. From the policy point of view a significant reduction of Crown Court Work might follow.[84] Magistrates would be able to displace the presumption by committing cases to the Crown Court if they found special circumstances of exceptional gravity. Excluded from the presumption would be cases in which the defendant had no previous conviction for an offence of dishonesty, where there would be an absolute right to elect trial in the Crown Court.[85] This proposal seems to meet the principal thrust of the earlier parliamentary opposition, but it runs into a separate group of objections based on equality of treatment and unfair discrimination. The Royal Commission's recommendation—to the effect that magistrates should make the decision, that one relevant factor would be 'loss of reputation', and that this would 'often be relevant only to first offenders'—has attracted criticism for the same reason. Thus Lord Taylor states: 'I do not accept that a defendant with a criminal record has, by that token, a weaker claim to jury trial. On the contrary, he or she may well feel specially vulnerable. "Round up the usual suspects" may not be just an old joke.'[86] The Lord Chief Justice went on to say that, if it came to a choice between a monetary limit and the 'socially divisive regime that may well result from the Commission's more sweeping proposal', the former should be preferred. 'Insignificance of the offence is a fairer test than insignificance of the offender'. The James Committee used a similar argument against giving the power to magistrates' courts: magistrates would be required to have regard to the consequences of conviction for the particular

---

[83] For critical discussion of this part of the Bill, see [1977] Crim. LR 65 and 125.

[84] RCCJ Report, para. 6.16, notes that removing trial by jury from offences of theft, deception, and handling of property under £100 would reduce the Crown Court workload by some 10%.

[85] Home Office, *The Distribution of Business between the Crown Court and Magistrates' Courts* (1986).

[86] Taylor, 'Criminal Justice after the Royal Commission'.

defendant, and this might make them appear biased if they committed well-to-do defendants to the Crown Court and retained lower-class defendants for summary trial.[87] This argument about social class becomes closely intertwined with the point about previous convictions, since it is assumed that most middle-class defendants will have no previous convictions. The only way of avoiding the reproach of inequality of treatment is to select an arbitrary limit, probably one of monetary value, and this will revive anxieties about the quality of magistrates' justice—for middle-class defendants.

6. Implications for Victims

What implications, if any, does the debate about mode of trial have for the rights and interests of victims? Three matters stand out. One is that Crown Court trial usually means a longer delay before the case is dealt with. This may prolong the victim's anxiety, both generally and particularly in cases where the defendant is on bail and the victim is worried about this. A second is that the greater formality of the Crown Court might put the victim in greater awe of the proceedings. There are allied matters such as the waiting facilities, which might be better at some Crown Courts, but many of these factors vary geographically and according to their impact on particular victims. The third factor is much less subjective: it is that victims are far less likely to be awarded compensation in the Crown Court than in magistrates' courts.[88] This is not simply a reflection of the fact that the Crown Court imposes more custodial sentences and compensation orders are rarely combined with custody. Even taking that into account, Crown Court judges appear to be less willing to make compensation orders, despite the requirement in the Criminal Justice Act 1988 that they should consider this in every case involving injury, loss, or damage. The Royal Commission recognizes the point but makes no recommendation.[89] The proper approach is to seek to eliminate this anomaly by improved training of judges and counsel, emphasizing the prosecutor's responsibility for raising the issue of compensation.[90]

---

[87] James Report, para. 59.

[88] Hedderman and Moxon, *Magistrates' Court*, 32.

[89] RCCJ Report, para. 6.8.

[90] See now the *Statement on the Treatment of Victims and Witnesses by the Crown Prosecution Service*, discussed in Ch. 6 above, which affirms this responsibility (para. 14). For judicial authority, see *Panayioutou* (1989) 11 Cr. App. R. (S) 535 and *Hartrey* (1993) 14 Cr. App. R. (S) 507.

7. Discriminatory Practices

Evidence of different modes of trial for defendants from ethnic minorities is inconclusive. Two studies in Leeds suggest that magistrates commit for trial at the Crown Court a higher proportion of defendants from an Afro-Caribbean background than whites, and one of the studies suggests that Afro-Caribbeans are also more likely than whites to elect.[91] A study in London courts suggests that Afro-Caribbean defendants are significantly more likely to exercise their right to Crown Court trial.[92] This accords with Hood's finding that a higher proportion of Afro-Caribbean defendants plead not guilty in the Crown Court,[93] since presumably those who intend to plead guilty would be much more likely (following the usual pattern) to choose Crown Court trial. Once again, therefore, we find a close connection between plea and mode of trial. There is insufficient information on whether magistrates are more likely to commit Afro-Caribbeans to the Crown Court, but the probability that more Afro-Caribbeans choose the Crown Court suggests that abolition of the defendant's right of election might amount to indirect discrimination, and would certainly be so perceived. It would, to put matters crudely, result in many Afro-Caribbeans being tried unwillingly in courts in which the decision-makers are predominantly white and middle class. It may be fair to assume that the proportion of magistrates' courts sitting with one member from an ethnic minority is lower than the 35 per cent of juries that contain at least one member of an ethnic minority,[94] and this may account for the greater faith of non-white defendants in trial by jury.

8. Reforming the System for Determining Mode of Trial

It is apparent that the question of mode of trial raises acute conflicts between policy and principle. The fundamental argument of policy is an economic and managerial one, that the country cannot afford to pay for the continuing expansion of Crown Court trial. That must be a matter of political judgement, and one on which opinions might differ.

[91] I. Brown and R. Hullin, 'A Study of Sentencing in the Leeds Magistrates' Court: The Treatment of Ethnic Minority and White Offenders', (1992) 32 *BJ Crim.* 41; T. Jefferson and M. Walker, 'Ethnic Minorities in the Criminal Justice System', [1992] *Crim. LR* 83, who suggest that Afro-Caribbeans are more likely to elect. The term 'Afro-Caribbean' is used throughout as a short way of denoting those from an Afro-Caribbean background.

[92] A. Shallice and P. Gordon, *Black People and White Justice* (1990), discussed by M. Fitzgerald, *Ethnic Minorities and the Criminal Justice System*, RCCJ Research Study 20 (1993), 21 and 45.

[93] R. Hood, *Race and Sentencing* (1992).

[94] The latter figure comes from Zander and Henderson, *Crown Court Study*, 241.

However, there is some political wisdom in accepting that as an inevitable starting-point and then discussing what can be done about it. Those who maintain steadfastly that the country ought to find the resources to try more people in the Crown Court at least have the advantage of avoiding the awkward questions that follow from the opposite view.

Two main ways of reducing committals for trials to the Crown Court have been discussed above. The first, reclassifying some offences to 'summary only' and retaining the existing system otherwise, is a relatively blunt instrument; but it would be likely to achieve the policy objective if it took away from the Crown Court many small-value property offences. The second, abolishing the defendant's right of election, seems rather less likely to achieve the policy objective unless accompanied by new guidelines and new attitudes in the magistrates' courts and, perhaps, in the Crown Prosecution Service. Both ways of reducing committals seem to emphasize the seriousness of the offence, whether intrinsically or in its consequences for the defendant, and pay little attention to the complexity of the case as a reason for Crown Court trial.

Whether the approach is to reclassify certain offences or to abolish the defendant's right to elect, many similar issues arise. Neither Parliament nor the Royal Commission pays sufficient attention to them. One is the quality of magistrates' justice, about which defendants and solicitors have generally been quite disparaging in the last twenty years. There is a widespread feeling that summary justice is too summary, and that magistrates' courts give insufficient opportunity for a full examination of the case.[95] Any policy of reducing the case-load of the Crown Court must be accompanied by renewed efforts to improve the quality, or at least the appearance of quality, in magistrates' justice. It is a significant reproach of the Royal Commission that it fails to grasp this issue, which is becoming ever more important as magistrates' courts are subjected to fresh scrutiny and new managerial regimes. Of course we cannot tell, because of lack of information, whether the disparity in acquittal rates between the two levels of court derives from the gullibility of juries, a bias in magistrates' courts towards the prosecution, or some other influence. But there may be implications for the presumption of innocence if one effect of any reform is to relegate

[95] It is noteworthy that the Justices' Clerks Society (in its evidence to the 1993 Royal Commission) pressed the argument for allocating cases according to the complexity of the issues rather than purely the seriousness of the case, which suggests a lack of confidence in lay magistrates as a tribunal for dealing with many of the cases that might otherwise come before them.

some defendants to a form of justice that inclines unfairly in favour of conviction. These implications become doubly serious if it is found that ethnic minority defendants have greater faith in Crown Court trial, not only because of its greater thoroughness but also because of the greater likelihood of finding a member of an ethnic minority on a jury than on a bench of magistrates.

Both alternatives would preserve considerable power for magistrates' courts, in determining mode of trial. The existence of local cultures, whether bolstered by the liaison judge, the justices' clerk, or the chairman of the bench, would make implementation of either approach uneven unless measures were taken to counteract this. Lord Taylor, in his critique of the Royal Commission, refers to the importance of preserving the independence of the individual judge;[96] but it is that very independence that helps to generate, or at least to preserve, the local diversity that is to objectionable on this issue. Mode of trial decisions should be based on criteria of seriousness, or on the complexity of the case, or the defendant's choice—but not a personal policy or a local policy that is not justified by special local conditions. Some would argue that these sources of inconsistency might be avoided by transferring the decision to the Crown Prosecution Service or to justices' clerks, but in either case there would need to be clear guidelines and proper accountability. Even if decisions were not thus transferred, we have seen that the CPS wields considerable power in practice through its choice of charges, although there is now an internal memorandum instructing prosecutors not to alter charges after mode of trial has been determined either by the court or by the defendant's election.[97]

The two approaches also raise some different issues, however. The social discrimination argument has been pressed most strongly: if the decision on mode of trial is left to magistrates—or, for that matter, to the CPS or to justices' clerks—then it may well be made on grounds of what the Royal Commission described as 'loss of reputation', and this may mean that middle-class defendants are more likely than others to benefit from the more thorough hearings and higher acquittal rate in the Crown Court. This line of reasoning militates in favour of reclassification as the avenue of reform, since at least that is neutral in relation to class, ethnic origin, and other factors. Reclassifying property offences according to monetary value is likely to give rise to cries of arbitrariness—e.g. jury trial if £100 is stolen but summary trial if it is

[96] Taylor, 'Criminal Justice after the Royal Commission'.
[97] This memorandum, which was issued in 1993, suggests that cases such as those discussed in s. 3 of this chapter no longer occur.

merely £99—but it is fair to say that these have not inhibited the use of monetary limits for criminal damage since 1977.

The Royal Commission is justified in challenging references to jury trial as a 'right': save in a mere historical sense, this cannot withstand scrutiny because the right is claimed only for a fluctuating class of crimes of intermediate gravity. The difficulty with its proposals is that it fails to attend to the practical steps necessary to achieve its policy objective of reducing the number of Crown Court trials. It ignores the need to make several improvements in the operation of the magistrates' courts. Far from being a proposal based on pragmatic reasons, its very lack of pragmatism in addressing concerns about summary justice should lead to its rejection. Abolition of the defendant's right to jury trial for either-way offences can be contemplated, but not without far more changes to the operation of magistrates' courts and the Crown Court than are envisaged in the Commission's report.

9

Plea

ONE of the key decisions for people who are prosecuted is how to plead. With the exception of special pleas such as *autrefois convict* and *autrefois acquit* in cases where the defendant pleads that he or she has previously been tried for the offence,[1] and the rare plea of not guilty by reason of insanity, defendants have a choice of two: guilty or not guilty. We have seen from the previous chapter that decisions on plea may influence decisions on mode of trial, in so far as most of those wishing to plead guilty to either-way offences prefer the case to be heard in the magistrates' court whereas those wishing to plead not guilty to either-way offences tend to elect Crown Court trial. The research also showed that many of those who choose Crown Court trial nevertheless change their pleas to guilty and are therefore not tried. The reasons for changes of plea are one of the issues for this chapter.

If the defendant pleads not guilty, the case goes to trial. If the defendant pleads guilty, there is no trial. Instead, the prosecution gives a statement of facts in court and, unless the defence disputes this statement to an extent that requires some form of hearing to resolve the matter,[2] the judge or magistrates will proceed to sentence the defendant. The European Convention on Human Rights declares that 'everyone is entitled to a fair and public hearing', that 'everyone charged with a criminal offence shall be presumed innocent until proven guilty according to law', and that everyone shall have the right 'to examine or have examined witnesses against him'.[3] In some countries these rights are thought so fundamental that they cannot be waived: the unavailability of the guilty plea is regarded as a guarantee of defendants' rights.[4] In France, for example, there is no such thing as a plea of guilty: the court must examine the dossier to ensure that there is sufficient

---

[1] For discussion, see *Archbold's Criminal Pleading: Evidence and Practice* (1993 edn.), paras. 4.142 f.; A. Choo, *Abuse of Process and Judicial Stays of Criminal Proceedings* (1993), ch. 2.

[2] See the leading case of *Newton* (1982) 4 Cr. App. R. (S) 388, and the discussion by A. Ashworth, *Sentencing and Criminal Justice* (1992), 281–4.

[3] Art. 6: see Ch. 3.3, above.

[4] M. Damaska, 'Evidentiary Barriers to Conviction and Two Models of Criminal Procedure: A Comparative Study', (1973) 121 *U. Pa. LR* 506.

evidence of guilt. That rigid approach has now been called into question by the Delmas-Marty Commission,[5] and it seems possible that some matters may in future be dealt with on a guilty plea. In the Netherlands, on the other hand, no such reform appears to be contemplated: the ascertainment of guilt is for public officials to accomplish, not for defendants to concede, and the court must review and check the dossier.[6] In Germany there is no guilty plea, but there are forms of 'plea bargain' in which a defendant may confess to the judge in order to gain a reduction in the sentence.[7] In England and Wales there is not even the appearance of a review by the court, although in Crown Court cases the judge may read the papers quickly before dealing with a case on a guilty plea. In essence, the guilty plea constitutes a waiver by the defendant of the right to be tried.

This chapter begins with an inquiry into the percentage of defendants who plead guilty. It then considers some of the principal reasons for changes of plea, looking at charge bargains (where the defendant agrees to plead guilty in exchange for the prosecution reducing the level of the charge or the number of charges), at fact bargains (where the defendant agrees to plead guilty only on the basis that the prosecution will put forward a particular version of the facts), and at plea negotiation (where the change of plea is motivated by considerations of sentence). The various proposals for reform are then evaluated in the light of defendants' rights and the supposed advantages to the system.

1. The Rate of Guilty Pleas

In the magistrates' courts the rate of guilty pleas is well over 90 per cent. Most of these are relatively minor matters, three-quarters being summary offences that almost always end in a fine. A contested trial in a magistrates' court is therefore fairly rare: even among either-way offences heard in magistrates' courts the rate of guilty pleas is 91 per cent.[8] We saw in the preceding chapter that the acquittal rate in the

---

[5] Commission Justice Pénale et Droits de l'Homme, *La Mise en état des affaires pénales* (1991), 10.

[6] H. Lensing and L. Rayar, 'Notes on Criminal Procedure in the Netherlands', [1992] *Crim. LR* 623.

[7] J. Herrmann, 'Bargaining Justice: A Bargain for German Criminal Justice?', (1992) 53 *U. Pittsburgh LR* 755; L. Leigh and L. Zedner, *A Report on the Administration of Criminal Justice in the Pre-trial Phase in France and Germany*, RCJ Research Study 1 (1992), 43.

[8] D. Riley and J. Vennard, *Triable-Either-Way Cases: Crown Court or Magistrates' Court?*, HORS 98 (1988), 6.

early 1980s was 30 per cent in magistrates' courts compared with 57 per cent in the Crown Court.[9]

In the Crown Court the rate of guilty pleas is now around 70 per cent, having risen gradually from about 60 per cent in 1980. The statistics have constantly shown for several years a distinct difference in guilty plea rates from circuit to circuit. The Northern circuit has a guilty plea rate in excess of 80 per cent, whereas on the South-Eastern circuit the rate is 50 per cent and in London itself only 40 per cent. No clear explanation for these divergences has been found. The acquittal rate of those who plead not guilty seems to be roughly the same among the various circuits, around 55–60 per cent, although that is a percentage of a much larger number in the South East than in the North. The cultures of some provincial Bars could be different from that in London: if there are fewer barristers, they may be expected to know one another and to know the limited pool of judges rather well, and may therefore be able to give much more confident predictions of the outcome to their clients.

Why do so many defendants plead guilty and forgo their right to be tried? Some years ago Bottoms and McClean conducted interviews with over 200 defendants who pleaded guilty either at a magistrates' court or at the Crown Court. When they asked why the defendant pleaded guilty, about two-thirds answered that it was because they were guilty. Indeed, some 70 per cent of these admitted to the police from the beginning that they were guilty.[10] The circumstances in which some of the remainder pleaded guilty will be discussed later, but the important point here is that a majority of those who plead guilty accept their guilt without demur.

What about those who change their plea? There is little information about plea-changers in the magistrates' courts,[11] but for the Crown Court there are statistics on what are termed 'cracked trials'. A cracked trial is one that is listed as a not guilty plea, with court time set aside for a contested trial, and in which the defendant changes to a guilty plea after the case has been listed, i.e. at a fairly late stage. Some trials 'crack' on the day of the hearing, others a day or two before. Cracked trials cause considerable concern to administrators, since they cause listing difficulties (even though there are usually one or two other trials waiting to come on) and consequently they may cause a wastage of scarce resources, namely court time, judicial time, and public money.

[9] J. Vennard, 'The Outcome of Contested Trials', in D. Moxon (ed.), *Managing Criminal Justice* (1985).

[10] A. E. Bottoms and J. D. McClean, *Defendants in the Criminal Process* (1976), 115.

[11] J. Baldwin, *Pre-Trial Justice* (1986), 92–7.

They also cause unnecessary inconvenience and even anxiety to victims and other witnesses who are brought to court on what turns out to be a fruitless journey. The scale of the problem is evident from the findings of the recent Crown Court survey: of the 65 per cent of cases that were guilty pleas, only 39 per cent were originally listed as guilty pleas and the remaining 26 per cent were made up of 'cracked trials' which were originally listed as not guilty pleas.[12] Some 31 per cent were listed as not guilty pleas and did go to trial, which confirms that the rate of 'cracking' of cases that begin as not guilty pleas is little short of one-half (i.e. 26 per cent compared with 31 per cent). That is a national figure, however, and other research suggests that it masks considerable variations between regions.[13] The question is: why do so many defendants who apparently start out with the intention of contesting their guilt subsequently change their minds and admit it?

2. Pleading Not Guilty

We have seen that a small minority of defendants in magistrates' courts plead not guilty throughout, but that in the Crown Courts it is around 30 per cent who exercise their right to be tried. More do so in London, fewer in the North-East. Why do they persist in their pleas of not guilty, whilst others change their pleas? Once again, the most obvious answer is that they maintain that they are not guilty. It seems that around 60 per cent of defences involve a denial of the basic facts:[14] around one in six of these are alibi defences, and perhaps one-quarter are claims of mistaken identification.[15] The other 40 per cent of defences accept the basic facts but contest guilt on the basis of justification or lack of culpability. Some three-quarters of these seem to amount to a denial of *mens rea*, and almost all the remaining one-quarter claim self-defence.

Just as it seems likely that some people who are innocent eventually plead guilty, so it also seems likely that some who are guilty plead not guilty. They may do so for a variety of personal reasons, ranging from over-confidence to shame at the offence and an unwillingness to admit it publicly in any circumstances (e.g. with serious sexual offences). It is possible, though, that some defendants are alive to the possibility that they have a chance of gaining an acquittal if prosecution witnesses fail to attend court to give evidence. It is recognized that some defendants

---

[12] M. Zander and P. Henderson, *Crown Court Study*, RCCJ Research Study 19 (1993), 95–6; the study probably under-recorded the numbers originally listed as guilty pleas, since the national average rate of guilty pleas is around 70 rather than 65%—see ibid. 248.

[13] P. Robertshaw, '"Cracked Trials": What is Happening?', [1992] *Crim. LR* 867; to similar effect, the Seabrook report (below, n. 32).

[14] Zander and Henderson, *Crown Court Study*, 121.   [15] Ibid. 75 and 92.

who change their pleas to guilty on the day of the trial do so because they see that the prosecution witnesses are at the court. Presumably there are others who, seeing that the prosecution witnesses have not arrived, persist in their plea of not guilty, with the result that the case collapses. Whilst no study has identified the numbers involved, it seems entirely plausible that some defendants do benefit from windfalls of this kind.[16]

3. Charge Bargains

The term 'charge bargaining' is used here to encompass two distinct kinds of case. The first is where a defendant faces two or more charges and signifies an intention to plead not guilty to them. It is then possible for the prosecution to drop one or more of the others. Either the prosecution or the defence may suggest this way of resolving the matter. Many of these are cases where several distinct offences are alleged, but some will be cases in which the prosecution has charged a person with both theft and handling stolen goods in the expectation that there would be a conviction of only one offence. The second kind of case is where the defendant faces a serious charge and signifies an intention to plead not guilty to it. It may be possible for the prosecution to drop the serious charge in exchange for a plea of guilty to a less serious charge. Much depends on the criminal law. At some points the law seems to be ready-made for this kind of charge bargain: for example, a defendant might intend to plead not guilty to grievous bodily harm with intent, contrary to section 18 of the Offences against the Person Act 1861, but might be willing to plead guilty to the lesser offence. of grievous bodily harm contrary to section 20 of the same Act. The same applies if the original charge is under section 20, and the defendant is willing to plead to the lesser offence under section 47. It is not unknown for defendants charged with murder to offer a plea of guilty to manslaughter: this is often done in cases of diminished responsibility, but may also be done on other grounds. With other serious offences such as rape and robbery the law itself does not provide an apparent lesser alternative, but there might be circumstances in which rape is reduced to indecent assault or robbery to theft. The *Code for Crown Prosecutors* cites as a common example 'burglary reducing to theft by virtue of a denial of the element of trespass'.[17]

In what proportion of cases do charge bargains of these kinds take

[16] Cf. the reasons for prosecution decisions to discontinue cases and for directed acquittals, in Ch. 6.2, above.

[17] Crown Prosecution Service, *Code for Crown Prosecutors* (1992), para. 11.

place? As many as seventy-seven of the 112 defendants in McCabe and Purves's sample who changed their plea at a late stage pleaded guilty to only part of the original indictment,[18] whereas in Baldwin and McConville's sample it was only eleven out of 121 late guilty pleaders[19] and in Bottoms and McClean's sample only three out of sixty-eight.[20] Most of the recent research on cracked trials does not provide details of the nature of any negotiation that took place, but some 51 per cent of those in Hedderman and Moxon's sample who changed their plea stated that they did so in the expectation that some charges would be dropped or reduced, resulting in a lighter sentence.[21] It may therefore be assumed that one or other form of charge bargain is a fairly frequent phenomenon.

What are the advantages and disadvantages for the prosecution? The chief benefit is that they are assured of at least one conviction, and do not have to risk the hazards of trial, with an acquittal rate of some 57 per cent in the Crown Court. In view of the possibility that witnesses may fail to turn up or may alter their story, or that the jury will be swayed by some non-legal factor, it is tempting for the prosecution to settle for a certain conviction. The disadvantage is that the resulting conviction may not give a proper reflection of the gravity of the offending behaviour. In principle this is to be avoided, although the *Code for Crown Prosecutors* does not recommend this approach in undiluted form:

The overriding consideration will be to ensure that the court is never left in the position of being unable to pass a proper sentence consistent with the gravity of the defendant's actions . . . Administrative convenience in the form of a rapid guilty plea should not take precedence over the interests of justice, but where the court is able to deal adequately with an offender on the basis of a plea which represents a criminal involvement not inconsistent with the alleged facts, the resource advantages both to the Service and to the courts generally will be an important consideration.[22]

Shorn of its double negatives, this seems to suggest that it is proper to accept a plea of guilty to a lesser offence if the maximum sentence for that offence is not too low compared with the seriousness of what the defendant did. Thus, for example, if the defendant enters a plea of not guilty to a charge of causing grievous bodily harm with intent (which carries a maximum sentence of life imprisonment), and the defendant

[18] S. McCabe and R. Purves, *By-Passing the Jury* (1972).
[19] J. Baldwin and M. McConville, *Negotiated Justice* (1977), ch. 2.
[20] Bottoms and McClean, *Defendants in the Criminal Process*, 126–7.
[21] C. Hedderman and D. Moxon, *Magistrates' Court or Crown Court?*, HORS 125 (1992), 24.
[22] *Code for Crown Prosecutors*, para. 11.

then offers to plead guilty to the lesser offence of inflicting grievous bodily harm (which carries a maximum sentence of five years' imprisonment), the prosecutor should reflect on whether the five-year maximum is appropriate for what was done. In practice, courts hardly ever pass sentences approaching five years for this offence, and sentences longer than three years are rare.[23] Assuming that the prosecutor believes that there are reasonable prospects of establishing that the grievous bodily harm was caused with intent—and that belief should be held, otherwise the charge ought to be reduced without any question of bargaining—he or she must decide whether a sentence in the three- to four-year range would be adequate. It might be argued that, since many sentences for the more serious offence of causing grievous bodily harm with intent are in the three- to four-year range too, the only effect of accepting the plea may be that a less serious conviction is entered on the offender's criminal record. However, the Court of Appeal has stated that a sentencer must have regard to the fact that the plea of guilty is only to the lesser offence and must not sentence on a different basis.[24] In so far as this is true, and a plea to a lesser offence invariably leads to a lesser sentence, this should mean that many offenders receive a sentence lower than they would have done if the prosecution had proved the higher offence at trial. In addition to this, of course, the defendant would receive a sentence discount for pleading guilty, which would not have been granted on conviction after a trial. There is the further possibility that a lower custodial sentence will enable the defendant to benefit from automatic early release.[25] The disadvantage to the prosecution would therefore be that some offenders would be sentenced less severely than they deserve, and that victims' opinions and public confidence generally may be adversely affected as a consequence.

What are the advantages and disadvantages from the defendant's point of view? These depend on whether the defendant has committed an offence and, if so, what offence(s). It is easy to say that, if the defendant has really committed the higher offence, a plea of guilty to a lesser offence brings a benefit to the defendant in terms of a lower sentence. What is more debatable is the kind of case in which the defendant may be said to have been overcharged in order to put pressure on him or

[23] Cf. *McLoughlin* (1985) 7 Cr. App. R. (S) 67 (three years too long when plea of guilty to s. 20, not s. 18), with *Moore* (1991) 13 Cr. App. R. (S) 130 (three years upheld, fortunate not to have been charged with s. 18 offence).

[24] e.g. *McLoughlin* (1985) 7 Cr. App. R. (S) 67, *Stewart* (1990) 12 Cr. App. R. (S) 15.

[25] Those serving sentences of less than four years are conditionally released after serving one-half, whereas those serving four years or longer only receive parole at the discretion of the Parole Board: see A. Ashworth, *Sentencing and Criminal Justice* (1992), 233–40.

her to plead guilty to the lesser charge. Research has not focused on the extent to which such cases occur: prosecutors tend to deny that they do, whereas defendants and lawyers acting for the defence are confident that this does happen from time to time. Overcharging is contrary to the *Code for Crown Prosecutors*,[26] as one might expect of an official document, but whether supervision within the Crown Prosecution Service is sufficiently active to ensure that such cases are rare aberrations is hard to assess. One could certainly see that it might operate to the defendant's disadvantage in certain cases where an injury is caused that fulfils the definition of a wound. If the prosecution charge the defendant with wounding with intent, the defence might succeed in having it reduced to unlawful wounding. But if the original charge was unlawful wounding, the defence might succeed in having it reduced to assault occasioning actual bodily harm. The starting-point may therefore matter. The position is even worse for the defendant who maintains innocence of all charges: the course of pleading guilty to a lesser charge promises not only a lower sentence for the lesser offence but also a further discount for pleading guilty. If counsel's advice is that pleading guilty to a lesser charge is likely to result in a non-custodial sentence whereas conviction after a trial might result in custodial sentence whereas conviction after a trial might result in custody, a defendant may succumb to the pressure to forgo a perfectly reasonable defence. The dependence of the defendant on his or her legal representatives is considerable, and this brings issues of professional ethics to the fore.

4. Fact Bargains

Relatively little attention has been devoted to this class of case, which may be said to lie half-way between charge bargains and the straightforward plea bargains to be discussed in the next section. There is, however, evidence that in some cases there has been an agreement by the defendant to change the plea to guilty on the faith of a promise by the prosecution to state the facts of the case in a particular way. An agreement not to mention a particular aggravating feature, for example, or not to mention the part played by another (such as a friend or spouse) may be sufficient to persuade the defendant to plead guilty. Again, the principal advantage for the prosecution is that they secure a conviction in the case, even though the 'public interest' may be said to lose because the sentence is based on facts less serious than those that

---

[26] Para. 12.

actually occurred. There is also the discount for pleading guilty, which will lower the sentence further. The defendant, on the other hand, stands to benefit from these sentence reductions—although it can only be counted as a benefit if he or she is actually guilty of a more serious version of the offence than that put to the court.

The *Code for Crown Prosecutors* deals not with this type of case but with the opposite situation, stating that 'having accepted a plea, the Crown Prosecutor must not then open the case on the basis that what the defendant actually did was something more serious than appears in the charge'.[27] Though formally unregulated, the practice of stating the facts more favourably to the accused can have implications for victims. In the *Victim's Charter* it is stated that prosecutors 'must be ready to intervene to correct any misleading speech in mitigation, particularly where attempts are made to denigrate the character of the victim'.[28] However, in one widely publicized case this plainly did not happen. The complainant in a rape case discovered that, although the offender had pleaded guilty, he pleaded guilty only on the basis that she consented to intercourse when it began and subsequently changed her mind. On inquiring how this version of facts was put forward, she learnt that this was the basis on which the plea of guilty was negotiated—in effect, to a version of the offence which was much less serious, and which in her view was a travesty of the true facts. Presumably the prosecution was concerned to avoid a trial, perhaps because of a belief that the victim would not attend court to give evidence or might not be a convincing witness, or possibly in order to spare the victim the distress of having to give evidence.

It might be added that, where there is a dispute about the factual basis of a guilty plea, there is provision for the judge to hold a post-conviction hearing to determine the issue. Known as *Newton* hearings,[29] these involve the hearing of evidence from both sides, in general applying the same rules of evidence as would apply at trial. The judge then determines the issue, and this becomes the basis for sentence. It might therefore be possible for a defendant who is not offered a fact bargain by the prosecution to plead guilty with a view to contesting the prosecutor's version of the facts in a *Newton* hearing. This, of course, is more hazardous than relying on the prosecutor to present the facts favourably in the first place.

[27] *Code for Crown Prosecutors*, para. 11.
[28] Home Office, *Victim's Charter* (1990), 17–18: the whole thrust of those paragraphs is that the *defence* may seek to minimize the defendant's role. Cf. now Crown Prosecution Service, *Statement on the Treatment of Victims and Witnesses* (1993).
[29] The leading case is *Newton* (1982) 4 Cr. App. R. (S) 388.

5. Plea Bargains

One of the main reasons for dealing first with charge bargains and fact bargains is that it leaves for separate consideration those cases in which the defendant intends to plead not guilty to the charge and then, at a late stage, alters the plea to guilty. These are cases where there is no question of reducing the number or level of the charges, and no bargain about the factual basis on which the case will be put forward. The essence seems to be that the defendant trades a chance of acquittal for a lower sentence than would have been received in the event of a conviction.

Thus far the discussion has proceeded on the assumption that a defendant who pleads guilty should receive mitigation of sentence for doing so. That is indeed the principle enunciated by the Court of Appeal:[30] it is well known to counsel and to many defendants. The discount is often said to be about one-third of the sentence that would have been appropriate on a conviction, and a discount of one-quarter is certainly well established in the precedents.[31] However, there is evidence that some judges merely pay lip-service to the discount and do not give much effect to it, with the result that sentences on conviction and after a guilty plea vary from court to court.[32] Moreover, its precise impact on the sentence in a particular case depends on the judge's starting-point. Apart from the few offences for which sentencing guideline judgments have been handed down, much turns on the judge's view of the facts and particular approach to sentencing. The strong impression of one researcher was that the identity and sentencing reputation of the judge or recorder are key factors in decisions on plea.[33]

In some cases, especially where the sentencer's reputation is not known, defence counsel might wish to discover the judge's preliminary view about the likely sentence. In the leading decision of *Turner* (1970),[34] the Court of Appeal laid down various rules to govern the conduct of judges and counsel in these matters. The first rule is that defence counsel should be free to give advice to the defendant, if necessary in strong terms, about the best approach. The second is that defendants should have freedom of choice, having heard the advice.

---

[30] Ashworth, *Sentencing and Criminal Justice*, 130–1.

[31] For a selection of authorities, see D. A. Thomas, *Current Sentencing Practice* (1982), pt. A. 8.

[32] P. Robertshaw and A. Milne, 'The Guilty Plea Discount', (1992) 31 *Howard JCJ* 53; Bar Council, *The Efficient Disposal of Business in the Crown Court*, Report of the working party chaired by Robert Seabrook, QC (1992), hereinafter the Seabrook Report.

[33] J. Bredar, 'Moving up the Day of Reckoning: Strategies for Attacking the Problem of "Cracked Trials"', [1992] *Crim. LR* 153.

[34] [1970] 2 QB 321.

The third is that defence counsel should be able to see the judge, and vice versa, on matters relating to trial and sentence, but that this should only be done when really necessary. And fourth, the judge should never indicate the likely sentence, except to say that the sentence will take the same form whether the defendant pleads guilty or is convicted.

The warning by Lord Parker, CJ, in *Turner* that visits by counsel to the judge's private room should be kept to a minimum has not been heeded. There is a long series of Court of Appeal decisions quashing convictions for breaches of the rules. Twice in 1990 the Court of Appeal lamented the frequency of such visits, with Lord Lane, CJ, stating that 'no amount of criticism, no number of warnings, and no amount of exhortation seems to be able to prevent that happening'.[35] The principal difficulty is that, if counsel discloses to the defendant that he or she has been to see the judge, any advice then given to the defendant might appear to be based on what the judge said. In *Pitman* the judge indicated that if the defendant changed his plea to guilty as charged there would be substantial mitigation, even though the defendant wished to argue that he was guilty not of reckless driving but of the less serious offence of careless driving.[36] In *Turner* counsel stated or implied that the judge had indicated that the sentence on the defendant would be non-custodial if he pleaded guilty but custodial if convicted after a trial.[37] In both cases the Court of Appeal held that this placed improper pressure on the defendant in deciding on plea. The problems were of a different kind in *Smith*, where counsel said that the judge had undertaken to give a non-custodial sentence in the event of a guilty plea but the judge recollected no such undertaking. The Court of Appeal insisted that there should be a tape recorder or shorthand writer for any such meetings.[38] This would at least prevent disputes about what was said, but the deeper problem is whether such meetings should take place at all. Bypassing the trial may also mean bypassing the rights of certain parties.

However, it would be wrong to assume that the reported appellate decisions convey a full picture of daily practice. Whilst some judges are clearly doing what the Court of Appeal says they should not do, other judges refuse to see counsel for this purpose.[39] It appears that practice

[35] *Pitman* (1990) The Times 31 Oct.; the second case was *Smith* (1990) 90 Cr. App. R. 413, per Russell, LJ.
[36] *Pitman* (1990) The Times 31 Oct. For discussion, see P. Curran, 'Discussions in the Judge's Private Room', [1991] *Crim. LR* 79.
[37] [1970] 2 QB 321.   [38] (1990) 90 Cr. App. R. 413.
[39] JUSTICE, *Negotiated Justice: A Closer Look at the Implications of Plea Bargains* (1993), 3.

is variable, and this is manifestly unsatisfactory in terms of equality of treatment of like cases. The Seabrook Report maintained that some judges are not honouring the principle that a guilty plea should attract mitigation of one-quarter or one-third.[40] Large-scale surveys of sentencing show that those who plead guilty receive a discount on average of 22 per cent[41] or 31 per cent,[42] but it remains possible that there are variations from court to court. At around 10 per cent of courts it appears that defendants pleading guilty receive more severe sentences than those convicted after a trial.[43] The reasons for this may vary—judges may not be giving the proper discount for guilty pleas, defendants who go to trial may be able to put their offence in a more favourable light[44]—but once again the facts suggest a failure to accord equality of treatment. We saw in the last chapter that many defendants elect trial in the Crown Court with the intention of pleading not guilty, and then change their plea to guilty at the last minute. In some cases this may simply be a way of ensuring that a larger part of the inevitable custodial sentence is served on remand, with its attendant privileges. In other cases it may be that a defendant does not receive 'realistic' advice until the day of the trial, for in the survey by Zander and Henderson some 70 per cent of those who changed their plea met the trial counsel only on the day of the trial.[45] Some 94 per cent of those who received legal advice on plea and who changed their mind followed the advice they received, often because it conformed with their own view, but sometimes because of persuasion by counsel.[46]

What is the balance of advantages of plea bargains for the State? They contribute to the smooth running of the system by bringing speed and a reduction of the cost and resources needed to deal with the cases. They ensure a conviction, and avoid the hazards of trial which at present produce an acquittal rate of 57 per cent. In the present system these advantages come at the price of a sentence reduction: it could be claimed that offenders who benefit from the sentence discount are receiving a lower sentence than they deserve (on the basis of harm and culpability), purely for reasons of speed and cost.[47] Those who believe that sentencing should be based on preventive grounds, such as deterrence or inca-

---

[40] Seabrook Report, 12.
[41] D. Moxon, *Sentencing Practice in the Crown Court*, HORS 103 (1988), 32.
[42] R. Hood, *Race and Sentencing* (1992), 125.   [43] JUSTICE Report, 2.
[44] Bottoms and McClean, *Defendants in the Criminal Process*, found that 3% of defendants in the Crown Court pleaded not guilty, even though they knew they were guilty, in order to have the opportunity for mitigating factors to be brought out fully.
[45] Zander and Henderson, *Crown Court Study*, 55.   [46] Ibid. 96–8.
[47] See Ashworth, *Sentencing and Criminal Justice*, 130–3; cf. also the effect of parole and early release, outlined in n. 25 above.

pacitation, would also regard the discount as detracting from its primary purpose. It would be difficult to calculate whether these losses to
the system are justified by the advantages, because that would also
involve a calculation of how many defendants would persist in a not
guilty plea if there were no sentence discount for pleading guilty.

What is the balance of advantages for victims? In general guilty pleas
spare victims the anxiety of having to give evidence in court, and the
unpleasantness of hearing all the details of the crime analysed at length
in public. For those victims who do give evidence (a minority, because
of the large numbers of guilty pleas), the process is often stressful.[48]
But the advantage of avoiding this anxiety is purchased at the price of
sentence reductions, and victims may share some of the disquiet about
undeserved mitigation or reduced protection described in the previous
paragraph.

What is the balance of advantages for defendants? The primary
benefit is the discount for pleading guilty, which in general promises a
substantial reduction in the length of a custodial sentence and may in
some cases result in the passing of a non-custodial rather than a custodial sentence.[49] Another significant benefit is that the defendant may
use the choice of plea to reap the greatest advantage from conditions
before the trial: a defendant remanded in custody who believes that a
custodial sentence is inevitable may delay the guilty plea until the last
moment, benefiting from the privileges of a remand prisoner as long as
possible without forfeiting any or much mitigation, whereas other
defendants may speed up the process of disposal by entering a guilty
plea at an early stage. These, however, are only advantages for the
guilty defendant. From the point of view of other defendants, these are
disincentives that pull against a justifiable challenge to the prosecution
case, which might be said to be embodied in the presumption of innocence. Among these are innocent defendants who feel pressure to
plead guilty, because they may not obtain an acquittal and it might
appear best to 'cut their losses' in the hope of receiving a non-custodial
sentence. Estimates of the number of innocent defendants who take
this course vary: Zander and Henderson's figures suggest that up to
11 per cent of guilty pleaders claim innocence,[50] and earlier research

[48] e.g. J. Morgan and L. Zedner, *Child Victims* (1992), 141–3; J. Shapland, J. Willore, and
P. Duff, *Victims in the Criminal Justice System* (1985), 63–7.

[49] Moxon, *Sentencing Practice in the Crown Court*, 32, found that 55% of those convicted on a not guilty plea received immediate custody, compared with 48% of those
pleading guilty. Thus a guilty plea may sometimes make the difference between a custodial sentence and a community sentence.

[50] Zander and Henderson, *Crown Court Study*, 138–42; cf. M. McConville and
L. Bridges, 'Convicting the Innocent', (1993) 143 *NLJ* 160.

suggested that as many as 18 per cent of guilty pleaders were 'possibly innocent' of one or more charges.[51] There is an important question of definition here, since a person may have an arguable defence and yet be advised that running the defence is not worth the loss of discount. If so, this raises squarely the issue of whether a defendant may be said to have a right to have the prosecution case proved in court and, if so, whether the sentence discount does not impose an unfair disincentive to exercising this right. Moreover in practice there may be problems over the accuracy of counsel's advice to the defendant, for we have seen that the practice of judges is somewhat variable and may not be easy for counsel to predict.

6. The Path of Reform

There is much that is unsatisfactory in current rules and practices. Charge bargains are an unavoidable aspect of any system that includes graduated criminal offences (more serious, less serious) and that allows multiple charging. Graduated offences are right in principle,[52] and it is often justifiable to charge more than a single offence. But the result is to place pressure on defendants to plead guilty to something as a kind of compromise. Fact bargains seem to have arisen through the absence of controls on the way in which the prosecution states the facts before sentence on a guilty plea: if the statement is unfairly adverse to the defendant it can be challenged, but if it is unfairly favourable, there seems to be no check. Plea bargains appear to operate in a kind of half-light, with some judges prepared to see counsel in order to give an indication of sentence and others not, and with a difficulty of predicting the sentence in any individual case. Defendants may be given advice by their counsel, sometimes in strong terms, but the basis of this may not be completely accurate. In effect, there is an element of gambling in defendant's decision-making here: the roulette wheel has taken the place of the rule of law. From the defendant's point of view, all three forms of bargain raise fundamental questions about the implications of the presumption of innocence and about the privilege against self-incrimination. From the public point of view, these practices enable some defendants who are guilty to 'play the system', for example by waiting until the day of trial in order to see whether key witnesses attend before signifying plea, in a manner that raises questions about the public interest in law enforcement.

Existing practices could be improved by certain changes. One obvi-

[51] Bottoms and McClean, *Defendants in the Criminal Process*, 120.
[52] For elaboration, see A. Ashworth, *Principles of Criminal Law* (1991), 59–73.

ous improvement, proposed by the Court of Appeal, is that a proper record should be kept of any meeting between the judge and counsel on these matters.[53] Another is that when judges pass sentence they should be required to indicate the effect of the guilty plea on the sentence: this would have the advantage of bringing some of the judge's calculations into the open, giving the Court of Appeal more information on which to review them and allowing the public to see clearly the extent of the discounts given.[54] It is not known whether judicial objections that this is not feasible involve a denial that the proper course is to deduct the discount from a provisional sentence calculated by reference to other aggravating and mitigating factors, or embarrassment at the possibility that sentence calculations might be made public. A related change would be to decide on whether, and to what extent, the discount should operate in magistrates' courts. This has been a long-running question and, whilst there are now clear statements in favour of magistrates giving the discount,[55] the extent of its practical impact remains uncertain. If the obligation to indicate what sentence would have been given after a conviction were to be imposed on magistrates when they sentence someone who pleads guilty, this would add further complications to the sentencing task performed by lay justices. In view of the relatively low level of magistrates' court sentences, which are already well below Crown Court sentences for comparable offences,[56] there is a strong case for excluding the discount from the magistrates' courts.

From the administrative and economic points of view, the most urgent problem is the evident waste of resources stemming from cracked trials. When a plea of guilty is entered only on the day of the trial, this often means that counsel, jurors, and the judge are left without work to do. When cracked trials run at a rate of 40 per cent, and yet there are long waiting times for contested trials, it becomes not only an administrative nightmare but also an impediment for those defendants who do wish to fight their case. The obvious solution would be to bring forward the time at which plea is indicated, in a way that enables courtrooms and personnel to be used for trials that really are contested rather than lying empty in consequence of the cracking of trials. Two broad methods of solving this problem may be considered. One is the

[53] In *Smith* (1990) 90 Cr. App. R. 413.

[54] This has been proposed, in one form or another, in the Seabrook Report and in the JUSTICE Report at 18.

[55] The Magistrates' Association, *Sentencing Guidelines* (rev. edn., 1993), 3: 'a timely guilty plea may be regarded as a mitigating factor for which a sentencing discount of approximately one-third might be given.'

[56] Hedderman and Moxon, *Magistrates' Court*, 27.

introduction of a graduated sentence discount that encourages an early plea, and the other is the introduction of a procedure for obtaining a provisional indication of sentence from the judge.

The Royal Commission on Criminal Justice follows the Seabrook Report in recommending a graduated sentence discount.[57] The Royal Commission Report points out that there is already appellate authority in favour of this,[58] but this authority, like *Turner*, seems not to be followed faithfully: research shows that some judges give a greater discount for a late guilty plea.[59] Under the proposals the full discount of one-third would be given for a guilty plea entered at the committal stage, and then the amount of the discount would be reduced so as to provide a much smaller discount for those who plead guilty on the day of the trial.[60] This has several advantages. It recognizes clearly that the reason for the discount is an economic or 'system' justification, and ought to banish from judicial discourse the notion that it reflects the defendant's remorse.[61] Since the justification is economic, it is much more logical to tie the amount of the discount to the scale of the economic benefits—not in any mechanistic sense, but at least to the extent of distinguishing between committal stage, any pre-trial review or hearing, and the day of the trial. Judges would have clear guidance on the amount of discount to be given. And it ought to operate as an incentive to consider the plea fully at an early stage, thereby maximizing the benefit to the system by reducing the wastage of court time. Before sentencing guidelines on the discount for pleading guilty are issued, fresh attention should be given to the categories of case in which the discount may be withheld, since some of the justifications offered in *Costen* are unpersuasive.[62]

The disadvantages of the proposed scheme, however, are no less impressive. How seriously should one take the possibility that innocent defendants may be tempted by the incentives to 'cut their losses' and plead guilty?[63] The Royal Commission, appointed in the wake of several miscarriages of justice, simply declares: 'Against the risk that

[57] RCCJ, *Report*, Cm. 2263 (1993), paras. 7.45–7.47.
[58] *Hollington and Emmens* (1986) 82 Cr. App. R. 281, per Lawton, LJ, approved by Lord Lane, CJ, in *Costen* (1989) 11 Cr. App. R. (S) 182.
[59] Moxon, *Sentencing Practice in the Crown Court*, 33.   [60] Seabrook Report, 12.
[61] This reason was given in the leading case of *De Haan* [1968] 2 QB 108, where it was quite unconvincing on the facts.
[62] *Costen* (1989) 11 Cr. App. R. (S) 182, discussed by Ashworth, *Sentencing and Criminal Justice*, 130–1.
[63] The Royal Commission Report mentions the views of defence barristers on the guilt or innocence of their lay clients (para. 7.43) but fails to refer to the views of the defendants themselves, as set out in Zander and Henderson's *Crown Court Study*, 138–42, and discussed above, nn. 50–1 and accompanying text.

defendants may be tempted to plead guilty must be weighed the benefits to the system and to defendants of encouraging those who are in fact guilty to plead guilty. We believe that the system of sentence discounts should remain.'[64] The reasons behind this confident expression seem to be that the numbers of innocent guilty-pleaders may be small and that counsel invariably tell them that they should not plead guilty if they are innocent. The problem with the latter point is that counsel also draw the defendant's attention to countervailing forces at the same time, notably the sentence discount. Moreover, establishing an incentive to decide on plea at an early stage places pressure on defendants at the time when knowledge of the case against them is likely to be least, and when a prediction of the probable sentence on a plea and on conviction at trial would be most difficult. This leads us to the second plank of the Royal Commission's approach, the 'sentence canvass'.

If counsel are to be able to advise their lay clients properly on the likely sentence, rather than simply stating the existence of the discount, they would need to overcome the difficulty of predicting sentence without knowledge of the judge's approach and of all the necessary facts. The Royal Commission, broadly following the Seabrook Report, recommends that the judge should give an indication of the highest sentence on a guilty plea, if approached by defence counsel. This involves a reversal of one of the cardinal principles in *Turner*, but the Royal Commission was encouraged by the support of 88 per cent of defence barristers, 86 per cent of prosecution barristers, and 67 per cent of judges for a reform that would 'permit full and realistic discussion between counsel and the judge about plea and especially sentence'.[65] Most defendants in the Crown Court seem to know about the sentence discount,[66] but the Royal Commission starts from the proposition that defendants are more interested in 'the actual sentence and in particular whether it will be custodial or not'.[67] Their proposal for a procedure of 'sentence canvass' has five main elements. First, it should take place only at the request of defence counsel on instructions from the defendant. Second, it may take place at the preparatory hearing, at a hearing called specially for the purpose, or during the trial. Third, both sides should be represented and either a recording or a note should be made. Fourth, the only question the judge may answer is, 'what would be the maximum sentence if my client were to plead guilty at this stage?' Fifth, the judge may decline to answer the question where this might be especially difficult or might prejudice others, such as co-defendants.

[64] RCCJ Report, para. 7.44.
[66] Ibid. 146 (62%).
[65] Zander and Henderson, *Crown Court Study*, 145.
[67] RCCJ Report, para. 7.49.

Eschewing points of detail, we may consider two possible problems with this approach. One is the difficulty that judges might experience in making these predictions. The Royal Commission goes some way towards resolving this, by emphasizing that the indication is only of the 'maximum' sentence that would be given and by providing that each counsel should make a brief statement of facts and mitigation before the judge decides. Under the Criminal Justice Act 1991 the pre-sentence report will be important in many cases and is unlikely to have been prepared if the defendant has signified the intention of pleading not guilty. The effect of the pre-sentence report might be to lead the court towards a community sentence rather than a custodial sentence. In the absence of this, both the judge and the defendant may be handicapped in their decision-making. The other possible problem concerns the degree of voluntariness in the defendant's decision. This will be analysed further in the next section, but the Royal Commission's proposals do leave the matter in some doubt. The Royal Commission accepts 'that to face defendants with a choice between what they might get on an immediate plea of guilty and what they might get if found guilty by the jury does amount to unacceptable pressure'.[68] Yet their proposal is, in effect, that defendants will be told the judge's view of what the highest sentence on a guilty plea would be. They are then likely to ask counsel to predict what the sentence would be on a conviction after a trial, knowing that the sentence on a guilty plea will be significantly lower. In *Turner* the court held that: 'a statement that on a plea of guilty he would impose one sentence but that on a conviction following a plea of not guilty he would impose a severer sentence is one that should never be made.'[69] This, the court held, would constitute undue pressure on the accused. Thus the pressure would be unacceptable if the judge gave a view on both eventualities but is acceptable if the judge gives one and counsel the other. The Royal Commission seems to agree with this. No doubt counsel will perform the duty of advising the defendant not to plead guilty if he or she is not guilty, but this advice may well be overshadowed by the other considerations pressing forward.

Both the Seabrook Committee and the Royal Commission have been concerned particularly with the problem of late guilty pleas and cracked trials. Both have made other recommendations aimed at alleviating the wastage of money and of the time of court officials, witnesses, counsel, police, and others. The Royal Commission, for example, recommends a new form of preparatory hearing in the Crown

---

[68] RCCJ Report, para. 7.50.   [69] [1970] 2 QB 321, at 327.

Court, alterations in practices of brief allocation at the Bar, and a new structure for fees that places emphasis on preparatory work.[70] It may be asked whether these might have a significant effect without the need to alter the *Turner* rules or, more radically, with the abolition of the sentence discount. There has been a marked reluctance to speculate on the effects of abolishing the discount for pleading guilty. The prevailing view is that defendants would then plead not guilty in their thousands, swamping the courts and gravely compromising the quality of justice as delays lengthen, victims are made anxious, witnesses forget, and so forth. It might be thought that this is confirmed by findings that more than half of Crown Court defendants regard the discount as important to their decision to plead guilty rather than not guilty.[71] However, those findings are set in the context of a system in which the discount is well established and thought to be normal. No doubt, if defendants had been asked whether they would have pleaded guilty if there were no discount, many would have said no. But in Scotland there is not and has not been a discount for pleading guilty, and yet the criminal courts suffer no worse delays than those in England and Wales.[72] Of course there are tremendous difficulties in cultural change, and it does not follow that because something works in Scotland it would work in England and Wales if the system were altered. Altering the system would cause resistance, since many people believe that the discount is a right or a necessity and might well act accordingly. However, if it is concluded that such a fundamental social and legal change would be right in principle, that conclusion and the reasons for it should be stated clearly and authoritatively. It might then take some time to accomplish the change, but the goal would be known and the sentence discount—which ought to be reduced straight away—would be temporary. These arguments will be continued in Section 7 below.

7. Four Principles

From the vantage-point of Scotland, Sheriff-Principal Nicholson writes that 'it would be quite unacceptable that, in a legal system which presumes innocence and which permits every person to go to trial, a person who was found guilty after trial should be punished more severely simply because he had not pleaded guilty'.[73] The same point was made

[70] The RCCJ recommendations are summarized at [1993] Crim. LR 637.

[71] Hedderman and Moxon, *Magistrates' Court*, 24; Zander and Henderson, *Crown Court Study*, 146.

[72] S. R. Moody and J. Tombs, 'Plea Negotiations in Scotland', [1983] *Crim. LR* 297.

[73] C. G. B. Nicholson, *The Law and Practice of Sentencing in Scotland* (1st edn., 1981), 219.

by the Lord Justice-Clerk in *Strawhorn* v. *McLeod*: referring to the sentence discount, he held that 'in our opinion no such inducement should be offered to accused persons. In this country there is a presumption of innocence and an accused person is entitled to go to trial and have the Crown to establish his guilt if the Crown can.'[74] Yet English law calmly and openly breaches this principle, and the breach would be exacerbated if the Royal Commission's recommendations were to be implemented. To argue the point by quibbling with the references to 'more severe' punishment for contesting the case would be unconvincing. It may be conceded that the sentence following conviction should be regarded as the 'normal' sentence and the sentence on a guilty plea as discounted, but the upshot is still that pleading not guilty has a price. The point will become clearer as we consider the four issues of principle raised by the Royal Commission report but, sadly, not confronted within it.

1. *The presumption of innocence*: we have already noted that Article 6 (2) of the European Convention on Human Rights declares that 'everyone charged with a criminal offence shall be presumed innocent until proved guilty according to law'.[75] One implication of this seems to be that a defendant has a right to put the prosecution to proof. No one should be recorded as guilty of an offence until the prosecution have proved that guilt, and 'any doubt should benefit the accused'.[76] It should be open to the defendant to waive the right to be tried, unless one takes the purist view that the judiciary ought to check in every case that there is sufficient evidence of guilt.[77] If waiver of the right to be tried is permitted, and if we are serious about the presumption of innocence, anything that represents a standing incentive to waive the right would seem to contradict or weaken the presumption of innocence. It is one thing to allow defendants to choose whether or not to be tried; it is quite another thing to try to buy out their insistence on being tried. Yet this is exactly what the discount for pleading guilty is designed to do—to act as an incentive to forgo one's right to be tried and to have the prosecution prove guilt. In the United States the Supreme Court has taken the view that a sentence discount for pleading guilty does not undermine the Fifth Amendment right not to plead guilty: although in *United States* v. *Jackson* (1968) the Court held that the objectives of the Government 'cannot be pursued by means that needlessly chill the exercise of basic constitutional rights', subsequent decisions have held that the sentence discount falls outside this ban, doubtless influenced

[74] 1987 SCCR 413, at 415.   [75] Ch. 2.4.

[76] *Barbera, Messegue and Jabardo* A. 146 (1989) 33.

[77] See n. 4 above and accompanying text.

by the belief that plea bargaining is essential to the smooth functioning of American criminal justice.[78]

Another argument against the sentence discount is this. If there is a fundamental right to be presumed innocent until proved guilty, it is surely wrong that exercise of this right by someone who is subsequently convicted at the trial should result in a sentence that is higher than would have been the case on a guilty plea. The Court of Appeal described the present English position beautifully in an early sentencing decision: 'This court feels that it is very improper to use language which may convey that an accused is being sentenced because he has pleaded not guilty or because he has run his defence in a particular way.'[79] Improper as it may be to use such language, the effect of the discount for pleading guilty is that the person convicted after a trial does receive a longer sentence for that reason. Whether or not one expresses it in terms of forgoing mitigation, the exercise of the right to be tried has its cost. Indeed, if one accepts that the discount may be as much as one-third, this means that a person convicted after a trial may legitimately receive a sentence 50 per cent longer than someone who pleads guilty. No wonder that Sheriff-Principal Nicholson describes the system as unacceptable.

The Royal Commission might defend itself by arguing that it took a pragmatic view. Cracked trials have to be reduced, as a matter of administrative necessity, and talk of defendants' rights does nothing to ease this pressing problem. Certainly it would be wrong for the advocates of rights to argue that it behoves us to take every possible step to ensure that innocent persons are never convicted. That would result in an immense investment of resources into criminal trials that might cripple the economy. But to dismiss that extreme position is not enough. As Dworkin argues, there is a strong case for maintaining that at all points in criminal justice our procedures should put the proper value on the fundamental harm of wrongful conviction.[80] What is the proper value may be a matter of debate, but the argument here is that to operate as a standing incentive a substantial sentence discount for defendants who waive their right to trial goes too far. It fails to take the presumption of innocence seriously. The strongest counter-arguments are the 'cultural block' view, which is that the discount is so ingrained in our culture that taking it away might well alter behaviour significantly, and the 'unfair advantage' view, which is that defendants

---

[78] See *Brady* v. *US* (1970) 397 US 742, and *Corbitt* v. *New Jersey* (1978) 439 US 212.

[79] *Harper* [1968] 2 QB 108.

[80] R. M. Dworkin, 'Principle, Policy, Procedure' in C. Tapper (ed.), *Crime, Proof and Punishment* (1981), 212.

may be encouraged to insist on trial in the hope that witnesses may fail to attend or forget or change their story, with the result that guilty persons would benefit from a windfall that was unfair on society (including any victim of the offence). These points are pursued below.

2. *The privilege against self-incrimination*: this privilege finds a place in the US Constitution but not, as such, in the European Convention on Human Rights. However, in the decision in *Funke, Cremieux and Miailhe* v. *France*[81] the European Court recognized the link between the presumption of innocence in Article 6 (2) and this privilege, referring to 'the right of anyone charged with a criminal offence to remain silent and not to incriminate himself'. In the context of English law this has direct implications for the law on the admissibility of confessions and for the permissibility of judicial comment on a defendant's decision to remain silent. As the Royal Commission recognizes, there is now considerable literature on the phenomenon of false confessions.[82] A majority of the Commission took the view that existing safeguards under the Police and Criminal Evidence Act 1984 are sufficient, whilst three members of the Commission insisted that a conviction should never be based on a confession unless there is supporting evidence.[83] The Commission as a whole accepts the terms of section 76 of the 1984 Act, that a confession should not be admitted if it was obtained in consequence of anything said or done which was likely, in the circumstances existing at the time, to render it unreliable. Setting aside the criticism that this test needs amendment,[84] one might argue that *pari passu* a plea of guilty should not be upheld if it was obtained in consequence of what might be described as a substantial inducement; indeed, the argument would be that the legal system should not provide such an inducement.

The Royal Commission comes even closer to self-contradiction when its approach to the right to remain silent under police questioning is considered. Once again, its members divided on the question whether it would be right for the law to permit a jury or magistrates to draw an adverse inference from the defendant's failure to answer questions or to mention a point subsequently relied upon in defence. A minority of two thought that courts should be invited to draw appropriate inferences, whereas the majority held 'that the possibility of an increase in the convictions of the guilty is outweighed by the risk that the extra pressure on suspects to talk in the police station and the adverse inferences invited if they do not may result in more convictions of the inno-

---

[81] A. 256 (1993).   [82] RCCJ Report, para. 4.32.   [83] Ibid., paras, 4.85–4.87.
[84] J. Jackson, 'The Royal Commission on Criminal Justice: The Evidence Recommendations', [1993] *Crim. LR* 817, at 826–8.

cent'.[85] Consistency would require that the Royal Commission took the same stance on the discount for pleading guilty, since it is intended to, and probably does, exert extra pressure on defendants at the stage of deciding on plea. But the Royal Commission says little about this, once it has made the point that its own survey results may overestimate the numbers of innocent people pleading guilty.[86] The Report states:

Provided that the defendant is in fact guilty and has received competent legal advice about his or her position, there can be no serious objection to a system of inducements designed to encourage him or her so to plead. Such a system is, however, sometimes held to encourage defendants who are not guilty of the offence charged to plead guilty to it nevertheless . . . This risk cannot be wholly avoided and, although there can be no certainty as to the precise numbers . . . it would be naive to suppose that innocent persons never plead guilty because of the prospect of the sentence discount.[87]

The only relevant point made subsequently is that the risk to the innocent must be 'weighed against' the benefit of encouraging the guilty to plead guilty.[88] The Royal Commission does accept that particular care should be taken during plea negotiations with vulnerable defendants who would be entitled to the support of an 'appropriate adult' at a police station[89]—rather a weak gesture towards this group, but at least an acknowledgement that the analogy with confessions is a fair one. The Commission's general assumption appears to be that counsel will safeguard the defendant's interests, but leave might be taken to doubt this. Even the *Turner* rules allow that counsel may give his or her advice, if necessary, in strong terms. That might easily be perceived as pressure by a defendant, especially one unfamiliar with the Crown Court. The decision in *Turner* distinguishes between statements believed to come directly from the judge, which were thought to exert unfair pressure, and counsel's own 'best advice', which was not thought unfair.[90] The findings of Baldwin and McConville's research in the 1970s were that over half of those who change their plea to guilty at a late stage were responding to what they perceived as pressure from their barrister.[91] In the absence of fuller research—and it is fair to point out that far more research has been done into false confessions than into decisions to change plea—little should be made of this distinction. After all, the 'person in authority' requirement in the law of confessions was abandoned in 1984: it no longer matters where the 'things said or

---

[85] RCCJ Report, paras. 4.20–4.25.   [86] Ibid., para. 7.43.
[87] Ibid., para. 7.42.   [88] Ibid., para. 7.45.   [89] Ibid., para. 7.51.
[90] [1970] 2 QB 321.
[91] Baldwin and McConville, *Negotiated Justice*, 28; cf. also Bottoms and McClean, *Defendants in the Criminal Process*, 79 and 130.

done' come from, so long as they tend to render the confession unreliable.

3. *The right to be treated fairly and without discrimination*: we have seen that Article 14 of the European Convention on Human Rights insists that the rights in the Convention 'shall be secured without discrimination on any ground such as sex, race, colour'. Would this principle be breached, either in the letter or in the spirit, if it were found that the operation of a particular criminal justice system routinely discouraged members of a particular ethnic minority from disputing their guilt?

Consider the available evidence in England and Wales. All studies that have included data on defendants' plea show that both persons from an Afro-Caribbean background and those from an Asian background tend to plead not guilty at a higher rate than whites. It also appears that Afro-Caribbeans are more likely to be acquitted, which may be regarded as vindicating their pleas.[92] Roger Hood found that not only do Afro-Caribbeans tend to plead not guilty more frequently than whites but that, when convicted, they tend to receive longer sentences largely because they have forfeited the discount for pleading guilty.[93] This can be regarded as a form of indirect discrimination: a general principle (the sentence discount) has a disproportionate impact on members of ethnic minorities simply because they exercise a right (the right to be tried and to be presumed innocent until convicted). The Royal Commission seems to recognize this, but merely expresses its support for 'the recommendation made by Hood that the policy of offering sentence discounts should be kept under review'.[94] In fact, Hood argued that 'it is time [i.e. now] to consider all the implications of a policy which favours so strongly those who plead guilty'.[95] The Commission goes on to state that careful ethnic monitoring of sentences is needed to detect whether there are sentencing patterns that are unfavourable to particular minority groups. However, Hood has established that there are such patterns, and he raised the issue of principle—should we persist with the sentence discount? It is unfortunate that the Commission tackles neither of the key issues here.

4. *The right to a 'fair and public' hearing*: Article 6 (1) of the European Convention declares that 'everyone is entitled to a fair and public hearing', and goes on to describe the limited situations in which 'the press and public may be excluded from all or part of the trial'. One character-

---

[92] For a useful summary, see M. Fitzgerald, *Ethnic Minorities and the Criminal Justice System*, RCCJ Research Study 20 (1993), 26.

[93] Hood, *Race and Sentencing*, 125.   [94] RCCJ Report, para. 7.58.

[95] Hood, *Race and Sentencing*, 182.

istic of cases in which there is a guilty plea is that there is no real public hearing. An added characteristic of cases in which there is a plea bargain is that the crucial negotiation takes place in the absence not only of the public but also of the accused. The High Court of Australia has spoken strongly against these private meetings between judge and counsel, disapproving even the limited contact allowed by the *Turner* rules on the ground that this is inconsistent with 'the common law rule which requires a court to administer justice in public'.[96] Whilst plea negotiation involving counsel and/or the judge may or may not infringe the European Convention, it certainly detracts from the spirit of Article 6 (1). A defendant's fate is determined by words spoken in private, of which only some are relayed to the defendant by counsel. In some American jurisdictions a change of plea is only accepted if the defendant meets the judge and is questioned about the motivation behind the change, so that the judge is satisfied that it is a voluntary change. That, too, takes place in private, but at least it involves the defendant in person.

8. Conclusion

From the point of view of principle there are powerful arguments in favour of abolishing the sentence discount for those who plead guilty. It is certainly against the spirit of four fundamental rights and freedoms recognized under the European Convention on Human Rights—the assumption of innocence, the privilege against self-incrimination, the right to equality of treatment, and the right to a fair and public hearing—and is probably against the letter of two of them. It treats the question of sentence as a negotiable commodity—not directly, in England and Wales, since judge and counsel would rarely discuss specific sentences, but indirectly to the extent that the sentence may reflect not the harm and culpability of the defendant's conduct but the outcome of negotiations. Some of these points of principle have been recognized in Germany, although the Federal Constitutional Court appears not to have faced the arguments squarely.[97]

It is unfortunate that the Royal Commission on Criminal Justice saw no reason to re-examine the justifications for the sentence discount for pleading guilty. Presumably it adopted the widespread view among practitioners that abolition of the discount is unthinkable because of its probable consequences. Courts would soon be overwhelmed by defendants exercising their right to trial, and the system would grind

---

[96] *R.* v. *Tait and Bartley* (1979) 24 ALR 473, at 488.
[97] Herrmann, 'Bargaining Justice', at 767–8.

expensively to a halt. But this has not happened elsewhere. Scotland has survived without any general principle that a guilty plea merits a reduced sentence. Other European countries operate satisfactorily without the discount. In Philadelphia, the fourth largest city in the United States, there is no principle of sentence discount for pleading guilty. The result is that most defendants in felony cases do opt for trial, many of these being 'bench trials' by judge alone, which can be dealt with fairly quickly. This shows that, even in a country in which plea bargaining has come to be regarded as endemic, it is in fact merely a policy choice.[98] It could be eliminated or reduced substantially. That might entail costs, but that throws down the challenge to simplify criminal procedure generally. Alschuler, who has studied plea bargaining in the United States extensively over a long period, argues that changes in criminal procedure could make for a fairer system that afforded the opportunity of trial to every defendant.[99] To liken plea bargaining to torture may smack of exaggeration,[100] but the arguments of principle set out in Section 6 make a powerful case for considering these radical alternatives in England and Wales, bearing in mind the interests of victims and the strains of giving evidence.

A starting-point would be to reconsider the guilty plea itself. Rarely has it been considered whether we should remove the possibility of a guilty plea from, say, indictable cases. It may be true that some other European countries are beginning to see the merits of guilty pleas in certain types of case, but there is little evidence that serious consideration has ever been given in England to the arguments for abolishing guilty pleas in some cases. Is judicial scrutiny of the factual basis of a case thought unnecessary, or beneficial in an ideal world, or simply prohibitively expensive? Have the foundations for each of these views been examined? Then it would be necessary to examine the justification for the sentence discount itself. Apart from the reasons already given, it is no argument that the possibility of charge reduction would be unaffected by any abolition of the discount. That is true, and will remain as an incentive to certain innocent defendants to 'cut their losses'. But that is an argument in favour of judicial scrutiny of guilty pleas; and, in any event, the existence of some unavoidable compromises of principle does not absolve one from avoiding those that can be avoided. Any fundamental re-examination ought also to extend to aspects of sentencing. There would be a need for more sentencing

---

[98] S. Schulhofer, 'Is Plea-Bargaining Inevitable?', (1984) 97 *Harv. LR* 1037.

[99] Among his many writings, see particularly A. Alschuler, 'Implementing the Criminal Defendant's Right to Trial', (1983) 50 *U. Chi. LR* 931.

[100] J. Langbein, 'Torture and Plea-Bargaining', (1978) 46 *U. Chi. LR* 3.

guidelines for particular offences, and it would be necessary to assess the impact on sentence levels of abolishing the discount. There would be no reason for raising sentence levels overall, but the size of current differences between sentences after guilty pleas and those after trials makes it important to consider where the new levels should be set.

The sentence discount is not the only structural incentive to plead guilty. There is also the 'tit-for-tat' rule in cross-examination of a defendant who gives evidence: if the defence attack the character of one or more witnesses for the Crown, the prosecution may in turn attack the defendant's character.[101] In practice this means that if the defence question a police officer with a view to suggesting that he or she attributed to the defendant words that were not spoken ('verbals') or 'planted' evidence on the defendant, this opens the way for the defendant to be cross-examined about any previous convictions. It is a rule that inhibits defendants with previous convictions from both attacking Crown witnesses and giving evidence, and leaves them with a choice of tactics that is bound to involve some sacrifice. If this is combined with the sentence discount, the effect may be to create strong pressure to plead guilty.

Pending a proper official review of criminal procedure in the light of plea, some sentence discount will remain prudent in the short and medium terms, even if regrettable. The most important step is to ensure that it impinges as little as possible on the four principles outlined above. The Royal Commission regards 'cracked trials' as the nub of the problem and orients its proposals in that direction, with little more than a passing nod to the issues of innocence and race. A preferable approach would be to regard innocence and race as worthy of special consideration, ensuring that any reforms improve the protection of innocent defendants and those from ethnic minorities. This is not to ignore the unnecessary anxiety for victims and witnesses and the waste of resources resulting from late changes of plea. But it should mean that prominence is given to the problem of pressure on defendants to plead guilty, both from the amount of discount available and from the advice of counsel. The Seabrook Committee's proposal that judges should signify the effect of the discount on a particular sentence should be followed. Graduated sentence discounts have their advantages, but the overall amounts of the discount should be reduced significantly. The best reason for allowing any discount to remain on the day of the trial is to spare those victims who have been damaged psychologically or who are afraid from having to give evidence.

[101] Criminal Evidence Act 1898, s. 1 (*f*) (ii), discussed by A. A. S. Zuckerman, *The Principles of Criminal Evidence* (1989), ch. 13.

The Royal Commission's proposal for 'sentence canvass' at the instance of the defence has the merit of recognizing the importance of knowing what the particular judge or recorder is likely to do: sadly, the consensus of practitioners is that there is insufficient consistency (and probably insufficient guidance) to allow confident predictions without this. However, the proposed system has the disadvantage that the judge will only indicate a maximum, without taking account of mitigation or the pre-sentence report, and raises the possibility that a defendant who finds the judge's indication unacceptable might decline in the hope that a further canvass might take place before another judge. Even the existing system has elements of circus about it: in his research report on serious fraud, Levi castigates the bargaining practices that came to his attention:

The haphazard structure under which discussions sometimes take place in camera without solicitors (including in-house SFO lawyers), police or defendant being present gives rise to enormous problems, maximises incoherence, and generates no precedent for dealing consistently and fairly with cases.[102]

Other changes in the short term must therefore be to increase the amount of guidance on sentencing, in the shape of guideline judgments; to reduce the amount of the sentence discount; and to require judges to state the exact effect that the discount had upon the sentence they pass. Changes such as these might smooth the transition to an altered system of criminal procedure that does not rely on tempting defendants to forgo their rights.

[102] M. Levi, *The Investigation, Prosecution and Trial of Serious Fraud*, RCCJ Research Study 14 (1993).

Part III

Conclusions

10

Criminal Process Values

CHAPTERS 4 to 9 of the book have discussed six key stages of decision-making in the criminal process, making reference to issues of policy and principle in the relevant law and practices. It is time now to reflect more generally upon the values that appear to dominate the English criminal process, the values that ought to dominate it, and how change might be brought about.

1. The Avoidance of Criminal Trials

Early in the first chapter a distinction was drawn between three types of decision at the pre-trial stage—processual decisions, which are concerned with the progress of the case from arrest through to court, or as far as the case goes; dispositive decisions, which divert a case from the process of prosecution and trial and which may impose a kind of penalty; and the temporal decision, remand, which determines whether or not the defendant should be at liberty between first court appearance and trial. Whilst there is often a tendency to regard these decisions as discrete rational determinations, it will have become apparent that they cannot be assessed properly without having regard to the system or process of which they form part. Thus, for example, each decision is shaped by the flow of information to the decision-maker and by the way in which 'facts' and opinions are selected, constructed, and communicated. Additionally, each decision-maker may be not only subject to rules or guidelines, as the case may be, but also influenced by an occupational culture and by the expectations of others both within and outside the system. It is therefore important not to neglect the serial view of decisions, noting that decisions by the public and by ordinary police officers or by the personnel of regulatory agencies may have considerable implications for later determinations; that decisions on charge may have implications for mode of trial; that decisions on mode of trial may have implications for remand and for plea; and so forth. As a result of the exploration of decision-making in the chapters above, it should be clear that central concepts such as 'the facts', 'innocence', and 'guilt' are sometimes not objective phenomena

(as often assumed), but rather compromises or value-judgements ema-
nating from the practices and pressures of the process.

Little has been said, in the foregoing chapters, about the differences
between accusatorial and inquisitorial systems of criminal justice. The
English criminal process is fundamentally accusatorial in orientation,
eschewing the idea of an impartial inquiry into the case by a neutral
official in favour of the notion that the truth emerges from an adversarial process in which the prosecution constructs a case for convicting
the defendant and he or she attempts to undermine or discredit that
case. One reason for not dwelling on this contrast of systems is what
may be termed the 'theory of convergence'—suggesting that the trend
in Europe has been away from a clear dichotomy of approaches and
towards a unified framework.[1] The convergence is said to have been
assisted by the European Convention on Human Rights and the judgments of the Court: the Convention emphasizes the rights of the individual defendant, in a way that typifies accusatorial systems (for
example, the various rights enumerated in Article 6, included the right
to confront each witness), but it also promotes some principles associated with an inquisitorial approach, such as equality of arms and the
duty of disclosure. It may be added that, quite apart from any influence
exerted by the European Convention, the 'ideal type' of an accusatorial
or an inquisitorial criminal procedure is hard to find in Europe. The
example of forms of plea bargaining in Germany was given in Chapter
9, and various restrictions on questioning in court by English advocates
(emphasizing that judges should intervene more often and more
firmly) suggest a movement away from accusatorial ideals, although
with few active inquisitorial powers for the judge.[2] Yet, whilst there are
pitfalls in classifying systems as accusatorial or inquisitorial,[3] some
effects may flow from a particular characterization of the role of the
prosecutor in the different systems. It is at least possible that the ethical orientation of a prosecutor in an inquisitorial system differs from
that of a prosecutor in an accusatorial system, because of the different
procedural contexts in which they operate. However, the point should
not be pressed too far, since it is well known that the rules and the
rhetoric of a system may not determine the actual practices followed by

---

[1] N. Jorg, S. Field, and C. Brants, 'Are Inquisitorial and Adversarial Systems
Converging?', in C. Harding (ed.), *The Europeanisation of Criminal Justice* (1994), ch. 1.

[2] See J. Jackson, 'Two Methods of Proof in Criminal Procedure', (1988) 51 *MLR* 549,
J. Jackson, 'The Royal Commission on Criminal Justice: The Evidence Recommendations', [1993] *Crim. LR* 817.

[3] Cf. the well-known work of M. Damaska, *The Faces of Justice and State Authority*
(1976).

officials. Some evidence for that proposition was given as early as Chapter 3, and has been consolidated in subsequent chapters.

It has also become evident that, whereas the rhetoric of criminal procedure tends to place emphasis on trial by jury according to the laws of evidence, the practice is otherwise. Most cases are heard in magistrates' courts, not in the Crown Court with a jury. The vast majority of cases—over 90 per cent in magistrates' courts and over 70 per cent in the Crown Court—proceed on a plea of guilty, which means that no trial of guilt ever takes place. In no sense is this a 'natural' or 'unavoidable' phenomenon: the system is structured so as to produce it. There are incentives towards the avoidance of trials, incentives that do not exist in some other legal systems. The most notable of these is the sentence discount for a plea of guilty, up to one-third off the sentence that would otherwise be given for the offence. In recent years there have been increasing fiscal pressures towards having fewer cases dealt with in the Crown Court and more in the magistrates' courts, manifested (for example) in the reclassification of certain offences as 'summary only' in 1988. It also remains possible that either the charging policy of some police or prosecutors, or the disposition of CPS prosecutors and their counsel, favours the striking of bargains in order to secure guilty pleas where possible. Indeed, the high rates of guilty pleas and 'cracked trials' suggest that both the prosecution and the defence often favour this course.

It is not only for cases that are pursued to conviction that the system tends strongly towards trial-avoidance. The trend towards diversion is designed to take cases out of the formal criminal process and to dispose of them separately. Predominant among these dispositive decisions are the police caution, the different forms of 'caution plus', the various warnings and compounded penalties used by the 'regulatory' agencies, and discontinuances by the Crown Prosecution Service that are followed by a caution or (if the recommendation of the 1993 Royal Commission is implemented) by a prosecutor fine. The foundations of the movement towards diversion may be located in different theoretical considerations: the painful consequences of being prosecuted may themselves be too severe a response to some forms of wrongdoing; encounters with the court system may create stigma and disadvantage; and diversion is far less expensive than court proceedings. Although some may suspect that considerations of cost weigh most heavily in inclining policy-makers towards diversion, the advantage on this occasion is that economic savings may also result in procedures that achieve a more proportionate response to non-serious law-breaking.

It would be wrong, however, to overlook the disadvantages. On a general plane, a widely used discretion not to prosecute may be regarded as undermining the principle of legality and the idea of the rule of law, and serious consideration should be given to the decriminalization of some forms of conduct. On a more specific plane, existing methods of diversion are often inseparable from incentives for the suspect or defendant to accept them. Rather like the discount for pleading guilty, the incentive to accept a caution—combined, of course, with a statement that the suspect must not admit to anything that he or she did not do—may prove powerful in practice as a way of terminating one's involvement with the criminal justice system quickly and without the anxiety of a court appearance. However, the European Court has insisted and English law generally provides that anyone who does not wish to accept diversion can decline and invite the prosecution to bring the case before a court.[4] This requires a certain self-confidence and resilience but, if diversion is to remain as a feature of the criminal process (which it certainly should do), suspects should be provided with safeguards, such as access to legal advice and a principle that any sentence the court passes on a finding of guilt should not be more onerous than the penalty voluntarily rejected by the defendant.

These remarks are at a general level, and the practical operation of the system may vary according to whether the offence in question is shop theft or serious fraud, manslaughter or a breach of the Health and Safety regulations. However, one observation that applies generally is the absence of any overall strategy. There is no aspiration to treat like cases alike, that most elementary proposition of justice, and different agencies continue to operate in different ways. The police and the CPS have their different powers and their different spheres, although the National Standards for cautioning are closely parallel to the Code for Crown Prosecutors. The regulatory agencies follow their differing paths and priorities. These variations, not to mention the discretionary power within each of them, leave open the possibility of practices that discriminate on irrelevant grounds such as class, social position, race, and gender. There is no common starting-point, no conception that people who commit offences of similar seriousness should receive similar responses (unless there are strong grounds for doing otherwise), and no real attempt to provide guidance on the relative seriousness of the various types of offence. Like sentencing, diversion décisions are dispositive. Unlike sentencing, there are no open hearings and the principles relating to specific types of offence are hardly developed at all.

---

[4] See Ch. 3 n. 66 and accompanying text.

The absence of an aspiration to treat like cases alike is also manifest in local variations of policy. National Standards on cautioning were issued as such in 1990, but the previous Home Office circulars had failed to prevent variations both between police forces and between divisions within the same police force.[5] National Mode of Trial guidelines were promulgated in 1991, but it is not yet known whether these have succeeded in removing or even reducing the sturdy independence of some local liaison judges, justices' clerks, and benches.[6] Local variations in remand decisions, in plea rates, and in the practices of some regulatory agencies are also long-standing. It would be inadvisable to stifle all local variation, particularly when several worthwhile innovations in the criminal process have originated in local schemes (e.g. bail information schemes, Public Interest Case Assessment schemes). But it is no less wrong to tolerate what, in effect, are declarations of local independence in matters of criminal justice policy. It is unjust that a person who is (rightly or wrongly) suspected of a certain offence in one area should be treated in a significantly different way from a person in a similar person in another area. Local variations in practice should be monitored and local variations in policy should only be permitted if clear justifications can be found: this would expose the unwarranted whilst enabling experimental schemes to be introduced.

Both processual and dispositive decisions, as we have seen, tend towards the avoidance of trials. The prosecution, chiefly in the form of the CPS, play a central role in this. It is they who have the power to take key processual decisions, discontinuing cases that are either too weak evidentially, or too slight in terms of public interest, to justify bringing to court. They also have some control over dispositive decisions, in so far as the police ask for advice before cautioning or the CPS remit discontinued cases to the police with a view to a caution. Of course, the earlier warning about the dangers of regarding a single decision as if it were a discrete rational determination are applicable here. Much of the 'input' received by the CPS comes from the police, who therefore exert considerable practical influence through their construction of case files. Some of the working practices of the CPS may be shaped by local magistrates or justices' clerks or the local judiciary. But, to the extent that the CPS move towards an 'intrinsic merits' approach in which they take key decisions about charge, mode of trial, and plea by

[5] R. Evans and C. Wilkinson, 'Variations in Police Cautioning Policy and Practice in England and Wales', (1990) 29 *Howard JCJ* 155, discussed in Ch. 5.4.

[6] These local 'cultures' were mentioned as recently as 1993 by the Criminal Justice Consultative Committee, *Mode of Trial Decisions and Sentencing* (1993), 8; see above, Ch. 8.2.

reference to legal policy rather than local practice, they would be
assuming a quasi-judicial function in the criminal process. It remains
to be seen whether the CPS has the quantity and quality of staff to
undertake such functions successfully.

One person who perhaps does not have the central role that would
be appropriate is the defendant. Under existing practice in both the
Crown Court and magistrates' courts, and under the scheme of 'sentence canvass' proposed by the 1993 Royal Commission, the defendant
is excluded from plea negotiations themselves and has to depend on
the mediated words of legal representatives.[7] Direct information for
the defendant is relatively rare, and this places much emphasis on the
quality of legal representation. There is growing evidence that this is
variable, and that it is not always motivated by a desire to secure the
defendant's rightful advantages but is sometimes diluted by a desire to
curry favour with the police, or to obtain the maximum fee for the minimum work, or not to 'pull the stops out' for a client deemed
unworthy.[8] Moreover, in relation to decisions on mode of trial, as we
saw in Chapter 8, some of the advice offered by defence solicitors may
result in defendants electing Crown Court trial and then receiving a
sentence much heavier than would have been imposed in a magistrates' court—advice perhaps given in order to earn greater fees, or
because of a misapprehension about the relative sentencing levels of
the courts, or for other reasons. A defendant who cannot rely on his or
her legal representatives for full support and good advice is, given the
other disadvantages outlined in Chapter 4 and elsewhere, in a particularly vulnerable position.

2. The Principled Approach

The scourge of many debates about criminal justice policy is the concept of 'balance'. As it is often expressed, notably by the 1993 Royal
Commission, the 'balancing' of conflicting interests is presented as if
there is no particular weighting of or priority among the interests. They
are all matters to be taken into consideration, and somehow a 'balance'
emerges. Sometimes the process is given an apparent respectability by
quoting probabilities that a certain consequence will ensue—for example, the low risk of innocent people being convicted. The existence of a
low risk on one side of the equation may be thought to tip the scales in
that direction, but herein lies the difficulty. It should not merely be a
matter of utilitarian weighing, of calculating the balance of advantages,

[7] See J. Baldwin, *Pre-trial Justice in Magistrates' Courts* (1986).
[8] M. McConville and J. Hodgson, *Standing Accused* (1993), 273 and 281.

but rather a matter of social weighting, which involves deciding on principled priorities among the various interests. For this it is necessary to begin with a clear conception of the rights and duties that should be relevant.

It was argued in Chapter 2 that one of the most basic rights is the right of an innocent person not to be convicted. In Dworkin's theory the two rights associated with this are the right to procedures that place a proper valuation on moral harms (a right stated in broad and negotiable terms, yet which insists on the classification of certain harms as moral harms), and the right to consistent treatment within the declared policies. To this we added a third right, the right to be subjected to the minimum of restriction and inconvenience during the criminal process before conviction. All these rights remain at a rather general level, however, and do not cover in any specific form the many decisions to be taken in the criminal process. At this point it is possible to transfer the argument, as it were, from the philosophical level to a statement of positive law in the shape of the European Convention on Human Rights and Fundamental Freedoms. We saw in Chapter 3 that the European Convention, as interpreted by the judgments of the European Court of Human Rights, establishes a number of rights relevant to the criminal process: the right not to be subjected to torture or inhuman or degrading treatment, the presumption of innocence, the principles of legality, the presumption of liberty save for reasonable arrest or lawful detention, the right to a prompt court appearance, the right to prepare one's defence properly, the right to trial without unreasonable delay, the principle of equality of arms, the principle of non-discrimination, and the right to privacy.

In what way should this list of rights be used? First, it should be recognized that it cannot be regarded as exhaustive. It makes no reference to the rights of victims, although there are other declarations of the Council of Europe that do so. For many purposes it would be better if these rights of victims were incorporated into the European Convention on Human Rights, lest the separation should obscure their importance, but the process of declaring the rights of victims should be approached with circumspection. As argued in Chapters 2 and 7, the right to compensation, the right to respect, and the right to protection (at the remand stage) should be emphasized. Any procedural rights or powers that go further and incorporate the victim into decision-making should be rejected not merely as inappropriate but also on the ground that they may cast too great a burden on victims and increase the risk of intimidation. Second, it should be recognized that even within the European Convention some of the rights have greater force or priority than others. The most strongly weighted rights, then, are the right not to be subjected to torture or inhuman or degrading treatment (Article 3) and the right not to be held guilty of an offence that did not exist at the time of the act or omission charged (Article 7). These are absolute: there can be no justification for failing to observe them. On the other hand, we have seen that the right to privacy in Article 8 allows for derogation when 'necessary in a democratic society in the interests of national security, public safety . . . etc'. We have also seen that Article 15 allows member states to derogate from other obligations, notably Articles 5 and 6, 'in time of war or other public emergency threatening the life of the nation . . . to the extent strictly required by the exigencies of the situation'.[9] The text of the European Convention demonstrates not only the importance of assigning weight or priority to the different rights and duties but also, in conjunction with the judgments of the Court, the practical possibility of doing so.

The contrast with the approach of the 1993 Royal Commission is marked. The Commission's terms of reference required it to have regard to 'securing the conviction of those guilty of criminal offences and the acquittal of those who are innocent, having regard to the efficient use of resources'.[10] At no stage in the Report is it stated how the Commission approached the question of priority among the three objectives in its terms of reference. In response to those who have criticized the Commission for giving undue weight to the reduction of public expenditure and insufficient weight to the protection of the innocent, one member of the Commission has stated that 'each [objective] had to be given its proper weighting in regard to every topic'.[11] This is a defective method, in that there is no suggestion of a clear standpoint from which the Commission began its deliberations on these issues of principle: no doubt the Commission might argue that this would have been a profitless exercise in abstraction, but that would miss the significance of the European Convention and its imperatives. Even if the Commission did follow some such method, its Report is defective in failing to articulate how its method was applied to each of the key decisions it reached. All too often the Report refers to the 'balance' favouring one solution rather than another, as if this were some ineffable mystery that requires no supporting explanation about how the conclusion was reached. Moreover, the assumption seems to be that in practice one can only decide on a policy by assessing the bal-

---

[9] See the discussion in Ch. 3.4.

[10] RCCJ Report, Cm. 2263 (1993), p. i, and paras. 1.5–1.10.

[11] M. Zander, 'Where the Critics got it wrong', [1993] NLJ 1338. Cf. N. Lacey, 'Missing the Wood . . .', in M. McConville (ed), Criminal Justice in Crisis (1994).

ance between different considerations. When there are so many conflicting interests how could one do otherwise?

The principled approach, evident from the structure of the European Convention and the judgments of the Court, does not adopt the utilitarian concept of balancing. Rather, it assumes that certain individual rights should be respected absolutely, and that several other individual rights should only be sacrificed in certain extreme circumstances. The process is different from balancing: it involves regarding certain principles as inviolable or as subject to derogation only where there is special justification, and then controlling the derogation so that it is kept to a minimum. Of course the European Convention says nothing about the interest of the community in ensuring that the guilty are convicted, and it would wrong to conduct an argument, let alone to recommend policy, without recognizing this as a fundamental justification for having a formal criminal process. However, recognition of this fundamental justification does not return the discussion to the realms of balancing. It is clearly implicit in the European Convention that the individual rights it declares may operate to restrict the interest of the community in convicting the guilty, and that this of itself is not a sufficient reason to deny the rights. Once again the difference between a utilitarian form of balancing and a rights-based approach is evident. The 'balancing' approach tends to regard conviction of the guilty and acquittal of the innocent as matters to be weighed together, and empirical evidence of the effect of certain existing or changed procedures on convictions or acquittals would be important. The principled approach would assign priority to certain individual rights, and would then insist that any derogations be reasoned and minimal. Empirical evidence also plays a key role in this process, since it is important to verify claims about changes that are said to be 'necessary for public safety', or whatever community argument is advanced. For example, evidence such as that from research studies for the 1993 Royal Commission about the infrequency of 'ambush defences' or the infrequency of acquittals in cases where the defendant has relied on the right of silence[12] should play an important part in assessing the strength of the arguments for derogation. Empirical evidence would continue to play a part in the monitoring of procedures, to ensure that they further rather than frustrate the values of the process: disclosure by the prosecution may be viewed as a prime example of the principle of 'equality of arms', but if it comes to be used as a defence tactic to delay proceedings or even to lead to the

---

[12] See Ch. 4.1.13.

dropping of prosecutions, questions must be asked about the appropriateness of the rules.[13]

There remains the point that the European Convention does not constitute an exhaustive statement of relevant rights. There are some central issues in the criminal process on which it contains little guidance at all, even apart from victim-related matters. There is little on the appropriate sanctions for breach by officials of rights declared either by the Convention or in domestic law. The Convention has little to say about dispositive decisions, and relatively little about the appropriate principles for remand decisions. There is nothing on such issues as confessions, controls on questioning by investigators, corroboration requirements, and mode of trial. On other issues, such as guilty pleas, there is no direct provision. However, this should not mean that in spheres not expressly covered by the European Convention there should be a return to 'balancing', even if it were conducted by a more explicit process than that evident from the Report of the 1993 Royal Commission. On some issues the spirit of the European Convention is clear, and is being developed already by the decisions of the European Court—for example, the presumption of innocence declared by Article 6 (2) has been held to support the right of silence.[14] At the very least the spirit of the Convention should be allowed to flow into the areas not covered, and to indicate directions in which the law and practice ought to move. It was argued in Chapter 9 that this would cast strong doubt on both existing practices of plea negotiation and the Royal Commission's proposals. A more difficult issue, as argued in Chapter 8, is whether the European Convention has any implications for the debate on mode of trial.

3. Discrimination and Non-discrimination

The principle of equality before the law, or non-discrimination, is often declared to be a fundamental element in the administration of justice. There are, however, certain difficulties with this. On the one hand it may tend to overlook the case for special treatment of certain groups—positive discrimination, aimed at insulating the vulnerable from pressures with which they cannot fairly be expected to cope. We have seen that there is a strong case for special procedures to protect juveniles

---

[13] Quite apart from the recommendations of the 1993 Royal Commission on disclosure (on which see J. Glynn, 'Disclosure', [1993] *Crim. LR* 841), there is growing concern about the difficulty of protecting sensitive information held by the prosecution: see C. Pollard, 'A Case for Disclosure?', [1994] *Crim. LR* 42.

[14] See the decision in *Funke, Cremieux and Miailhe* v. *France* A. 256 (1993), discussed in Ch. 3.3.

and the mentally disordered, and also for special assistance for those who do not understand the English language well enough. These and other claims for positive discrimination must be kept under constant review. On the other hand, the widespread lip-service to the principle of non-discrimination declared in Article 14 of the European Convention and alluded to in section 95 of the Criminal Justice Act 1991 must not lead us to neglect research and other inquiries into whether the practice conforms to the law. The recent introduction in England and Wales of a system for the collection of evidence on certain of these matters should not lead us to forget the evidence that people from an Afro-Caribbean background may be disadvantaged in decisions to prosecute or caution, decisions on mode of trial, and in the process of plea negotiation. The extent of discrimination on grounds of sex is unclear, but studies of sentencing suggest that it would be unwise to take at face value the apparently lenient treatment of women and girls.

Rather less sharply defined and less widely discussed in official documents than race and sex discrimination is class bias, or discrimination according to factors connected with social class or wealth. It is evident from Chapter 4 that any systematic examination of the prosecution policies of the police compared with those of the so-called regulatory agencies would reveal a diversity of approaches, amounting in general to a less formal, less public, and less severe response to law-breaking by employers, taxpayers, and others in established ways of life. It is hardly surprising that statistics about the social background of offenders show a predominance of those from the lower socio-economic groups when the enforcement process is skewed against those groups and in favour of those from the higher occupational categories. However, dealing with this presents a structural problem of immense proportions. The 1993 Royal Commission was content to approve non-criminal resolutions of certain fraud cases, without examining the wider social issues underlying this dispensation. Those who adopt a desert or retributive approach would probably argue that the first task should be to decide on the relative seriousness of all these offences, whether 'white-collar', 'normal', 'financial', 'commercial', 'domestic', or however they may be labelled. The second task might then be to ensure that the criminal law is invoked at a certain level of seriousness, whatever the context of the offence, and not below that level. This would represent an attempt to achieve equality before the law, preventing the use of the criminal process for relatively minor offences by impecunious or poorly connected defendants when at the same time corporate or wealthy defendants benefit from a less vigorous approach.

That enterprise would not be easy to achieve, however, for many reasons. Among those reasons are the ways in which certain regulatory offences are drafted, and the possibility that wealthy or corporate 'deviants' might deploy their considerable resources to devise means of 'creative compliance' with the law.[15]

Important as it is to tackle unfair discrimination in the criminal law, in the enforcement process, and in criminal procedure, one cannot overlook the difficulty of doing so within a society many of whose institutions and practices may be said to lean towards unfair discrimination. So far as policing is concerned, for example, 'the young "street" population has always been the prime focus of police order maintenance and law enforcement work. The processes of racial disadvantage in housing, employment and education lead young blacks to be disproportionately involved in street culture.'[16] This demonstrates the folly of regarding the criminal process as something separate from wider social issues and capable of separate treatment. It also demonstrates the folly of regarding issues of race as separate from other issues of general social policy. Similar arguments could be made about gender. This is not to deny the importance of efforts to remove discrimination from the criminal process, but it is to argue that there are structural factors that make it likely that some discriminatory effects might be found even if the law and its enforcers were scrupulously fair in their own actions.

4. Promoting the Principles

How should the principled approach outlined in section 2 of this chapter be put into practice? Lawyers would tend to look to a network of rules or to a system of legal regulation as the means of advancing the desired principles. It has often been remarked that many stages in the criminal process are characterized by wide swaths of little-regulated discretion, from which it is assumed that the path of reform involves restrictions on or the complete removal of discretion. However, this would be naïve. It would be to assume that the existence of rules eliminates the practices that discretion allows. There are plenty of examples of rules being circumvented or neutralized, for instance by the police (Chapter 4), by Crown Prosecutors (Chapter 6), and by counsel and judges (Chapter 9). From the point of view of observance, it is doubtful that rules enacted in primary legislation will necessarily be more suc-

[15] D. McBarnet and C. Whelan, 'The Elusive Spirit of the Law: Formalism and the Struggle for Legal Control', (1991) 54 *MLR* 848.

[16] R. Reiner, *The Politics of the Police* (2nd edn., 1992), 169.

cessful than guidelines within or outwith the ambit of secondary legislation.

This is not to deny the social and symbolic importance of placing certain standards firmly in primary legislation. This is probably the strongest reason in favour of enacting the European Convention on Human Rights into United Kingdom domestic law:[17] despite the arguments against trusting with the power to override legislation a judiciary little experienced in constitutional review, and despite the arguments for amending the European Convention considered above, enactment soon would be an important declaratory step. A more mundane question is how best to ensure that the principled approach dictates day-to-day decisions by officials involved in the criminal process. It is quite possible that discretion is more appropriate than a structure of rules and exceptions, because many of the decisions (e.g. prosecute or caution, remand on bail or in custody, magistrates' court or Crown Court) require a range of factors to be taken into consideration.[18] On the other hand, the use of presumptions or elements of the rule-and-exception approach should be incorporated where possible. The aim should be to supply some guidance, in the form of rules, presumptions, or guidelines, to provide for the most frequent and the most difficult factual combinations that come before the decision-makers. The problem of deciding on the most appropriate and most effective techniques of guidance should not be allowed to overshadow the question of who should determine the policies and the priorities reflected in the guidance. In principle these should be determined by accountable bodies applying the general principles embodied in primary legislation. One of the difficulties exposed in Chapters 5 and 6 is that there is no overall strategy linking the police and the so-called regulatory agencies on matters of selective law enforcement: this, as urged in section 3 of this chapter in relation to discriminatory practices, must be rectified if the process is to achieve an acceptable level of fairness.

In terms of decision-making in the criminal process, then, the leading principles should be declared in primary legislation. Detailed guidance should be drafted by broadly based bodies drawing members from different parts of the criminal process, and should be incorporated in delegated legislation or other codes with statutory authority.

[17] See above, Ch. 3.3, and Sir Harry Woolf, *Protection of the Public: A New Challenge* (1990), 120–2, Sir Nicolas Browne-Wilkinson, 'The Infiltration of a Bill of Rights', [1992] *PL* 397, Sir John Laws, 'Is the High Court the Guardian of Fundamental Constitutional Rights', [1993] *PL* 59, and Sir Thomas Bingham, 'The European Convention on Human Rights: Time to Incorporate', (1993) 109 *LQR* 390.

[18] See D. Galligan, 'Regulating Pre-trial Decisions', in I. Dennis (ed.), *Criminal Law and Criminal Justice* (1987).

There should be frequent review of the appropriateness of certain groups taking certain decisions, for example the police taking the decision to charge, and magistrates taking the decision on mode of trial. Both policy decisions and individual decisions should be open to challenge, whether by appeal or by judicial review. This requires a substantial change in the English approach,[19] but it would recognize the considerable importance of decisions taken at the early stages of the criminal process. At present the possibilities of appeal increase as the case progresses further, and those possibilities are particularly strong if there has been a trial. Yet the early stages may be no less powerful in their influence over a case, and the decisions may be taken in private without the giving of reasons. The principle of 'equality of arms' must be spread into these early decisions: some steps have been taken, in the shape of lay visitors to police stations, legal aid, access to legal advice in the police station, duty solicitor schemes, and so forth, but it is essential to lay greater emphasis on what occurs at these early stages and on the quality of legal advice available to defendants when they make what may turn out to be crucial choices. One essential part of achieving change would be to alter the fee structure in the legal aid system to reward preparation and early advice more respectably, so as to attract admitted solicitors more to police station work.[20]

This focus on the early stages of the process is central to the issue of miscarriages of justice. One of the most widely anticipated recommendations of the 1993 Royal Commission was that there should be the creation of a special body to investigate alleged miscarriages of justice after the normal appeal process has been exhausted, a Criminal Cases Review Authority. The need for some such body is evident from the cases of miscarriage of justice discussed in Chapter 1, but those cases show that it is no less important to take steps to ensure that errors are reduced to a minimum in the first place. The use of unfair interviewing techniques by the police, the alteration or falsification of records of what defendants said, the suppression of evidence favourable to the defendant (particularly by the Forensic Science Service), and several other unacceptable practices were revealed by the brief discussion of those notorious cases.[21] The rules must be changed, and so must the practices. Nor should it simply be a matter of 'fire-brigade' responses to points that have already caused controversy: thus, for example, the Royal Commission's failure to declare that any unrecorded statement

---

[19] Cf. G. Richardson, *Law, Process and Custody: Prisoners and Patients* (1993), chs. 2, 3, and 4, with N. Lacey, 'The Jurisprudence of Discretion', in K. Hawkins (ed), *The Uses of Discretion*, 380f.

[20] Cf. McConville and Hodgson, *Standing Accused*, 279.   [21] Ch. 1.3.

attributed to the defendant should be inadmissible in court leaves open an obvious opportunity for miscarriages of justice.[22]

The path of reform should pay particular attention to the practices and procedures in the early stages of the process. The principles should be declared clearly, not simply in terms of police ethics but also spelling out the importance of such matters as investigating before questioning wherever possible and following up exculpatory claims no less vigorously than inculpatory possibilities. The provision of thorough training, guidance, and supervision are essential ingredients. There will always, in a system dependent on human beings, be departures from proper practice and genuine errors. Even if suitable measures to prevent such miscarriages have been taken, there will be a need to address the question of official responses. Professional disciplinary procedures must operate effectively according to public criteria: there have been doubts about the adequacy of arrangements for the disciplining of solicitors, but one of the more constructive aspects of the Report of the 1993 Royal Commission is its recognition of the shortcomings of police disciplinary procedures and its recommendation of improvements.[23] However, more attention should be paid to professional standards and professional discipline at the Bar. The Royal Commission formed the view that the 'last-minute culture' of the criminal Bar, under which briefs are returned late and counsel has little opportunity for thorough preparation or proper discussion with client, victim, or witnesses, will be difficult to dislodge. Whether the proper solution is to try to break the culture or to try to reshape it,[24] fuller investigation should be made of the possibility that prosecutions and defendants are disadvantaged by the criminal Bar's approach. The confidence expressed by most barristers in their ability to deal with preparations satisfactorily at the last minute, even though supported by many other professionals,[25] should be taken as the starting-point for further research rather than as grounds for concluding that all is well.

A separate question concerns the effect that deviations from proper procedure should have on the progress of an individual case. Much has been made, both by academics[26] and latterly by some British judges,[27]

---

[22] See Ch. 4.1.5.   [23] RCCJ Report, paras. 3.96–3.103.

[24] Compare RCCJ Report, para. 7.36, with the Note of Dissent by Professor Zander, para. 47.

[25] M. Zander and P. Henderson, *Crown Court Study*, RCCJ Research Study 19 (1993), paras. 2.4.8, 2.4.13, 2.5.4, and 2.5.13.

[26] e.g. A. A. S. Zuckerman, *The Principles of Criminal Evidence* (1989), A. Choo, *Abuse of Process* (1993).

[27] Notably the speech of Lord Lowry in *R. v. Horsferry Road Magistrates' Court, ex p. Bennett* [1993] 3 WLR 90.

of the 'integrity principle'. The argument is that the integrity of the court, or more widely of the criminal justice system, would be compromised if it were to act on evidence that had been obtained as a result of a departure from proper procedure. At one level the argument is persuasive, and the imagery of 'tainting' or 'the fruit of the poisoned tree' seems apposite. Yet in other respects the integrity principle leaves certain questions unanswered.[28] Should every departure from procedure, no matter how small or inconsequential, be regarded as calling into question the integrity of a court or the whole system? If not, by what criteria can we tell whether integrity is compromised? Questions of this kind raise a doubt whether the integrity principle can be a satisfactory operating standard for the courts: attractive as it is in clear and gross cases, it needs considerable refinement if it is to be suitable for the general run of situations.[29] The disciplinary principle cannot withstand careful scrutiny, since the actions or remarks of judges have no formal disciplinary consequences for the police or other investigative authority in general, or for the particular investigator. Professional discipline is and should be the concern of tribunals constituted for that purpose, as mentioned above. In practice the disciplinary principle amounts to nothing more than a principle of public censure, a symbolic practice of criticizing the conduct of an investigator or investigative agency in court, often bolstered by reporting in the mass media. More relevant to the objective of promoting a principled approach to criminal justice is the protective principle: that a court should not act on evidence if that would deprive the defendant of a protection that should have been assured. In other words, a deviation from procedures may only be overlooked if it can be regarded as 'technical', not because it is intrinsically small but rather because it has not prejudiced, or, alternatively, has not prejudiced significantly, the defendant. The defendant should not be disadvantaged by an investigator's non-observance of the procedures.

It will be apparent that, even if the appropriateness of the protective principle is accepted, its implementation depends on a considerable value-judgment if the term 'significant' is introduced into its formulation. A strong version of the principle would exclude any such qualification, and is to be preferred if rights are to be respected fully. However, in terms of practical politics there may be some pressure to

[28] One question, raised above in Ch. 2.2, but not pursued here, is whether the concept of integrity incorporates the social value placed on the conviction of the guilty, as certain American judges have maintained.

[29] Cf. Zuckerman, *The Principles of Criminal Evidence*, 350–2, referring to the 'balancing process' necessary to determine whether integrity or 'legitimacy' is sufficiently compromised, and the discussion above in Ch. 2.2.

qualify the principle so as to avoid losing 'good' convictions for a procedural departure that really had little effect on the defendant's exercise of rights. That would require some kind of judgement to be reached, but it is clearer what is at stake when dealing with ordinary cases under the protective principle than under the integrity principle. What neither the protective principle nor the principle of integrity settles is the most appropriate consequences of breach. Rarely is it suggested that there should be a complete defence to criminal liability (although this has been argued to be appropriate for entrapment[30]), but in many cases a decision to stay the prosecution on the ground of abuse of process will have a similar effect, whereas the better-established remedy of excluding evidence is less powerful and may occasionally leave room for a conviction based on other admissible evidence.[31] One might then ask why the prevention of conviction is regarded as the benchmark of appropriateness if the protection of the defendant from unfair disadvantage is the rationale. Ideally, the strength of the response should be in some way proportionate to the degree of disadvantage to the defendant (which, to re-emphasize, is not the same as the degree of the departure from proper procedure).

The promotion of a principled approach therefore requires not only the provision of training, guidance, and supervision but also sufficient and appropriate remedies in cases where the principles are not put into practice. However, the discussion of occupational cultures which began in Chapter 3 and continued in subsequent chapters makes it plain that there is, at the very least, a risk that these measures will fail. The risk of failure would be greatest where the particular occupational culture is adverse and strong. It is therefore necessary to attempt to reshape the occupational cultures of some of those working within the criminal process. As outlined in Chapter 3, this means not only setting out the principles that ought to be respected but tackling the often well-entrenched arguments for ignoring individual rights that hold sway within some professions. Ideas such as 'society expects us to fight crime with our hands tied behind our back' must be carefully and persuasively unpicked. This means incorporating into training the reasons for respecting rights, and reorienting professional goals and official performance indicators in a way that reveres and rewards respect for rights over the mere obtaining of convictions. None of this means that convicting the guilty is unimportant; rather, it emphasizes that this worthy goal should be achieved by fair processes. This is not just a

---

[30] See Ch. 4.1.1.

[13] Choo, *Abuse of Process*, ch. 4; see also s. 76 (4) of PACE, which allows a court to admit evidence of matters discovered in consequence of an inadmissible confession.

matter of ensuring that this country upholds the European Convention
on Human Rights, although that is constitutionally important. It is also
something that people in general regard as an essential element in a
criminal justice system. To set against the belief of some politicians
that public confidence in the system would be threatened by thorough-
going respect for human rights (not that it is often thus expressed) are
the findings of social psychologists such as Tom Tyler, which insist that
the fairness of procedures is no less valued and may be more highly
valued than the outcomes of those procedures.[32] Tyler found that
people 'focus more on their opportunities to state their case than they
do on their influence over decisions',[33] and even goes so far as to claim
that 'if people receive fair procedures, outcome is not relevant to their
reactions. If they do not, it is.'[34]

5. The Criminal Process of the Future

In this chapter some reformist proposals have been advanced in
relation to the selected stages of the criminal process discussed earlier
in the book. Any such set of detailed proposals is likely to have a modest effect if other aspects of the criminal justice system remain little
changed, and any changes in the criminal justice system may have a
modest effect if various social structures and policies remain little
changed. Moreover, considerations of cost and public expenditure
must be taken into account by anyone who forsakes the cover of academic discussion to venture some policy proposals. Recognizing cost as a
constraint does not, however, argue against fundamental change. The
Report of the 1993 Royal Commission is pervaded by managerial and
fiscal concerns, but the tendency is largely to consider expenditure in
relation to discrete stages in the process. The annual budget of the
whole system—including police, prosecutors, courts, legal aid, prisons,
and so forth—is immense. One approach would be to consider a five-
year reorientation of expenditure which would enhance human rights
to the greatest extent without increasing the overall budget. Rather
than discussing a 'balance' at each stage of the process, the approach
would be to meet the challenge of ensuring or maximizing respect for
rights with a minimum loss of convictions of the guilty, looking critically at the roles of the various professional groups, at their powers,
and at their practices. In addition to debating the rights of victims, the
approach would be to examine methods of preventing crime that
promise fewer victims (and fewer offenders), such as the wider avail-

[32] T. R. Tyler, *Why People Obey the Law* (1990).   [33] Ibid. 126.   [34] Ibid. 101.

ability of pre-school education, improved housing, and other changes in social policy. The inquiry thus strays into spheres of expenditure other than criminal justice, but this is inevitable and proper. Even if the debate could be confined within criminal justice, this approach would place the benefits of, say, pre-trial legal representation in a proper perspective rather than simply seeing it as an extra expense. It would, however, require careful examination of dispositive decisions, their justification, and their public impact: the potential for saving public money by diverting offenders from the formal process is obvious, but considerations of proportionality, effectiveness, individual rights, and public confidence ought not to be neglected.

The 1993 Royal Commission had the opportunity to establish a blueprint for criminal justice at the millennium, and to propound a vision of criminal justice that could rise up from the failures exposed to the world in the early 1990s. In the event it purported to eschew theory and produced a range of proposals informed largely by managerial concerns, interspersed with occasional gestures towards defendants' rights and victims' rights. At a time when senior judges have begun to lobby strongly in favour of incorporating the European Convention on Human Rights into English law,[35] the Royal Commission's failure to discuss the issues from that point of view seems extraordinary. Yet so fickle is the world of politics that, at the time of writing, some of the Commission's recommendations appear almost revolutionary when compared with the statements and proposals for legislation emerging from the Home Office. The need to insist on a principled approach can rarely have been greater.

[35] See above, n. 17.

Index